Lecture Notes in Computer Science 6142

Commenced Publication in 1973
Founding and Former Series Editors:
Gerhard Goos, Juris Hartmanis, and Jan van Leeuwen

W0193055

Laurence Tratt   Martin Gogolla (Eds.)

Theory and Practice of Model Transformations

Third International Conference, ICMT 2010
Málaga, Spain, June 28 - July 2, 2010
Proceedings

 Springer

Volume Editors

Laurence Tratt
Middlesex University
Engineering and Information Sciences
The Burroughs, London, NW4 4BT, United Kingdom
E-mail: laurie@tratt.net

Martin Gogolla
University of Bremen
Computer Science Department Database Systems Group
D-28334, Bremen, Germany
E-mail: gogolla@informatik.uni-bremen.de

Library of Congress Control Number: 2010928208

CR Subject Classification (1998): D.2, F.3, D.3, C.2, K.6, D.2.4

LNCS Sublibrary: SL 2 – Programming and Software Engineering

ISSN   0302-9743
ISBN-10   3-642-13687-7 Springer Berlin Heidelberg New York
ISBN-13   978-3-642-13687-0 Springer Berlin Heidelberg New York

springer.com

© Springer-Verlag Berlin Heidelberg 2010
Printed in Germany

Typesetting: Camera-ready by author, data conversion by Scientific Publishing Services, Chennai, India
Printed on acid-free paper   06/3180

Preface

Model transformations are the glue that tie modelling activities together. If you've used modelling in anger then, whether you know it or not, you've used model transformations. They come in all shapes and sizes from moving models between different tools to generating implementations. Model transformations have humble beginnings—at one point, not long ago, it was said by many 'in the know' that the way forward in model transformations was to use XSLT. That this idea now raises a wry smile shows how far the model transformation community has come in a short time. Where once model transformations were hacked together in a variety of unsuitable languages, we now have a number of powerful, dedicated languages and theories at our disposal.

Since 2008, the ICMT conference series has played a huge part in advancing the subject, and this third edition was no different. The theories and languages presented at ICMT have allowed principled model transformations to play an ever greater part in real systems. Of course there is still much more to do: we need our model transformations, languages, and theories to scale further, allow greater expressivity, be more flexible, and aid reusability; and we lack empirically backed studies of model transformations in use. Doubtless you can think of other gaps. Yet, though some real-world challenges lie just beyond our reach, each year sees once-daunting problems conquered. Much of that progress is now driven by ICMT, and this year's edition showed how model transformations are increasingly being used in previously unfamiliar areas.

ICMT prides itself on transparency: 63 abstracts yielded 58 full submissions, of which 17 were eventually accepted—a 29% acceptance rate. Every paper was reviewed by at least three Programme Committee members. The resulting paper discussion and selection process was lively and detailed, reflecting the strength of the submissions. We were fortunate to have an invited paper and keynote from Stefano Ceri, which provides motivation for modelling and model transformations in a new, exciting, and challenging area.

For each of us, being Chair for this third edition was an honor. Many people helped make this conference what it is. We thank the Programme Committee for their hard work, particularly those who took on extra duties. The Publicity Chair Dennis Wagelaar did a wonderful job at advertising the conference. The ICMT Steering Committee were consistently wise and supportive and some went further than we could reasonably have hoped: Alfonso Pierantonio ran the ICMT 2010 website; Antonio Vallecillo, who doubled as Organizing Chair for the TOOLS Federated Conference as a whole, did wonders in communications; and Richard Paige provided much advice based on his experience as last year's

PC. Last, but certainly not least, we thank ICMT's lifeblood—those who submitted papers. To all these people we give wholehearted thanks!

April 2010   Laurence Tratt
                                                                        Martin Gogolla

Organization

Conference Committee

Programme Chair	Laurence Tratt (Middlesex University, UK)
Conference Chair	Martin Gogolla (University of Bremen, Germany)
Publicity Chair	Dennis Wagelaar (V.U. Brussel, Belgium)
Steering Committee	Jean Bézivin (INRIA, Nantes, France)
	Jeff Gray (University of Alabama, USA)
	Richard Paige (University of York, UK)
	Alfonso Pierantonio (University of l'Aquila, Italy)
	Antonio Vallecillo (University of Málaga, Spain)

Programme Committee

Kelly Androutsopoulos
Orlando Avila-Garcia
Luciano Baresi
Jordi Cabot
Antonio Cicchetti
Tony Clark
Charles Consel
Davide Di Ruscio
Gregor Engels
Piero Fraternali
Jesús García-Molina
Reiko Heckel
Howard Ho
Zhenjiang Hu
Frédéric Jouault
Gerti Kappel
Stuart Kent
Guenter Kniesel
Dimitris Kolovos
Vinay Kulkarni

Ivan Kurtev
Thomas Kühne
Esperanza Marcos
Marc Pantel
Francesco Parisi-Presicce
Vicente Pelechano
Ivan Porres
Nicolas Rouquette
Andreas Rummler
Bernhard Rumpe
Andy Schürr
Bran Selic
Jim Steel
Gabriele Taentzer
Yasemin Topaloglu
Daniel Varro
Eelco Visser
Jens Weber
Jon Whittle
Andreas Winter

Additional Reviewers

E. Balland	S. Hidaka	I. Rauf
S. Barat	C. Huemer	R. Raventós
J. Bézivin	M. Löwe	S. Roychoudhury
E. Biermann	E. Legros	J. Sánchez-Cuadrado
P. Boström	P. Liegl	M. Schindler
P. Brauner	M. Look	M. Seidl
P. Brosch	T. Lundkvist	C. Soltenborn
H. Cichos	R. Machado	H. Song
R. Clarisó	J. Manuel Vara Mesa	M. Tisi
R. Drogemuller	J. Mercadal	D. Truscan
A. Egesoy	R. Mohan	A. Vallecillo
Q. Enard	K. Nakano	G. Varro
J. Fons	J. Oliver Ringert	G. Wachsmuth
B. Güldali	R. Paige	I. Weisemoeller
C. Gerth	L. Patzina	M. Wimmer
A. Haber	I. Ráth	
B. He	A. Radwan	

Table of Contents

Search Computing: A Model-Driven Perspective

Marco Brambilla[1], Stefano Ceri[1], and Massimo Tisi[2]

[1] Politecnico di Milano, Dipartimento di Elettronica ed Informazione,
V. Ponzio 34/5, 20133 Milano, Italy
{mbrambil,ceri}@elet.polimi.it
[2] AtlanMod, INRIA & Ecole des Mines de Nantes,
rue Alfred Kastler, BP 20722, F-44307 Nantes Cedex 3, France
massimo.tisi@inria.fr

Abstract. Search Computing is a novel discipline that focuses on exploratory search of multi-domain Web queries like "Where can I attend an interesting conference in my field close to a sunny beach?". The approach is based on the interaction between cooperating search services, using ranking and joining of results as the dominant factors for service composition. This paper sketches the main characteristics of search computing and discusses how software engineering and model-driven engineering are challenged by the search computing problems. We present Search Computing applications from a model-driven perspective, in terms of (1) the models describing the objects of interest, (2) the specification of applications through model transformations, and (3) the definition of a domain specific language (DSL) defined for the specification of search query plans. This work provides a first exploration of MDE approaches applied to search computing and poses a set of challenges to the model transformation community.

Keywords: Search Computing, software engineering, search engine, conceptual models, model transformations, MDE, MDD, ATL.

1 Introduction

Search has become the most adopted way to access information over the Internet. Users are asking for queries that are more and more challenging for search engines, in several senses: the user search activity assumes the form of an interaction process instead of a single query; the single query itself becomes more complex (in terms of amount and extension of information the user asks for); and the information to be retrieved is often hidden in the so called "deep Web", which contains information perhaps more valuable than that which can be found on the surface Web.

In addition to general-purpose search engines, different classes of search systems have emerged to cover this information need, including meta-search engines, which query several engines and build up a unified result set, and vertical search engines, which aggregate domain-specific information from a fixed set of relevant sources and let users pose more sophisticated queries (e.g., finding proper combinations of flights, hotels, and car rental offers).

L. Tratt and M. Gogolla (Eds.): ICMT 2010, LNCS 6142, pp. 1–15, 2010.

However, an entire class of information needs remains to be supported: the case in which a user performs a complex search process [1], addressing different domains, possibly covered by distinct vertical search engines. This kind of search can be performed by separately looking for each individual piece of information and then mentally collating partial results, to get a combination of objects that satisfies the needs, but such a procedure is cumbersome and error prone.

We define search computing [6] as the new class of search applications aimed at responding to multi-domain queries, i.e., queries over multiple semantic fields of interest, by helping users in their ability to decompose queries and manually assemble complete results from partial answers. Search computing is especially effective for improving the visibility and economical value of so-called long-tail content, which can be used to produce highly customized search solutions (e.g., travel planners for wine enthusiasts, of event finders for niche music lovers).

Search computing applications are characterized by data sources usually heterogeneous and distributed, and multi-domain queries are answered by selecting a subset of those sources and by joining the responses, that are produced as combined and ranked results.

The contribution of this paper is to provide models and model transformations for search computing. In particular, we model and describe the main objects of interest for search computing applications, and how they can be transformed according to MDE practices. The need for explicitly formalizing the metamodels and transformation is multifold: (1) formalized metamodels contribute to the definition of a shared knowledge and vision upon search computing, a crucial achievement given that the discipline is new and needs to establish a common understanding among practitioners; (2) model transformations are essential to grant interoperability among the various tools devised for developing search computing applications[1]; (3) model transformations also play a central role in laying the foundations of the discipline, since they provide a formalized representation of the intended semantics of the interactions between models. This being said, MDE cannot be the only approach to be adopted. Indeed, various functional and non-functional requirements must be considered too (e.g., performance issues, distribution and scalability, complexity and acceptance, and so on). Therefore, some aspects of the approach need to be implemented with other kinds of technology in their final production version. Nonetheless, the effort of defining a MDE perspective on the field is a core asset for the success of the approach. In this work we provide a set of metamodels for the main concepts involved in search computing and we define a prototype of transformation between the query models and the query plan models. However, several further challenges and activities are still open. We have planned some of them in our future research agenda, while we leave others as open research problems for the MDE community.

The paper is organized as follows: Section 2 gives an overview of the approach; Section 3 discusses the services, query and result models and the associated transformations; Section 4 delves into the details of a DSL (domain specific language) devised for the specification of query plans; Section 5 describes the details of the core

---

[1] This can be achieved by applying the usual practices, for instance based on tool-specific syntax injection in the Ecore space, and subsequent model transformations implemented in ATL.

model transformation that generates the query plans; Section 6 discusses the related works and Section 7 proposes some challenges.

2 Overview of the MDE Approach to Search Computing

Search computing relies on a very limited set of core concepts, whose usage and transformations generate actual search applications and allow their executions. Fig. 1 shows an overview of the main concepts and associated transformations.

The **service mart model** provides the scaffolding for wrapping and registering data sources. Data sources can be heterogeneous (examples are: a Web site wrapper, a Restful data source, a WSDL web service, a data source exposed by means of the Yahoo! Query Language [http://developer.yahoo.com/yql/], etc.); registration requires a standardization of their interface, so to comply with a service invocation protocol. A service mart is defined as an abstraction (e.g., Hotel) of one or more Web service implementations (e.g., Bookings and Expedia), each capable of accepting queries and of returning results, possibly ranked and chunked into pages. A connection is defined as an input-output relationship between pairs of service marts that can be exploited for joining them (e.g., the declaration that the output city of the Hotel service mart can be used as an input destination to the Trip service mart).

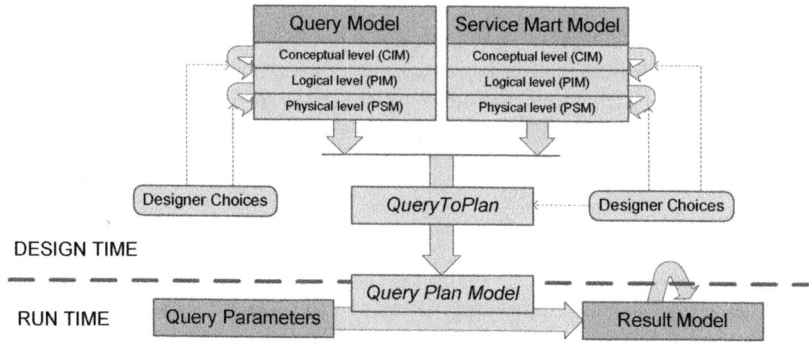

Fig. 1. Overview of the MDE approach to Search Computing

The **query model** describes the structure of a parametric search query: a query can be executed, saved, modified, and reused. Together with the service mart model, it represents the starting point for defining a search computing application: through appropriate model transformations (*QueryToPlan* transformation), executable **query plans** can be generated for describing procedural workflows for query execution. The query plan generation can be implemented in different ways, from trivial solutions to complex query optimization strategies that produce an optimized query execution plan. Furthermore, such plans can be fine tuned by designers, who can apply their own preferences and/or constraints to the transformation that generates the query plan.

At runtime an execution engine actually performs the query plan, which can be seen in turn as a model transformation that produces the model of the **query results** starting from the model of the **input parameters** submitted by the end users, by combining the outputs produced by **service calls**, computing the global ranking of results, and producing the corresponding query output.

The output itself is conformant to a result model. Results can evolve and blend dynamically according to the user choices, to support exploratory search processes [2]. Such processes can be seen as sequences of model transformations to apply **views** upon the result model.

Besides the main transformation flow, a plethora of model transformations can be applied locally at each step of the flow. For instance, at service and query level a set of transformations are defined from conceptual level (CIM) to logical level (PIM) and from logical level to physical level (PSM) at the purpose of defining default mappings between the different levels of abstractions. Such mappings can be manually overridden by the designer, who can impose his own choices; otherwise, if the designer prefers to stick at high level with his design, our automatic transformations map his choices to the detailed choices that are needed for running the application.

In the next sections we define the models describing the main objects involved in Search Computing applications.

Running example. For illustration, throughout the paper we use a running example, in which a user plans a leisure trip, and wants to search for upcoming concerts (described in terms of music type, e.g., Jazz, Rock, Pop, etc.) close to a specified location (described in terms of kind of place, like beach, lake, mountain, seaside, and so on), considering also availability of good, close-by hotels. Additionally, the user can expand the query with information about available, nearby good quality restaurants for the candidate concert locations, the news associated to the event, photos that are taken close to the location, and possible options to combine further events scheduled in the same days and located in a close-by place with respect to the first one.

3   Service Marts Model

The core model of Search Computing is devoted to service marts, which are abstractions that represent the properties (attributes and data types) of Web objects in a standardized way. Service marts are described in the Marts package of Fig. 3. Every service mart definition includes a name and a signature (a collection of exposed attributes). Attributes are strongly typed and can be atomic (i.e., defined by single-valued, basic types), composed (i.e., defined by a set of sub-attributes), or multi-valued (i.e., allowing multiple instances). The association between service marts is expressed by **connection patterns** (composition package of Fig. 3). Every pattern has a conceptual Name and a *logical specification*, consisting of simple comparison predicates between pairs of attributes of the two services, which are interpreted as a conjunctive Boolean expression, and therefore can be implemented by joining the objects returned by calling service implementations[2].

---

[2] The service mart model is currently being extended to support textual partial matching, type coercion, and connections based on proximity (giving special support to time, space, and money distances).

Besides the conceptual definition of service marts, the Patterns package of Fig. 3 describes a lower level characterization, whereby each service mart is associated with one or more access patterns. An **access pattern** is a specific signature of the service mart in which each attribute is denoted as either input (I) or output (O), depending on the role that it plays in the service call. In the context of logical databases, an assignment of I/O labels to the attributes of a predicate is called predicate adornment [5], and thus access patterns can be considered as adorned service marts. Moreover, an output attribute can be designed as ranked (R), if the service results are ordered based on the value of that attribute (e.g., the number of stars for hotel retrieval service mart).

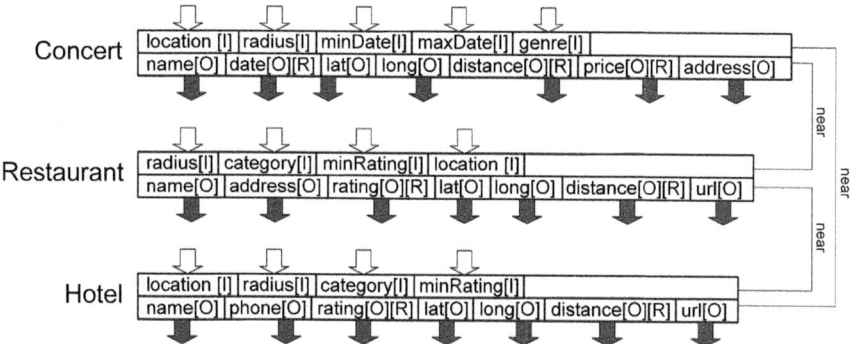

Fig. 2. Three access pattern examples for concerts, restaurants, and hotels

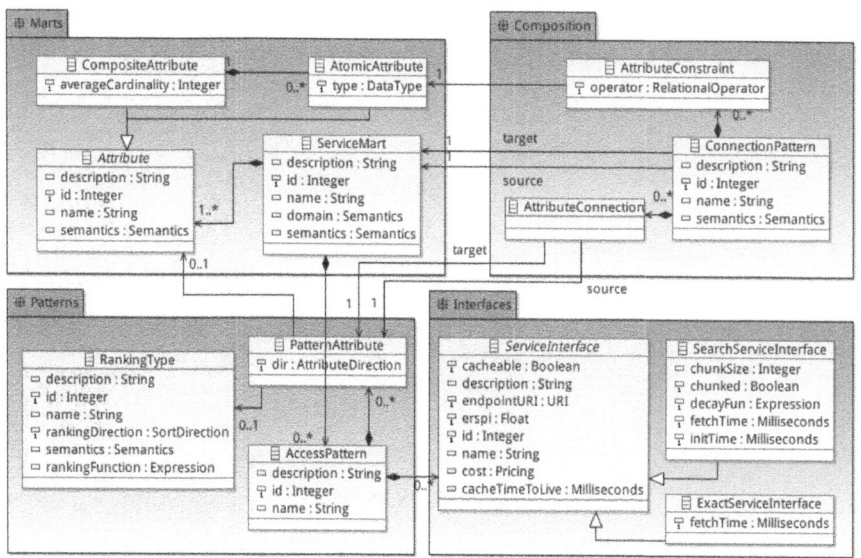

Fig. 3. Service mart model

Finally, **service interfaces** (Interfaces package of Fig. 3) describe the physical implementations of services. Two categories of service interfaces are possible: *search service* (i.e., one producing ranked sets of objects) or an *exact service* (i.e., services producing unranked objects[3]). Service interfaces are characterized by the following properties: **chunk descriptors** (a *chunked* service is a stateful service returning objects "one subset at a time", so as to enable the progressive retrieval of all the objects in the result set); **chunk size** (number of result instances in the chunk); **cache descriptors** (it indicates if a service interface is *cacheable* and in such case what is the cache *decay*, i.e. the Time To Live of the internal cache of data source objects maintained by the service); and **cost descriptors** (a cost characterization expressed as the *response time* and/or as the *monetary cost of invocation*).

Running example. Three examples of access patterns for concerts, restaurants, and hotels of the running case are shown in Fig. 2. Input [I], output [O] and ranking [R] attributes are highlighted.

4 Query Model

A *Search Computing query* is a conjunctive query over services. The query is a *declarative description* of the user request and is provided in input to the system and is used as starting point for generating procedural query plans to be executed by the system at the purpose of producing a result. Fig. 4 shows that a query can be defined at an abstract level (*AccessPatternLevelQuery*) or at physical level (*InterfaceLevelQuery*). A query is composed by a set of clauses can refer to the service mart level (and thus

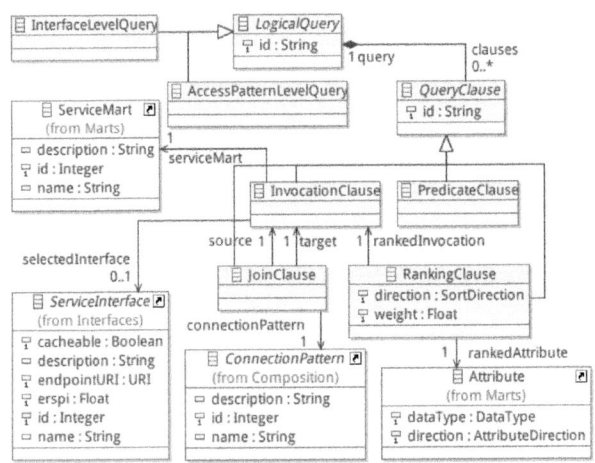

Fig. 4. Query model

---

[3] The term "exact" refers to the fact that a service returns the objects that exactly satisfy some condition and are equivalent (e.g., the actors of a movie). Search service instead typically return objects that satisfy some condition approximately and are therefore ranked for relevance (e.g., nearby theatres). The distinction is inherent to the service.

requires automatic translation down to the concrete service interfaces) or at the Service Interface level. Clauses can cover various aspects: *invocation* clauses select the services to be invoked, *predicate* clauses specify restriction conditions over the service outputs (i.e., assign a static value to a parameter), *join* clauses declare the connection patterns to be used for joining service results, and *ranking* clauses define the ranking criteria for the results.

Running example. An example of complex query is "Where can I find a jazz concert in San Francisco close to a nice vegetarian restaurant and to a good hotel?". A designer is expected to define a general structure that captures queries of this kind and provides a graphical representation, as shown in Fig. 5 as an *AccessPatternLevelQuery*. In the example, three *InvocationClauses* declare which are the marts to be involved (Concert, Restaurant and Hotel); a *TransformationClause* (gray circle in the schema) converts the objects {Concert.lat, Concert.long} into a location object; two *JoinClauses* define the connection between the services, based on the location of the extracted data: the location generated from {Concert.lat, Concert.long} is used to restrict the results of Restaurant and Hotel; and several *PredicateClauses* restrict the results based on the user inputs, which are fed into some input slots of the services. Finally, a *RankingClause* is defined on the distances and on the ratings of hotels and restaurants as a linear combination of attributes.

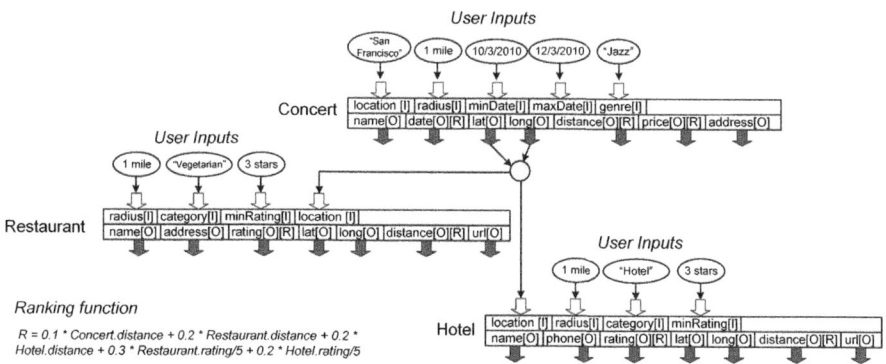

Fig. 5. Query example over concerts, restaurants, and hotels

5 Query Plan Model

A *query plan* is a well-defined scheduling of service invocations, possibly parallelized, that complies with their service interface and exploits the ranking in which search services return results to rank the combined query results. A query plan (see Fig. 6) is a DAG (direct acyclic graph) composed by nodes (i.e., invocations of services or other operators) and edges, which describe the execution flow and the data flow between nodes. Several types of nodes exist, including service invocators, sorting, join, and chunk operators, clocks (defining the frequency of invocations), caches, and others. The plans are specified through Panta Rhei *Domain Specific Language* [4].

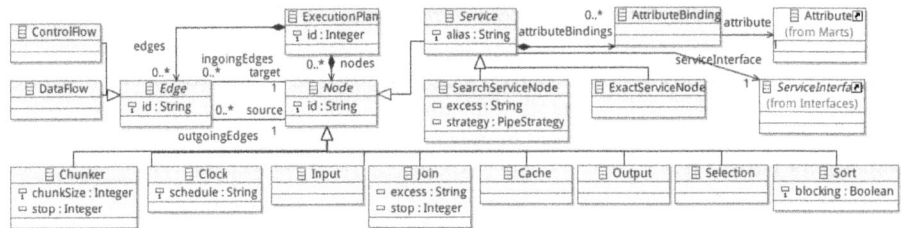

Fig. 6. Query plan model

Running example. As an example of query plan model expressed in Panta Rhei, Fig. 7 shows a join of two search services for extracting a list of *Concerts* and *Restaurants*, whose invocations are performed in parallel. The clock function is set to $(1,2,10)^n$, which means – by looking at the first two entries of the clock function - that at each clock cycle the *Concert* service is called (at most) once and the *Restaurant* service is called (at most) twice. Results are cached and then joined by suitable join units, which execute the join of search engine results [3]. If the executions of the branches are unbalanced the clock is notified and stops sending pulses until the 1/2 ratio is re-established. The execution of service calls and joins continues according to the joiner's strategy until 10 result instances are built. At this point, the plan continues with 10 invocations of a service extracting for each extracted pair a list of close-by *Hotels*, which are in turn joined with the previous result, thus producing the complete query response.

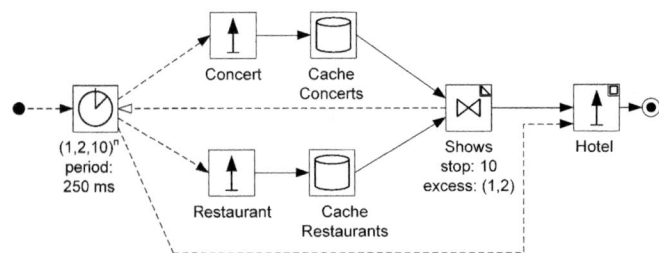

Fig. 7. Example of query plan according to the *SeCo Panta Rhei* DSL

6   Model Transformations

The SeCo runtime environment needs to offer performance and scalability guarantees that are hardly enforced by modern model transformation languages. On the other side, we are successfully experimenting model transformation languages at development and deployment time for the integration of SeCo with heterogeneous tools. Search Computing is an articulated framework that involves several actors with different tasks. Actors have access to the system using separate interfaces and store their information in different formats (e.g. XML, json, SQL). MDE and model-transformations provide an ideal platform for integrating the Search Computing ecosystem. In this section we want to show that model transformations can also be effectively used to specify the core algorithms of Search Computing.

6.1 Applicability of Model Transformations in the Context of Search Computing

Once the artifacts of Search Computing have been represented in the MDE technical space, transformations can be used to manage in a unified way the configuration and the execution of the SeCo system. Using model transformations in SeCo have benefits during the configuration phase of the application and service repository, and also during the query execution and visualization.

At configuration time, model transformations can especially be used in the **service adaptation phase**, for integrating existing services in SeCo. Service adaptation is necessary in the majority of cases, in which the data required by the application are already present on the Web, but the Web services that expose them do not adhere to the service mart interface. The adaptation is performed by service publishers, which generally need programming skills for the construction of data and protocol adaptation components. In several simple cases, the adapter of the service can be defined using a transformational approach, specifying, by model transformation rules, the mapping from the schema provided by the service and the service mart. For instance, a set of transformations can be defined from Service Mart to Access Pattern to Service Interface, at the purpose of defining default mappings between the different levels of abstractions. Such mappings can be manually overridden by the designer, who can impose his own choices; otherwise, if the designer prefers to stick at high level with his design, automatic transformations map his choices to the detailed choices that are needed for running the application.

Several works address the application of model transformations to service adaptation. Model transformations can be useful in all the phases of the SeCo development lifecycle. The **configuration of a SeCo application** is performed directly online, by accessing the configuration tools that manipulate the runtime model of service repository and applications. During the **execution of the query**, model transformations can be used to explicitly represent the logic of the mappings: from the model of the query structure to the query plan, from the query results to their visualizations as views.

Representing these logics as explicit mappings, with respect to hardcoded implementations, makes them more readable and maintainable and more suitable to automatic manipulation, for example for runtime adaptation by higher-order model transformations.

6.2 Query to Plan Transformation

While service adaptation and tool integration aspects are being deeply studied in literature, we show in this section the use of model transformations for the internal logic of the SeCo system. As a first study we perform the definition, by ATL [14] transformation rules, of a mapping between the basic query model, composed only of Service Invocation Clauses and Join Clauses, and the query plan. The query model is structurally very different from the query plan. The first is a declarative representation of the static structure of the input query, while the second is a procedural, dynamic representation of the query process.

The transformation rules are organized in two, ideally sequential, phases:

- In a first phase an ATL helper (i.e. a functional program) encapsulates the scheduling algorithm of the execution plan. The function produces a representation of a partial order of the clauses (as a Map that connects each clause to the next one to be processed) to be used during the generation of the output model. Several very different scheduling algorithms can be used in this phase, and the transformation structure allows to easily swap the preferred one, also at runtime.
- The second phase performs the actual generation of the output model, the Pantha Rhei query plan. In this phase the following mappings are assumed:
  - o Invocation clauses become Service invocation nodes,
  - o Join clauses become parallel joins or pipe joins
  - o The connections between the nodes are generated based on the ordering calculated in the first phase.

In our running case, a Higher Order Transformation (HOT) could be used to automatically modify the logic of the plan. For instance, we implemented the transformation rules that modify the generation algorithm to remove any caching node (and keep the graph correctly connected). This HOT can be composed with similar ones, e.g., that plug alternate algorithms to derive the scheduling of the clauses or the clock parameters.

Some implementation details of the transformation are reported in Appendix A.

7   Related Work

SeCo largely takes inspiration from model-driven engineering. All the SeCo artifacts are modeled as conceptual entities and are managed by model-driven design tools and transformations. The existing works in the field, which include general-purpose MDE techniques and web-specific languages and tools (e.g., WebML [7], OO-HMETHOD [10], UWE [13], and others), do not consider the search-specific aspects of application development and in particular completely ignore the need for an intermediate role between the user and the developer (that we call expert user) that has the duty of configuring search applications starting from basic services. None of the tools for object-oriented design, including the ones focusing on databases (e.g., Oracle JDeveloper 10g [http://www.oracle.com/tools]), on Web applications design (e.g., Code Charge Studio [http://www.codecharge.com], WebRatio [www.webratio.com]), and standard application design (e.g., Rational Rapid Developer or jABC, Java Application Building Center), explicitly support the design of search applications. From various tools, SeCo borrows the ideas of *visual composition* of the applications and *automatic deployment* of the running prototype. Mashup approaches are even more inspiring in this sense, since they exactly comply with the SeCo expert users need of an easy online toolsuite to quickly configure and deploy applications. The most famous mashup environments are Yahoo Pipes and Microsoft Popfly (recently discontinued), together with several scientific investigations still ongoing (e.g., spreadsheet based mashup frameworks [12]).

In this work we make use of the AmmA framework [14] to experiment with model transformations for search algorithms. While several applications of model transformations have been documented (for example in [17]) there are not many applications of MDE in the search domain. Some approaches have addressed the problem of searching UML models but they usually exploit an XML format for indexing seamlessly UML models, text files, and other sources [9]. The paper [15] proposes a retrieval framework allowing designers to retrieve information on UML models based on XMI representation through two query modalities: inclusion and similarity. Schemr [8] implements a search algorithm, based on a combination of text search and schema matching techniques, as well as a structurally-aware scoring methods, for retrieving database conceptual models with queries by example and keyword-based. Finally, [19] gives a classification of several use cases for HOTs. Within this classification, SeCo could use adaptation HOTs.

Although several other transformations exist in SeCo, in this paper we have especially focused our attention on specific use of ATL for the generation of a procedural query plan starting from a declarative specification of the query. Our current prototype applies a naïve transformation approach, although much more complex policies can be implemented, for optimizing the resulting plan. The use of rules in data management is not new: actually, a whole branch of research exists on *rule-based query plan optimization*, that dates back to the mid-Eighties [11][16][18]. In this sense, one significant contribution of SeCo could consist in porting those approaches to the modern model transformation approaches.

8   Conclusions

Search Computing is a novel proposal for supporting multi-domain search. In this paper we proposed a MDE perspective on search computing, that is useful for building a shared vision on the objects and tasks of interest for the framework, so as to lower the entrance barrier as much as possible. The metamodels and model transformations presented in this paper help establishing a common understanding on the core search computing issues and lay the bases for future tool interoperability and industrial-strength implementation of search computing systems. Our framework integrates several interacting models, thereby partitioning the design space and responsibilities to different roles and expertise, in a non-trivial way; the model-driven approach shall replace programming wherever possible, yielding flexibility and efficiency in application development.

Although a preliminary investigation in the MDE field has been carried out, search computing still poses several major challenges to the model transformation community. The main ones are:

- *Transformations to facilitate the development of Web service adapters.* There are several ways for extracting data from sources (ranging from queries to data sets in the hidden web to interchange data formats such as XML or JSON to wrapping technologies over Web sites) and these have to be interfaced to search integration systems. A framework based on model transformations enables the specification of simple mappings for data extraction, possibly making use of the latest proposals in Model Transformations, such as Model Weaving or Transformations by Example.

- *Transformations for building views of the results.* Research about views and viewpoints on models, i.e. the use of model transformations to filter or change the representation of a given data set, can be used as a start point for designing expressive user interfaces helping the browsing and combination of results.
- *Search on query models.* The availability of query models allows us to consider the domain of the queries themselves as a search target, thereby computing some of their properties, such as the most typical queries and their relationship to usage patterns.
- *Search process orchestration in light of model transformations.* The orchestration of search processes, exemplified in this paper with the Pantha Rhei DSL, can be seen as a model transformation. A generalized vision on the problem and a wider and more general set of languages still need formalization, so as to represent query plans as composition of operations on models.

Acknowledgements. This research is part of the Search Computing (SeCo) project, funded by the European Research Council (ERC), under the 2008 Call for "IDEAS Advanced Grants", a program dedicated to the support of frontier research. The project lasts from November 2008 to October 2013.

References

[1] Agrawal, P., Widom, J.: Confidence-Aware Join Algorithms. In: ICDE 2009, pp. 628–639 (2009)

[2] Bozzon, A., Brambilla, M., Ceri, S., Fraternali, P.: Liquid Query: Multi-Domain Exploratory Search on the Web. In: WWW 2010, Raleigh, USA, April 2010. ACM, New York (2010) (in print)

[3] Braga, D., Campi, A., Ceri, S., Raffio, A.: Joining the results of heterogeneous search engines. Information Systems 33(7-8), 658–680 (2008)

[4] Braga, D., Ceri, S., Corcoglioniti, F., Grossniklaus, M.: Panta Rhei: A Query Execution Environment. In: Ceri, S., Brambilla, M. (eds.) Search Computing Challenges and Directions. LNCS, vol. 5950, pp. 244–268. Springer, Heidelberg (2010)

[5] Calì, A., Martinenghi, D.: Querying Data under Access Limitations. In: ICDE 2008, pp. 50–59 (2008)

[6] Ceri, S., Brambilla, M. (eds.): Search Computing Challenges and Directions, March 2010. LNCS, vol. 5950. Springer, Heidelberg (2010)

[7] Ceri, S., Fraternali, P., Bongio, A., Brambilla, M., Comai, S., Matera, M.: Designing Data-Intensive Web Applications, December 2002. Morgan Kaufmann, USA (2002)

[8] Chen, K., Madhavan, J., Halevy, A.: Exploring schema repositories with schemr. In: SIGMOD 2009: Proc. of the 35th SIGMOD Int. Conf. on Management of data, New York, NY, USA, pp. 1095–1098. AC (2009)

[9] Gibb, F., McCartan, C., O'Donnell, R., Sweeney, N., Leon, R.: The integration of information retrieval techniques within a software reuse environment. Journal of Information Science 26(4), 211–226 (2000)

[10] Gómez, J., Cachero, C., Pastor, O.: Conceptual Modeling of Device-Independent Web Applications. IEEE MultiMedia 8(2), 26–39 (2001)

[11] Haas, L.M., Freytag, J.C., Lohman, G.M., Pirahesh, H.: Extensible query processing in Starburst. ACM SIGMOD Record 18(2), 377–388 (1989)
[12] Kongdenfha, W., Benatallah, B., Vayssière, J., Saint-Paul, R., Casati, F.: Rapid development of spreadsheet-based web mashups. In: WWW 2009, pp. 851–860. ACM, New York (2009)
[13] Knapp, A., Koch, N., Moser, F., Zhang, G.: ArgoUWE: A CASE Tool for Web Applications. In: EMSISE Workshop (2003)
[14] Kurtev, I., Bezivin, J., Jouault, F., Valduriez, P.: Model-based DSL frameworks. In: Companion to the 21st ACM SIGPLAN symposium on Object-oriented programming systems, languages, and applications, Portland, Oregon, USA, p. 616. ACM, New York (2006)
[15] Llorens, J., Fuentes, J.M., Morato, J.: Uml retrieval and reuse using xmi. In: IASTED Software Engineering, Acta Press (2004)
[16] Lohman, G.M.: Grammar-Like Functional Rules for Representing Query Optimization Alternatives. In: ACM SIGMOD 1988 (1988)
[17] Mens, T., Van Gorp, P.: A taxonomy of model transformation. In: Proceedings of the International Workshop on Graph and Model Transformation (GraMoT 2005), vol. 152, pp. 125–142 (2005)
[18] Pirahesh, H., Hellerstein, J.M., Hasan, W.: Extensible/rule based query rewrite optimization in Starburst. In: ACM SIGMOD 1992, pp. 39–48 (1992)
[19] Tisi, M., Jouault, F., Fraternali, P., Ceri, S., Bezivin, J.: On the Use of Higher-Order Model Transformations. In: Proceedings of the Fifth European Conference on Model-Driven Architecture Foundations and Applications (ECMDA), p. 1833. Springer, Heidelberg (2009)

Appendix A – Model Transformation from SeCo Queries to Plans

In this appendix we report some details of the main declarative transformation rules written in ATL [14] for transforming Query models into Plan models. A big part of the transformation complexity is related to the correct inter-connection of the building blocks generated by the transformation rules. To connect to the following element each rule makes a call to a getNextEdge() helper. The helper returns the next edge, based on a partial order of the clauses, computed at the beginning of the transformation.

The recursive helper that computes the partial order encapsulates the scheduling logic of the execution plan. It produces a representation of this schedule as a Map that connects each clause to the next one to be processed. The following example of scheduling algorithm tries to process every ParallelJoin before any PipeJoin:

```
helper context LQ!LogicalQuery def : schedule(map : Map(LQ!QueryClause, LQ!QueryClause)) :
Map(LQ!QueryClause, LQ!QueryClause) =
let parallelJoin:LQ!JoinClause = self.clauses->any(j |
  not map.getValues().includes(j) and j.isParallelJoin) in
  if (not parallelJoin.oclIsUndefined()) then
    self.schedule(map->
    including(thisModule.getLastFrom(map, parallelJoin.source), parallelJoin)->
    including(thisModule.getLastFrom(map, parallelJoin.target), parallelJoin))
  else let pipeJoin:LQ!JoinClause = self.clauses->any(j |
    not map.getValues().includes(j) and j.isPipeJoin) in
    if (not pipeJoin.oclIsUndefined()) then
      self.schedule(map->
      including(thisModule.getLastFrom(map, pipeJoin.source), pipeJoin)->
      including(thisModule.getLastFrom(map, pipeJoin.target), pipeJoin))
    else map endif endif;
```

The complexity of the transformation logic is lowered assuming, in our exemplary algorithm, a one-to-one correspondence between InvocationClauses and ServiceInvocations (i.e. each service involved in the query gets called only once in the execution plan). The rest of the transformation is then built around these key rules. A starting rule sets the ExecutionPlan container of the target model, and produces the first and last elements of the query execution plan, namely an Input node, an Output node, a Clock and the needed edges. The setup of the clock values is an important part of the algorithm that is factored out of the transformation rule by two helpers, calculating respectively the period (clockPeriod) and the schedule (clockSchedule) of the Clock.

Finally the main logic of the transformation is contained in the generation of the target model topology, defined in Pantha Rhei by using two kinds of connections, i.e. ParallelJoin and PipeJoin. Joins in the query execution plan are defined to implement JoinClauses in the query model. We define two ATL helpers to detect if the JoinClause is going to generate a ParallelJoin or a PipeJoin. ParallelJoins are generated when two services have a set of common attributes as output (e.g. latitude and longitude for the Restaurant and the Hotel):

```
helper context LQ!JoinClause def : isParallel : Boolean =
   self.connectionPattern.attributeConnections->
       forAll(c | c.patternAttribute1.dir = #OUT and c.patternAttribute2.dir = #OUT);
```

A PipeJoin has to be generated whenever the transformation engine is analyzing JoinClauses that refer to attributes with opposite directions (e.g. the output coordinates of the concert are given as input to the restaurant service).

```
helper context LQ!JoinClause def : isPipe : Boolean =
   self.connectionPattern.attributeConnections->
       forAll(c | c.patternAttribute1.dir = #OUT and c.patternAttribute2.dir = #IN);
```

ParallelJoins require the generation of a join node and of a caching mechanism for the services to invoke in parallel:

```
rule ParallelJoin {
   from
      join: LQ!JoinClause ( join.isParallelJoin )
   to
      inSourceControlFlow : EP!ControlFlow (
         target<-sourceCache
      ),
      inTargetControlFlow : EP!ControlFlow (
         target<-targetCache
      ),
      sourceCache: EP!Cache,
      targetCache: EP!Cache,
      sourceCacheControlFlow : EP!ControlFlow (
         source<-sourceCache,
         target<-joinNode
      ),
      targetCacheControlFlow : EP!ControlFlow (
         source<-targetCache,
         target<-joinNode
      ),
      clockDataFlow : EP!DataFlow (
         source <- joinNode,
         target <- thisModule.resolveTemp(join."query",'clock')
      ),
      joinNode : EP!Join (
```

```
     outgoingEdges <- Sequence{join.getNextEdge()}
   )
 }
```

In the case of PipeJoins, the Pantha Rhei syntax only requires that an edge is drawn from the source to the target invocations. We implement this transformation by extending the generation rule for the target invocation and adding the edge for the pipe to it.

```
rule searchServiceInvocationPipes extends searchServiceInvocations {
   from
       invocation: LQ!InvocationClause ( invocation.getNext().isPipeJoin and
          invocation.selectedInterface.oclIsKindOf(LQ!SearchServiceInterface))
   to
       inControlFlow: EP!ControlFlow (
          target <- service
       )
 }
```

We remark that the declarative specification of the transformation rules is readable and concise. Moreover it is easily manageable, for instance using Higher-Order Transformations to customize the transformation logic by adding cross-cutting concerns. In our running case, an HOT could be used to modify the caching logic of the plan. For instance, the following transformation rules could be used to modify the generation algorithm to remove any caching node (and keep the graph correctly connected). This HOT can be composed with similar ones, e.g. that plug alternate algorithms to derive the scheduling of the clauses or the clock parameters.

```
rule RemoveCacheNode {
   from
       i : ATL!OutPatternElement ( i.type = 'EP!Cache' )
 }
rule RemoveCacheEdge {
   from
       i : ATL!OutPatternElement ( i.type = 'EP!ControlFlow' and
       i.bindings->exists(b | b.propertyName='source' and
       if (b.value.oclIsKindOf(ATL!VariableExp))
       then b.value.name='sourceCache' or b.value.name='targetCache' else false endif ))
 }
rule RedirectCacheEdge {
   from
       b : ATL!Binding ( b.propertyName='target' and (b.value='sourceCache' or b.value='targetCache')
   to
       b1 : ATL!Binding (
          propertyName<-'target',
          value<-'joinNode'
       )
 }
```

The current prototype of the whole ATL transformation can be downloaded at:
`http://dbgroup.como.polimi.it/brambilla/SeCoMDA`

Domain-Specific Composition of Model Deltas

Maider Azanza[1], Don Batory[2], Oscar Díaz[1], and Salvador Trujillo[3]

[1] University of the Basque Country, San Sebastián, Spain
{maider.azanza,oscar.diaz}@ehu.es
[2] University of Texas at Austin, Austin, Texas, USA
batory@cs.utexas.edu
[3] IKERLAN Research Centre, Mondragon, Spain
strujillo@ikerlan.es

Abstract. We present a general approach to the incremental development of model-based applications using endogenous transformations, i.e. transformations whose input and output models conform to the same metamodel. Our work describes these transformations as model deltas that, when composed, deliver a complete model. We establish a relationship between a metamodel and its corresponding delta metamodel, show how model deltas can be defined as model changes (additions), explain how deltas can be composed using domain-specific composition algorithms, and propose metamodel annotations to specify these algorithms. We present different case studies as proofs of concept.

1 Introduction

Model Driven Engineering (MDE) conceives software development as transformation chains where models are the artifacts to be transformed. Transformations which map abstract models to executables have received the most attention [30]. An *initialModel* of an application is conceived and then is mapped, level by level, until a platform-specific model is reached. The main challenges are mapping between levels, where each level has its own distinct metamodel, and balancing trade-offs between alternative transformation strategies, e.g. addressing non-functional requirements. These transformations, that have different input and output metamodels, are *exogenous*.

The creation of *initialModels* has itself been the subject of research. Viewpoints have been used to address distinct perspectives of a target system [20]. In UML, class diagrams, state machine diagrams and activity diagrams capture different perspectives of the same application. Each viewpoint has its own distinct metamodel. But even viewpoints can be too coarse-grained to be units of development. *Object-oriented (OO)* programming faces similar problems when modularity is arranged by classes, rather than by concerns. Individual concerns crosscut distinct classes, complicating both development and maintenance [14].

Likewise, an *initialModel* integrates many distinct concerns of an application. Ease of maintenance encourages concerns to be both explicit and specified

L. Tratt and M. Gogolla (Eds.): ICMT 2010, LNCS 6142, pp. 16–30, 2010.

separately as model transformations, so that the *initialModel* itself is the result of a chain of *endogenous* transformations, i.e. transformations whose input and output models conform to the *same* metamodel. A consequence is that an *initialModel* is constructed incrementally by composing different endogenous transformations c_i, one per concern, starting from a base: $initialModel = c_3(c_2(c_1(baseModel)))$. This is the essense of *incremental development* [35].

Incremental development is not new. Collaborations have been proposed to support role-based designs in the incremental development of OO programs where each role contributes attributes and operations to achieve the role's purpose [31]. Classes are then "incrementally" extended by the roles they endorse. Incremental development is also at the heart of feature-oriented programming [5]. Here, the notion of feature displaces that of role as the design driving force. Products are then incrementally constructed by composing the features the product will exhibit. This paper inherits from these approaches. The primary difference stems from the artifacts being incrementally defined (i.e. initialModels), and the mechanism realizing the increments (i.e. endogenous transformations).

Current model transformation languages (e.g. ATL [15], ETL [19], RubyTL [11]) can specify any transformation. They were designed to handle arbitrarily complex mappings between different metamodels. Our experience and that of many others suggests that typical endogenous transformations are much simpler [3,23,24,32].

In this paper, we explore endogenous transformations characterized by:

- *Model Deltas.* Transformations are expressed as changes (additions) to models that when composed with a base model, deliver a complete model.
- *Domain-specificity.* Domain-specific composition algorithms are essential [3,24,28,36]. To this end, we annotate the domain metamodel to specify composition algorithms. We show that this light-weight approach offers a practical and powerful way to integrate domain-specific composition algorithms seamlessly into a development environment.

We implement our ideas using the *Epsilon Merging Language (EML)* [18] and present different case studies as proofs of concept[1].

2   Big Picture

Incremental development is widely known to handle design complexity and improve design understandability [35]. Although any artifact can be developed incrementally, the greatest benefits are observed when families of related artifacts are developed. This occurs in *Software Product Lines (SPL)* [10].

In an SPL, features can be seen as endogenous transformations [5]. A *feature* is an increment in program functionality that customers use to distinguish one program from another. SPL programs are constructed from a pre-planned set of

---

[1] Our composition engine and examples used in this paper are available for download at http://www.onekin.org/andromeda

features, which map (Java) programs to (Java) programs. A particular program in an SPL is produced by applying features to an initial program.

A product line in an MDE setting is a set of models. The *baseModel* corresponds to the above mentioned initial program and expresses the greatest common denominator of all SPL members. In many product lines, *baseModel* is simply the empty model $\emptyset$ [6].

Figure 1a shows a metamodel MM and its *cone of instances* (i.e. the set of all models that conform to MM). A subset of the cone is a set of models that belongs to a product line PL (e.g. $m_2...m_4$ belong to PL, m_1 is not a member, and all $m_1...m_4$ conform to MM). Note that the empty model $\emptyset$ and model m_A are outside the cone of MM,

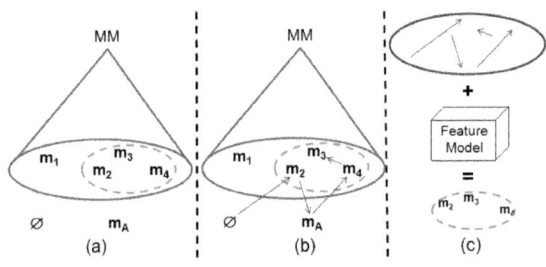

Fig. 1. Models, Endogenous Transformations and Product Lines

meaning that $\emptyset$ and m_A do not conform to MM.

Figure 1b shows feature realizations (i.e. endogenous transformations) as *arrows*[2] that map one model to another. An important property about arrows is that a composition of two or more arrows is yet another arrow [6]. Further, observe that a composition of arrows may produce an intermediate model (m_A) that does not conform to MM. Only the members of PL (m_2, m_3 and m_4) are required to conform to MM, regardless of the steps needed to obtain them. The members of PL are produced by composing arrows starting from $\emptyset$ and this collection of arrows defines the features of PL.

A specification of all legal compositions of features in a product line is a *feature model* [16]. Every model in PL's product line has a derivation (i.e., composition of arrows starting from $\emptyset$) that is expressed by the PL's feature model. Figure 1c illustrates the SPL perspective: a collection of arrows (features) plus a feature model (that constrains how these arrows can be composed) yields the set of models of a product line.

The relationships among arrows described above are very general; they hold for *all* implementations. The key questions in mapping arrows to an implementation are: *(i)* how is an arrow specified?, *(ii)* if arrows are themselves models then, what is an arrow metamodel? *(iii)* how are arrows composed? and *(iv)* how can domain-specific arrow composition algorithms be defined? The next sections address these issues.

---

[2] The term comes from Category Theory. Arrows are maps between objects. In an MDE setting arrows can be implemented using endogenous or exogenous transformations depending on their function. In this work we are interested in arrows that build SPLs (i.e. endogenous transformations) that implement deltas. See [6] for a description of the links between MDE, SPLE and Category Theory.

3   A Questionnaire SPL and Its Arrows

Fig. 2. Feature Model for the CSSPL

Questionnaires are a common research instrument in Social Sciences as a means to gather information. A set of questions is presented to respondents and a research hypothesis is validated against their answers. Although the Web is an invaluable resource for conducting surveys, social scientists generally lack the technical knowledge to make their questionnaires accessible online. To overcome this, abstractions are defined to liberate domain experts from the technicalities of Web surveys and are transformed into actual Web implementations[3].

Similar questionnaires that are targeted to different population profiles are needed on a regular basis. A one-size-fits-all questionnaire is inappropriate. Our example focusses on *Crime and Safety Surveys* that assess citizens' feelings on the safety of their enviroment. Figure 2 shows the feature model for the *Crime and Safety Survey Questionnaire SPL (CSSPL)*[4]. Its features define how questionnaires vary in this domain. Specifically, *(i)* if the respondent is a female, she is given a *Sexual Victimization Block* apart from the *Base Questionnaire*, *(ii)* if he or she belongs to a minority, a *Hate Crime Block* is added and *(iii)* regarding age, adults are given the *Consumer Fraud Block* while minors receive the *School Violence Block*. Now questionnaire creation is not just a "single shot". Rather, a questionnaire is characterized in terms of features that customizes it for a target audience.

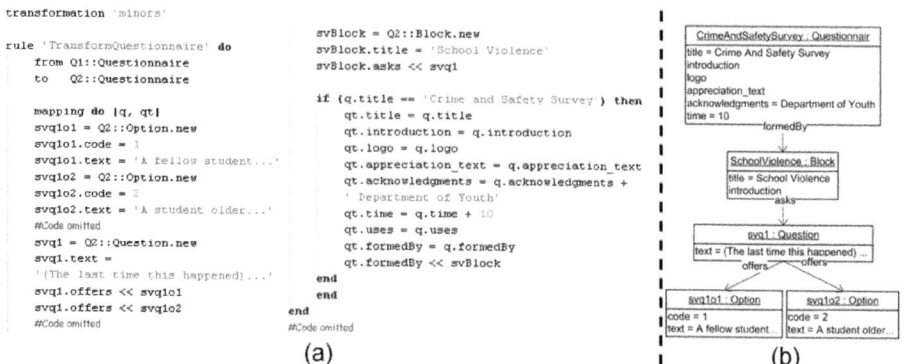

(a)   (b)

Fig. 3. Feature Implementation Options

---

[3] Examples of applications that cater to this need are ESurveyPro (http://www.esurveyspro.com) and Lime Service (http://www.limeservice.org).
[4] This *Questionnaire* family is inspired in the European Crime and Safety Survey (http://www.europeansafetyobservatory.eu/euics_fiq.htm).

There are two basic ways to implement a feature (i.e. an arrow that increments a model with certain functionality). One is to use a general-purpose transformation language. Figure 3a shows how the *Minor* feature is expressed in RubyTL. That is, how the *Department of Youth* should be added to the `acknowledgments` of the *Base Questionnaire*, how the estimated completion `time` is increased in 10 minutes, and the *School Violence Block* that should be included when the questionnaire is directed to minors. Another way is simply to create a *model delta* that defines the additions the *Minor* feature makes to a model (see Figure 3b). The latter brings the following advantages: *(i)* permits the checking of questionnaire constraints (e.g. `option codes` have to follow a certain format), *(ii)* makes features easier to understand and analyze [36] and *(iii)* separates *what* the feature adds from *how* it is added, thus making the *how* reusable for all questionnaire arrows. This advantages are revised in Section 7. Note that this definition of endogenous transformations is monotonic, features are not allowed to delete previously existing model elements.

4   Arrow Metamodels

Let M and MM be a model and its metamodel, respectively. Further, let AM and AMM stand for an arrow model and its arrow metamodel, respectively. This section presents a definition of AMM and its relationship with MM.

Figure 4 is a simplified *Questionnaire Metamodel* MM. Arrows (which to us represent fragments/additions to MM models) do not satisfy all constraints of MM. In the `Question` metaclass, for example, each question must have at least two options. An arrow can contribute just one or no option at all. This is the case for the *Minor* feature (see Figure 5), where question `atq2` has but one option. Once this feature is composed with the base, the result has four options, which is conformant with the questionnaire metamodel. Hence, an AMM can be created by eliminating constraints from MM.

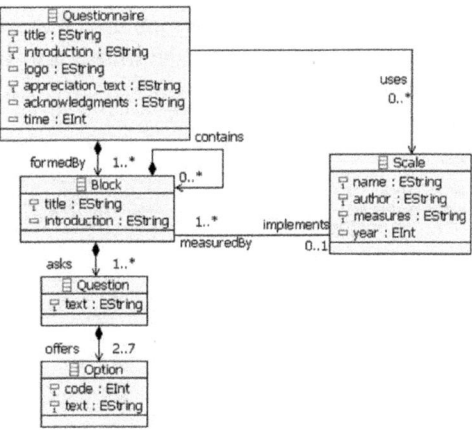

Fig. 4. Questionnaire Metamodel

However, not every constraint in the metamodel should be removed. Consider the `Question` metaclass which requires every question to have at most seven options. If any arrow adds more than seven options, every questionnaire created

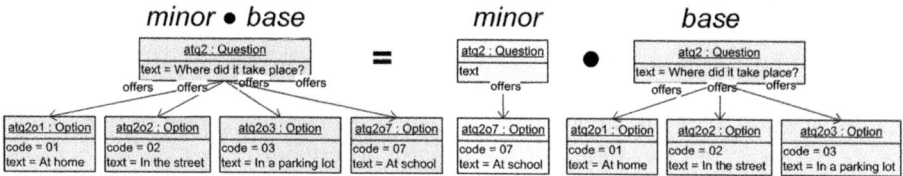

Fig. 5. Constraint Violation by the *Minor* Feature

using that arrow will not conform to the metamodel. Thus, this upper-bound constraint should be fulfilled by every arrow[5].

Two types of constraints are encountered when creating arrow metamodels:

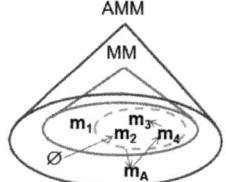

AMM

Fig. 6. AMM Cone

- *Arrow Constraints:* Constraints that can be validated for every arrow (e.g. upper-bounds, option codes have to follow a certain format, etc.). These constraints are kept in the AMM.
- *Deferred Constraints:* Constraints that can only be evaluated after *all* arrows are composed, i.e. when the entire product model has been assembled (e.g. lower-bounds)[6]. The AMM is obtained by removing these contraints from the metamodel.

Domain engineers should decide to which group each constraint belongs. An AMM can also be automatically generated from the product metamodel simply by removing all the metamodel's constraints except upper-bounds. However, the first option is preferrable as it detects more inconsistencies earlier in the process (i.e. at arrow creation time). We derived the AMM for the Questionnaire MM by removing eight lower-bound constraints.

Figure 6 shows the relationship between the cones of MM and AMM. Each model m_i in MM is equivalent to an arrow $\emptyset \rightarrow m_i$ in AMM. This means that the cone of AMM not only includes every model in the cone of MM, but other models and arrows as well (e.g., models $\emptyset$ and m_A, and arrow $m_A \rightarrow m_4$ and composite arrow $\emptyset \rightarrow m_A$). The close relationship between AMM and MM means that arrows are defined using the same concepts as models and, as they belong to an SPL, they are designed with composition in mind, the topic of the next section.

---

[5] This holds for composed arrows as well. If a composed arrow adds more than seven options, its use will also not conform to the the Question metaclass.

[6] This has a database counterpart. The database administrator defines a database schema with constraints. Additionally, the administrator can declare a constraint to be validated as soon as a database update happens (immediate mode) or wait till the end of the transaction, once all updates were conducted (deferred mode). The deferred mode allows for some constraints to be violated during a transaction execution, as long as the constraints hold at the end of the transaction.

5   Arrow Composition

Model composition has been defined as the operation M_{AB} = Compose (M_A, M_B, C_{AB}) that takes two models M_A, M_B and a correspondence model C_{AB} between them as input, and combines their elements into a new output model M_{AB} [7]. Arrow composition is a special case, where both M_A and M_B conform to the *same* metamodel. Further, the correspondence model C_{AB} is implicit as objects with the same name (or rather, identifier) in models M_A and M_B are, in fact, the same object. Arrow composition is performed by pairing objects of different fragments with the same name (identifier) and composing them.

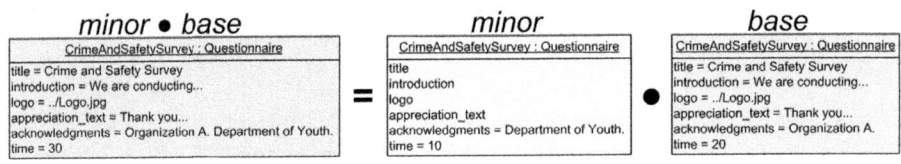

Fig. 7. Composition of Minor and Base Features

There are two distinct cases in object composition:

– *Generic:* This is the default, metamodel independent, composition [2,5]. The composition of a pair of objects equals the composition of their corresponding attribute pairs. The composition of a pair of scalar-valued attributes is this: if both have different non-null values, composition fails and an error is raised. Otherwise, the non-null value is the result. In the case of set-valued attributes (including references), their union is the result. Figure 7 presents different examples of this composition: title, introduction, logo and appreciation_text attributes.
– *Domain-Specific:* In a majority of cases, generic composition is sufficient. The remaining cases require a domain-specific composition method. Consider the acknowledgments and time attributes in the Questionnaire metaclass. An organization can fund all the study or only part of it. Figure 7 shows how the *base* study is funded by Organization A and the part regarding *minors* is funded by the Department of Youth. If objects were composed generically, an error would be raised as both objects have a different value in the acknowledgments attribute. However, the convention for questionnaires is to concatenate both acknowledgments as the result.
The time attribute is another example. It indicates the estimated time needed to complete the questionnaire. The *base* feature takes 20 minutes and the *minor* feature needs 10 more. The expected behavior would add both values to the result, not to raise an error.

A practical tool should allow domain engineers to annotate any class or attribute to indicate that a customized composition algorithm, rather than the default algorithm, is to be used. Additionally, since some algorithms are likely to be used in different domains (e.g. string concatenation), a set of keywords are provided to denote those recurrent algorithms as annotations on the metamodel, hereafter referred to as *built-in algorithms*. These annotations include: @concat (i.e. given two values V1 and V2, the composition delivers V1V2), @slash_concat (i.e. the composition delivers V1/V2), @sum (i.e. the composition delivers the addition of V1 and V2), @min (minimum value), and @max (maximum). Engineers can turn a domain-specific composition algorithm into a built-in algorithm by naming and including it in a composition-algorithm library.

Figure 8 depicts the annotated *Questionnaire* metamodel. Note that the acknowledgments attribute in *Questionnaire* and the introduction attribute in *Block* are annotated with @concat. This indicates that their values are to be composed by concatenation. Moreover, the time attribute in *Questionnaire* is annotated with @sum, meaning that composed contents should be added.

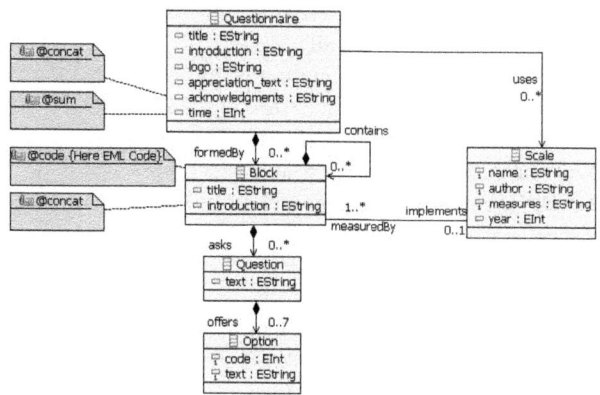

Fig. 8. Annotated Questionnaire Metamodel

When no built-in algorithm is sufficient, engineers must resort to describing domain-specific composition algorithms procedurally (hereafter called *ad-hoc algorithms*). This is the only case that requires knowledge of a transformation language, which in our case is EML. In the *Questionnaire* domain, blocks can be defined using a scale. When composing blocks with different scales, *Questionnaire* semantics dictate not to merge blocks but to keep them as separate sub-blocks[7]. We specify ad-hoc algorithms as a piece of EML code, and is an annotation that is attached to the *block* class[8] (see Figure 8).

5.1   Implementation

Given an annotated metamodel MM, our prototype automatically generates *Epsilon Merging Language (EML)* rules for composing arrows. EML is a rule-based language for merging models of diverse metamodels and technologies [18].

---

[7] Note that this domain specific composition is not limited to individual attributes as in the above examples; it applies to complete *Block* objects.

[8] This option is debatable. Another possibility is to embed the ad-hoc algorithm directly into the generated code using a "protected region", i.e. a piece of code that is not overridden when the code is newly generated. We prefer to have all composition algorithms specified in a single place: the metamodel. In our opinion, this facilitates understandability and maintainability.

The Object metaclass defines the core metamodel of our implementaion of *ANDROMEDA (ANnotation-DRiven Oid-based coMposEr for moDel Arrows)* (see Figure 9). Object instances are singled out by an explicit identifier that is used for object matching. Object holds the generic methods for match, merge, and copy methods. *Match* compares pairs objects and decides if they match. *Merge* merges two objects that match and *copy* copies objects for which no match has been found to the result.

This generic behavior can be specialized to cater for the composition peculiarities of the domain at hand. To this end, Object specializations are created for each domain metaclass (see Figure 9). Note how Questionnaire and Block override the generic merge method to address their own specific composition semantics.

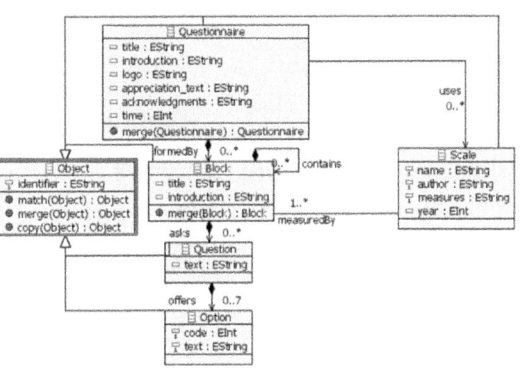

Generic behavior. This behavior is provided by AN-DROMEDA. The match method

Fig. 9. Extended Questionnaire Metamodel

is realized through an *Epsilon Comparison Language (ECL)* rule (see Figure 10a) [17]. This rule indicates that two Objects match if they are instances of the same class and have the same identifier. The merge method is supported through an EML rule (see Figure 10b). The rules applies to all Object instances. We also provide methods that define default merge behavior for attributes and references.

Domain-specific behavior. Domain-specific EML rules that extend the generic EML rules (rule extension is the counterpart of method inheritance) are **generated**. Metamodel annotations indicate that generic merging needs to be substituted by domain-specific merging. Three situations arise:

- *Generic Algorithm* (e.g. *Question* metaclass). See Figure 10c for an example. This rule extends the generic rule MergeObject for the *Question* metaclass by just reusing the default methods.
- *Built-in Algorithm* (e.g. *Questionnaire* metaclass). The annotations in the metaclass the metamodel (see Figure 8), the acknowledgments attribute is annotated with @concat and the time attribute is annotated with @sum. These annotations lead to the merge rule in Figure 10d where the generic merge of acknowledgments and time attributes is overridden by string concatenation and integer addition respectively.
- *Ad-hoc Algorithm* (e.g. *Block* class). The approach is similar to the built-in algorithm, but now the code embedded in the annotation is directly copied into the EML rule (see Figure 10e).

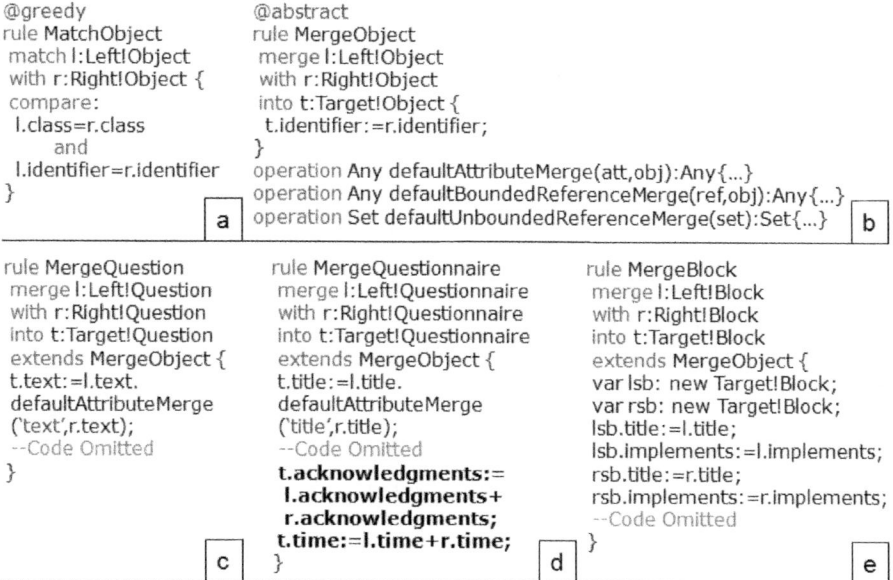

Fig. 10. Implementing composition through EML and ECL rules

6   Case Studies

Among the motivations for connecting arrows and product lines in Section 2 is to underscore the generality of their relationships. We believe our *CSS Questionnaire SPL (CSSPL)* is typical of a basic MDE product line, and we have explained how our tools handle it. But there are examples from other technical spaces [8] for which these same relationships can be demonstrated to hold.

The largest examples of feature-based compositions come from *Feature Oriented Programming (FOP)*, i.e. from the EBNF technical space [8]. SPLs in FOP are families of Java-based programs. *AHEAD Tool Suite (ATS)* is a set of tools to support FOP [5]. ATS was refactored into the *ATS Product Line (APL)*, i.e., ATS bootstraps itself by composing features of APL. Over time, ATS has grown to 24 different tools comprising over 200K LOC Java. In our case study, we focus only on model representations of the code that corresponds to features[9].

Features in APL are written in Jak, a superset of Java that supports features and metaprogramming [5]. We defined a bridge that translates an APL feature written in Jak into a model fragment that conforms to the Jak Arrow Metamodel and the other way around. By composing model fragments, we can produce a model of the ATS product line.

---

[9] Along with APL, we also created models for the *Graph Product-Line (GPL)*, a family of classical graph applications [21]. The results of GPL are not much different than what we report for APL and CSSPL. The GPL case study is available at http://www.onekin.org/andromeda

Interestingly, no constraint had to be removed from the Jak metamodel to produce its arrow metamodel: all constraints defined in the Jak metamodel where applicable to arrow models. Next, a composition algorithm was chosen for each element in the Jak metamodel.

Table 1 lists statistics about the *Jak Metamodel*, with statistics from the *Questionnaire metamodel (Qst)* for comparison purposes. The number of classes, attributes and references of each metamodel and the distribution of their composition types are listed. Note that Jak uses a large number of domain-specific composition algorithms. While this is not unexpected, what is interesting is that several of these algorithms worked on objects and not attributes.

Table 1. Jak and Questionnaire Metamodels

MM DATA	Jak	Qst
Classes	12	5
Attributes	18	15
References	25	7
Removed Constraints	0	8
Generic Comp.	37	23
D.S. Comp.	18	4

Table 2 compares the average size of CSSPL and APL features with their size in objects (a.k.a *Objs*) and references (a.k.a *Refs*). It also presents the average size for particular products we composed. Note that APL model arrows are on average four times larger than the arrows of CSSPL, and APL products are over fifty times larger than CSSPL products.

Table 2. CSSPL and APL Statistics

	Objs	Refs
CSSPL Features	22	21
APL Features	109	332
CSSPL Products	63	62
APL Products	3035	9394

Again, one of the advantages of the Jak case studies was to demonstrate our composition principles hold across different technical spaces. Another advantage was that we could verify the correctness of our compositions. Model arrows were composed to yield a certain product and then transformed into code. The same product was obtained by directly composing its code features and both results were compared using source equivalence to test for equality[10].

7   Perspective and Related Work

7.1   Perspective

We conceive model construction as a gradual composition of model arrows. Each arrow realizes an increment in application functionality (i.e. a feature), and the functionality of the final application is the added functionality of each of its arrows. Therefore, the characterization of our work is twofold. First, increments in functionality are embodied as deltas that are expressed in the same language as the final model. The benefits include:

- Certain domain constraints can be checked at arrow building time, allowing earlier error detection. It paves the way to safe composition, the assurance that all products of the SPL conform to the domain metamodel.

---

[10] Source equivalence is syntactic equivalence with two relaxations: it allows permutations of members when member ordering is not significant and it allows white space to differ when white space is unimportant.

- It separates what a feature adds from how it is added, thus making the composition algorithms reusable for all features that conform to the same metamodel.
- Declarativeness. Model arrows are easier to read and write than their transformation counterpart. Figure 3a shows the same *Minor* feature but now realized using a general-purpose transformation language, RubyTL [11]. Even to someone accustomed to reading transformation rules, it takes some time to grasp information that the transformation adds to the base model. When handling SPLs with hundreds of features, scalability is a main issue and declarativeness a major enabler.
- The Arrow Metamodel can be derived from the domain metamodel (e.g. *Questionnaire*) by removing constraints.

Second, our work also uses model superimposition as the default approach to model composition. Additionally, domain-specific composition semantics are captured through annotations in the domain metamodel. This improves the declarativeness of how the composition algorithms are captured. The benefits include:

- *Automatization*: The composition algorithm can be automatically generated. As a proof of concept, we showed the implementation that generates EML rules.
- *Understandability*: Anchoring composition annotations on the metamodel, permits designers to focus on the *what* rather than on *how* the composition is achieved.
- *Maintenance*: Additional composition algorithms can be added or removed with minimal effort. This could be of interest in the context of metamodel evolution where new metaclasses/attributes can be added that require customized composition algorithms [33].

Our work also raises research questions that are subject of future work. Generalizing our arrow definition to allow deletions is a case in point. We want to study in which cases is that deletion necessary and what its drawbacks are. Moreover, in an MDE setting endogenous transformations define only half of the picture. We are interested in transformations that map an arrow that is an instance of an arrow metamodel to an arrow that is an instance of another [6]. Another topic deals with safe composition: once all arrows are composed, the resulting model should fulfill all the constraints of the metamodel. We want to guarantee that all legal feature compositions yield models that satisfy all constraints of the metamodel, *but without enumeration*. Existing work suggests a direction in which to proceed [12,22,29].

7.2 Related Work

Implementation Approaches. Two main trends in implementing endogenous transformations can be identified: transformation languages vs. model deltas. Examples of the former include C-SAW [4], MATA [34] and VML* [36]. A transformation language is more versatile and it performs analyses that are presently outside our work. For example, MATA comes with support to automatically detect interactions between arrows. Since arrows in MATA are graph rules, the technique of critical pair analysis can be used to detect dependencies and conflicts between rules[11]. This versatility, however, comes at a cost: *(i)* it requires developers to be familiar with a graph transformation language and *(ii)* being defined in a different language, it reduces checking with respect to the domain metamodel that can be performed on the transformations. To ease the developers burden, MATA defines transformations between UML and the underlying graph rules. Nevertheless, these transformations must be defined for every metamodel at hand.

Traditionally SPL arrows are defined as model deltas — a set of additions — that are superimposed on existing models. Recently, several researchers have followed this trend, particularly using aspects to implement them [3,23,24,32]. To the best of our knowledge, none of these approaches defines a mechanism to check the conformance of arrows to their arrow metamodels. Interestingly, SmartAdapters [24] defines pointcuts as model snippets that conform to a metamodel that is obtained by eliminating all constraints from the domain metamodel, in a similar fashion to the way we define arrow metamodels [26]. However, no mention is made about an advice metamodel.

Along with aspects, collaborations are another candidate paradigm for realizing model deltas. Collaborations are monotonic extensions of models that encode role-based designs and are composed by superimposition [31]; collaborations are a centerpiece in recent programming languages (e.g. Scala [25]) and prior work on feature-based program development [5]. In contrast, aspects may offer a more general approach to express model deltas, where pointcuts identify one or more targets for rewriting (a.k.a. advising). However, the generality of aspects is by no means free: it comes at a cost of increased complexity in specifying, maintaining, and understanding concerns [1].

Domain-Specificity. There are a number of model delta composition tools, some using *Aspect Oriented Modeling (AOM)*, that are now available. XWeave [32] and Kompose [13] support only generic composition, although the latter has some limited support for domain specificities in the form of pre-merge and post-merge directives. Other approaches, e.g. SmartAdapters [24], VML* [36] and Feature-House [3], provide support for domain-specific composition. The first two require engineers to explicitly indicate how arrows are to be composed, while we strive to promote reuse by automatically generating as much as possible from the metamodel by leveraging metamodel annotations. FeatureHouse also accounts for domain specificities. However, it is restricted to tree composition, and domain-specific composition is limited to tree leaves. In contrast, our approach considers graphs rather than trees and composition can be simultaneously specified at different points within models.

Model Differences. Model arrows are closely related to the idea of model model differences [9,27]. The main distinction stems from their purpose, the former implement a feature in an SPL and are normally built separately while the latter are calculated as the difference between two models that conform to the same metamodel.

---

[11] It may be possible to define a corresponding analysis on model fragments.

8   Conclusions

MDE conceives software development as transformation chains where models are the artifacts to be transformed. We presented an approach to the incremental development of *initialModels* in an SPL setting. Models are created incrementally by progressively applying endogenous transformations that add increments in functionality. We depicted these transformations as arrows and implemented them as model deltas. We explained how arrows realize features in SPLs, how arrows conform to arrow metamodels, and how arrow metamodels are derivable from domain metamodels. The focus of our work stressed the need for domain-specific composition algorithms, and how they could be added to metamodels in a practical way. Further, our case studies illustrated the technical-space independence of our approach. We believe our light-weight approach offers a practical and powerful way to integrate domain-specific composition algorithms seamlessly into an MDE development environment.

Acknowledgments. We gratefully thank L. Vozmediano for her help with the questionnaires domain and J. De Sosa, M. Kuhlemann, R. Lopez-Herrejon, G. Puente and J. Saraiva for fruitful discussions during the preparation of this draft. This work was co-supported by the Spanish Ministry of Education, and the European Social Fund under contract MODELINE, TIN2008-06507-C02-01 and TIN2008-06507-C02-02. Batory's work was supported by NSF's Science of Design Project CCF-0724979.

References

1. Apel, S., et al.: Aspectual Feature Modules. IEEE TSE 34(2) (2008)
2. Apel, S., et al.: FeatureHouse: Language-Independent, Automated Software Composition. In: ICSE (2009)
3. Apel, S., et al.: Model Superimposition in Software Product Lines. In: Paige, R.F. (ed.) ICMT 2009. LNCS, vol. 5563, pp. 4–19. Springer, Heidelberg (2009)
4. Balasubramanian, K., et al.: Weaving Deployment Aspects into Domain-Specific Models. IJSEKE 16(3) (2006)
5. Batory, D., et al.: Scaling Step-Wise Refinement. IEEE TSE 30(6) (2004)
6. Batory, D., et al.: The Objects and Arrows of Computational Design. In: Czarnecki, K., Ober, I., Bruel, J.-M., Uhl, A., Völter, M. (eds.) MODELS 2008. LNCS, vol. 5301, pp. 1–20. Springer, Heidelberg (2008)
7. Bézivin, J., et al.: A Canonical Scheme for Model Composition. In: Rensink, A., Warmer, J. (eds.) ECMDA-FA 2006. LNCS, vol. 4066, pp. 346–360. Springer, Heidelberg (2006)
8. Bézivin, J., Kurtev, I.: Model-based Technology Integration with the Technical Space Concept. In: MIS (2005)
9. Cicchetti, A., et al.: A Metamodel Independent Approach to Difference Representation. In: JOT (2007)
10. Clements, P., Northrop, L.M.: Software Product Lines - Practices and Patterns. Addison-Wesley, Reading (2001)
11. Cuadrado, J.S., et al.: RubyTL: A Practical, Extensible Transformation Language. In: Rensink, A., Warmer, J. (eds.) ECMDA-FA 2006. LNCS, vol. 4066, pp. 158–172. Springer, Heidelberg (2006)

12. Czarnecki, K., Pietroszek, K.: Verifying feature-based model templates against well-formedness OCL constraints. In: GPCE (2006)
13. Fleurey, F., et al.: A generic approach for automatic model composition. In: MoD-ELS Workshops (2007)
14. Gottlob, G., et al.: Extending Object-Oriented Systems with Roles. ACM TOIS 14(3) (1996)
15. Jouault, F., Kurtev, I.: Transforming Models with ATL. In: Bruel, J.-M. (ed.) MoDELS 2005. LNCS, vol. 3844, pp. 128–138. Springer, Heidelberg (2006)
16. Kang, K., et al.: Feature-Oriented Domain Analysis (FODA) Feasibility Study. Technical report, CMU/SEI-90-TR-21, Software Engineering Institute (1990)
17. Kolovos, D.: Establishing Correspondences between Models with the Epsilon Comparison Language. In: Paige, R.F., Hartman, A., Rensink, A. (eds.) ECMDA-FA 2009. LNCS, vol. 5562, pp. 146–157. Springer, Heidelberg (2009)
18. Kolovos, D., et al.: Merging Models with the Epsilon Merging Language (EML). In: Nierstrasz, O., Whittle, J., Harel, D., Reggio, G. (eds.) MoDELS 2006. LNCS, vol. 4199, pp. 215–229. Springer, Heidelberg (2006)
19. Kolovos, D., et al.: The Epsilon Transformation Language. In: Vallecillo, A., Gray, J., Pierantonio, A. (eds.) ICMT 2008. LNCS, vol. 5063, pp. 46–60. Springer, Heidelberg (2008)
20. Kulkarni, V., Reddy, S.: Separation of Concerns in Model-Driven Development. IEEE Software 20(5) (2003)
21. Lopez-Herrejon, R., Batory, D.: A Standard Problem for Evaluating Product-Line Methodologies. In: Bosch, J. (ed.) GCSE 2001. LNCS, vol. 2186, pp. 10–24. Springer, Heidelberg (2001)
22. Lopez-Herrejon, R., et al.: Using incremental consistency management for conformance checking in feature-oriented model-driven engineering. In: VAMOS (2010)
23. Morin, B., et al.: A Generic Weaver for Supporting Product Lines. In: EA (2008)
24. Morin, B., et al.: Weaving Aspect Configurations for Managing System Variability. In: VAMOS (2008)
25. Odersky, M., et al.: An Overview of the Scala Programming Language. Technical report, EPFL (2004)
26. Ramos, R., et al.: Matching Model-Snippets. In: Engels, G., Opdyke, B., Schmidt, D.C., Weil, F. (eds.) MODELS 2007. LNCS, vol. 4735, pp. 121–135. Springer, Heidelberg (2007)
27. Rivera, J.E., Vallecillo, A.: Representing and Operating with Model Differences. In: TOOLS (2008)
28. Schaefer, I.: Variability modelling for model-driven development of software product lines. In: VAMOS (2010)
29. Thaker, S., et al.: Safe Composition of Product Lines. In: GPCE (2007)
30. Vallecillo, A., Gray, J., Pierantonio, A. (eds.): ICMT 2008. LNCS, vol. 5063. Springer, Heidelberg (2008)
31. VanHilst, M., Notkin, D.: Using Role Components to Implement Collaboration-Based Designs. In: OOPSLA (1996)
32. Völter, M., Groher, I.: Product Line Implementation using Aspect-Oriented and Model-Driven Software Development. In: SPLC (2007)
33. Wachsmuth, G.: Metamodel adaptation and model co-adaptation. In: Ernst, E. (ed.) ECOOP 2007. LNCS, vol. 4609, pp. 600–624. Springer, Heidelberg (2007)
34. Whittle, J., Jayaraman, P.: MATA: A Tool for Aspect-Oriented Modeling Based on Graph Transformation. In: MODELS Workshops (2007)
35. Wirth, N.: Program Development by Stepwise Refinement. Communications of the ACM 14(4) (1971)
36. Zschaler, S., et al.: VML* - A Family of Languages for Variability Management in Software Product Lines. In: SLE (2009)

Temporal Model-Based Diagnostics Generation for HVAC Control Systems

Marion Behrens and Gregory Provan

Complex Systems Lab, University College Cork, Ireland

Abstract. Optimizing energy usage in buildings requires global models that integrate multiple factors contributing to energy, such as lighting, "Heating, Ventilating, and Air Conditioning" (HVAC), security, etc. Model transformation methods can then use these global models to generate application-focused code, such as diagnostics or control code. In this paper we focus on using model transformation techniques to generate model-based diagnostics (MBD) models from "global" building systems models. This work describes the automated generation of models for MBD by considering control systems which are described through behavior that also relies on the state of the system.

Our approach contributes to model-driven development of complex systems by extending model consistency up to models for diagnostics. We transform hybrid-systems (HS) models into models based on propositional temporal logic with timing abstracted through sequentiality, and illustrate the transformation process through a simple example.

1 Introduction

One emerging area of research is developing software to improve the energy efficiency of buildings. To fully realize this goal, it is necessary to integrate the operation of all building systems, so that we can optimize the building's operation on a global setting. In this case, a global building model is necessary. We can then use such a global model to generate application-specific code, e.g., lighting controls, diagnostics, etc. This use of a global model to drive code generation for multiple applications will significantly reduce the cost of software development, as opposed to generating code for each application from scratch.

In this article we focus on using model transformation techniques to generate MBD models from "global" building systems models. This transformation process is a very challenging task, given the significant differences between the global and MBD models. The global (or source) model is defined using a hybrid-systems (HS) [1] language, which describes the continuous-valued dynamics of a range of building parameters, such as temperature and light levels, movement of people throughout the zones of the building, control of HVAC, lighting, etc. The MBD (target) model focuses on discrete system parameters governing *abnormal* operation of building components, such as the HVAC/lighting controllers and the associated equipment, e.g., chillers, pumps, fans, etc. Consequently, the model transformation process must extract just the diagnostic-related information from

L. Tratt and M. Gogolla (Eds.): ICMT 2010, LNCS 6142, pp. 31–44, 2010.

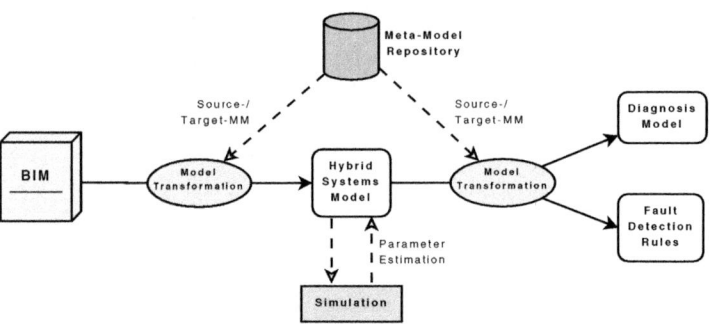

Fig. 1. Model-Transformation Context

the source model and further inject diagnostic-related information that is not contained in the source model, e.g. failure probabilities, from other sources.

Fig. 1 shows the global context of a framework for fault detection and diagnosis of building automation in which the transformation from HS models into models for diagnosis plays a key role. This framework has been roughly outlined in [2]. The figure shows how the source global model, which is provided by a building information modeling (BIM) tool, can be transformed. The BIM contains information about 3D objects, i.e. the building's geometry and quantities, properties and interconnection of building components, as well as information about the building control and a collection of data produced by components, e.g. sensors and actuators, during its life cycle. From the BIM we can extract an operational building model, represented as HS model. After simulating the system in order to assign parameters with estimated values, an MBD model can be generated from the refined HS model.

Our contributions are as follows:

1. We present a modeling methodology for HS models that extends existing approaches and enables the generation of MBD models.
2. We show how we can abstract the continuous-time dynamics of an HS model to create a discrete-event temporal model which can enable temporal diagnosis.
3. We illustrate our model-transformation approach through a detailed example of an on/off control system of a thermostat.

The article is organized as follows: In section 2 we describe the architecture of the model-transformation framework which we adopted. Section 3 describes the source models of the transformation (hybrid systems), and the target models of the transformation, temporal MBD models. Section 4 outlines the step-by-step transformation process from a HS model towards a model for temporal MBD.

2   System Architecture

Fig. 2 depicts the main features of the system architecture for our model transformation. This figure shows that we have two applications, a source and a target application, with a corresponding meta-model for each application.

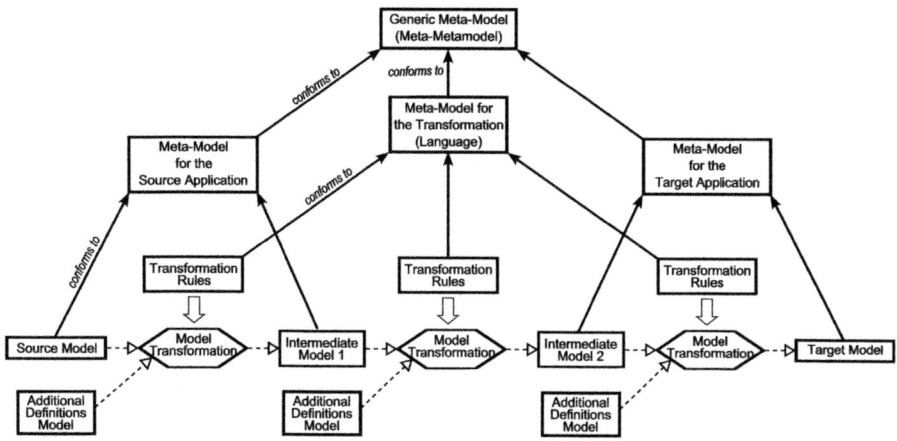

Fig. 2. Architecture of the Model Transformation

To generate a target model from a source model, two intermediate forms are taken. Enrichment of the models is essential to inject information that is specific to the target application. We inject these information through additional models that contain general parameters as well as parameters referring to specific elements of the model at each transformation step.

We use the theory of model transformation [3] to formalize our transformation process in terms of a rewrite procedure. Model transformations that translate a source model into an output model can be expressed in the form of rewriting rules. According to Mens et al. [3], the transformation we adopt is an exogenous transformation, in that the source and target model are expressed in different languages, i.e., hybrid-systems and propositional logic languages. The exogenous transformation step is encompassed by two endogenous transformation steps, in which the source and target model are expressed in the same language.

We adopt the definitions of [4] for meta-model mapping and instance.

Definition 1. *A meta-model mapping is a triple $\Omega = (S_1, S_2, \Sigma)$ where S_1 is the source meta-model, S_2 is the target meta-model and Σ, the mapping expression, is a set of constraints over S_1 and S_2 that define how to map from S_1 to S_2.*

Definition 2. *An* instance *of mapping $\otimes$ is a pair $\langle \check{S}_1, \check{S}_2 \rangle$ such that $\check{S}_1$ is a model that is an instance of S_1, $\check{S}_2$ is a model that is an instance of S_2 and the pair $\langle \check{S}_1, \check{S}_2 \rangle$ satisfies all the constraints Σ. S_2 is a translation of S_1 if the pair $\langle S_1, S_2 \rangle$ satisfies definition 1. Hence, we must specify an appropriate mapping, or set of rules Σ, to ensure that this holds.*

We assume a component-based framework for meta-model mapping, in which we map component by component. In other words, we assume that we can represent a model in terms of a connected set of components, where we call our set of components a component library $\mathcal{C}$. Further, we assume that for each component

$C_i \in \mathcal{C}$, we have an associated meta-model. Given that we are mapping from component library $\mathcal{C}_1$ to $\mathcal{C}_2$, we have two component libraries, with corresponding meta-model libraries, $S_1 = \{s_{1,1}, \ldots, s_{1,n}\}$ and $S_2 = \{s_{2,1}, \ldots, s_{2,m}\}$.

Given a component-wise transformation, we must then assemble the resulting transformed model Φ^T from the transformed components. In other words, given input components C_i and C_j, we can create the original model as $\Phi = C_i \otimes C_j$. We can then compose the transformed components, $\gamma(C_i)$ and $\gamma(C_j)$, to create the transformed model, using the model composition operator $\oplus$ for the transformed system. In this case, we have $\Phi^T = \gamma(\Phi) = \gamma(C_i) \oplus (C_j)$.

In order to apply this approach to model transformation, we need to represent our models in terms of their corresponding meta-models. The Eclipse Modeling Framework Project (EMF)[1] provides a generic meta-model called "Ecore" for describing meta-models. To implement our model transformation process, we use a suite of tools based on the Ecore model, i.e., Xtend for Model Transformation, Xpand for Code Generation and a workflow language, which were formerly developed under the openArchitectureWare (oAW)[2] platform and have now been integrated into the EMF. Mapping rules are expressed in Xtend, which is a general purpose transformation language that enables to build transformation rules over meta-model elements.

3   Source and Target Model Formalisms

3.1   Hybrid-Systems Model

A HS model can describe how a discrete controller can drive a system (plant) whose state evolves continuously. A HS describes the evolution of its state space over time. Each state can be either continuous, if it takes values in Euclidean space $\mathbb{R}^n$ for some $n \geq 1$, or discrete, if it takes values in a finite set $\{q1, q2, \ldots\}$.

Hybrid Systems Language. A hybrid automaton H is a mathematical model for describing an HS. It is a finite state machine (FSM) augmented with differential equations for continuous updates. The state of the system is a pair $S \equiv (x, q)$ in which $x = (x_1, \ldots, x_n)$ with $x_i \in \mathbb{R}$ is the set of n continuous state variables, and $q \in Q$ with $Q = \{q_1, q_2 \ldots\}$ is the discrete state. The discrete state might have multiple dimensions $q \in Q_1 \times \ldots \times Q_m$ when automata are extended to enable modeling of hierarchical behavior, but through indices over the Cartesian product of the finite sets Q_i, the discrete state can always be reduced to a single dimension. In the hybrid automaton, the discrete state can change only during a transition into another mode $q \to q'$ while the continuous state can also be updated through differential equations within a mode q. Discrete changes $E = \{S_{t+1} = g_{q \to q'}(S_t)\}$ are called *jumps* and continuous updates $F = \{\dot{S} = f_q(S)\}$ are refered to as *flows* [1].

---

[1] http://www.eclipse.org/modeling/
[2] http://www.openarchitectureware.org/

Composition of Hybrid automata. When developing large scale systems, the complexity of the system can be mastered by composing models of simple components, each described through a hybrid automaton. In such composition, hybrid automata $H_1, H_2, \ldots$ generally require an input $V = V_C \cup V_D$ and might provide an output $Y = Y_C \cup Y_D$ where C refers to continuous and D to discrete variables. Two components H_i and H_j can communicate through these interfaces. If an input variable v of H_j is renamed as an output variable y of H_i, that dimension of the state of H_i which is represented by y becomes visible to H_j.

Example: Thermostat. Our running example is a thermostat which controls the temperature of a room as in fig. 3 by turning a radiator on and off. On this activation the radiator increases its temperature towards a maximum heat and decreases its temperature respectively. This control pattern causes the air temperature to bounce between the minimum and maximum border of the defined range, and even beyond these borders (fig. 4), depending on the response time and thermal inertia.

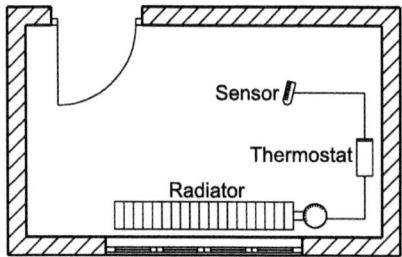

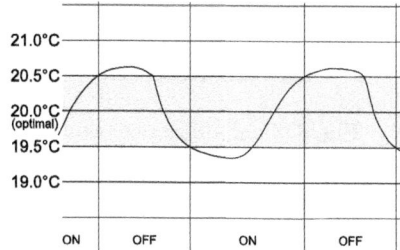

Fig. 3. Room with temperature sensor, thermostat and radiator

Fig. 4. Continuous flow of the air temperature in a range of $20.0 \pm 0.5°C$

A model for the thermostat is represented as a simple discrete automaton with a state $q \in \{\text{ON}, \text{OFF}\}$. The air temperature is defined to be optimal in a range of $\vartheta_{\text{opt}} \pm \theta$. Therefore the jump conditions between the modes ON and OFF are defined as

$$\sigma_{\text{ON} \to \text{OFF}} \Leftrightarrow x_1 \geq \vartheta_{\text{opt}} + \theta$$
$$\text{and} \quad \sigma_{\text{OFF} \to \text{ON}} \Leftrightarrow x_1 \leq \vartheta_{\text{opt}} - \theta .$$

The radiator has been modeled as a hybrid automaton as illustrated in fig. 5 with a discrete state $q \in \{\text{IncrTemp}, \text{HighTemp}, \text{DecrTemp}, \text{LowTemp}\}$ and a continuous state of dimension two: $x = (x_1, x_2)$, where x_1 denotes the air temperature in the room and x_2 refers to a local timer. When the radiator is in the state of HighTemp, the air temperature $x_1 \in \mathbb{R}$ in the room increases exponentially towards the hottest possible temperature T_H according to the differential equation $\dot{x}_1 = \text{rate}_H(T_H - x_1)$ for some $\text{rate}_H > 0$. When the radiator is in the state of LowTemp, the temperature of the room decreases exponentially towards the coldest possible temperature T_C according to the differential

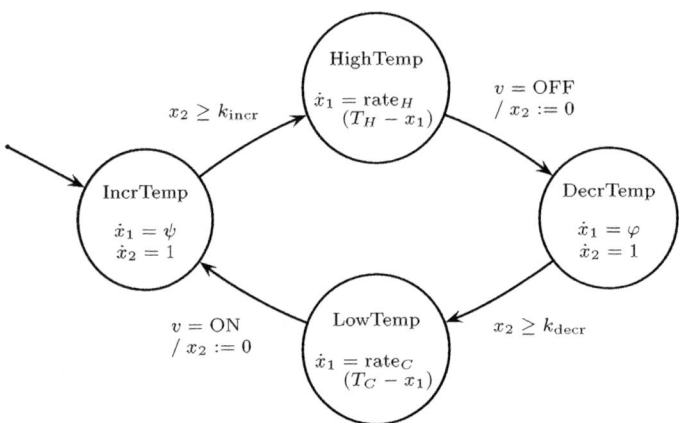

Fig. 5. Hybrid Automaton of the Radiator Component

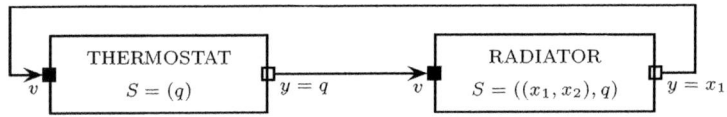

Fig. 6. Composition of two Components: Thermostat and Radiator

equation $\dot{x}_1 = \text{rate}_C (T_C - x_1)$ for some $\text{rate}_C > 0$. Between these steady modes, transitional modes DecrTemp and IncrTemp implement the switchover points by updating x_1 through some unspecified functions φ and ψ. The local timer $x_2 \in \mathbb{R}$ is reset to 0 when entering one of the transitional modes and updated through the differential equation $\dot{x}_2 = 1$. The jump conditions from the steady to the transitional modes refer to the state of the thermostat $v \in \{\text{ON}, \text{OFF}\}$, whereas the jump conditions from the transitional to the steady modes

$$\sigma_{\text{IncrTemp} \to \text{HighTemp}} \Leftrightarrow x_2 \geq k_{\text{incr}}$$

$$\text{and} \quad \sigma_{\text{DecrTemp} \to \text{LowTemp}} \Leftrightarrow x_2 \geq k_{\text{decr}}$$

ensure that the transient modes are activated for just the appropriate time interval.

3.2   Model-Based Diagnosis

Model-Based Diagnosis Language. Fault diagnosis is the process of analyzing non-nominal system behavior in order to identify and localize the components that are the root cause of a failure. Diagnosis is generally involved with fault detection, known as FDD (Fault Detection and Diagnosis). Fault detection is the indication of anomalies through verifying observed values of a real system on the basis of rules. Diagnosis then isolates the underlying faults.

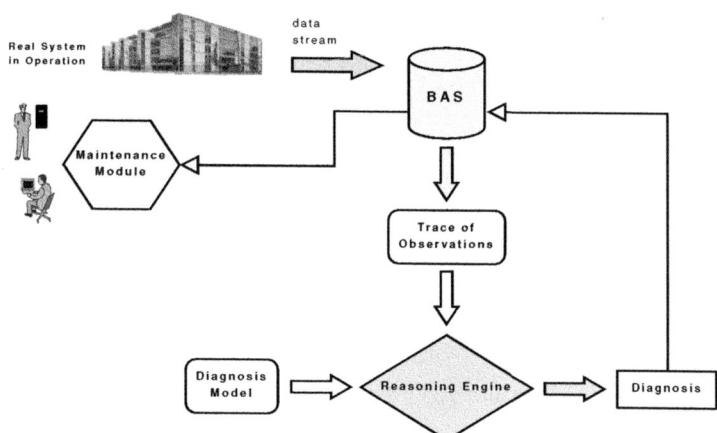

Fig. 7. Diagnosis Architecture

Fig. 7 illustrates how diagnosis is embedded in our framework for fault detection and diagnosis of building automation systems (BAS). Once a fault has been detected, the observed values are compared with the predicted state of the system using the diagnosis model. Through reasoning strategies implemented in MBD engines the malfunctioning components of the system can be located. Depending on the type of the diagnosis model the reasoning engine can even identify which type of failure occurred in each malfunctioning component. However, the generation of *strong* diagnosis models which describe not only the nominal but also the faulty behavior, and therefore allow the distinction between different failure types, is still work in progress. *Weak* models describe only the nominal behavior in relation to a boolean *health variable*, e.g. $h \Rightarrow (o \Leftrightarrow (i_1 \wedge i_2))$ for an and-gate with inputs i_1 and i_2, output o and the health variable h.

Most diagnoses in the intelligent building domain have a state- and time-dependent behavior. Taking a temporal dimension into account makes diagnosis significantly more complex than atemporal MBD with static models. Approaches for temporal MBD are distinguished between different temporal phenomena, categorized in [5]. We pursue an approach which abstracts timing by sequentialization. The diagnosis model describes the behavior of a system as a sequence of states. A diagnosis is no longer computed based on a single observation α_t over OBS made at a time t, but based on a sequence of observations.

We define a temporal diagnosis model using a standard temporal propositional logic [6]. A model for a diagnostic system, DS, consists of propositions P over a set of temporal variables V, a set of assumables (health variables) AS $\subseteq$ V and a set of observable variables OBS $\subseteq$ V. For modularity reasons we favor a modeling technique where each health variable h is encapsulated in a component $c \in$ COMPS with input and output parameters and instantiated by a superordinate component.

4   Transformation

This section describes each step of the transformation from an HS model to a model for temporal MBD. Fig. 8 illustrates the steps of the model-transformation process. In this work we present the transformation into a model for MBD for the case of dynamic systems with feedback control through the following transformation steps:

1. **Discrete Abstraction** of a HS model into a discrete-systems model.
2. **Generation of Propositions** from automata contained in the components of the discrete-systems model results in a dynamic, structured system description (DSSD).
3. **Temporal Unfolding** creates a structured system description (SSD) from a DSSD for a finite sequence of time slices.
4. **Code Generation** to receive a model executable with an MBD tool.

The intermediate models are (1) a discrete-systems model that is a discrete abstraction of a HS model and therefore conforms to the HS meta-model, (2) a dynamic, structured system description (DSSD) [7] is a system model that describes component behavior through temporal propositional logic, permits directed cycles of component interconnectivity and which conforms to the diagnosis meta-model, (3) a structured system description (SSD) [7] that is a special form of a DSSD with only acyclic component interconnectivity and therefore conforms to the same diagnosis meta-model. The meta-models and transformation rules are also documented in a technical report [8].

4.1   Summary of Transformation Approach

Our model transformation converts a model described in a HS language into a model described in a diagnosis language, using meta-modeling as the methodology. We first outline the entities that are transformed, and then describe the transformations in detail.

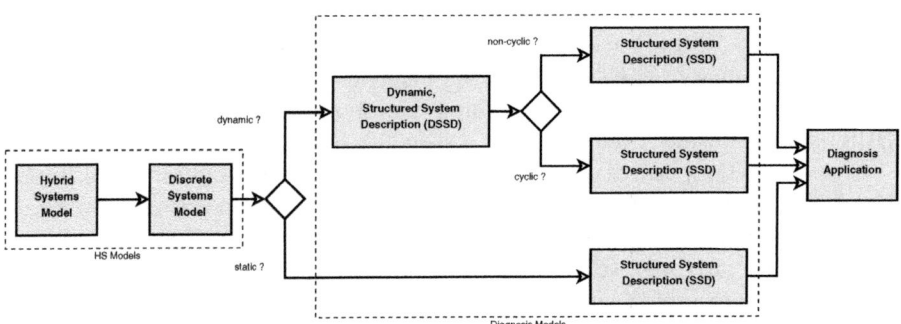

Fig. 8. Transformation Process

As described earlier, we can summarize a HS model using the tuple $\langle \mathcal{S}_H, \Delta_H \rangle$, where $\mathcal{S}_H = \{Q, X\}$ is the set of state-variables, where each state is represented by its discrete and continuous parts, $\{q, x\}$ respectively, for $x \in X, q \in Q$. $\Delta_H = \{E, F\}$ is the set of flow equations, with E being the discrete and F the continuous equations. Analogously, we can summarize a temporal diagnosis model using the tuple $\langle \mathcal{S}_D, \Delta_D \rangle$, where $\mathcal{S}_D = \{Q_D\}$ is the set of discrete state-variables. Δ_D is the set of discrete-valued temporal propositional equations.

To generate a diagnosis model, we transform $\mathcal{S}_H$ to $\mathcal{S}_D$, and Δ_H to Δ_D. We must handle the continuous-discrete transformation differently than the discrete-discrete transformation as presented in [9], and we outline some details below.

4.2   Discrete Abstraction

The initial system models are HS models which consist of components containing hybrid automata. With reasoning engines however, only a finite number of system states can be diagnosed. Therefore it is necessary to transform continuous behavior with an infinite number of system states into discrete behavior.

Discrete abstractions involves in the first step the replacement of numeric variables by finite sets of intervals. Second, we can substitute differential equations through additional modes and components. Finally we must evaluate the model and eventually add primitive components that have not yet been considered.

Discrete Abstraction of Domains. We follow the approach of Sokolsky and Hong [10] who define finite sets of *landmarks* to replace numeric variables with enumerative variables. After screening the HS for all occurrences of numeric variables, a finite set $L = \{l_1, \ldots, l_n\}$ is proposed as landmarks for each variable. The condition that landmarks for a variable v are completely ordered as claimed in [10], is fulfilled by the majority of control systems in intelligent buildings, and taken for granted throughout this paper.[3] Therefore we can define a finite set of disjoint intervals $\{(-\infty, l_1), [l_1, l_2), \ldots, [l_n, \infty)\}$ where $-\infty$ and ∞ represent the lower and upper bound of the domain.[4] After appropriate intervals have been specified for each numeric variable, all occurrences must be rewritten following the rules of interval arithmetics as described by Lunde [11].

Discrete Abstraction of Equations. For variables x_k that represent a dimension of the continuous state of the superordinate component of a HS architecture, discrete behavior needs to be added in order to represent x_k as part of the discrete state of the overall system. That means that for each interval of the discrete domain of x_k, as defined in the first step of the discrete abstraction, modes $q_1^k, \ldots, q_n^k$ must be added. For x_k that is updated in a hybrid automaton

---

[3] If this condition is not fulfilled, e.g. if for a numeric variable two landmarks were found, one is an expression and the other is a constant value in the range of that expression, total order is not assured. In such case, a structure type can be created to represent the discrete domain of the variable.

[4] The usage of inclusion or exclusion at the interval endpoints depends on the comparisons $(>, \geq, <, \leq, =, \neq)$ used with the landmarks.

H through a set of equations $\dot{x}_k = F_q(x_k)$ an additional automaton H' is created to represent x_k as its discrete state. In the new automaton H' the discrete state of H is queried by the jump conditions and therefore required as input to H'.

Local variables x_l that represent a dimension of the continuous state of a hybrid automaton without being connected to other components are substituted by splitting modes q of the hybrid automaton H into modes $q_1^l, \ldots, q_n^l$ only if x_l is observable in the real system. Other local variables and equations for their continuous updating are removed from the hybrid automata. The HS model, after completing the discrete abstraction, has at this point been transformed into a model of a purely discrete system with a finite number of possible states. The automata that model the behavior of each component are now plain FSM without the extension of differential equations.

Completion of Components. System models that are created for different purposes may be decomposed differently. For example, a model that has been created to simulate the behavior of a system is unlikely to contain components that "do nothing" from the simulation point of view. But especially fault-prone subsystems must be detached from others and partitioned as a separate component in order to generate a reliable diagnostics model. This might seem redundant in many cases, but necessary in order to separate, for example, a broken sensor from other malfunctioning components.

Example: Thermostat (cont.). In the following we illustrate the discrete abstraction through the example of a thermostat described as a HS model in 3.1.

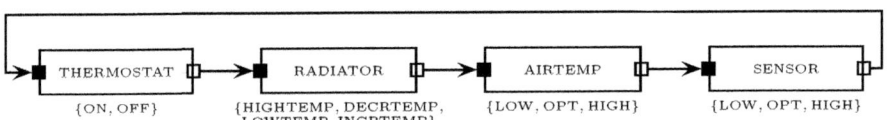

Fig. 9. Composition after Discrete Abstraction

In the source model for the single-zone heating system we identify the landmarks $l_1 = \vartheta_{\mathrm{opt}} - \theta$ and $l_2 = \vartheta_{\mathrm{opt}} + \theta$ for the variable x_1 which represents the air temperature. We define the discrete domain for x_1 through the intervals $I_1 = (-\inf, \vartheta_{\mathrm{opt}} - \theta]$, $I_2 = (\vartheta_{\mathrm{opt}} - \theta, \vartheta_{\mathrm{opt}} + \theta)$ and $I_3 = [\vartheta_{\mathrm{opt}} + \theta, \inf)$. Representing the intervals $\{I_1, I_2, I_3\}$ with an enumeration $\{\mathrm{LOW}, \mathrm{OPT}, \mathrm{HIGH}\}$, we must rewrite the occurrences of the variable in the model. For example, $x_1 \geq \vartheta_{\mathrm{opt}} + \theta$ becomes $x_1 = \mathrm{HIGH}$.

The composition of components in fig. 9 shows that we substitute x_1 globally through a new component AIRTEMP. Continuous updates of the numeric variable x_1 are substituted with an additional automaton in which each mode refers to an interval of the discrete domain of x_1. Transitions to activate these modes are controlled through a variable representing the discrete state of the RADIATOR component.

In our example the sensor that measures the air temperature that must be included additionally. Its behavior is modeled with the same modes LOW, OPT and HIGH as used already for the air temperature itself. For every state we add transitions in order to reach this state from every other state at the same condition.

4.3   Generation of Propositional Logic

In this transformation step we transform the FSM of each component into temporal logic propositions. The FSM consists of a set of modes M and a set of transitions Δ. Each transition $\delta \in \Delta$ is guarded by a condition c_δ.

The next state (output) of an FSM is a function of the condition (input) and of the current state of the FSM. Since the FSM is deterministic[5], it can be reduced to a canonical form. For each component we introduce a state variable x and define the following rule for generating propositions:

$$\bigwedge_{\delta \in \Delta} \left([x = \text{start}_\delta]_{t-1} \wedge [c_\delta]_t \Rightarrow [x = \text{end}_\delta]_t \right) \wedge$$

$$\bigwedge_{m \in \text{FSM}} \left([x = m]_{t-1} \wedge \neg \left(\bigvee_{\delta \in \text{out}_m} [c_\delta]_t \right) \Rightarrow [x = m]_t \right)$$

where $\text{start}_\delta / \text{end}_\delta$ is the mode from which the transition δ starts/ends, respectively. For a mode m, out_m denotes the set of all transitions that start from m.

Logical propositions generated with the above rule describe the nominal behavior of a component and are therefore logically equivalent to the system health $[h]_t$ at time t. The resulting model after this transformation step is a dynamic, structured system description (DSSD) as defined by Darwiche et al in [7]. We further assign values for the probability that the boolean health variable turns out to be true to instances of components.

Example: Thermostat (cont.). Applying the transformation rule for generation of temporal logic to the example, the following proposition is automatically generated for the thermostat component:

$$[h_{\text{THERMOSTAT}}]_t \Leftrightarrow (([x = \text{ON}]_{t-1} \wedge [v = \text{LOW}]_t) \Rightarrow [x = \text{OFF}]_t) \wedge$$
$$(([x = \text{OFF}]_{t-1} \wedge [v = \text{HIGH}]_t) \Rightarrow [x = \text{ON}]_t) \wedge$$
$$(([x = \text{ON}]_{t-1} \wedge \neg[v = \text{LOW}]_t) \Rightarrow [x = \text{ON}]_t) \wedge$$
$$(([x = \text{OFF}]_{t-1} \wedge \neg[v = \text{HIGH}]_t) \Rightarrow [x = \text{OFF}]_t)$$

Some components are described through a behavior that is independent of the previous state. These behaviors can be reduced to propositions that do not consider the previous value of the state variable x as shown for the sensor component of the example:

$$[h_{\text{SENSOR}}]_t \Leftrightarrow ([v = \text{LOW}]_t \Rightarrow [x = \text{LOW}]_t) \wedge$$
$$([v = \text{OPT}]_t \Rightarrow [x = \text{OPT}]_t) \wedge$$
$$([v = \text{HIGH}]_t \Rightarrow [x = \text{HIGH}]_t)$$

---

[5] We assume that the extended automata of the HS was deterministic, therefore its discrete abstraction is deterministic as well.

4.4   Temporal Unfolding of Cycles

In this step we transform the architecture of the DSSD which is a directed graph depicting component interconnectivity into an acyclic architecture. We adopt the approach of temporal unfolding described in Darwiche et al [7] for diagnosis of discrete event systems. We clone the whole cyclic system in each time slice and then disconnect each cycle between the same two components. For the removed connections we reassign the output port of the component from which the connection started to the input port of the target component in the next time slice.

It conveys a certain meaning which connection between components is cut in each clone and reassigned to the next time slice. Therefore, for each cycle at least one component must be flagged as *entry-point* before the transformation can run automatically. Models of HVAC control systems, as a general rule, contain components that represent embedded systems, sensors with very short response time and components that represent unobservable physical phenomena, e.g. the temperature of a medium, with a rather long response time. We advise that the component of the cycle to be flagged as entry-point should be the component of the system that takes most time to react. In most cases this is a component describing a slowly changing physical phenomenon. This results from the assumption that events from the real system are taken during the operation of the component with the longest response time.

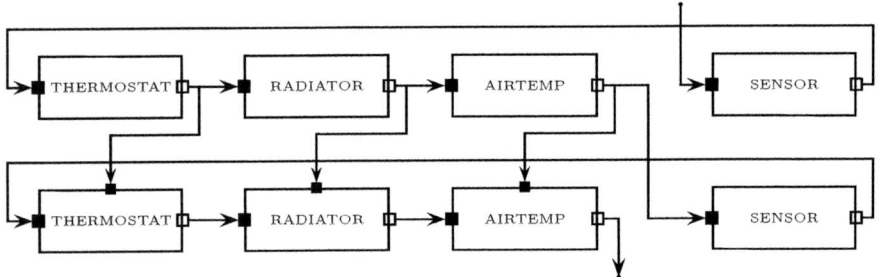

Fig. 10. Unfolded Composition

Example: Thermostat (cont.). We assume that observations of the system are provided by the thermostat that submits the sensor reading and the corresponding actuation command periodically or event-driven. Therefore we can choose either the air temperature or the sensor as entry point for the unfolding of components. Choosing a temporal unfolding of two time slices with the sensor as entry-point, the architecture of the unfolded model as shows in fig. 10 contains two instances of each component. Except the sensor component whose behavior could be reduced to an atemporal form as shown in 4.3, all components of the second time slice require the state variable of the instance in the first time slice as additional input.

5   Related Work

This section summarizes related work in three areas, hybrid systems transformations, auto-generation of diagnostics, and model transformation.

Due to the difficulty of analyzing hybrid systems models, a variety of transformations have been applied to these models, e.g., [12,13]. We focus on abstraction into a discrete model, which is similar to [10], which describe a qualitative version of the Charon modeling language and the transformation from a hybrid-systems model to its discrete abstraction. Our work is different in that the output model is a diagnosis model.

This work is related to work on the auto-generation of diagnostics. Our approach is different from most existing approaches, which generate models from diagnosis component models rather than abstract a diagnosis model from a more complex hybrid systems model. Among this class of approaches, we examine two particular papers. [14] describes a methodology of diagnostics generation for car subsystems, based on the assumption that models of car systems can be automatically composed from model libraries. [15] presents an approach to build models for temporal MBD for VHDL designs, in which they model the temporal behavior of VHDL by temporal unfolding of process execution, which is then converted into a component-connection model which can be used by a MBD reasoner.

Our work applies the theory of model transformation in a novel way. We propose an exogenous translation, for which the source and target are from different meta-models, and our target meta-model has the semantics of a temporal diagnosis model. This target model is unique in the model transformation literature, and it also extends prior work in which the target model was a static diagnosis model [9].

6   Conclusions and Future Work

This article has described an implemented framework for transforming hybrid systems models to temporal propositional logic diagnosis models. Our approach contributes to research in model-driven development of complex systems by extending model consistency up to models for diagnostics. We have illustrated the transformation process using the domain of HVAC, with an on/off thermostat control system.

This approach can make significant contributions to building automation systems. Instead of needing to create multiple models, and maintain consistency among multiple models, this transformation approach provides the methodology for creating a single generic model, and then creating component-based meta-models and transformation rules to automate the generation of the additional models needed for building automation applications.

We hope to extend this work in a variety of ways. First, we plan to extend the class of diagnosis models from the current approach, which describes only the correct behavior of a system, to models that define explicit fault behaviours. Second, we want to extend the current transformation rules, which only apply to systems with observable or unobservable components, to rules that can deal with observable and unobservable transitions in each state machine.

Acknowledgment

This work was funded by SFI grant 06-SRC-I1091.

References

1. Henzinger, T.A.: The theory of hybrid automata. In: LICS 1996: Proceedings of the 11th Annual IEEE Symposium on Logic in Computer Science, Washington, DC, USA, p. 278. IEEE Computer Society Press, Los Alamitos (1996)
2. Provan, G., Ploennigs, J., Boubekeur, M., Mady, A.: Using building information model data for generating and updating diagnostic models. In: Conf. on Civil Engineering and Computing (August 2009)
3. Mens, T., Czarnecki, K., Gorp, P.V.: A taxonomy of model transformations. In: Bezivin, J., Heckel, R. (eds.) Language Engineering for Model-Driven Software Development. Dagstuhl Seminar Proceedings, No. 04101 (2005)
4. Fagin, R., Kolaitis, P.G., Popa, L., Tan, W.C.: Composing schema mappings: Second-order dependencies to the rescue. ACM Trans. Database Syst. 30(4), 994–1055 (2005)
5. Brusoni, V., Console, L., Terenziani, P., Dupré, D.T.: A spectrum of definitions for temporal model-based diagnosis. Artificial Intelligence 102, 39–79 (1998)
6. Emerson, E.: Temporal and modal logic. Handbook of theoretical computer science 8, 995–1072 (1990)
7. Darwiche, A., Provan, G.: Exploiting system structure in model-based diagnosis of discrete-event systems (1996)
8. Behrens, M.: Model transformation: Hybrid systems to temporal diagnosis models. Technical report (2010), http://www.cs.ucc.ie/~mb20/
9. Behrens, M., Provan, G., Boubekeur, M., Mady, A.: Model-driven diagnostics generation for industrial automation. In: Proc. 7th IEEE International Conference on Industrial Informatics (June 2009)
10. Sokolsky, O., Hong, H.S.: Qualitative modeling of hybrid systems. Presented at the Monterey Workshop on Engineering Automation for Computer Based Systems (2001), http://repository.upenn.edu/cispapers/87
11. Lunde, K.: Object-oriented modeling in model-based diagnosis. In: Proceedings of the First Modelica workshop, Lund, Sweden (2000)
12. Antoulas, A., Sorensen, D., Gugercin, S.: A survey of model reduction methods for large-scale systems. Contemporary Mathematics 280, 193–219 (2001)
13. Mazzi, E., Vincentelli, A., Balluchi, A., Bicchi, A.: Hybrid system reduction. In: 47th IEEE Conference on Decision and Control, CDC 2008, pp. 227–232 (2008)
14. Dressler, O., Struss, P.: Generating instead of programming diagnostics. In: 25 Jahre Elektronik-Systeme im Kraftfahrzeug, Haus der Technik Fachbuch, vol. 50, pp. 159–169 (2005)
15. Köb, D., Peischl, B., Wotawa, F.: Debugging vhdl designs using temporal process instances. In: Chung, P.W.H., Hinde, C.J., Ali, M. (eds.) IEA/AIE 2003. LNCS, vol. 2718, pp. 402–415. Springer, Heidelberg (2003)

Synthesis of OCL Pre-conditions for Graph Transformation Rules

Jordi Cabot[1], Robert Clarisó[2], Esther Guerra[3], and Juan de Lara[4]

[1] INRIA - École des Mines de Nantes, France
jordi.cabot@inria.fr
[2] Universitat Oberta de Catalunya, Spain
rclariso@uoc.edu
[3] Universidad Carlos III de Madrid, Spain
eguerra@inf.uc3m.es
[4] Universidad Autónoma de Madrid, Spain
Juan.deLara@uam.es

Abstract. Graph transformation (GT) is being increasingly used in Model Driven Engineering (MDE) to describe in-place transformations like animations and refactorings. For its practical use, rules are often complemented with OCL application conditions. The advancement of rule post-conditions into pre-conditions is a well-known problem in GT, but current techniques do not consider OCL. In this paper we provide an approach to advance post-conditions with arbitrary OCL expressions into pre-conditions. This presents benefits for the practical use of GT in MDE, as it allows: (i) to automatically derive pre-conditions from the meta-model integrity constraints, ensuring rule correctness, (ii) to derive pre-conditions from graph constraints with OCL expressions and (iii) to check applicability of rule sequences with OCL conditions.

1 Introduction

The advent of Model Driven Engineering (MDE) has made evident the need for techniques to manipulate models. Common model manipulations include model-to-model transformations, as well as in-place transformations like refactorings, animations and optimisations. Many transformation languages and approaches have been proposed for in-place transformations, but much research is directed towards usable languages (e.g. able to take advantage of the concrete syntax of the language) providing good integration with MDE standards (e.g. UML, MOF, OCL) and that support some kind of analysis.

Graph transformation (GT) [7] is a graphical and declarative way to express graph manipulations with a rich body of theoretical results developed over the last decades. Its graphical nature has made it a common choice to define in-place manipulations for Domain Specific Visual Languages (DSVLs), taking the advantage that one can use the concrete syntax of the DSVL, making rules intuitive. However, further integration with technologies like OCL is still needed for its practical use in MDE. In this paper, we aim to advance in this direction.

L. Tratt and M. Gogolla (Eds.): ICMT 2010, LNCS 6142, pp. 45–60, 2010.

In particular, a recurring problem is the interaction of the applicability conditions of GT rules with the OCL invariants defined in the meta-models. In this way, one may consider that rules should be restricted enough in their applicability conditions to ensure that their application does not violate any meta-model constraint. If this is not the case, the system would fall in an inconsistent state and hence lead to an incorrect simulation or refactoring. However, it is tedious and error prone for the grammar designer to derive by hand from the meta-model invariants all application conditions required for each rule. Our goal is to automate such task. Hence, given an invariant I that a model M must satisfy after the application of a rule r, we generate the weakest invariant I' s.t. if the model satisfies it before applying r, then the resulting model will satisfy I. This core technique has many applications, like deriving rule pre-conditions from meta-model constraints and from graph constraints [7] equipped with OCL, as well as to test the applicability of rule sequences with arbitrary OCL conditions.

Paper organization. Section 2 presents motivating examples that benefit from our techniques. Section 3 introduces our techniques to advance OCL invariants to rule pre-conditions. Section 4 goes back to the examples, illustrating the advancement of OCL invariants for them. Section 5 comments possible optimisations for the method. Section 6 discusses related research and Section 7 concludes.

2   Motivating Examples

First we consider a DSVL for defining production systems. Its meta-model is shown to the left of Fig. 1. The meta-model defines machines with input and output conveyors, which may contain two different kinds of pieces. An OCL constraint ensures that conveyors do not hold more pieces than their capacity. The center of the same figure shows a model in abstract and concrete syntax.

Once we have defined the DSVL syntax, we can use GT rules to define its semantics. The rule to the right of Fig. 1 describes how machines behave, consuming and producing pieces. GT rules [7] are made of two graphs, the left and the right hand sides (LHS/RHS), which encode the pre- and post-conditions for rule application. Intuitively, a rule can be applied to a model whenever an occurrence of the LHS pattern is found in it. Roughly, the application of a rule consists in deleting the elements of $LHS - RHS$, and creating those of $RHS - LHS$.

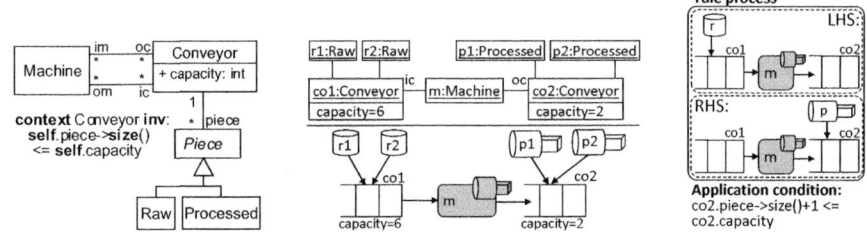

Fig. 1. Meta-model (left). Models in abstract/concrete syntax (center). A rule (right).

In our case, the rule application deletes the Raw piece and creates a Processed one in the output conveyor.

Considered in isolation, the rule could create a piece in a full output conveyor, violating the OCL integrity constraint of the meta-model. Hence, most approaches and tools require the inclusion of an *application condition* in the rule's LHS constraining the application of the rule to the case when the output conveyor has enough capacity (so that the resulting model is consistent with the meta-model). This is what we have done in the figure. However, this is a redundant work, as we are specifying a constraint for the same purpose *twice*: once in the meta-model and another time in the rule. Even worse, the designer has the burden of calculating an application condition that, given the rule's actions, forbids applying the rule if the execution breaks any meta-model constraint.

Hence, one important improvement in current practice is a mechanism to automatically derive OCL application conditions from the meta-model, in such a way that any possible rule application cannot break the meta-model constraints. This presents several advantages: (i) it notably reduces the work of the designer, (ii) it facilitates grammar and meta-model evolution, as a change in the constraints of the latter has less impact on the rules, as many application conditions are automatically derived (iii) it eliminates the risk of not adding appropriate conditions that would cause rule applications to violate the meta-model constraints, and (iv) it eliminates the risk of adding a too restrictive condition that would forbid applying the rule, even when its application would not break any constraint (i.e. a condition that is not the weakest). In fact, the OCL condition added to the rule in Fig. 1 is not the weakest. We solve this issue in Section 4.

The second motivating scenario is a refactoring of class diagrams. We assume the simple meta-model in Fig. 2, where classes contain properties, each of a given data type. For the sake of illustration, an invariant forbids attribute overriding, by disallowing classes to have properties with same name as properties in direct children (note that a real scenario would check this on indirect children too).

Fig. 2 (right) depicts rule *extract superclass* that, given two classes, creates a common superclass. As in the previous scenario, we would not like to calculate by hand the extra conditions needed for this rule to be applicable. In this case, the problematic situation is with the "0..1" cardinality constraint in the meta-model that forbids a class to have several parents. The following sections will show that our method treats such cardinality constraints uniformly as OCL constraints [9].

Fig. 3 shows another refactoring rule, *pull-up property*, which given two sister classes having a property with same name and type, pulls up such property to a common parent class. Again, the problem is to calculate the needed applicability

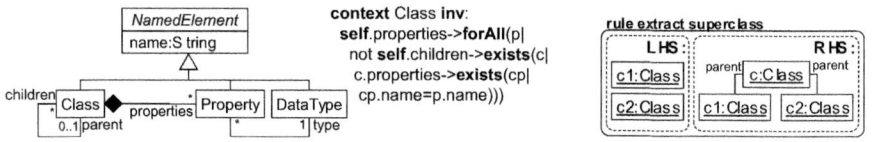

Fig. 2. Simple meta-model for class diagrams (left). Refactoring rule (right).

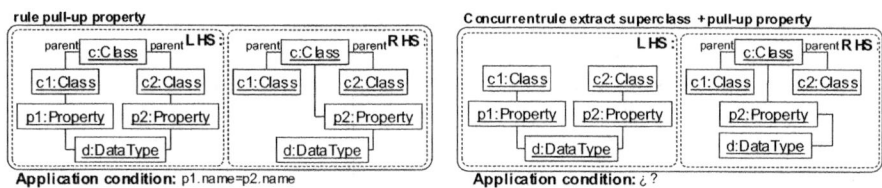

Fig. 3. Refactoring rule (left). Concurrent rule for both refactorings (right).

conditions, where the problematic part is the meta-model invariant, as the parent class may have other children containing a property with same name. Finally, it is common to apply two or more refactorings in sequence, e.g. we may only want to extract a common superclass if we can then apply the pull-up property refactoring. Hence, we need to calculate the applicability conditions of a sequence of rules. Neglecting OCL conditions, this can be done by calculating the concurrent rule [7], which includes the pre-conditions and effects of both rules, and is built by gluing the initial rules through common elements. In our case, the glueing is done through elements c1, c2 and c, and the resulting rule is shown to the right of Fig. 3. In this scenario we need our method to calculate the OCL application conditions of the concurrent rule. First, the application conditions of the second rule should be advanced to the first, and additional pre-conditions for the resulting rule should be derived from the meta-model constraints.

Altogether, we have seen that the use of GT rules in MDE necessitates techniques to manipulate OCL conditions. The next section presents our method to advance OCL conditions, and then Section 4 will look back again at these examples to explain how our method solves the problems we have pointed out.

3   Translating OCL Post-Conditions into Pre-conditions

This section describes how to advance constraints from the RHS of a rule into the LHS. The input of the procedure is a GT rule and an OCL constraint restricting the graph after applying the rule. This constraint can either be (1) an OCL invariant or (2) an arbitrary OCL boolean expression with explicit references to the objects of the RHS using their identifier. We will refer to this expression as the *post-condition*, even though it may not attempt to describe the effects of rule application (e.g. it could be an integrity constraint that should be preserved).

The output is an OCL boolean expression which constrains the graph before applying the rule. We refer to this new expression as the *pre-condition*, and we compute it performing several replacements on the OCL constraint being advanced, which depend on the actions performed by the rule. This computation should ensure that in any match where the rule is applicable, the pre-condition is satisfied before applying the rule iff the post-condition is satisfied after applying the rule. Formally, in any application $G \Rightarrow_r G'$ of the rule r on a graph G producing a graph G', $Pre(G) \leftrightarrow Post(G')$ should hold. This is similar to Dijkstra's notion of *weakest pre-condition*[5].

3.1 Overview

The computation of the weakest pre-condition proceeds in three steps: (1) static analysis of the rule, (2) preprocessing of the post-condition and (3) the final computation of the weakest pre-condition.

Static analysis of the rule: First we examine the rule to identify the list of *atomic graph updates* that occur when the rule is applied. This step is independent on the OCL post-condition being advanced, as we only need to compare the LHS and the RHS. Then, the following atomic graph operations can be identified: (1) deletion/creation of a link between two existing objects; (2) deletion of an object (and all its adjacent links); (3) update of an attribute value; and (4) creation of a new object (plus its adjacent links and attribute initialization).

As an example, the rule of Fig. 1 performs two atomic graph updates: deletion of object r and its link col-r; and creation of object p and its link co2-p.

Preprocessing the OCL post-condition: This step simplifies the OCL post-condition before converting it into a pre-condition. First, if the post-condition is an OCL invariant defined in a context type T, it is implicitly universally quantified over all objects of type T. In order to advance this constraint, it is necessary to make the quantification explicit by performing the following replacement:

$$\text{\textbf{context} } T \text{ \textbf{inv}: } exp \quad \Rightarrow \quad T\text{::allInstances()}\text{--}\text{>forAll}(v \mid exp')$$

where exp' is computed by replacing all references to the keyword *self* in exp with the variable v. After this expansion of invariants, we apply several transformations that simplify the constraint. For example, if-then-else expressions nested into other OCL constructs can be expanded as:

$$(\text{\textbf{if} } A \text{ \textbf{then} } B \text{ \textbf{else} } C \text{ \textbf{endif}}) \text{ op } D \quad \Rightarrow \quad \text{\textbf{if} } A \text{ \textbf{then} } (B \text{ op } D) \text{ \textbf{else} } (C \text{ op } D) \text{ \textbf{endif}}$$

This latter step is also performed whenever a replacement takes place.

Computing the weakest pre-condition: Finally, we transform the post-condition into a pre-condition, by applying a set of *textual replacement patterns* on the OCL post-condition. We have defined a collection of replacement patterns for each atomic graph update. These patterns capture the effect of an atomic graph update and modify the constraint accordingly, synthesizing the equivalent constraint before applying that update. Applying the replacement patterns for all the graph updates the rule performs yields the corresponding pre-condition.

There are two necessary requirements for the replacement we have defined:

- The replacement patterns for each atomic graph update should capture all OCL subexpressions which are relevant to that update. For example, if the update is the deletion of a link, we should consider all OCL navigation expressions that may potentially traverse this link.
- If an OCL constraint is well-formed before applying a replacement pattern, then the result of applying the replacement pattern should also be well-formed.

By "well-formed", we refer to syntactical and semantical correctness according to the OCL specification, e.g. correct types for each subexpression.

3.2 Basic Replacement Patterns

In this section, we focus on the replacement patterns for all atomic graph updates *except* the creation of new nodes (discussed in Subsection 3.3). The application of these replacement patterns works on the *abstract syntax tree* (AST) of the OCL post-condition. The leaves of this tree are constants (e.g. 1, 2, "hello"), variable names or type names. Each internal node is an operator (logic, arithmetic or relational) or an OCL construct (quantifier, operation call, etc).

In order to transform the post-condition for a single atomic update, we perform a bottom-up traversal of the AST: starting from the leaves and looking for matches of the replacement patterns defined for that update. Whenever a match is located in the AST, it is replaced according to the pattern and the traversal continues upwards, until the root of the AST is reached.

In order to identify the OCL subexpressions which are relevant to an atomic graph update, two items are considered: (1) the *operator* involved in the OCL expression and (2) the *type* of its operands. For example, updates dealing with the assignment of a new value to an attribute will affect expressions where the value of this attribute is being accessed. Regarding types, we will use the following notation: $T = T'$ if type T is equal to T', $T \sqsubset T'$ if T is a subtype of T', and $T \sqsubseteq T'$ if T is a subtype or is equal to T'.

Object deletion. Let us consider the deletion of an object x of type T. In order to advance the post-condition, the constraint should be modified to ensure that its evaluation does not take x into account, i.e., it is as if x did not exist.

In OCL, an object x can only be accessed from a collection of objects of its type T, its subtypes or supertypes. This access may use a quantifier (forAll, exists, ...) or an operation on collections (first, size, ...). This collection can be computed either from a "Type::allInstances()" expression or from a navigation expression. Therefore, we simulate the deletion by appending "excluding(x)" to any "allInstances()" expression or navigation expression of an appropriate type. Table 1 depicts the complete set of replacement patterns.

Notice that, due to how navigation expressions are being modified, these replacement patterns are implicitly encoding the deletion of all edges where x may participate. Therefore, replacement patterns for link deletion only need to be applied if both objects are preserved in the RHS.

Example 1. In a rule deleting an object x of type T, the post-condition:

```
T::allInstances()−>exists(t | t.isGreen)
```

is advanced to a pre-condition demanding some object *other than* x to be green thus ensuring that the rule is only applied when x is not the only green object:

```
T::allInstances()−>excluding(x)−>exists(t | t.isGreen)
```

Table 1. Replacement patterns for object deletion

	Ref	Pattern	Conditions	Replacement
LHS: `x:T` **RHS:**	OD1	A::allInstances()	$T \sqsubseteq A$ or $A \sqsubset T$	A::allInstances()−>excluding(x)
	OD2	exp.role	"role" is an association end of type A, with $T \sqsubseteq A$ or $A \sqsubset T$	exp.role−>excluding(x)

Attribute updates. Let us consider the update of attribute *attr* of an object x of type T, such that the new value is given by an OCL expression *new_val_exp*. In OCL, the value of an attribute can only be accessed through an expression of type AttributeCallExp, e.g. "object.attribute". Intuitively, to advance any post-condition, it is necessary that every time we refer to the attribute *attr* of an object of type T, we use *new_val_exp* instead, but only if we are referring to x. In Table 2, we present the replacement patterns that implement this concept.

Table 2. Replacement patterns for an update of an attribute

LHS: `x:T` **RHS:** `x:T`

Attribute computation:
x.attr' = new_value_exp

Ref	Pattern	Conditions	Replacement
At1	x.attr	None	new_val_exp
At2	exp.attr	$Type(exp) \sqsubseteq T$	**if** exp = x **then** new_val_exp **else** exp.attr **endif**

Link deletion. Let us consider the deletion of a link of association As between objects a (of type T_A) and b (of type T_B). We only consider scenarios where neither a nor b are deleted by this rule, because if any of them is deleted, the situation is already captured by the replacement patterns for object deletion.

Hence, we only need to modify navigation expressions traversing association As, so that they do not take the link $a - b$ into account. This can be implemented by appending "excluding(a)" to navigations going from T_B to T_A and "excluding(b)" to navigations going from T_A to T_B, as described in Table 3.

Example 2. In a rule deleting a link a-b, the post-condition:

> T_A::allInstances()−>exists(x | x.rb−>notEmpty())

states that at least one T_A object is connected to a T_B object. Advancing the invariant considers a a special case, as it may be connected to b in the LHS:

> T_A::allInstances()−>exists(x |
> (**if** x = a **then** x.rb−>excluding(b) **else** x.rb **endif**)−>notEmpty())

Link creation. Finally, we consider the creation of a link of an association As between objects a (of type T_A) and b (of type T_B). We assume that both a and b exist in the LHS, as the creation of objects is discussed in Section 3.3. We have

Table 3. Replacement patterns for link deletion, for navigations $T_A \rightarrow T_B$ (the symmetric patterns LD1b and LD2b for navigations $T_B \rightarrow T_A$ are omitted for brevity)

LHS: RHS:	Ref	Pat.	Conditions	Replacement
	LD1a	exp.rb	$Type(exp) \sqsubseteq T_A$	**if** exp = a **then** exp.rb−>excluding(b) **else** exp.rb **endif**
	LD2a	exp.rb	$Type(exp) = Set(T')$ with $T' \sqsubseteq T_A$	(exp−>excluding(a).rb)−> union(a.rb−>excluding(b))

to simulate the existence of an edge $a - b$ in navigation expressions that traverse association *As*. This is done by appending "including(b)" to navigations going from T_A to T_B, or "including(a)" to expressions going from T_B to T_A.

Example 3. In a rule adding a link a-b, the following post-condition:

T_A::allInstances()−>forAll(x | x.rb−>size() $\neq$ 5)

states that no object of type T_A can be connected to exactly 5 T_B objects. It would be advanced as follows, by treating object a in a distinct way:

T_A::allInstances()−>forAll(x |
(**if** x = a **then** x.rb−>including(b) **else** x.rb **endif**)−>size() $\neq$ 5)

Table 4. Replacement patterns for link creation, for navigations $T_A \rightarrow T_B$ (the symmetric patterns LC1b and LC2b for navigations $T_B \rightarrow T_A$ are omitted for brevity)

LHS: RHS:	Ref	Pattern	Conditions	Replacement
	LC1a	exp.rb	$Type(exp) \sqsubseteq T_A$	**if** exp = a **then** exp.rb−>including(b) **else** exp.rb **endif**
	LC2a	exp.rb	$Type(exp) = Set(T')$ with $T' \sqsubseteq T_A$	**if** exp−>includes(a) **then** exp.rb−>including(b) **else** exp.rb **endif**

3.3   Replacement Patterns for Creating Objects

New objects create a challenge, because there is no placeholder to designate them in the LHS. For example, a constraint like the following:

Conveyor::allInstances()−>forAll(x | x.capacity $\geq$ 0)

restricts all objects of type Conveyor. If a new Conveyor c is created by the rule, it should also satisfy this constraint. However, as new objects do not exist in the LHS, we cannot refer to them using an identifier. Thus, the expression:

Conveyor::allInstances()−>including(c) −>forAll(x | x.capacity $\geq$ 0)

is an invalid pre-condition, as identifier c is meaningless before rule application.

As a result, the transformation for advancing post-conditions becomes more complex in rules that create objects. Hence, we have to split it in two steps:

- In the first step, described in Table 5, we modify "allInstances()" and navigation expressions to take into account the newly created object. This transformation introduces references to the identifier of the new object that need to be removed in the next step. These direct references (and also those appearing previously in the post-condition) may be located in two types of expressions: collections including the new object and object expressions.
- The second step removes direct references to the new object by a set of replacements that either (i) move the reference upwards in the AST of the OCL expression, (ii) particularize OCL quantifiers that affect the new object, or (iii) rewrite the expression to avoid the reference. The iterative application of those replacements yields an equivalent expression without direct references.

The remainder of this section focuses on the second step. Tables 6 and 7 describe the replacements for collection expressions and object expressions, respectively. Due to space constraints, the collection of patterns is incomplete.

Collection expressions can be classified into three categories: simple queries (C1-3), iterators (C4-10) and operations involving objects or other collections (C11-19). For example, C2 indicates that the query "isEmpty()" can be replaced by "false" when it is applied to a collection containing the new object.

The transformation of iterators combines the evaluation of the expression on the new object and on the remaining elements of the collection. We denote by $Inst[var, exp]$ the replacement of all references to variable var with the identifier of the new object in the RHS. Then, a pattern like C4 for the existential quantifier establishes that either the old elements of the collection *or* the new object satisfy the condition. Applying $Inst$ introduces references to the new object, which are, again, further simplified using the patterns from Tables 6 and 7.

Table 5. Replacement patterns for object creation

	Ref	Pattern	Conditions	Replacement
LHS: a:TA	OC1	T::allInstances()	$T_B \sqsubseteq T$	T::allInstances()−>including(b)
RHS: a:TA ra rb	OC2	exp.rb	Type(exp) $\sqsubseteq T_A$	if exp = a then exp.rb −>including(b) else exp.rb endif
	OC3	exp.rb	Type(exp) = Set(T'), with $T' \sqsubseteq T_A$	if exp−>includes(a) then exp.rb −>including(b) else exp.rb endif
b:TB	OC4	b		See Tables 6 and 7.

Finally, collection expressions with subexpressions of type object or collection are *synchronisation points*: the replacement to be applied depends on whether the other subexpression also contains the new object. For example, if the object b is created, an expression like "b = b" is replaced by "true". However, we need to process both branches of the equality before reaching this conclusion. Hence, replacements should be applied bottom-up in the AST, stopping at synchronisation points until all sibling subexpressions in the AST have been processed.

Object expressions, described in Table 7, are defined similarly. For example, pattern O1 describes an attribute access, simply replaced by the attribute computation expression in the RHS. Again, object expressions which operate with other objects or collections are synchronisation points.

Table 6. Replacement patterns for collection expressions, where b is the identifier of the new object, *col* and *col'* are collection expressions, *exp* is an arbitrary expression, and COL_B is a shorthand for $col-> including(b)$

Ref	Pattern	Replacement
C1	COL_B->size()	col->size() + 1
C2	COL_B->isEmpty()	false
C3	COL_B->notEmpty()	true
C4	COL_B->exists(x | exp)	col->exists(x | exp) **or** $Inst[x, exp]$
C5	COL_B->forAll(x | exp)	col->forAll(x | exp) **and** $Inst[x, exp]$
C6	COL_B->collect(x | exp)	col->collect(x | exp)->including($Inst[x, exp]$)
C7	COL_B->one(x | exp)	(col->one(x | exp) **and not** $Inst[x, exp]$) **or** (**not** col->exists(x | exp) **and** $Inst[x, exp]$)
C8	COL_B->isUnique(x | exp)	col->isUnique(x | exp) **and** col->select(x | exp = $Inst[x, exp]$)->isEmpty()
C9	COL_B->any(x | exp)	**if** col->exists(x | exp) **then** col->any(x | exp) **else** b **endif**
C10	COL_B->select(x | exp)	**if** $Inst[x, exp]$ **then** col->select(x | exp) ->including(b) **else** col->select(x | exp) **endif**
C11	COL_B->count(exp)	1 (if exp = b) col->count(exp) (otherwise)
C12	COL_B->includes(exp)	true (if exp = b) col ->includes(exp) (otherwise)
C13	COL_B->excludes(exp)	false (if exp = b) col->excludes(exp) (otherwise)
C14	COL_B->including(exp)	col ->including(b) (if exp = b) col->including(exp)->including(b) (otherwise)
C15	COL_B->excluding(exp)	col (if exp = b) col->excluding(exp) ->including(b) (otherwise)
C16	COL_B->includesAll(exp)	col->includesAll(col') (if exp = col'->including(b)) col->includesAll(exp) (otherwise)
C17	exp->includesAll(COL_B)	false (if exp ≠ col'->including(b)) col'->includesAll(col) (otherwise)
C18	COL_B= exp or exp = COL_B	col = col' (if exp = col'->including(b)) false (otherwise)
C19	COL_B≠ exp or exp ≠ COL_B	col ≠ col'(if exp = col'->including(b)) true (otherwise)

Table 7. Replacement patterns for object expressions, where b is the identifier of the new object and *exp*, *exp1* and *exp2* are arbitrary expressions

Ref	Pattern	Replacement
O1	b.attrib	attribute_condition(attrib)
O2	b.role	Set{$a_1, \ldots a_N$}, where $a_1, \ldots a_N$ are the identifiers of the objects linked to x through "role" in the RHS
O3	b.oclIsTypeOf(A)	true if $T = A$; false otherwise
O4	b.oclIsKindOf(A)	true if $T \sqsubseteq A$; false otherwise
O5	b.allInstances()	T::allInstances()−>including(b)
O6	exp−>count(b)	1 (if exp = col−>including(b)) 0 (otherwise)
O7	exp−>includes(b)	true (if exp = col−>including(b)) false (otherwise)
O8	exp−>excludes(b)	false (if exp = col−>including(b)) true (otherwise)
O9	exp−>excluding(b)	col (if exp = col−>including(b)) exp (otherwise)
O10	b = exp or exp = b	true if b = exp; false otherwise
O11	b ≠ exp or exp ≠ b	false if b = exp; true otherwise
O12	Set{ exp1, ..., b, ..., exp2}	Set{ exp1, ..., exp2}−>including(b)

Example 4. Continuing with the previous example, the expression with references to "including(c)" can be transformed into the following (pattern C5, forAll):

Conveyor::allInstances()−>forAll(x | x.capacity $\geq$ 0) **and** (c.capacity $\geq$ 0)

This pattern has particularised the quantifier "forAll" for object c. Now pattern O1 replaces "c.capacity" by the value given to this attribute in the RHS, removing the last reference to the object. For example, if the RHS includes an attribute computation like: c.x' = 10, the final pre-condition would be:

Conveyor::allInstances()−>forAll(x | x.capacity $\geq$ 0) **and** (10 $\geq$ 0)

3.4 Putting Everything Together

Given a list of atomic graph updates corresponding to a rule, advancing a post-condition consists on applying the replacement patterns for each update in sequence. The order of application of the replacements is irrelevant for two reasons. First, each intermediate replacement produces a valid OCL expression. Second and most important, there is no overlap between updates: link creation/deletion updates are applied only when no object is being created/deleted, otherwise we use the object creation/deletion patterns.

Finally, we provide some remarks on the *correctness* and *completeness* of the method. Our method ensures that the resulting expression is well-formed, because each pattern ensures type consistency by replacing each matching expression with another one of a compatible type. Regarding the equivalence of pre- and post-conditions, a complete proof is out of the scope of this paper.

The method supports most of the OCL but the following features from the OCL 2.0 specification are unsupported:

- Calls to recursive query operations.
- OCL collections other than Set (i.e. Bag, Sequence, OrderedSet) and their operations (i.e. first, last, append, prepend, insertAt, sortedBy, at, indexOf, subSequence, subOrderedSet, asBag/Sequence/OrderedSet)
- The type Tuple and operations involving tuples, e.g. the cartesian product.

4   Back to the Examples

This section illustrates the transformation method using the examples we presented in Section 2. Firstly, we consider rule *process* in Fig. 1.

1. First we pre-process the OCL invariants, rewriting them to a global scope:

   > Conveyor::allInstances()−>forAll(v | $v.piece−>size() \leq v.capacity$) **and**
   > Piece::allInstances()−>forAll(z | $z.conveyor−>size() = 1$)

   where the second clause, constraining pieces, is derived from the cardinality constraints on the association between conveyors and pieces.
2. Now we extract the atomic actions the rule performs. In our case, it deletes object r (together with link co1-r) and it creates object p (with link co2-p).
3. Next, we apply the replacement patterns. We start by the replacements due to object deletion, which in addition incorporate the deletion of all adjacent edges (hence deletion of both r and co1-r). The resulting expression is:

   > Conveyor::allInstances()−>forAll(v |
   > $v.piece−>$excluding(r)$−>$size() $\leq$ v.capacity) **and**
   > Piece::allInstances()−>excluding(r)−>forAll(z | $z.conveyor−>size() = 1$)

   where we have applied patterns *OD2* and *OD1*.
4. In order to apply the patterns for the creation of object p and its adjacent link co2-p, we will consider both conditions in the conjunction separately. In the first condition, the expression $v.piece$ matches the pattern OC2:

   > Conveyor::allInstances()−>forAll(v |
   >   (**if** v.piece = co2 **then** v.piece −>including(p)
   >   **else** v.piece **endif**)−>excluding(r)−>size() $\leq$ v.capacity)

5. Before continuing, we can expand the conditional expression:

   > Conveyor::allInstances()−>forAll(v |
   >   **if** v = co2 **then** v.piece−>including(p)−>excluding(r)−>size() $\leq$ v.capacity
   >   **else** v.piece−>excluding(r)−>size() $\leq$ v.capacity **endif**)

6. Now we can apply pattern C15 (excluding), and then pattern C1 (size):

Conveyor::allInstances()−>forAll(v |
   if v = co2 **then** v.piece−>excluding(r)−>size() + 1 ≤ v.capacity
   else v.piece−>excluding(r)−>size() ≤ v.capacity **endif**)

Notice that this result is more complex than the condition stated in Fig. 1 (right), because it considers the possibility of a *non-injective* matching, i.e. co1 = co2. In this case, there is no size problem as the rule creates *and* deletes the piece on the same conveyor. This is achieved implicitly by the conditional and the call to "excluding(r)": if co1 = co2, then "v.piece" contains piece r and it is removed by the call "excluding(r)"; otherwise, "v.piece" remains unaltered. This case was not considered by the designer of the rule in Fig. 1 as it is not obvious from the invariant and the LHS. As a result, condition in Fig. 1 was too restrictive and forbade the execution of the rule in a correct scenario. This example illustrates the benefits of automating the approach.

7. Finally, we apply the replacements for the second part of the post-condition:

Piece::allInstances()−>excluding(r) −>forAll(z | z.conveyor−>size() = 1)

↓ Pattern OC1 (allInstances)

Piece::allInstances()−>including(p) −>excluding(r)
   −>forAll(z | z.conveyor−>size() = 1)

↓ Pattern C15 (excluding)

Piece::allInstances()−>excluding(r)−>including(p)
   −>forAll(z | z.conveyor−>size() = 1)

↓ Pattern C5 (forAll)

Piece::allInstances()−>excluding(r) −>forAll(z | z.conveyor−>size() =1)
and (p.conveyor−>size() = 1)

↓ Pattern O2 (navigation)

Piece::allInstances()−>excluding(r) −>forAll(z | z.conveyor−>size() = 1)
and (Set{co1}−>size() = 1)

↓ Set{co1}−>size() = 1 : the second condition in the **and** is true

Piece::allInstances()−>excluding(r) −>forAll(z | z.conveyor−>size() = 1)

The complete pre-condition generated from our post-condition is therefore:

Conveyor::allInstances()−>forAll(v |
   if v = co2 **then** v.piece −>excluding(r)−>size() + 1 ≤ v.capacity
   else v.piece −>excluding(r)−>size() ≤ v.capacity **endif**) **and**
Piece::allInstances()−>excluding(r)−>forAll(z | z.conveyor−>size() = 1)

5 Optimizations

When the post-condition *Post* being advanced is an integrity constraint, the problem becomes different to that of computing the weakest pre-condition: as *Post* is an invariant, it also holds before applying the rule. This can simplify the pre-condition being advanced, as it only needs to check the property *incrementally*, i.e. on the subgraph being modified by the rule. For instance, the conveyor capacity constraint could be reduced to:

$$co2.piece->excluding(r)->size() +1 \leq co2.capacity$$

since adding a piece to a conveyor (in this case *co2*) can only violate the invariant on that conveyor. Therefore, it is useless to iterate through all existing conveyors when checking rule applicability. As before, the *excluding(r)* operation is added to handle the special case in which *co1* and *co2* are matched to the same object in the host graph.

Extending our approach with the synthesis of incremental constraints would follow the general algorithms for deriving incremental constraints for UML/OCL models presented in [3], which we do not show for space constraints.

6 Related Work

There are previous works on moving constraints from the RHS to the LHS of GT rules. The idea was first proposed in [12], where post-conditions for rules where derived from global invariants of the form $\forall P \exists Q$, where P and Q are graphs. The approach generated a set of post-conditions for each rule from such invariants, and then applied the rule "backwards" to obtain the desired set of pre-conditions. In [6] the approach was generalized to adhesive high-level replacement systems. Again, constraints are graphical graph patterns which can be universally or existentially quantified, or combined using boolean operators. These works were extended in [10] to deal with nested conditions of arbitrary depth. This family of conditions has the same expressive power as first-order graph formulas [11].

These approaches have two main limitations w.r.t. our new technique: (1) lack of expressivity in the post-condition expressions (e.g. OCL expressions such as numerical constraints on attributes or cardinalities of collections are not supported) and (2) complexity of the advancement procedure (the procedure is described by categorical operations and needs an additional method to simplify redundant graph patterns as otherwise the graph constraints may become too large) that makes difficult their application in practice. In contrast, our technique is especially tailored to consider OCL expressions, and hence is very appropriate for its use in meta-modelling environments. Furthermore, the use of OCL allows the application of tools for the simulation, analysis and verification on UML/OCL models [1,2,8,15]. Regarding the drawbacks of our proposal, it is not complete (some OCL constraints have no translation for rules that create objects) and we do not have a formal proof of its correctness yet.

The work of [16] translates a subset of OCL to graph constraints, which can be used to synthesize local pre-conditions for rules. However, the covered OCL subset is limited, and their techniques suffer the drawbacks of [6,11,12].

For transformations not defined as GT, the computation of the weakest pre-condition has also been studied, e.g. to analyse the composition of refactorings [13]. The notion of "backward descriptions" defined in [13] captures our replacement patterns of OCL expressions.

Regarding information systems, in [4] the authors study the generation of weakest pre-conditions for basic operations that perform a single change on the system state, e.g. instance creation or attribute update. Rather than studying the generation of weakest pre-conditions for arbitrary operations and constraints (as it is done in this paper), a fixed catalog of typical integrity constraints as well as patterns for determining the weakest pre-condition with respect to each kind of basic operation are defined. The same problem, advancing integrity constraints as pre-conditions, is studied in [14] for set-based invariants described in B. This family of constraints (constraints involving intersections, unions, differences and tests for membership) is a subset of those considered in this paper, e.g. cardinalities of sets are not supported.

7   Conclusions and Future Work

We have presented a technique to automatically synthesize application conditions for GT rules. Application conditions are derived from the rule post-conditions such that host graphs satisfying the applicability conditions will surely be consistent with all post-conditions at the end of any possible rule execution. Rule post-conditions may come from the rule itself or, for instance, from the well-formedness constraints defined in the meta-model. As a salient feature of our approach, post-conditions may include arbitrary OCL expressions and hence is a step towards the integration of GT and MDE.

As further work we would like to adapt this technique to other transformation languages (e.g. QVT and ATL), to combine it with techniques to advance graphical post-conditions and to reuse it as part of more complex scenarios like the automatic generation of concurrent rules. We also plan to study in more detail the possible optimizations commented above to simplify and improve the efficiency of the generated conditions and to provide tool support.

Acknowledgements. Work funded by the Spanish Ministry of Science and Innovation through projects "Design and construction of a Conceptual Modeling Assistant" (TIN2008-00444/TIN - Grupo Consolidado), "METEORIC" (TIN2008-02081), mobility grants JC2009-00015 and PR2009-0019, and the R&D program of the Community of Madrid (S2009/TIC-1650, project "e-Madrid"). We would like to thank the anonymous referees and the members of the Conceptual Modeling Group (GMC) at UPC for their useful comments.

References

1. Cabot, J., Clarisó, R., Guerra, E., de Lara, J.: A UML/OCL framework for the analysis of graph transformation rules. Soft. and Syst. Mod. (2010) (to appear)
2. Cabot, J., Clarisó, R., Riera, D.: Verification of UML/OCL class diagrams using constraint programming. In: MoDeVVa 2008. ICST Workshop, pp. 73–80 (2008)
3. Cabot, J., Teniente, E.: Incremental integrity checking of UML/OCL conceptual schemas. Journal of Systems and Software 82(9), 1459–1478 (2009)
4. Costal, D., Gómez, C., Queralt, A., Teniente, E.: Drawing preconditions of operation contracts from conceptual schemas. In: Bellahsène, Z., Léonard, M. (eds.) CAiSE 2008. LNCS, vol. 5074, pp. 266–280. Springer, Heidelberg (2008)
5. Dijkstra, E.W.: Guarded commands, nondeterminacy and formal derivation of programs. Communications of the ACM 18(8), 453–457 (1975)
6. Ehrig, H., Ehrig, K., Habel, A., Pennemann, K.-H.: Theory of constraints and application conditions: From graphs to high-level structures. Fundamenta Informaticae 74(1), 135–166 (2006)
7. Ehrig, H., Ehrig, K., Prange, U., Taentzer, G.: Fundamentals of Algebraic Graph Transformation. Springer, Heidelberg (2006)
8. Gogolla, M., Bohling, J., Richters, M.: Validating UML and OCL models in USE by automatic snapshot generation. Soft. and Syst. Mod. 4(4), 386–398 (2005)
9. Gogolla, M., Richters, M.: Expressing UML class diagrams properties with OCL. In: Clark, A., Warmer, J. (eds.) Object Modeling with the OCL. LNCS, vol. 2263, pp. 85–114. Springer, Heidelberg (2002)
10. Habel, A., Pennemann, K.-H.: Nested constraints and application conditions for high-level structures. In: Kreowski, H.-J., Montanari, U., Orejas, F., Rozenberg, G., Taentzer, G. (eds.) Formal Methods in Software and Systems Modeling. LNCS, vol. 3393, pp. 293–308. Springer, Heidelberg (2005)
11. Habel, A., Pennemann, K.-H.: Correctness of high-level transformation systems relative to nested conditions. Math. Struct. Comp. Sci. 19(2), 245–296 (2009)
12. Heckel, R., Wagner, A.: Ensuring consistency of conditional graph rewriting - a constructive approach. In: ENTCS, vol. 2 (1995)
13. Kniesel, G., Koch, H.: Static composition of refactorings. Sci. Comput. Program. 52(1-3), 9–51 (2004)
14. Mammar, A., Gervais, F., Laleau, R.: Systematic identification of preconditions from set-based integrity constraints. In: INFORSID 2006, pp. 595–610 (2006)
15. Queralt, A., Teniente, E.: Reasoning on UML class diagrams with OCL constraints. In: Embley, D.W., Olivé, A., Ram, S. (eds.) ER 2006. LNCS, vol. 4215, pp. 497–512. Springer, Heidelberg (2006)
16. Winkelmann, J., Taentzer, G., Ehrig, K., Kuster, J.M.: Translation of restricted OCL constraints into graph constraints for generating meta model instances by graph grammars. In: ENTCS, vol. 211, pp. 159–170 (2008)

From State- to Delta-Based Bidirectional Model Transformations

Zinovy Diskin, Yingfei Xiong, and Krzysztof Czarnecki

Generative Software Development Lab,
University of Waterloo, Canada
{zdiskin,yingfei,kczarnec}@gsd.uwaterloo.ca

Abstract. Existing bidirectional model transformation languages are mainly state-based: a transformation is considered composed from functions whose inputs and outputs only consist of original and updated models, but alignment relationships between the models are not specified. In the paper we identify and discuss three major problems caused by this under-specification. We then propose a novel formal framework based on a graphical language: models are nodes and updates are arrows, and show how the three problems can be fixed.

1 Introduction

A bidirectional transformation (BX) synchronizes two models by propagating updates between them. To date, there exist a large number of bidirectional transformation systems [1,2,3,4,5,6] synchronizing different kinds of models. Despite their diversity, BX systems are based on few underlying principles and enjoy several simple mathematical models [1,7,8] formulated within similar formal frameworks. The main idea is to consider BX composed from *propagating* functions ppg that take the updated model B' on one side and, if necessary, the original model A on the other side, and produce the updated model $A' = \mathsf{ppg}(B', A)$.

A fundamental feature of these frameworks is that they are *state-* rather than *update-based*. That is, propagation procedures take states of models before and after updates as input and ignore how updates were actually done. Freedom from operational details allows loose coupling between synchronizers and applications and is technologically beneficial [9]. However, it requires a mechanism for model alignment, i.e., relating objects in the before- and after-states of the updated model. For example, QVT [6], Boomerang [2] and FSML [10] use external keys: chosen sets of attributes such that objects having the same key values are considered to be the same.

We may model alignment by a binary operation dif that takes two models and produces a delta (an update) between them. Then a general schema of update propagation (roughly) takes the form

$$(\mathsf{DifPpg}) \qquad \mathsf{ppg} \stackrel{\mathrm{def}}{=} \mathsf{dif}\,;\mathsf{ppg}_\Delta,$$

where ";" denotes sequential composition and ppg_Δ is an operation that takes a delta between models and computes an updated model on the other side. However, existing state-based synchronization frameworks and tools "hide" DifPpg

L. Tratt and M. Gogolla (Eds.): ICMT 2010, LNCS 6142, pp. 61–76, 2010.
© Springer-Verlag Berlin Heidelberg 2010

decomposition: the formalisms only specify the behavior of function ppg and correspondingly deltas do not occur into tools' interfaces.

Discovering updates (operation dif) and propagating updates (operation ppg_Δ) are two different tasks that must be treated differently and addressed separately. Mixing them in one state-based operation ppg leads to theoretical and practical problems. In this paper we will show that state-based framework have the following deficiencies: (a) inflexible interface for BX tools, (b) ill-formed transformation composition, and (c) an over-restrictive law regulating interaction of transformations with update composition.

To be concrete, we discuss these problems within the context of update propagation across views and the state-based framework of *lenses* [1], but basic ideas of our discussion can be generalized for symmetric synchronization frameworks [7,8] too.

To support the separation of dif and ppg_Δ theoretically, we develop an algebraic theory of operation ppg_Δ, whose input and output are states of the models together with updates between them. Making updates explicit leads to a novel specification framework, in which model spaces are graphs: nodes are models and arrows are deltas. The latter can be interpreted either operationally (edit logs or directed deltas) or structurally (relations between models or symmetric deltas); the latter interpretation is central for the present paper. We will follow a common mathematical terminology and call a symmetric delta between the original and updated state of a model an *update mapping*. Thus, both models and update mappings are first-class citizens, and we call BXs specified in this framework update-based BXs, or more specifically, *update-based lenses(u-lenses* in short). We prove several basic results about u-lenses, and show that they present an essential generalization of ordinary lenses.

The structure of the paper is as follows. In the next section, we consider a simple example showing that different update mappings may lead to different synchronization results. We then identify and discuss three problems caused by the absence of update mappings in the lens framework. In Section 3, we introduce u-lenses and discuss their properties. In Section 4, we discuss how u-lenses relate to s-lenses and allow us to manage the three problems. Related work is discussed in Section 5.

2   Problems of State-Based Bidirectional Transformations

We interpret the term "model" as "a state of the model" and will use the two terms interchangeably.

2.1   Model Synchronization via Lenses: A Missing Link

We first remind the basic motivation and definition of lenses. Lenses are an asymmetric BX framework: in the two models being synchronized, one model (the view) is determined by the other (the source). We have a set of source models **A**, a set of view models **B**, and two propagation functions between them, get and put, whose arities are shown in Fig. 1a. Function get (meaning "get the view") takes a source model $A \in \mathbf{A}$ and computes its view $B \in \mathbf{B}$. Function put takes an updated view model $B' \in \mathbf{B}$ and the original source $A \in \mathbf{A}$ and computes an updated source $A' \in \mathbf{A}$ ("puts the view back"). Function put is a special case of propagation function ppg (not ppg$_\Delta$) discussed in Section 1.

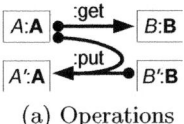

(a) Operations

Definition 1 (adapted from [1]). A *well-behaved (wb) lens* is a tuple $l = (\mathbf{A}, \mathbf{B}, \mathsf{get}, \mathsf{put})$ with $\mathbf{A}$ and $\mathbf{B}$ sets called the *source* and the *view space* of the lens, and get: $\mathbf{A} \rightarrow \mathbf{B}$ and put: $\mathbf{B} \times \mathbf{A} \rightarrow \mathbf{A}$ are functions such that the laws GetPut and PutGet in Fig. 1b hold for any $A \in \mathbf{A}$ and $B' \in \mathbf{B}$. (We write A.get and put(B, A) for the values of get and put to ease readability.) We write $l\colon \mathbf{A} \rightleftarrows \mathbf{B}$ for a lens l with the source space $\mathbf{A}$ and the view space $\mathbf{B}$.

(GetPut) $A = \mathsf{put}(A.\mathsf{get}, A)$
(PutGet) $(\mathsf{put}(B', A)).\mathsf{get} = B'$
(PutPut) $\mathsf{put}(B'', \mathsf{put}(B', A))$
$= \mathsf{put}(B'', A)$

(b) Equational laws

Fig. 1. Lens operations and laws

A wb lens is called *very well-behaved*, if for any $A \in \mathbf{A}$, $B', B'' \in \mathbf{B}$ the PutPut law holds as well.

In Fig. 1 and below, we use the following notation. Given a function $f\colon X \rightarrow Y$, we call a pair (x, y) with $y = f(x)$ an *application instance* of f and write $(x, y):f$ or $x \xrightarrow{:f} y$. For a binary $f\colon X_1 \times X_2 \rightarrow Y$, an application instance is a triple (x_1, x_2, y) with $y = f(x_1, x_2)$. We will also often write a pair (x, y) as xy.

Figure 2 shows a transformation instance in the lens framework. The source model specifies Person-objects with their first and last names and birthdates. Each person belongs to a department, which has a department name. The get function extracts a view containing the persons from the "Marketing" department and omits their birthdate. The put function reflects the updates on the view back into the source.

Note the change from Melinda French ($p1$) in state B to Melinda Gates ($p1'$) in state B'. This change can be interpreted as the result of two different updates: (u1) person $p1$ is renamed, or (u2) person $p1$ is deleted from the model and another person $p1'$ is inserted. These updates can be described structurally (rather than operationally) by specifying a binary *sameness* relation $R_\simeq$ between the states. For update (u1), $R_\simeq = \{p_1 p'_1, p_2 p'_2\}$, and for (u2), $R_\simeq = \{p_2 p'_2\}$, where xy denotes pair (x, y). We will call sameness relations or similar correspondence specifications *update mappings*. The latter allow us to specify updates lightly without involving full update operation logs.

A reasonable put-function should translate (u1) into renaming of Melinda French in the source, whereas (u2) is translated into deletion of Melinda French from the source followed by insertion of a new person Melinda Gates with attribute Birth set to Unknown. Thus, the results of translation A' should be different, $A'(u1) \neq A'(u2)$, despite the same argument states (B', A). The difference may be more serious than just in the attribute values. Suppose that the model also specifies Cars to be owned by Persons, and in the source model there

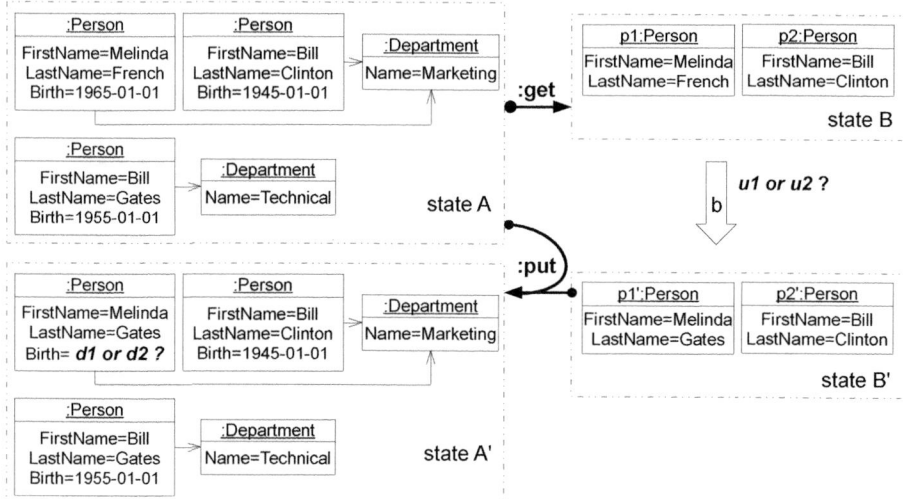

Fig. 2. Running Example

was a Car object with a single owner Melinda French. Then the backward translation of update (u2) must remove this Car-object as well. Thus, states $A'(u1)$ and $A'(u2)$ will have different sets of objects.

2.2   Inflexible Interface

At first glance, a state-based BX looks more flexible than an update-based, as a state-based BX frees users from specifying update mappings. However, since different update mappings lead to different synchronization results, we may want to control how to discover updates from two states or from an operation log. In these cases, we need the interface of update-based BX.

If we have an update-based procedure ppg_Δ, we can construct a state-based BX by composing it with operation dif, where dif can be a manually-implemented procedure or one of existing model difference tools [11,12,13]. In contrast, given a state-based ppg, we cannot easily build an update-based BX because it is not easy to extract ppg_Δ from the whole ppg (unless decomposition DifPpgis given explicitly). As a result, state-based BXs are in fact less flexible.

2.3   Ill-Formed Sequential Composition

Compositionality is at the heart of lenses' applications to practical problems. Writing correct bidirectional transformation for complex views is laborious and error-prone. To manage the problem, a complex view is decomposed into a sequence of simple components, say, model $B = B_n$ is a view of B_{n-1}, which is a view of $B_{n-2},...$, which is a view of $B_0 = A$, such that for each component view a correct lens can be found in a repository. A lens-based language provides the

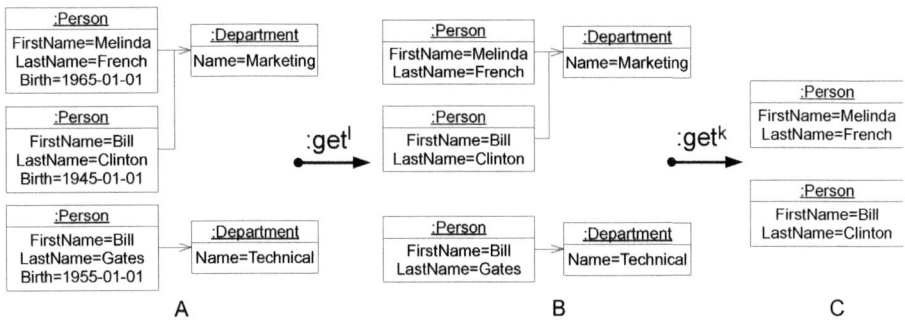

Fig. 3. Sequentially composed transformation

programmer with a number of operators of lens composition. Sequential composition is one of the most important operators, and a fundamental result states that sequential composition of wb lenses is also wb.

Definition 2 (Lens' composition [1]). Given lenses $l: \mathbf{A} \rightleftarrows \mathbf{B}$ and $k: \mathbf{B} \rightleftarrows \mathbf{C}$, their *sequential composition* $(l; k): \mathbf{A} \rightleftarrows \mathbf{C}$ is defined as follows. For any $A \in \mathbf{A}$, $A.\text{get}^{(l;k)} = A.\text{get}^l.\text{get}^k$, and for any pair $(C', A) \in \mathbf{C} \times \mathbf{A}$, $\text{put}^{(l;k)}(C', A) = \text{put}^l(B', A)$ where B' stands for $\text{put}^k(C', A.\text{get}^l)$.

Theorem 1 ([1]). *Sequential composition* $(l; k)$ *is a (very) well-behaved lens as soon as both lenses* l *and* k *are such.*

For example, transformation in Fig. 2 can be implemented by composing two transformations in Figure 3. The first one (transformation l) removes the attribute Birth, and the second one (transformation k) extracts a list of persons from the "Marketing" department. In the backward propagation, both transformations rely on their dif component to recover updates from models. Suppose both dif procedures use key to recover update. Procedure dif^l uses the key {FirstName, LastName}, and dif^k uses a smaller key {FirstName}, which, nevertheless, works well for the Marketing Department (cf. Fig. 3C).

Ignoring updates may lead to incorrect BX composition. Suppose Melinda French has married and become Melinda Gates as shown in Figure 4C'. Transformation k will successfully discover this update, and modify the last name of Melinda to Gates in model B'. However, when transformation l compares B and B', dif^k will consider Melinda Gates as a new person because her last name is different. Then ppg_Δ^k will delete Melinda French in the source model A and insert a new person with an unknown birthday thus coming to state A'. The result is wrong because the update produced by k and the update discovered by l are different, and hence the two transformations should not be composed.

This example shows a fundamental requirement for sequential composition: two transformations are composable only when they agree on update mappings on the common intermediate model (B in our case). However, this requirement is never specified (and is difficult to specify) in existing state-based frameworks.

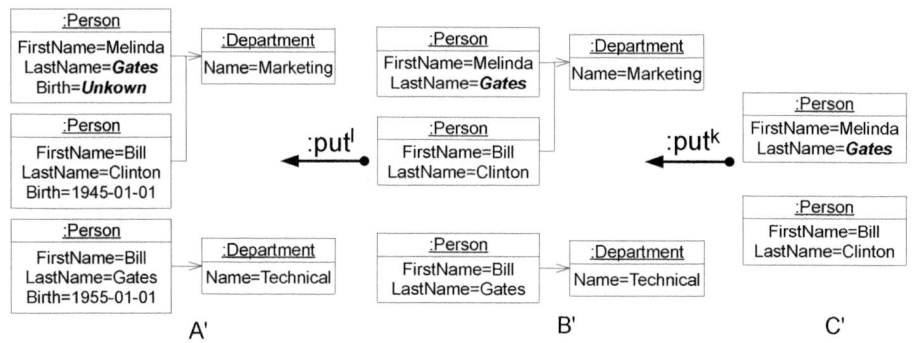

Fig. 4. A wrong putting back

2.4   PutPut: Over-Restrictive State-Based Version

The most controversial law of the basic lens framework is PutPut (Fig. 1b). It says that an updated view state B'' leads to the same updated source A'' regardless of whether the update is performed in one step from B to B'' or with a pair of smaller steps $B-B'-B''$ through an intermediate state B'. This seems to be a natural requirement for a reasonable backward propagation put, but many practically interesting BXs fail to satisfy the law.

Consider our running example. Suppose that in a view B (Fig. 5) the user deletes Melinda French and comes to state B'. The put-function deletes Melinda in the source as well and results in state A'. If later the user inserts back exactly the same person in the view, the put-function will insert this new person in the source and set attribute Birth to Unknown (state A'' in the figure). However, since the states B and B'' are equal, PutPut-law prescribes the states A and A'' be also equal. However, the birthdate of Melinda was lost in state A' and cannot be recovered in A''. Hence, for a quite reasonable transformation shown in Fig. 5, PutPut fails.

To analyze the problem, we present function put as composition dif;put$_\Delta$ and consider the effect of PutPut componentwise.

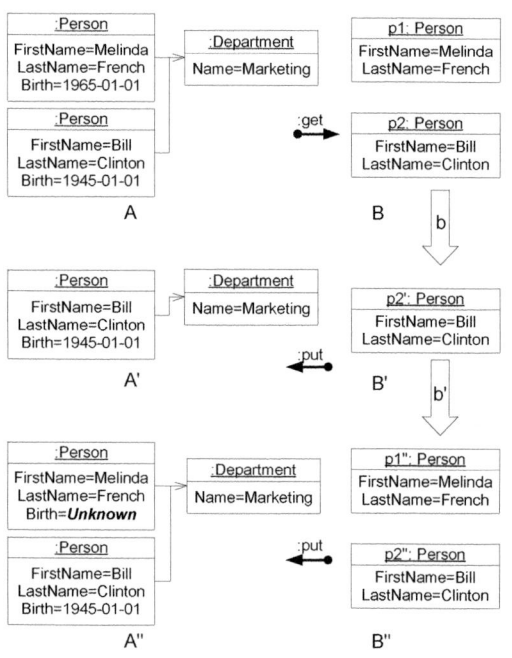

Fig. 5. Violation of PutPut

For pure propagation put_Δ, PutPut requires preservation of update composition: If we first propagate b and then propagate b', we should get the same result of propagating $b; b'$, where ";" indicates sequential composition of updates. For alignment dif, PutPut requires $\mathsf{dif}(B, B'') = \mathsf{dif}(B, B'); \mathsf{dif}(B', B'')$. Although the constraint on put_Δ holds well for the example, its counterpart on dif is unrealistic. For two identical models, B and B'', it is quite reasonable that dif returns the identity update. However, update b is a deletion and update b' is an insertion. Their composition $b; b'$ is different from the identity update. Formally, by specifying updates with sameness relations we have $R_\sim = \{p_2 p_2'\}$ for b and $R_\sim' = \{p_2' p_2''\}$ for b'. Sequential composition of $R_\sim$ and $R_\sim'$ as binary relations is relation $R_\sim \otimes R_\sim' = \{p_2 p_2''\}$ that is smaller than the identity update $\{p_1 p_1'', p_2 p_2''\}$ (and indeed, information that objects p_1 and p_1' are the same is beyond updates b and b'). As $b; b'$ is not identity, we cannot expect that the corresponding composition on the source $a; a'$ is identity, even though propagation ppg_Δ preserves composition.

This example shows a serious defect of the PutPut-law. In fact, it constrains both the alignment (dif) and the propagation (put_Δ). Although the latter requirement is not too restrictive in practice, the former is rarely satisfied. Hence, PutPut often fails due to dif rather than put_Δ. To improve PutPut, we should only constrain pure propagation put_Δ to be defined in an update-based framework for BX.

3   U-Lenses: Update-Based Bidirectional Transformations

We build our formal framework for update-based BX in an incremental way. First we define updates abstractly as arrows between models, and thus come to the notion of a model space as a graph. Then we define an *update-based* lens (*u-lens*) as a triple of functions $(\mathsf{get}_0, \mathsf{get}_1, \mathsf{put})$ satisfying certain equational laws. Functions get_0 and get_1 send nodes (models) and arrows (updates) in the source space to, respectively, nodes and arrows in the view space. Function put formalizes the ppg_Δ component of put in state-based lenses, mapping the arrows in the view space back to the arrows in the source space, and this mapping is parameterized by nodes (original models) in the source. To distinguish u-lenses from ordinary lenses working only with states, we call the latter *s-lenses*.

Since updates can be composed, our model spaces are graphs with composable arrows, or *categories*. Mappings between categories are normally compatible with composition and exhibit remarkable algebraic properties that have been studied in category theory. Not surprisingly, the u-lens framework is essentially categorical. Nevertheless, our presentation will mainly be arranged in set- rather than category-theoretical way to make comparison with s-lenses easier. Yet we employ simple categorical notions where their usage provides especially compact and transparent view of the formalities. Explanations of these categorical notions are displayed in boxes marked as "Background".

3.1 Building the Definition: Models and Updates

Representations of model updates can be classified into two main groups: *directed deltas* and *symmetric deltas* [14]. In the former, an update is basically a sequence of edit operations (add, change, delete). In the latter, an update is a specification of the common part of the before- and after-states of the model (while deleted and added parts are given by "subtracting" the common part from the before- and after-states). A typical representative of the second group is our *update mappings*, that is, triples $a = (A, R_{\sim}, A')$ with A and A' being states of the model and $R_{\sim}$ a sameness relation (the common part) between them. More details can be found in [15].

Whatever representation is used, updates have the following properties.

1. An update has a source model and a target model.
2. There may be multiple updates between two models.
3. A model can be updated to any model conforming to the same metamodel.
4. Updates can be composed sequentially. For the operational representation, if an edit sequence a updates model A to A', and another edit sequence a' updates A' to A'', then the composed update from A to A'' is concatenation of a and a'. For the structural representation, composition of $a = (A, R_{\sim}, A')$ and $a' = (A', R'_{\sim}, A'')$ is $(A, R_{\sim} \otimes R'_{\sim}, A'')$ with $\otimes$ denoting relational composition. We write $a; a'$ for the composition of updates a and a'.
5. For any model A, there is a "no-change" update, which we call *idle* and denote by $\mathbf{1}_A$. Operationally, an idle update is given by the empty edit sequence. Structurally, the idle update $\mathbf{1}_A$ is the identity mapping $(A, \{(e, e) : e \in A\}, A)$.

These considerations suggest to abstract updates as arrows between models, which can be composed. Hence, a model universe appears as a graph (points 1,2) with composable arrows (4), which is connected (3) and reflexive (5) — see Background below for precise definitions (where we write "a set X of *widgets*" instead of "a set X of abstract elements called *widgets*"). Identity loops should be required to be neutral wrt. composition since idle updates are such. In addition, we require arrow composition in our abstract model to be associative (both concatenation of edit sequences and relational composition are associative).

Definition 3. A *model space* is a connected category, whose nodes are called *models* and arrows are *updates*.

Background: Graphs. A *graph* $\mathbf{G}$ consists of a set of *nodes* $\mathbf{G}_0$ and a set of *arrows* $\mathbf{G}_1$ together with two functions $\partial_s \colon \mathbf{G}_1 \to \mathbf{G}_0$ and $\partial_t \colon \mathbf{G}_1 \to \mathbf{G}_0$. For an arrow $a \in \mathbf{G}_1$, we write $a \colon A \to A'$ if $\partial_s a = A$ and $\partial_t a = A'$ and call nodes A the *source* and A' the *target* of a. A graph is *connected*, if for any pair of nodes A, A' there is at least one arrow $a \colon A \to A'$. A *reflexive* graph is additionally equipped with operation $\mathbf{1} \colon \mathbf{G}_1 \to \mathbf{G}_0$ that assigns to each node A a special arrow-loop $\mathbf{1}_A \colon A \to A$ called *identity*.

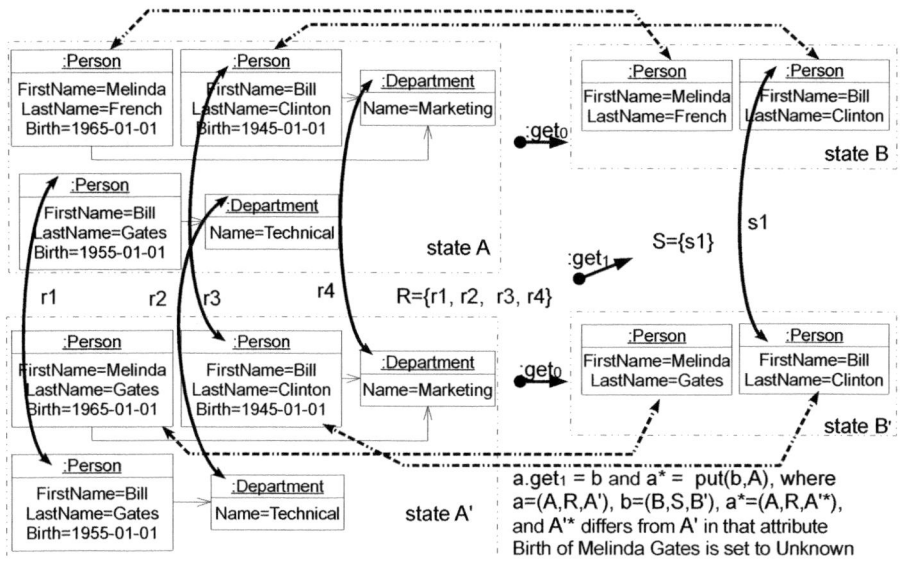

Fig. 6. Translation of update mappings

Background: Categories. A *category* is a reflexive graph with well-behaved composition of arrows. In detail, a category is a pair $\mathbf{C}=(|\mathbf{C}|,;)$ with $|\mathbf{C}|$ a reflexive graph and ; a binary operation of arrow composition, which assigns to arrows $a\colon A \to A'$ and $a''\colon A' \to A''$ an arrow $a;a'\colon A \to A''$ such that the following two laws hold: $a;(a';a'') = (a;a');a''$ for any triple of composable arrows Associativity, and $1_A;a = a = a;1_{A'}$ Neutrality of identity wrt. composition.

We write $A\in\mathbf{C}$ for a node $A\in|\mathbf{C}|_0$, and $a\in\mathbf{C}$ for an arrow $a\in|\mathbf{C}|_1$.

3.2 Building the Definition Cont'd: Views and Update Translation

---

Background: Functors. Let $\mathbf{A}$ and $\mathbf{B}$ be categories. A *semi-functor* $f\colon \mathbf{A} \to \mathbf{B}$ is a pair (f_0,f_1) of functions $f_i\colon \mathbf{A}_i \to \mathbf{B}_i$, $(i{=}0,1)$ that preserves 1) the incidence relations between nodes and arrows, $\partial_x f_1(a){=}f_0(\partial_x a)$, x = s, t, and 2) identities, $f_1(1_A) = 1_{f_0(A)}$. A semi-functor is called a *functor* if 3) composition is also preserved: $f_1(a;a') = f_1(a);f_1(a')$.

In the state-based framework, model spaces are sets and a view is a function $get\colon \mathbf{A} \to \mathbf{B}$ between these sets. In the update-based framework, model spaces are graphs and a view get consists of two components: a function on nodes $get_0\colon \mathbf{A}_0 \to \mathbf{B}_0$ computing views of source models, and a function on arrows $get_1\colon \mathbf{A}_1 \to \mathbf{B}_1$ translating updates in the source space to updates in the view space. The idea of function get_1 is illustrated by Fig. 6, in which vertical arrows denote pairs of elements from the sameness relations, and horizontal arrows denote traceability links. Roughly, function get_1 maps the links in the update

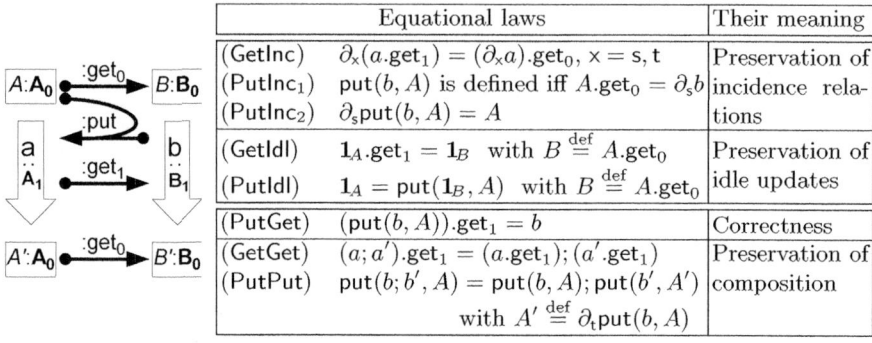

	Equational laws	Their meaning
(GetInc)	$\partial_x(a.\text{get}_1) = (\partial_x a).\text{get}_0, \ x = s, t$	Preservation of
(PutInc$_1$)	$\text{put}(b, A)$ is defined iff $A.\text{get}_0 = \partial_s b$	incidence rela-
(PutInc$_2$)	$\partial_s \text{put}(b, A) = A$	tions
(GetIdl)	$1_A.\text{get}_1 = 1_B$ with $B \stackrel{\text{def}}{=} A.\text{get}_0$	Preservation of
(PutIdl)	$1_A = \text{put}(1_B, A)$ with $B \stackrel{\text{def}}{=} A.\text{get}_0$	idle updates
(PutGet)	$(\text{put}(b, A)).\text{get}_1 = b$	Correctness
(GetGet)	$(a; a').\text{get}_1 = (a.\text{get}_1); (a'.\text{get}_1)$	Preservation of
(PutPut)	$\text{put}(b; b', A) = \text{put}(b, A); \text{put}(b', A')$	composition
	with $A' \stackrel{\text{def}}{=} \partial_t \text{put}(b, A)$	

Fig. 7. U-lens operations and laws

mapping $a\colon A \to A'$ accordingly to how function get_0 maps the elements in the models A and A'. Thus, given a view mechanism, the same view definition determines both get-functions.[1]

Evidently, the pair $(\text{get}_0, \text{get}_1)$ should preserve the incidence between models and updates (as prescribed by GetInc-law in Fig. 7), and map idle updates to idle updates (GetIdl-law). In other words, it is reasonable to assume that update translation is a semi-functor.

A backward translation is given by a function $\text{put}\colon \mathbf{B}_1 \times \mathbf{A}_0 \to \mathbf{A}_1$, which takes an update in the view space and produces an update in the source. Similarly to ordinary lenses, it also takes the original source model as its second argument to recover information missing in the view. An example of put is implicit in Fig. 6, where the the update $a^* = \text{put}(b, A)$ is not shown to avoid clutter but specified in the right lower corner of the figure. Note that $a^* \neq a$ because birthdates are lost in the view and update mapping S specifies Melinda Gates as a new object.

The backward translation must satisfy three technical laws ensuring that the formal model is adequate to the intuition : PutInc$_1$, PutInc$_2$ and PutIdl. Applying put to a view update $b\colon B \to B'$ and a source A, we of course assume that B is the view of A, i.e., $A.\text{get}_0 = B$ as prescribed by PutInc$_1$-law in Fig. 7. Thus, though function put is partially defined, this partiality is technical and ensures right incidence between updates and models: this gives us the "only if" half of the law PutInc$_1$. On the other hand, we require that for any update b that holds the required incidence of A, the backward translation is defined, which gives us the "if" half of the law. In this sense, PutInc$_1$ is analogous to totality requirement in the lens framework [1]. Similarly, we must require that the result of put is to be an update of model A, hence, the PutInc$_2$ law. In addition, it is reasonable to require that idle updates in the view space are translated into idle updates. as stated by PutIdl-law.

Five laws introduced above state the most basic properties of get and put operations, which ensure that the formal model is adequate to its intended

---

[1] Action of a view definition on update mappings can be shown by categorical arguments with a precise formal definition of queries [16]. How it can be done for XML schemas as models and relational deltas as updates is shown in [17].

meaning. Other laws specified in Fig. 7 provide more interesting properties of update propagation, which really constrain the transformational behavior.

The PutGet-law ensures the correctness of backward propagation. It is similar to the corresponding s-lens law, but is defined on updates rather than states. The incidence laws allow us to deduce PutGet for states from PutGet for updates. We do not require GetPut-law because some information contained in update $a\colon A \to A'$ is missing from its view $\mathsf{get}_1(a)$ and cannot be recovered from a's source A. As for the s-lens' law GetPut, its actual meaning is given by ours PutIdl-law, and the name GetPut for this law may be misleading.

Finally, GetGet and PutPut state compatibility of update propagation with update composition.

Definition 4 (u-lens). An *update-based lens (u-lens)* is a tuple $l = (\mathbf{A}, \mathbf{B}, \mathsf{get}, \mathsf{put})$, in which $\mathbf{A}$ and $\mathbf{B}$ are model spaces called the *source* and *target* of the u-lens, $\mathsf{get}\colon \mathbf{A} \to \mathbf{B}$ is a semi-functor providing $\mathbf{B}$-views of $\mathbf{A}$-models and their updates, and $\mathsf{put}\colon \mathbf{B}_1 \times \mathbf{A}_0 \to \mathbf{A}_1$ is a function translating view updates back to the source so that laws PutInc_1 and PutInc_2 in Fig. 7 are respected.

An u-lens is called *well-behaved* (we will write wb) if it also satisfies PutIdl and PutGet laws. A wb u-lens is called *very well-behaved* if it satisfies GetGet and PutPut.

We will write $l\colon \mathbf{A} \rightleftarrows \mathbf{B}$ for a u-lens with source $\mathbf{A}$ and target $\mathbf{B}$, and denote the functions by get^l and put^l. Note that for a very wb u-lens, get^l is a functor between categories $\mathbf{A}$ and $\mathbf{B}$.

3.3 Sequential Composition of U-Lenses

As we discussed in Section 2.3, sequential composition of lenses is extremely important for their practical applications. In the present section we will define sequential composition of u-lenses and prove that composition of two (very) wb u-lenses is also a (very) wb u-lens as soon as the components are such.

> **Background: Functor composition.** Given two semi-functors between categories, $\mathsf{f}\colon \mathbf{A} \to \mathbf{B}$ and $\mathsf{g}\colon \mathbf{B} \to \mathbf{C}$, their composition $\mathsf{f};\mathsf{g}\colon \mathbf{A} \to \mathbf{C}$ is defined componentwise via function composition: $(\mathsf{f};\mathsf{g})_i = \mathsf{f}_i; \mathsf{g}_i$, $i = 0, 1$. Evidently, $\mathsf{f};\mathsf{g}$ is a semi-functor again. Moreover, if f and g are functors, their composition is also a functor (the proof is straightforward).

Definition 5. Let $l\colon \mathbf{A} \rightleftarrows \mathbf{B}$ and $k\colon \mathbf{B} \rightleftarrows \mathbf{C}$ be two u-lenses. Their *sequential composition* is an u-lens $(l; k)\colon \mathbf{A} \rightleftarrows \mathbf{C}$ defined as follows. Forward propagation of $(l; k)$ is sequential composition of semi-functors, $\mathsf{get}^{(l;k)} \stackrel{\mathrm{def}}{=} \mathsf{get}^l; \mathsf{get}^k$

Backward propagation is defined as follows. Let $c\colon C \to C'$ be an update in space $\mathbf{C}$, and $A \in \mathbf{A}$ a model such that $A.\mathsf{get}_0^{(l;k)} = C$, that is, $B.\mathsf{get}_0^k = C$ with B denoting $A.\mathsf{get}_0^l$. Then $\mathsf{put}^{(l;k)}(c, A) = \mathsf{put}^l(b, A)$ with $b = \mathsf{put}^k(c, B)$.

Theorem 2. *Sequential composition of two (very) wb u-lenses is also a (very) wb u-lens as soon as the components are such.*

Proof. The get-part of the theorem is evident: sequential composition of semi-functors (functors) is a semi-functor (functor). The put-part needs just an accurate unraveling of Definition 5 and straightforward checking of the laws.   □

4   U-Lenses with Alignment: Fixing the Problems

We will first define the notion of u-lens with alignment and show how it is related to the s-lens formalism. Then we will review the three main problems of state-based synchronization within the u-lens framework.

4.1   From U- to S-Lenses

Definition 6. An *alignment* over a model space $\mathbf{A}$ is a binary operation dif: $\mathbf{A}_0 \times \mathbf{A}_0 \to \mathbf{A}_1$ satisfying the incidence law DifInc in Fig. 8. Alignment is *well-behaved (wb)* if the DifId-law holds, and *very wb* if, in addition, DifDif holds too.

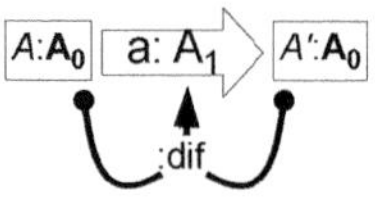

(DifInc)	$\partial_s \mathrm{dif}(A, A') = A, \; \partial_t \mathrm{dif}(A, A') = A'$
(DifId)	$\mathrm{dif}(A, A) = \mathbf{1}_A$
(DifDif)	$\mathrm{dif}(A, A'); \mathrm{dif}(A', A'') = \mathrm{dif}(A, A'')$

Fig. 8. Alignment operations and laws

In most practically interesting cases, alignment is wb but not very wb; we have only introduced the latter notion for analysis of s-lens's PutPut.

Definition 7 (ua-lenses). An *u-lens with alignment (ua-lens)* is a pair $\ell = (l, \mathrm{dif})$ with $l = (\mathrm{get}, \mathrm{put})$: $\mathbf{A} \rightleftarrows \mathbf{B}$ an u-lens and dif an alignment over $\mathbf{B}$. An ua-lens is called **(a)** *well-behaved (wb)* if its both component are such, **(b)** *very wb* if l is very wb, and **(c)** *very-very wb* if alignment is also very wb.

Theorem 3. *Any ua-lens ℓ gives rise to an s-lens ℓ_0. Moreover, if ℓ is (very-very) wb, then ℓ_0 is also (very) wb.*

Proof. Given a ua-lens $\ell = (\mathrm{get}, \mathrm{put}, \mathrm{dif})$: $\mathbf{A} \rightleftarrows \mathbf{B}$, we define an s-lens ℓ_0: $\mathbf{A}_0 \rightleftarrows \mathbf{B}_0$ as follows. For any models $A \in \mathbf{A}_0$ and $B' \in \mathbf{B}_0$, we set $A.\mathrm{get}^{\ell_0} \stackrel{\mathrm{def}}{=} A.\mathrm{get}^\ell_0$ and $\mathrm{put}^{\ell_0}(B', A) \stackrel{\mathrm{def}}{=} \partial_t \mathrm{put}^\ell(\mathrm{dif}^\ell(A.\mathrm{get}^\ell_0, B'), A)$. It is easy to check that s-lens laws in Fig. 1b follow from the alignment laws in Fig. 8 and u-lens laws in Fig. 7. In more detail, given the incidence laws for alignment and u-lenses, laws DifId and u-lens PutId imply s-lens GetPut, u-lens PutGet ensures s-lens PutGet, and DifDif together with u-lens PutPut provide s-lens PutPut.   □

Note that to obtain a very wb s-lens, we need both very wb alignment and very wb u-lens. This is a formal explication of our arguments at the end of Section 2.4 that PutPut-law often fails due to non-very wb alignment rather than propagation procedures as such. Nevertheless, the following weakened version of PutPut holds.

Theorem 4. *Any very wb ua-lens satisfies the following conditional law:*

(PutPut!) if difdif$(A.\mathsf{get}_0, B', B'')$ then putput(A, B', B'') for all $A \in \mathbf{A}$, $B', B'' \in \mathbf{B}$,

where difdif *and* putput *denote the following ternary predicates:*
difdif(B, B', B'') *holds iff* dif(B, B'); dif$(B', B'') =$ dif(B, B'')*, and*
putput(A, B', B'') *holds iff s-lens* PutPut *(see Fig. 1) holds for* (A, B', B'').

Proof. Given difdif(B, B', B'') with $B = A.\mathsf{get}$, the u-lens PutPut together with incidence laws provide putput(A, B', B'').   □

Theorem 4 shows that the notion of very wb ua-lens is a reasonable formalization of BX compatible with updates, and Theorem 3 shows that this notion is stronger than wb s-lens but weaker than very wb s-lens.

4.2   Review of the Three Problems

U-lenses allow us to manage the problems identified in Section 2 in the following way.

First, the possibility to build an s-lens from ua-lens (Theorem 3) shows the flexibility of u-lenses. Second, when the get and put functions of two u-lenses are composed (Definition 5), they must match on update mappings (arrows) rather than only on models (nodes) thus providing continuity of composition wrt. updates. Third, PutPut-law for u-lenses and based on it PutPut!-law for ua-lenses (Theorem 4) are much more adequate to the intended behavior of BXs than state-bases PutPut. Particularly, many useful BXs that satisfy the former would violate the latter (e.g., that one presented in Fig. 5). However, we can still find useful transformations that violate u-lens PutPut.

For instance, we can modify example considered in Fig. 5 in the following way. Suppose that the view also shows persons' birth years. When putting the updated year back, function put uses the month and the day of the month in the original source to restore the whole birthdate. Now, if a person's birthdate is 1984-02-29, changing the year to a non-leap one, say, 1985, in state B' will be propagated back to the date 1985-?-? in state A'. Changing the year in the view back to 1984 in state B'' gives us the identity update $b''=b; b'=1_B : B \rightarrow B$ (as $B = B''$) to be propagated back into identity $a''=1_A : A \rightarrow A$ (as $A = A''$). However, update $a' : A' \rightarrow A''$ cannot restore the lost date 02-29 and hence $a; a' \neq a''$. Yet removing PutPut from the list of u-lens laws is also not a good solution because it frees BXs from any obligations to respect somehow update composition. We plan to attack this problem in a future work.

5   Related Work

A well-known idea is to use incremental model transformations operating with updates to speed up synchronization, e.g., [18]. However, semantics of these approaches is state-based and updates are only considered as an auxiliary technological means. Ráth et al. [19] propose change-driven model transformations that map updates to updates, but they only concern uni-directional transformations, consider updates only operationally, and do not provide a formal framework.

Many BX systems conform to a formal framework. Focal is based on basic s-lenses [1], QVT [6] can be modeled in a "symmetric lens" framework [7], and MOFLON [20] is built upon TGGs [5]. These frameworks are state-based and thus have the problems we described.

Some researchers motivated by practical needs have realized the limitation of the state-based approach and introduced update modeling constructs into their frameworks. Xiong et al. enrich a state-based framework with updates to deal with situations where both models are modified at the same time [3,21]. Foster et al. augment basic lenses with a key-based mechanism to manage alignment of sets of strings, coming to the notion of *dictionary* lens [2]. However, even in these richer (and more complex) frameworks updates are still second-class entities. Transformations still produce only states of models, and the transformation composition problem persists. This problem is managed in the recent framework of *matching* lenses [22], where alignment is explicitly separated from transformation. However, even in the novel frameworks addressing alignment, updates are still second-class entities and the BX laws are state-based. As a result, laws for updates have to be expressed through states, making the framework very restrictive. For example, if we build a model transformation as a matching lens, the source model and the view model must have the same number of objects for each object type.

Close to ours is work by Johnson and Rosebrugh, who consider the view update problem in the database context and employ category theory (see [16] and reference therein). For them, updates are also arrows, a model space is a category and a view is a functor. However, in contrast to the lens-based frameworks including ours, in which models are points without internal structure, for Johnson and Rosebrugh models are functors from a category considered as a database schema to the category of sets and functions. This setting is too detailed for our goals, complicates the machinery and makes it heavily categorical. Also, while we are interested in the laws of composition (of transformations and within a single transformation via PutPut), they focus on conditions ensuring existence of a unique update policy for a given view. Further, they do not consider relations between the update-based and state-based frameworks, which are our main concern in the paper.

6   Conclusion

The paper identifies three major problems of the state-based bidirectional transformation (BX) frameworks: inflexible interfaces, ill-formed composition of transformations and over-restricting PutPut-law. It is shown that these problems can be managed (though the third one only partially) if propagation procedures are decomposed into alignment followed by pure update propagation. Importantly, the latter inputs and outputs not only models but also update mappings between them. We have developed the corresponding algebraic framework for an asymmetric BXs determined by a view, and called the basic structure *u-lens*.

In the u-lens framework, updates are arrows to be thought of as update mappings. They may be considered as light structural representation of updates: updates mappings do the alignment job yet keep us away from the complexities of full update operation logs. This shows that being non-state-based does not necessarily mean being operation-based: it means being update-arrow-based with an open possibility to interpret arrows as required by applications.

Acknowledgements. Thanks go to Michal Antkiewicz for his contributions to the initial version of the paper, and to anonymous referees for valuable comments. Financial support was provided by the Ontario Research Fund.

References

1. Foster, J.N., Greenwald, M.B., Moore, J.T., Pierce, B.C., Schmitt, A.: Combinators for bidirectional tree transformations: A linguistic approach to the view-update problem. ACM Trans. Program. Lang. Syst. 29(3), 17 (2007)
2. Bohannon, A., Foster, J.N., Pierce, B.C., Pilkiewicz, A., Schmitt, A.: Boomerang: Resourceful lenses for string data. In: Proc. 35th POPL (2008)
3. Xiong, Y., Liu, D., Hu, Z., Zhao, H., Takeichi, M., Mei, H.: Towards automatic model synchronization from model transformations. In: ASE, pp. 164–173 (2007)
4. Matsuda, K., Hu, Z., Nakano, K., Hamana, M., Takeichi, M.: Bidirectionalization transformation based on automatic derivation of view complement functions. In: ICFP, pp. 47–58 (2007)
5. Schürr, A., Klar, F.: 15 years of triple graph grammars. In: ICGT, pp. 411–425 (2008)
6. Object Management Group: MOF query / views / transformations specification 1.0 (2008), http://www.omg.org/docs/formal/08-04-03.pdf
7. Stevens, P.: Bidirectional model transformations in QVT: semantic issues and open questions. Software and System Modeling 9(1), 7–20 (2010)
8. Diskin, Z.: Algebraic models for bidirectional model synchronization. In: Czarnecki, K., Ober, I., Bruel, J.-M., Uhl, A., Völter, M. (eds.) MODELS 2008. LNCS, vol. 5301, pp. 21–36. Springer, Heidelberg (2008)
9. Foster, J.N., Greenwald, M., Kirkegaard, C., Pierce, B., Schmitt, A.: Exploiting schemas in data synchronization. J. Comput. Syst. Sci. 73(4), 669–689 (2007)
10. Antkiewicz, M., Czarnecki, K., Stephan, M.: Engineering of framework-specific modeling languages. IEEE Transactions on Software Engineering 99 (RapidPosts), 795–824 (2009)
11. Alanen, M., Porres, I.: Difference and union of models. In: Stevens, P., Whittle, J., Booch, G. (eds.) UML 2003. LNCS, vol. 2863, pp. 2–17. Springer, Heidelberg (2003)
12. Xing, Z., Stroulia, E.: UMLDiff: an algorithm for object-oriented design differencing. In: ASE, pp. 54–65 (2005)
13. Abi-Antoun, M., Aldrich, J., Nahas, N., Schmerl, B., Garlan, D.: Differencing and merging of architectural views. In: ASE, pp. 47–58 (2006)
14. Mens, T.: A state-of-the-art survey on software merging. IEEE Trans. Software Eng. 28(5), 449–462 (2002)
15. Diskin, Z., Czarnecki, K., Antkiewicz, M.: Model-versioning-in-the-large: Algebraic foundations and the tile notation. In: ICSE 2009 Workshop on Comparison and Versioning of Software Models, pp. 7–12 (2009), doi:10.1109/CVSM.2009.5071715

16. Johnson, M., Rosebrugh, R.: Constant complements, reversibility and universal view updates. In: Meseguer, J., RoCsu, G. (eds.) AMAST 2008. LNCS, vol. 5140, pp. 238–252. Springer, Heidelberg (2008)
17. Liefke, H., Davidson, S.: View maintenance for hierarchical semistructured data. In: Kambayashi, Y., Mohania, M., Tjoa, A.M. (eds.) DaWaK 2000. LNCS, vol. 1874, p. 114. Springer, Heidelberg (2000)
18. Giese, H., Wagner, R.: From model transformation to incremental bidirectional model synchronization. Software and Systems Modeling 8(1), 21–43 (2009)
19. Ráth, I., Varró, G., Varró, D.: Change-driven model transformations. In: Schürr, A., Selic, B. (eds.) MODELS 2009. LNCS, vol. 5795, pp. 342–356. Springer, Heidelberg (2009)
20. Amelunxen, C., Königs, A., Rötschke, T., Schürr, A.: MOFLON: A standard-compliant metamodeling framework with graph transformations. In: Rensink, A., Warmer, J. (eds.) ECMDA-FA 2006. LNCS, vol. 4066, pp. 361–375. Springer, Heidelberg (2006)
21. Xiong, Y., Song, H., Hu, Z., Takeichi, M.: Supporting parallel updates with bidirectional model transformations. In: Paige, R.F. (ed.) ICMT 2009. LNCS, vol. 5563, pp. 213–228. Springer, Heidelberg (2009)
22. Barbosa, D.M.J., Cretin, J., Foster, N., Greenberg, M., Pierce, B.C.: Matching lenses: Alignment and view update. Technical Report MS-CIS-10-01, University of Pennsylvania (2010)

A Constructive Approach to Testing Model Transformations

Camillo Fiorentini[1], Alberto Momigliano[1],
Mario Ornaghi[1], and Iman Poernomo[2]

[1] Dipartimento di Scienze dell'Informazione, Università degli Studi di Milano, Italy
{fiorenti,momiglia,ornaghi}@dsi.unimi.it
[2] Department of Computer Science, King's College London, Strand, London WC2R2LS, UK
iman.poernomo@kcl.ac.uk

Abstract. This paper concerns a formal encoding of the Object Management Group's Complete Meta-Object Facility (CMOF) in order to provide a more trustworthy software development lifecycle for Model Driven Architecture (MDA). We show how a form of constructive logic can be used to provide a uniform semantics of metamodels, model transformation specifications, model transformations and black-box *transformation tests*. A model's instantiation of a metamodel within the MOF is treated using the logic's realizability relationship, a kind of type inhabitation relationship that is expressive enough to characterize constraint conformance between terms and types. These notions enable us to formalize the notion of a correct model instantiation of a metamodel with constraints. We then adapt previous work on snapshot generation to generate input models from source metamodel specification with the purpose of testing model transformations.

1 Introduction

While model transformations have the potential to radically change the way we write code, the actual development of transformations themselves should be conducted according to standard software engineering principles. That is, transformations need to be either certified via some kind of formal method or else developed within the software development lifecycle. Currently the latter is the norm and, consequently, effective testing techniques are essential.

However, as observed in [3], the field currently lacks adequate techniques to support model transformation testing: testing techniques for code do not immediately carry across to the model transformation context, due to the complexity of the data under consideration [7]. In fact, test case data (test models) consists of metaobjects that conform to a given metamodel, while satisfying the precondition of the transformation's specification and additional constraints employed to target particular aspects of the implementation's capability. A metamodel itself has a particular structural semantics, consisting of a range of different constraints over a graph of associated metaclasses. It is therefore a non-trivial task to automatically generate a suitable range of instantiating metaobjects as test data.

The subject of this paper is a uniform framework for treating metamodels, model transformation specification and the automation of test case generation of data for

L. Tratt and M. Gogolla (Eds.): ICMT 2010, LNCS 6142, pp. 77–92, 2010.
© Springer-Verlag Berlin Heidelberg 2010

black-box testing of model transformations to validate their adherence to given specifications. We argue that such a uniform treatment is necessary for ensuring trusted testing of model transformations. Transformations are powerful and, consequently, dangerous when wrong: this is due to the systematic, potentially exponential, range of errors that a single bug in a transformation can introduce into generated code. But this danger can be counter-acted by effective model transformation testing, which demands that test models 1) are actual instances of their classifying metamodels and 2) satisfy the transformation specification preconditions and the tester's given contractual constraints for generation. In a standard approach, a number of different languages and systems may be involved: the MOF for defining metamodel types and constraints, a model transformation specification and implementation language and a system for generating test models that meet demands 1) and 2) above. Some of these paradigms may be conflated, but in general there will be some approaches with an inherent semantic gap. For example, one may employ Kermeta to define transformations and their specification, with MOF metamodels imported separately: a test case generation framework might be written in the former language, but would have its own separate semantics for understanding metamodel instantiation and the meaning of a transformation specification. As a result of employing semantically distinct languages and systems, one may end up without a formal guarantee that the generation approach actually does what it is meant to do.

This paper offers such a formal guarantee by employing a uniform formalism for representing MOF-based models and metamodels and their interrelationship (Section 2), model transformation specification and implementation and test-case generation (Section 3). We employ *constructive* logic to do this, since this formalism is inherently endowed with the ability to treat (meta)data, functions and their logical properties uniformly. Our encoding in logic is inspired by the relationship between models-as-terms and metamodels-as-types introduced in [14] following the Curry-Howard paradigm. The logic language corresponds to the metalevel, i.e., metamodels are represented by special logical formulae that satisfy the following property: if F_M is the formula representing a metamodel M, then terms of type F_M, which we call *information terms*, are encodings of the (valid) metamodel instances of M. Thus test case generation can be seen as information terms generation and the transformations themselves are specified as relationships between those terms.

Our work adheres to the transformation development approach of Jezequel et al., where design-by-contract and testing are used as a means of increasing trust [17]. The idea is that a transformation from models in a *source* language *SL* into model in a *target* language *TL* is equipped with a contract, consisting of a pre-condition and a post-condition. The transformation is tested with a suitable data set, consisting of a range of source models that satisfy the pre-condition, to ensure that it always yield target models that satisfy the post-condition. If we produce an input model that violates the post-condition, then the contract is not satisfied by the transformation and the transformation needs to be corrected. Our view of black-box testing of model transformations follows the framework given in Fig. 1, where a transformation Tr takes a source model *SM* as input, written in a source modelling language *SL*, and outputs a target model *TM*, written in a target language *TL*. The transformation is defined as a general mapping

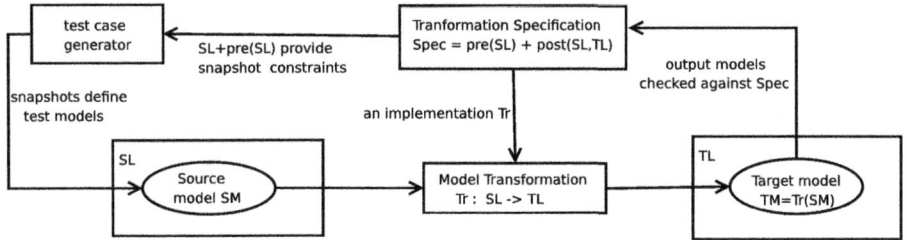

Fig. 1. Framework for testing transformation against contractual specifications

from elements of the *SL* that satisfy the pre-condition to elements of the *TL* that are required to satisfy the post-condition. A test case generator produces an appropriate set of source models: the transformation can then be tested by checking that each of the resulting target models preserve the contract (more precisely, are consistent with it). In our uniform approach we use the contract itself as an oracle. This does not entail, in general, that the contract can be used to perform the transformation. For example, it might express a loose relation, admitting a family of consistent implementations.

This paper thus proposes a solution to the open problem of how to derive in a fully declarative way an appropriate data set of source models for a given source language, pre-condition, post-condition and transformation. We will show how constructive logic enables a form of *meta-object snapshot generation* to solve this problem. Our approach is inspired by ordinary object-oriented snapshot generation [13], where objects are generated to satisfy given class specifications, for analogous same validation purposes.

2   A Constructive Encoding of the MOF

Model transformation test cases are generated according to constraints given over MOF-based metamodels. Our approach takes advantage of an approach to the uniform representation of both metamodel structure and semantics in relying on constructive logic, after the fashion of CooML's approach [6, 13] and the constructive encoding of the earlier MOF in [14]. This constructive encoding has been shown to have a number of advantages as a formalisation of the MOF. In particular, realizability semantics can naturally treat metamodel instantiation, where classifiers are considered as instances of other classifiers: a feature that is prominent in the MOF itself (model instances are classification schemes, but themselves instantiate a metamodel scheme). This section sketches the principle of the constructive encoding, showing how the structure of meta-models can be understood as set theoretic signatures with a constructive *realizability* semantics to formalize instantiation. This realizability semantics will then be exploited in the next sections for test generation. The implication of our final result will be that the encoding presented here is a uniform framework for both reasoning about models and metamodels, for writing model transformations and also for generating test cases.

A metamodel for a modelling language has a definition as a collection of associated MOF metaclasses. For example, the full UML specification, like all OMG standards, has been defined in the CMOF. In Example 1 we present a very simple example of metamodel transformation, which will be used through the paper.

Example 1. Fig. 2 (a) and (c) shows two metamodels M_1 and M_2. The metamodel instances of M_1 represent models for simple composite structures, those of M_2 for tables. We are looking for a transformation of the Component meta-objects ct into Table meta-objects t with columns corresponding to the attributes linked to ct and to the composite containing ct.[1] For example, the metamodel instance I_2 in Fig. 2(d), modelling a Person according to the Table metamodel, corresponds to I_1 in Fig. 2(b), modelling a Family according to the Composite metamodel. Beside the multiplicity constraints shown in the meta-models, other constraints regard the name and id meta-attributes. Those will be discussed in Section 3.

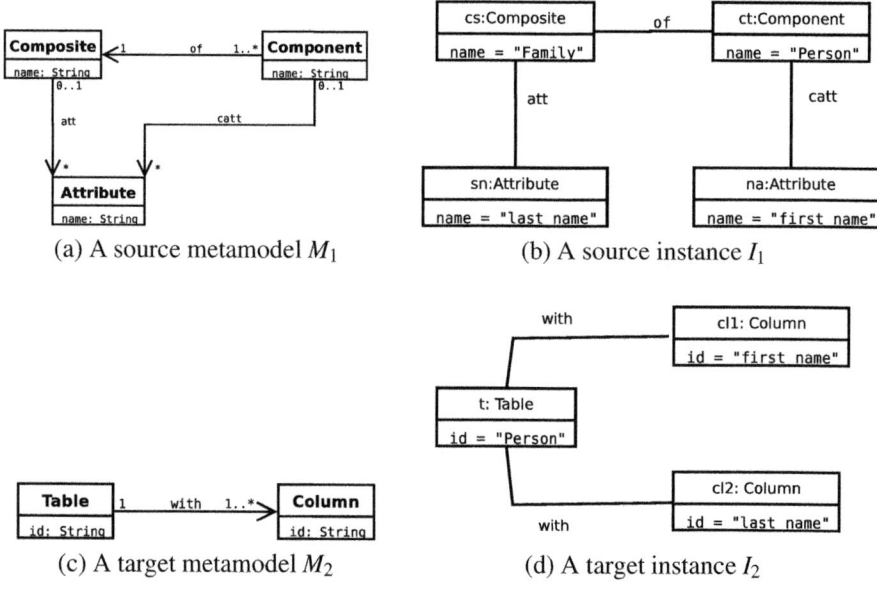

(a) A source metamodel M_1 (b) A source instance I_1

(c) A target metamodel M_2 (d) A target instance I_2

Fig. 2. A source and a target metamodel

2.1 Encoding the Structure of Metamodels

We now describe a simple set-based encoding of the *structure* of metamodels and metaobject instantiations. Once we have established this encoding, we will turn our consideration to *semantics* and constraint conformance, using a constructive logic formalism.

Since we are only concerned with creating metaobject test cases for transformations, we need not deal with representing methods within class types and, for reasons of space, we consider the subset of the CMOF that permits a UML class-style representation of metamodel grammars.

---

[1] This is inspired by the UML2RDB challenge transformation proposed in [4], for whose details we refer to *op. cit.*

Definition 1 (Signature for metamodel). *Assume* Class, Association, AssociationEnd *and* Property *are the meta-metaclasses for metaclasses, associations, association ends and properties in the CMOF. Take any metamodel M that consists of a set of (possibly associated) metaclasses:*

$$M : Set(\text{Class}) \times Set(\text{Association}) \times Set(\text{AssociationEnd}) \times Set(\text{Property})$$

Let M_{Class} denote $Set(\text{Class})$, $M_{\text{Association}}$ denote $Set(\text{Association})$ and so on. Then, the signature $Sig(M)$ for M is defined as $\langle \text{Sort}_M, \text{Rel}_M, \text{Op}_M \rangle$, where Sort_M is a set of sort names,[2] Rel_M is a set of relations, Op_M is a set of sorted operations and defined to be the minimal tuple of sets satisfying the following conditions:

- *$\{T_C \mid C \in M_{\text{Class}}\} \subseteq \text{Sort}_M$, where T_C is a unique sort name corresponding to a metaclass $C \in M_{\text{Class}}$.*
- *Every data type T used within a* Property *of any $C \in M_{\text{Class}}$ or $A \in M_{\text{Association}}$ is taken as a sort in the signature: $T \in \text{Sort}_M$.*
- *There is a set of distinguished relations $\{isLive_C : T_C \mid C \in M_{\text{Class}}\} \subseteq \text{Rel}_M$.*
- *For each $A \in M_{\text{Association}}$, such that A.ownedEnd.Property.type $= T_1$ and A.memberEnd.Property.type $= T_2$, $A : T_1 \times T_2 \in \text{Rel}_M$.*
- *For every $C \in M_{\text{Class}}$ and at $\in$ C.ownedAttribute such that at.type $= T$, $at : T_C \times T \in \text{Rel}_M$.*

Example 2. The signature for the metamodel M_1 of Fig. 2(a) takes the following form, for $C \in \{Component, Composite, Attribute\}$:

$$Sig(M_1) = \langle \{T_C, String\}, \{isLive_C : T_C, of : T_{Component} \times T_{Composite},$$
$$att : T_{Composite} \times T_{Attribute}, catt : T_{Component} \times T_{Attribute}, name : T_C \times String\},$$
$$OP_{String} \rangle$$

Remark 1. Observe that both attributes and associations are formalized in the same way. An attribute of a metaclass is understood as a relationship that holds between an element of the metaclass sort and elements of the data type sort. Sorts $T_C \in \text{Sort}_M$ are intended to denote the range of metaclasses for a given metamodel M. As we shall see, their semantics is taken to range over an infinite domain of possible instantiating metaobjects. However, every given metamodel instance contains a finite number of metaobjects. The predicate $isLive_C$ is consequently intended to always have a finite interpretation, denoting the set of the metaobjects of metaclass C that are operational or are alive in the metamodel instance. Note that multiplicities other than 1 or $*$ (including important kinds of multiplicities such as ranges) are not dealt with through the signature. Instead, these will be treated in the same way as metamodel constraints, as part of a larger, logical metamodel specification, defined next. Finally, subclassing can be understood as a subset relation among the live objects and inheritance can be imposed by suitable axioms. We have not considered this issue here, to focus on our constructive logical approach.

Before defining our logic, we first formulate a *value-based* semantics for metamodel signatures $Sig(M)$, based on the usual notion of $Sig(M)$-interpretation.

---

[2] To avoid confusion with other uses of the concept of a Type in the MOF, we use the term "sort" within our formalisation to denote classifying sets.

Definition 2 (Values). *Let* $T \in Sort_M$. *The set of* values *of* T, *denoted by* $dom(T)$, *is defined as follows: if* T *is a data type, then* $dom(T)$ *is the set of values inhabiting it; if* T *is the type of a class* C, *then* $dom(T) = oid(C)$, *where* $oid(C)$ *is the set of object identifiers of class* C.

Note that here we assume that data type *values* are represented by ground terms of $Sig(M)$ and that oids are constants of $Sig(M)$. Values are the same in all the possible metamodel instances. Specific metamodel instances differ according to their representation of specific interpretations of the predicates $isLive_C$, An and at.

Definition 3 (Metamodel interpretation). *Take any metamodel* M *with signature* $Sig(M)$. *A metamodel interpretation is a* $Sig(M)$*-interpretation* **m** *such that:*

1. *sorts are interpreted according to Definition 2 and data type relations and operations are interpreted according to the implemented data types.*
2. *Each predicate* $isLive_C$ *is interpreted as a finite sub-domain* $\mathbf{m}(isLive_C) \subset dom(T_C)$; *intuitively,* $\mathbf{m}(isLive_C)$ *contains the metaobjects of class* C *that constitute* **m**.
3. *Each association* $An : T_1 \times T_2$ *is interpreted as a relation* $\mathbf{m}(An) \subseteq \mathbf{m}(isLive_{T_1}) \times \mathbf{m}(isLive_{T_2})$.
4. *Each attribute* $at : T_C \times T$ *is interpreted as a functional relation* $\mathbf{m}(at) \subseteq \mathbf{m}(isLive_{T_C}) \times dom(T)$.

We treat the interpretation of sorts and data types in **m** as predefined, i.e., independently of the specific metamodel instance. The latter can be reconstructed from the interpretation of $isLive_C$, An and at. We represent this information with the model-theoretic notion of *diagram*:

Definition 4 (Diagram). *Given an interpretation* **m** *and values* $v_1, \ldots, v_n$, *a diagram* Δ *of a relation* r *is the set of closed atomic formulas* $r(v_1, \ldots, v_n)$ *that are true in* **m**.

We will use diagrams as a *canonical representation of metamodel instances*.

Example 3. The metamodel instance I_1 of the metamodel M_1 in Figure 2 (d) is represented by the diagram:

$$\Delta_{M_1} = \{ \; isLive_{Composite}(cs), \; isLive_{Component}(ct), \; isLive_{Attribute}(sn), \; isLive_{Attribute}(na),$$
$$of(ct, cs), \; att(cs, sn), \; catt(ct, na), \; name(cs, \texttt{"Family"}), \; name(ct, \texttt{"Person"}),$$
$$name(sn, \texttt{"last\_name"}), \; name(na, \texttt{"first\_name"}) \}$$

2.2   Encoding the Constraints of Metamodels

Signatures formalize the metamodel structure and diagrams formalize the possible instantiations of this structure. However, a metamodel is not just a structure: it also includes constraints. A diagram is correct if it represents an instantiation that satisfies the constraints. How do we formalize a metamodel with constraints and the notion of correct diagram? That is, when can we say that all the information contained in the relational assertions of a diagram yields an actual metamodel instantiation, in the sense of conforming to the structure of the metamodel and its associated constraints?

We do this via a form of constructive logic. Essentially, we define a *realizability* relationship [18] between a logical formula F and what we call an *information term* τ (see [6] for more details), denoted $\tau : F$, yielding a notion of "information content" $\mathrm{IC}(\tau : F)$, both to be defined next. Roughly, we will use $\tau : F$ to construct instance diagrams and $\mathrm{IC}(\tau : F)$ to validate them. The realizability relationship forms a kind of type inhabitation relationship that is sufficiently powerful to include constraint satisfaction, essential for developing formal notions of provably correct instantiating model.

Definition 5 (Information terms and content). *Given a metamodel signature $Sig(M)$, the set of* information terms τ, *(well-formed) formulas F over $Sig(M)$ and information content $\mathrm{IC}(\tau : F)$ are defined as follows:*

term τ	formula F	$\mathrm{IC}(\tau : F)$
t	$true(K)$	$\{K\}$
$\langle \tau_1, \tau_2 \rangle$	$F_1 \wedge F_2$	$\mathrm{IC}(\tau_1 : F_1) \cup \mathrm{IC}(\tau_2 : F_2)$
$j_k(\tau_k)$	$F_1 \vee F_2$	$\mathrm{IC}(\tau_k : F_k) \quad (k = 1, 2)$
$(v_1 \mapsto \tau_1, \ldots, v_n \mapsto \tau_n)$	$\forall x \in \{y : T \mid G(y)\}.F$	$\{\{y : T \mid G(y)\} = \{v_1, \ldots, v_n\}\} \cup$ $\bigcup_{i=1}^{n} \mathrm{IC}(\tau_i : F[v_i/x])$
$e(v, \tau)$	$\exists x : T . F$	$\mathrm{IC}(\tau : F[v/x])$

where t is a constant, K any first-order formula, $v \in dom(T)$, $\{v_1, \ldots, v_n\}$ is a finite subset of $dom(T)$ and G is a generator, *namely a special formula true over a finite domain.*

Remark 2. Although the intuitive meaning of each of the formulas should be clear, some explanations are required for $true(\cdot)$ and for bounded universal quantification. The predicate $true(K)$ designs a metalogical assertion that the formula K is known to be true and that K, used as an assertion about a metamodel, does not require any specific information to be used in the construction of a metamodel instance (the idea was originally introduced in [12]). The information content is K: i.e., K is the minimal assumption needed to prove K. Regarding universal quantification, the associated information term defines both the domain $\{y : T \mid G(y)\} = \{v_1, \ldots, v_n\}$ and a map from this domain to information terms for F. In a metamodel signature, the formulas $isLive_C(x)$ is an example of generator. This corresponds to the assumption that a metamodel instance contains finitely many metaobjects.

If we consider universally bounded quantification $\forall x \in \{y : T \mid G(y)\}.F$ as semantically equivalent to $\forall x : T.G(x) \to F$ and $true(K)$ as equivalent to K, our formulas can be viewed as a subset of the ordinary (many sorted) first-order formulas and $\mathbf{m} \models F$ can be defined as usual. Furthermore, we may use any first-order formula as an argument of $true$. We will use formulas F to formalize constraints over metamodels and information terms to guarantee that F contains all the information needed to construct *valid* diagrams, i.e. if it is the diagram of a metamodel interpretation $\mathbf{m}$ that satisfies the constraints – we shall formalize this in Def. 7. We will represent a metamodel M by a $Sig(M)$-formula $Spec(M)$, where the latter encodes the constraints of the metamodel M so that if $\mathrm{IC}(\tau : Spec(M))$ is (model-theoretically) consistent then the corresponding diagram is valid.

Consequently, with the aim of testing a transformation Tr, with input metamodel M_1 and output metamodel M_2, if we can generate a set of $\tau_j : Spec(M_1)$ with valid information content, we can generate the corresponding diagrams, which may then be fed into the transformation as test cases. Furthermore, if we specify the precondition of Tr as $true(Pre_{Tr})$ and its postcondition as $true(Post_{Tr})$, then we can use $Spec(M_1)$, $Spec(M_2)$, $true(Pre_{Tr})$ and $true(Post_{Tr})$ to check the correctness of Tr, i.e., to supply a test oracle.

We now define $Spec(M)$ and introduce some notation: for an atom B, $B(s^*)$ is an abbreviation of $\forall y : T.B(y) \leftrightarrow y \in s$ and $B(!x)$ an abbreviation of $\forall y : T.B(y) \leftrightarrow y = x$.

Definition 6 (Metamodel specification). *Given a metamodel signature $Sig(M)$, we represent each class C of M by a formula of the following form, where square brackets indicate optional sub-formulae:*

$$Spec(C) = \forall x \in \{y : T_C \mid isLive_C(y)\}.$$
$$\exists z_1 : Set(T_{C_1}).true(A_1(x,z_1^*) [\land K_1(x,z_1)]) \land \cdots \land$$
$$\exists z_m : Set(T_{C_m}).true(A_m(x,z_m^*) [\land K_m(x,z_m)]) \land$$
$$\exists v_1 : T_{at_1}.true(at_1(x,!v_1)) \land \cdots \land$$
$$\exists v_n : T_{at_n}.true(at_n(x,!v_n) [\land true(K_C)])$$

1. $A_i : T_C \times T_{C_i}$ $(0 \le i \le m)$ *are the relations of* Rel_M *corresponding to the associations;*
2. K_i $(0 \le i \le m)$ *are "multiplicity constraints" on the associations A_i;*
3. $at_j : T_C \times T_{at_j}$ $(0 \le j \le n)$ *are the relations of* Rel_M *corresponding to the attributes of C;*
4. K_C *is a formula that we call the "class constraint" of C.*

A metamodel M is specified by the $Sig(M)$-formula

$$Spec(M) = Spec(C_1) \land \cdots \land Spec(C_l) [\land true(K_G)] \tag{1}$$

where $C_1, \ldots, C_l$ are the metaclasses of M and K_G is an optional formula that we call the "global constraint" of M.

We switch to a "light notation", where we use generators $isLive_C$ as sorts.

Example 4. The specification of the metamodel M_1 described in Example 2 is $Spec(M_1) = F_{Cmt} \land F_{Cms} \land F_{Att} \land true(K)$, where:

$$F_{Cmt} = \forall x : isLive_{Component}(x).$$
$$\exists sc : Set(Composite).true(of(x,sc^*) \land size(sc) = 1) \land$$
$$\exists sa : Set(Attribute).true(catt(x,sa^*) \land \forall a \in sa.catt(!x,a)) \land$$
$$\exists s : String.true(name(x,!s) \land cattNames(x,s))$$

$$F_{Cms} = \forall x : isLive_{Composite}(x).$$
$$\exists sa : Set(Attribute).true(att(x,sa^*) \land \forall a \in sa.att(!x,a)) \land$$
$$\exists s : String.true(name(x,!s) \land attNames(x,s))$$

$$F_{Att} = \forall x : isLive_{Attribute}(x). \exists s : String.true(name(x,!s))$$

We omit the specification of K for conciseness; informally, it states that different attributes linked to the same component/composite must have different names. In F_{Cmt}, the constraint $size(sc) = 1$ encodes the multiplicity 1 of the target association end of of, while $\forall a \in sa.catt(!x,a)$ refers to the multiplicities $0..1$ of the source association ends of catt. The encoding of multiplicity constraints is standard, i.e., it can be fully automated. The other constraints are encoded in Prolog, for reasons that will be explained at the end of the section. For example, the constraint $cattNames(x,s)$ is defined by the clause:

$$\texttt{false} \leftarrow isLive_{Attribute}(a) \wedge catt(x,a) \wedge name(x,s)$$

i.e., it is false that there is an attribute a linked to component x whose name is s; the constraint $attNames(x,s)$ is similar.

Let $\tau : Spec(M)$ be an information term for a specification of a metamodel M. We distinguish between a "diagram part" IC_D and a "constraint part" IC_C of the information content. The latter contains the multiplicity constraints, the class constraints and the global constraint, while the former contains the domain formulas $isLive_C(o_i)$ for $\{y : T_C | isLive_C(y)\} = \{o_1, \ldots, o_n\}$, the association formulas $An(o,s^*)$ and the attribute formulas $at(o,!v)$. The diagram part allows us to define a bijective map δ from the information terms for $Spec(M)$ into the instance diagrams for M, by means of the following conditions:

1. Domain formulas: $isLive_C(o_i) \in \delta(\tau)$ iff $isLive_C(o_i) \in IC_D(\tau : Spec(M))$;
2. Association formulas: $An(o,o') \in \delta(\tau)$ iff $An(o,s^*) \in IC_D(\tau : Spec(M))$ and $o' \in s$;
3. Attribute formulas: $at(o,d) \in \delta(\tau)$ iff $at(o,!d) \in IC_D(\tau : Spec(M))$.

Example 5. Consider the specification $Spec(M_1)$ of Example 4 and the information term $\tau_1 = \langle \tau_{1_1}, \tau_{1_2}, \tau_{1_3}, t \rangle$, where:

$$\tau_{1_1} : F_{Cmt} = (ct \mapsto e(\{cs\}, \langle t, e(\{na\}, \langle t, e("\texttt{Person}",t) \rangle) \rangle))$$
$$\tau_{1_2} : F_{Cms} = (cs \mapsto e(\{sn\}, \langle t, e("\texttt{Family}",t) \rangle))$$
$$\tau_{1_3} : F_{Att} = (sn \mapsto e("\texttt{last\_name}",t), na \mapsto e("\texttt{first\_name}",t))$$

The diagram and constraint part of $IC(\tau_1 : Spec(M_1))$ are:

$$IC_D = \{ \ isLive_{Component}(ct), \ isLive_{Composite}(cs), \ isLive_{Attribute}(sn), \ isLive_{Attribute}(na),$$
$$of(ct,\{cs\}^*), \ catt(ct,\{na\}^*), \ att(cs,\{sn\}^*), \ name(ct,!"\texttt{Person}"),$$
$$name(cs,!"\texttt{Family}"), \ name(sn,!"\texttt{last\_name}"), \ name(na,!"\texttt{first\_name}") \}$$
$$IC_C = \{ \ size(\{cs\}) = 1, \ \forall a \in \{na\}.catt(!ct,a), \ \forall a \in \{sn\}.att(!cs,a),$$
$$cattNames(ct,"\texttt{Person}"), \ attNames(cs,"\texttt{Family}") \}$$

The diagram $\delta(\tau_1)$ coincides with Δ_{M_1} of Example 3. Clearly, we could start from Δ, reconstruct IC_D and, from the latter, reconstruct τ_1. We can consider the diagram part as the "encoding" of the pure UML part of an UML model, as depicted in part (b) of Fig. 2.

IC_C does not play any role in the definition of the map δ, but encodes the constraints. In the above example, the constraint part is satisfied: $size(\{cs\}) = 1$ is true and one can easily see that the other formulas in IC_C are also true. We will say that τ_1 *satisfies the constraints.*

Definition 7 (Constraint satisfaction). *Let* $\tau : Spec(M)$ *be an information term for a specification of a metamodel M: we say that* τ *(and* $\delta(\tau)$*) satisfies the constraints iff* $\Delta = \delta(\tau)$ *is the diagram of a metamodel instance* $\mathbf{m}_\Delta$ *of M such that* $\mathbf{m}_\Delta \models IC_C(\tau : Spec(M))$.

Let $\mathbf{m}_\Delta$ be as in the above definition. We can prove that $\mathbf{m}_\Delta \models IC(\tau : Spec(M))$ hence the valid metamodel instances of M are models (in the sense of logic) of $Spec(M)$. Finally, the following sufficient condition for satisfying the constraints can be proven:

Theorem 1. *Let* $\tau : Spec(M)$ *be an information term for a specification of a metamodel M, Ax any set of axioms that are true over all the metamodel-instances and* $K = \bigwedge IC_C(\tau : Spec(M))$. *Then:*

a) if $Ax \cup IC_D(\tau : Spec(M)) \vdash K$, *then* τ *(and* $\delta(\tau)$*) satisfies the constraints;*
b) if $Ax \cup IC_D(\tau : Spec(M)) \vdash \neg K$, *then* τ *(and* $\delta(\tau)$*) does not satisfy the constraints.*

In Ax we have the axioms for the data types (integers, strings, sets, ...) and the general assumptions on the oids and on the metamodel instances. Assume we have a *possible* term $\tau : Spec(M)$. To establish that the diagram $\delta(\tau)$ is a valid metamodel instance we could apply Theorem 1 and we could attempt to derive a proof using a suitable inference system for Ax; alas, this is hardly predictable if Ax and constraints are full first-order formulae. We need a tractable constraint language. The constraints concerning multiplicities are recognized and checked in the generation phase. To express and check the other constraints, we rely on Horn clauses. We distinguish between problem domain and absurdity clauses. The former are definite clauses implementing data types (strings, sets, bags, ...) and encoding the general properties of the MOF. The latter have the form false ← *Body*, with intended meaning $\neg\exists \mathbf{x}. Body$. By the properties of definite programs, one can prove:

a) if false finitely fails, then for every absurdity constraint false ← *Body*, $\neg\exists \mathbf{x}. Body$ is satisfied;
b) if false succeeds, then $\neg\exists \mathbf{x}. Body$ is falsified for some constraint.

For example, the constraint part of the information term of Example 5 contains two absurdity constraints, namely *cattNames*(*ct*, "Person") and *attNames*(*cs*, "Family") and false finitely fails, since there is no attribute with name "Person" or "Family". Had the diagram contained such an attribute, false would had succeeded.

3   Testing via Model Generation

In this Section we show how our setup allows us to:

1. generate input test models that meet the precondition for a model transformation;
2. check that, after the input models have been transformed, the transformation post-condition is met.

In this way, we are able to provide a constructive model transformation testing framework in accord with the concepts of Fig. 1.

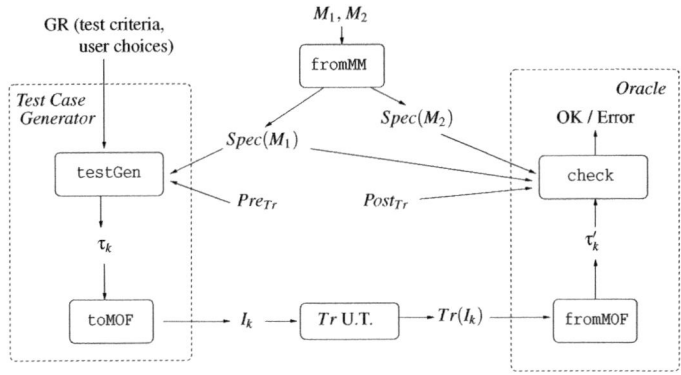

Fig. 3. Testing transformations

The System. The architecture of our system is outlined in Fig. 3 with two main units (*Test Case Generator* and *Oracle*) cooperating. The module testGen generates a set of information terms that are translated into test cases for the transformation undergoing testing (*Tr* U.T.) by the module toMOF. The inputs of testGen are the specification $Spec(M_1)$ of the source metamodel M_1, the transformation specifications precondition, encoded by a constraint Pre_{Tr} and a set *GR* of *generation requests* provided by the user to implement *test criteria*. The generated information terms $\tau_k : Spec(M_1) \wedge true(Pre_{Tr})$ are translated into test cases $I_k = \text{toMOF}(\tau_k)$. The transformation *Tr* U.T. is then run using such test cases. Note that we are *agnostic* about how models are represented — as abstracted in the fromMM module — as well as *Tr* U.T. is implemented: the framework could translate from arbitrary metamodelling language and feed test cases into a transformation written in any language. However, the transformation can also be assumed to be written in the *same* constructive language as the metamodel specification and information terms (together with the modules themselves) because the logic may rely on a λ-calculus rather than realizability. The reader is referred to [14] for details of such an encoding.

The translated metamodel instances are checked using the module fromMOF, which attempts to reconstruct the information terms corresponding to the transformation output model $Tr(I_k)$ and the check module, which tries to validate $Post_{Tr}$. The two modules work together as a test *oracle*: if fromMOF fails, then the results do not respect the types or the invariants prescribed by $Spec(M_2)$, while if check fails, then only $Post_{Tr}$ is violated.

The testGen module supports *exhaustive* (EGen) and *random* generation (RGen). In RGen, objects, attribute values and links are generated randomly, albeit consistently with the *GR* and the constraints. EGen, instead, generates all consistent information terms, which are *minimal* w.r.t. the constraints and a given population As emphasized in [7], the generation of "small test-cases" is crucial to make the understanding of each test case easier and to allow an efficient diagnosis in presence of errors. Finally, *data-centric* test criteria such as those considered in *op. cit.* can be expressed as generation requests.

Before delving into the specifics of the generation algorithm behind testGen, we illustrate how the architecture would operate over the source metamodel M_1 and the target metamodel M_2 shown in Fig. 2.

Example 6. The specification $Spec(M_1)$ is the one of Example 4, while $Spec(M_2) = F_{Tab} \wedge F_{Col} \wedge K_{Tab}$, where:

$$F_{Tab} = \forall t : isLive_{Table}(t).$$
$$\exists cl : Set(Column).true(with(t,cl^*)) \wedge \exists s : String.true(id(t,!s) \wedge id(!t,s))$$
$$F_{Col} = \forall cl : isLive_{Column}(cl).\exists s : String.true(id(cl,!s))$$

and the constraint K_{Tab} states that the id's occurring in a table are pairwise distinct. Let Tr be a transformation mapping M_1-instances into M_2-instances informally defined as follows:

- *Pre-condition.* Each Composite object is linked to a unique Attribute via att.
- *Post-condition.* For every Composite object cs and every Component ct of cs there is a corresponding Table t such that:
  - t.id is equal to ct.name;
  - for every Attribute a linked to ct by catt there is a corresponding Column cl linked to t by with, so that cl.id is equal to a.name;
  - for every Attribute a linked to cs by att there is a Column cl linked to t by with such that cl.id is equal to a.name.

For example, the metamodel instance I_1 of M_1 is transformed into $I_2 = Tr(I_1)$ of M_2 (see Fig. 2). The formal specification of Tr contains formulas such as:

$$toTable(ct,t) \leftrightarrow isLive_{Component}(ct) \wedge isLive_{Table}(t) \wedge \exists s : String.name(ct,s) \wedge id(t,s)$$
$$false \leftarrow isLive_{Component}(ct) \wedge \neg(\exists t : isLive_{Table}(t).toTable(ct,t))$$

For the experiments discussed in Table 1, we have implemented Tr in Prolog. To generate the test cases, we supplied (beside $Spec(M_1)$ and the precondition) the following generation requests, whose precise syntax we omit for the sake of space:

- *PR* (Population Requests): generate at most 2 composites, exactly 2 components and at most 8 attributes.
- *MR* (Multiplicity Requests): a snapshot must contain at most 2 components linked to a composite (via of) and at most 2 attributes linked to a component (via catt). No MR is needed for the association ends with multiplicity 1 or 0..1.
- *AR* (Attribute Requests). These are: (AR_a) all the objects have distinct name; (AR_b) there are at least two Attribute with the same name.

We use those requests to deal with *coverage* criteria such as those introduced in [7], adapting previous work on test adequacy criteria for UML. For example, "Association-end-Multiplicities" (a test case for each representative multiplicity pair) can be implemented by MR's, whereas "Class Attribute" (a test case for each representative attribute value) by AR's. In our experiment we have used *partition analysis* of the input domain, for example into (1a) the snapshots where all the objects have distinct names and (1b) those containing at least two distinct attributes with the same name. For (1a) and (1b)

Table 1. Experimental results

Experiment	Module	Input	Result	Time (sec.)
1a	Test Case Generator	$Spec(M_1)$, Pre_{Tr}, PR, MR, AR_a	18 test cases I_k	0.7
	Oracle	18 translations $Tr(I_k)$	9 failed	0.31
1b	Test Case Generator	$Spec(M_1)$, Pre_{Tr}, PR, MR, AR_b	118 test cases I_k	5.9
	Oracle	118 translations $Tr(I_k)$	76 failed	1.9
2	testGen	$Spec(M^*)$, GR^*, Pre^*	144 τ_k^*	4.4

we have relied on EGen, with the above PR to avoid a combinatory explosion of the number of minimal snapshots.

The experiments have been conducted with an Intel 2.2 GHz processor T7500 operating with 2GB of RAM and the results are summarized in Table 1. EGen for (1a) has been performed according to the generation requests PR, MR and AR_a. We have obtained 18 test cases. Running Tr and the oracle, 9 of the 18 test cases failed. EGen for (1b) used PR, MR and AR_b and yielded 118 test cases. Again we ran Tr and the

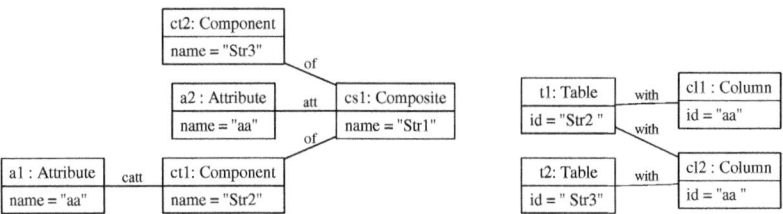

Fig. 4. Failed test cases

oracle; 76 test cases failed. As illustrated by the sample test cases in Fig. 4, two kinds of errors were detected:

1. The column cl2 corresponding to a2 occurs in both the tables t1 and t2 corresponding to ct1 and ct2 resp., i.e., the multiplicity 1 of with.Table is violated.
2. The table t1 corresponding to ct1 contains two columns with id = "aa".

Error 1 was reported in all 9 failed test cases of (1a) and can be traced back to a wrong implementation of Tr. Error 2 can be discovered only by (1b) and requires a stronger precondition. Without exhaustive generation for the (1a, 1b)-partition, the above errors could not have been revealed. We believe that the combination of exhaustive generation of the *minimal* information terms with domain partition testing, using the latter to avoid combinatory explosion, could be profitable line of research.

In the testGen module, the information terms are generated in two phases. In the first one, some existential parameters are left *generic* (this is possible thanks to the constructive structuring of the information). In the second phase, the generic parameters are instantiated according to a strategy, e.g. RGen/EGen. As a rule of thumb, one leaves generic those existential parameters that give rise to a combinatory explosion of the number of solutions. In particular, in the first phase of experiments (1a, 1b) we used *PR* and *MR* leaving name open; we obtained 18 generic solutions in 0.01 sec. In the second phase of (1b), the names were instantiated according to AR_b (at least two attributes with name "aa" and the other ones distinct): we obtained 118 test cases. As another larger example, we have formalized the UML metamodel considered in [16] (denoted with star in the table) and we have generated 144 generic terms in 4.4 sec.

4   Related Work and Conclusions

The relevance of snapshot generation (SG) for validation and testing in OO software development is widely acknowledged and has yielded several animation and validation tools supporting different languages. USE [8] has been the first system supporting automatic SG; differently from us, SG is achieved procedurally, requiring the user to write Pascal-like procedures in a dedicated language. Not coincidentally, USE performances are very sensitive to the *order* of objects and attribute assignments [2]. Alloy [9] is the leading system [2] for generation of instances of invariants, animation of the execution of operations and checking of user-specified properties. Alloy compiles a formula in first-order relational logic into quantifier-free booleans and feeds to a SAT solver. Alloy's original design was quite different from UML, but recent work [1] has brought the two together. Baudry et al. have developed a tool that maps metamodel descriptions in the Ecore framework into Alloy, delegating to the latter the generation of model snapshots [15]. Their approach is focused on generation of models solely from metamodel encoding. Our approach could be used to enhance their result, through our use of realizability to tighten the relationship among (meta)models and their transformations. On the other hand, they have extensively investigated the issue of the quality and adequacy of test models, both in term of generation strategies and of mutation analysis [15]. We have already adopted a version of their *domain partition* strategy to guide test generation and plan to refine it towards the filtering of *isomorphic* and thus useless test models.

Another close relative is FORMULA [10], a tool supporting a general framework for model-based development. Similarly to us, it is based on logic programming, more specifically model generation, employing abduction over non-recursive Horn logic with stratified negation. Model transformations are also encoded logically. Since abduction can be computationally expensive, we plan to compare it with our realizability-based SG, as the FORMULA setup may give us a hook to more general domain-specific modeling languages.

Our particular approach to snapshot generation builds on work by three of the present authors [6, 13] for object-oriented test case generation, but is now extended and combined with a first-order variant of the constructive encoding of the MOF and model transformations by the other author [14]. By combining the two approaches, we obtain the first universal encoding of its kind. Further, our logic supports the "proofs as programs" paradigm, where a constructive proof π of $TR \vdash F_1 \rightarrow F_2$ represents a program P_π mapping the realizers of F_1 into realizers of F_2, TR being a set of transformation formulae. Hence validation naturally leads to formal *certification* via proof assistants. This is indeed the object of future work.

A number of authors have attempted to provide a formal understanding of metamodelling and model transformations. We refer to [14] for a review. In particular, rule-based model transformations have a natural formalization in graph rewriting systems [11]: for example, Ehrig et al. have equipped graph grammars with a complex notion of instance generation, essentially adding a means of generation directly into graph rewriting [5]. As with our work, their formalism permits a uniform semantics of model transformations, specification and test generation, although with a fairly heavy mathematical overhead. However, their approach is by definition applicable within a rule-based paradigm: in contrast, because our tests are contractual and based in the very generic space of constructive logic, we need not restrict ourselves to rule-based transformations.

While full verification of model transformations can be as difficult to achieve as in ordinary programming, the power of model transformations demands some formal guarantee that any transformation algorithm actually produces the tests that we expect: in particular, that tests cases are of appropriate metamodel types and satisfy generation constraints/requests. We have developed a constructive encoding of the MOF that facilitates this via a uniform, single-language treatment of models, metamodels, instantiation, transformation specification, test case generation constraints *and* test cases generation. To the best of our knowledge, a similar approach has not been explored before. Our implementation relies on a fairly naive encoding of the MOF in logic and needs future work to be readily integrated into other tool sets: in particular, we need to investigate how standard visual representations of metamodels and transformations might complement the approach, together with an automatic translations from OCL into our logic for constraint representation. There are further optimisations that can be done to improve the constraint solver: for example, isomorphic solutions are reduced but, currently, not eliminated; divide and conquer strategies such as modularization of tests could be employed to overcome the potential combinatory explosion for large metamodels. Our approach can currently be considered as one way of integrating formal metamodelling perspectives with snapshot generation for testing. While formal metamodelling opens up the possibility of full transformation verification, from a practical perspective, testing is likely to remain an integral component of transformation development for the long term. However, by following an approach such as ours, formal metamodelling can still be exploited to generate test data in a way that is guaranteed to preserve consistency with required constraints. For this reason, we see this work as opening up a very promising line of research for the formal metamodelling community.

References

1. Anastasakis, K., Bordbar, B., Georg, G., Ray, I.: On challenges of model transformation from UML to Alloy. Software and System Modeling 9(1), 69–86 (2010)
2. Aydal, E.G., Utting, M., Woodcock, J.: A comparison of state-based modelling tools for model validation. In: Paige, R.F., Meyer, B. (eds.) TOOLS (46). Lecture Notes in Business Information Processing, vol. 11, pp. 278–296. Springer, Heidelberg (2008)
3. Baudry, B., Dinh-Trong, T., Mottu, J.-M., Simmonds, D., France, R., Ghosh, S., Fleurey, F., Traon, Y.L.: Model transformation testing challenges. In: ECMDA workshop on Integration of Model Driven Development and Model Driven Testing (2006)

4. Bézivin, J., Rumpe, B., Schürr, A., Tratt, L.: Model transformations in practice workshop. In: Bruel, J.-M. (ed.) MoDELS 2005. LNCS, vol. 3844, pp. 120–127. Springer, Heidelberg (2006)
5. Ehrig, K., Küster, J.M., Taentzer, G.: Generating instance models from meta models. Software and System Modeling 8(4), 479–500 (2009)
6. Ferrari, M., Fiorentini, C., Momigliano, A., Ornaghi, M.: Snapshot generation in a constructive object-oriented modeling language. In: King, A. (ed.) LOPSTR 2007. LNCS, vol. 4915, pp. 169–184. Springer, Heidelberg (2008)
7. Fleury, F., Steel, J., Baudry, B.: Validation in model-driven engineering: Testing model transformations. In: MoDeVa 2004 (Model Design and Validation Workshop associated to ISSRE 2004), Rennes, France (November 2004)
8. Gogolla, M., Bohling, J., Richters, M.: Validating UML and OCL models in USE by automatic snapshot generation. Software and System Modeling 4(4), 386–398 (2005)
9. Jackson, D.: Software Abstractions: Logic, Language, and Analysis. The MIT Press, Cambridge (2006)
10. Jackson, E., Sztipanovits, J.: Formalizing the structural semantics of domain-specific modeling languages. Software and Systems Modeling (2009)
11. Königs, A., Schürr, A.: Multi-domain integration with MOF and extended triple graph grammars. In: Bezivin, J., Heckel, R. (eds.) Dagstuhl Seminar Proceedings Language Engineering for Model-Driven Software Development, Dagstuhl, Germany. No. 04101 (2005)
12. Miglioli, P., Moscato, U., Ornaghi, M., Usberti, G.: A constructivism based on classical truth. Notre Dame Journal of Formal Logic 30(1), 67–90 (1989)
13. Ornaghi, M., Benini, M., Ferrari, M., Fiorentini, C., Momigliano, A.: A constructive object oriented modeling language for information systems. ENTCS 153(1), 67–90 (2006)
14. Poernomo, I.: Proofs-as-model-transformations. In: Vallecillo, A., Gray, J., Pierantonio, A. (eds.) ICMT 2008. LNCS, vol. 5063, pp. 214–228. Springer, Heidelberg (2008)
15. Sen, S., Baudry, B., Mottu, J.-M.: On combining multi-formalism knowledge to select models for model transformation testing. In: ICST, pp. 328–337. IEEE Computer Society, Los Alamitos (2008)
16. Sen, S., Baudry, B., Mottu, J.-M.: Automatic model generation strategies for model transformation testing. In: Paige, R.F. (ed.) ICMT 2009. LNCS, vol. 5563, pp. 148–164. Springer, Heidelberg (2009)
17. Traon, Y.L., Baudry, B., Jezequel, J.-M.: Design by contract to improve software vigilance. IEEE Trans. Softw. Eng. 32(8), 571–586 (2006)
18. Troelstra, A.S.: Realizability. In: Buss, S.R. (ed.) Handbook of Proof Theory, ch. 4, pp. 407–473. Elsevier, Amsterdam (1998)

From Sequence Diagrams to State Machines by Graph Transformation

Roy Grønmo[1,2] and Birger Møller-Pedersen[1]

[1] Department of Informatics, University of Oslo, Norway
[2] SINTEF Information and Communication Technology, Oslo, Norway
{roygr,birger}@ifi.uio.no

Abstract. Algebraic graph transformation has been promoted by several authors as a means to specify model transformations. This paper explores how we can specify graph transformation-based rules for a classical problem of transforming from sequence diagrams to state machines. The transformation rules are based on the concrete syntax of sequence diagrams and state machines. We introduce tailored transformation support for sequence diagrams and a novel graphical operator to match and transform combined fragments.

1 Introduction

Although sequence diagrams and state machines are used in different phases and are made with different diagram types, there is a great deal of overlap between the two specifications. The behavior defined by the sequence diagrams should also be recognized as behavior by the state machines.

There has been a lot of efforts to transform from sequence diagram-like specification languages to state-based languages (e.g. [11,17,18,14]). None of the previous approaches takes full advantage of the combined fragments that were introduced in UML 2.

The combined fragments in UML 2 includes possibilities to model conditional behavior (`alt` operator) and loops (`loop` operator), and these can have guard expressions and be arbitrarily nested. A combined fragment is displayed with a rectangle that spans the involved lifelines, an operator type shown in the top left corner of the rectangle, and dashed horizontal lines as operand separators in cases with multiple operands.

In this paper we specify a transformation from sequence diagrams to state machines where the specified rules are based on the concrete syntax of sequence diagrams and state machines. Our approach differs from the traditional model and graph transformation approaches, where transformations are specified in relation to the abstract syntax. We claim that this is more user-friendly since the specifier does not need to have knowledge of the metamodels and the associated abstract syntax. This is particularly useful for sequence diagrams where the abstract syntax is complicated and quite different from the concrete syntax.

Within the concrete syntax we introduce a *fragment operator* that allows us to specify the matching and transformation of combined fragments with an

L. Tratt and M. Gogolla (Eds.): ICMT 2010, LNCS 6142, pp. 93–107, 2010.

unknown number of operands. Our rules are mapped to traditional graph transformation rules and the transformation takes place in the AGG tool [15].

The remainder of this paper is structured as follows. In Section 2 we briefly
introduce sequence diagrams and state machines and how they can be used together in a modeling process; Section 3 describes preliminaries on graph transformation; Section 4 explains how we can define transformation rules based on the
concrete syntax of sequence diagrams and state machines; Section 5 presents the
specialized transformation formalism for sequence diagrams and our set of transformation rules from sequence diagrams to state machines; Section 6 compares
our approach with related work; and finally Section 7 concludes the paper.

2   Using Sequence Diagrams and State Machines in a Modeling Process

Figure 1 shows a sequence diagram and a corresponding state machine to represent the behavior of the second lifeline object (GasPump) in the sequence diagram. The sequence diagram has two lifelines with the types User and GasPump,
and two messages with the signals insertCard and requestPin. A lifeline,
visualized with a rectangle and a dashed line below, represents an interacting entity on which events take place in an order from top to bottom on the
dashed line. Each message is represented by two events, a send event (at the
source of the message arrow) and a receive event (at the target of the message
arrow).

In this paper we only use sequence diagrams with asynchronous messages,
although our transformation apparatus works for both synchronous and asynchronous messages. Asynchronous messages fits nicely with the event-based
nature of state machines, unlike sequence diagrams with synchronous messages
that have a procedural nature. We omit the optional rectangles to visualize when
a lifeline is active, since these are more relevant for synchronous messages.

A state machine, consistent with the GasPump lifeline, has an initial state with
a transition leading to the state named Idle. The Idle state has one outgoing
transition, with insertCard as its trigger and requestPin as its effect, going to
the final state.

The semantics of a sequence diagram can be described as a set of *positive
traces* and a set of *negative traces* [13]. *Positive traces* define valid behavior
and *negative traces* define invalid behavior, while all other traces are defined

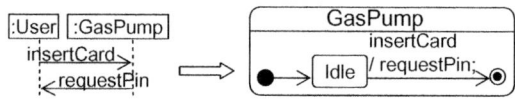

Fig. 1. Consistency between sequence diagram and state machine

as inconclusive. In the sequence diagram of Figure 1, there is exactly one positive trace: ⟨*send insertCard, receive insertCard, send requestPin, receive requestPin*⟩

Negative traces are described by special operators (e.g. **neg**), which are not used in the diagram of Figure 1. Hence, all other traces than the single positive trace, are inconclusive.

The set of sequence diagrams describing a system will normally have a nonempty set of inconclusive traces, which we call a *partial specification*. An actual implementation may choose to implement the inconclusive traces as either positive or negative. A state machine on the other hand, has no inconclusive traces and is thus a *complete specification*.

Since the set of sequence diagrams is only a partial specification, the automatically produced state machines are only intended to be a good starting point for a manual refinement. This makes it important that the produced state machines are readable.

We prescribe a modeling process consisting of four steps, starting with the early phase of simple sequence diagrams and ending with the final state machines that can be used to generate Java code as described in [7].

Step 1 - Initial modeling. Scenarios can easily be described with intuitive and simple diagrams showing example executions. These initial sequence diagrams should not be too detailed and they should use few or no combined fragments, since this could be counterproductive in the idea and brainstorming phase. Similar behavior may occur in several diagrams.

Step 2 - Detailed modeling. Combined fragments are used to manually merge similar behavior from multiple diagrams into a single diagram. The merging into a single diagram can always be achieved by using enough combined fragments. For convenience, unrelated scenarios involving the same lifeline can be kept in several diagrams, followed by a transformation that merges all lifelines into the same diagram. This transformation can introduce one outermost `alt` operator with one operand for each of the unrelated scenarios.

The step 2 artefact represents a *contract* which an implementation must fulfill. We interpret all the positive traces as mandatory behavior which must be implemented, while the negative traces describe prohibited behavior.

Step 3 - Generate State Machine. Our automated generation makes a state machine that accepts all positive traces from the sequence diagrams. Inconclusive traces are not implemented, and these traces become negative initially, but they can be changed to positive in step 4.

Step 4 - Refine State Machine. In step 4, the modeler refines the generated state machines so that they are detailed enough to express a full implementation. Furthermore, the modeler may also freely increase the number of implemented traces, but restricted to those that are inconclusive in the contract. Any modification of the state machines should be checked to see if the modification represents a breach of contract. Brændshøi has implemented an automated tool that checks if a state machine is a 'proper implementation' of a set of sequence diagrams [1].

The rest of the paper focuses on our transformation rules to support step 3.

3   Preliminary: Algebraic Graph Transformation

We provide the known formal foundation of algebraic graph transformation [12].

Definition 1 (Graph and graph morphism). *A graph $G = (G_N, G_E, src, trg)$ consists of a set G_N of nodes, a set G_E of edges, two mappings $src, trg : G_E \rightarrow G_N$, assigning to each edge $e \in G_E$ a source node $src(e) \in G_N$ and target node $trg(e) \in G_N$.*

A graph morphism $f : G_1 \rightarrow G_2$ from one graph to another, with $G_i = (G_{E,i}, G_{N,i}, src_i, trg_i), (i = 1, 2)$, is a pair $f = (f_E : G_{E,1} \rightarrow G_{E,2}, f_N : G_{N,1} \rightarrow G_{N,2})$ of mappings, such that $f_N \circ src_1 = src_2 \circ f_E$ and $f_N \circ trg_1 = trg_2 \circ f_E$ (preserve source and target). A graph morphism $f : G_1 \rightarrow G_2$ is injective if f_N and f_E are injective mappings.

Only injective graph morphisms will be relevant in this paper.

Definition 2 (Rule). *A graph transformation rule $p : L \xleftarrow{l} I \xrightarrow{r} R$ consists of three graphs L(LHS), I(Interface) and R(RHS) and a pair of injective graph morphisms $l : I \rightarrow L$ and $r : I \rightarrow R$.*

Definition 3 (Match and Dangling Condition). *Given a graph G and a rule $p : L \xleftarrow{l} I \xrightarrow{r} R$. Then an occurrence of L in G, i.e. an injective graph morphism $m : L \rightarrow G$, is called* match.

The function isMatch : $L, G, (L \rightarrow G) \rightarrow$ Bool returns true if and only if $L \rightarrow G$ is a match of L in G. A match m for rule p satisfies the dangling condition if no node in $m(L \setminus l(I))$ is incident to an edge in $G \setminus m(L \setminus l(I))$.

Definition 4 (Derivation Step). *Given a graph G, a graph transformation rule $p : L \xleftarrow{l} I \xrightarrow{r} R$, and a match $m : L \rightarrow G$, then there exists a derivation step from the graph G to the graph H if and only if the dangling condition is satisfied. H is constructed as follows:*

1. *Remove the image of the non-interface elements of L in G, i.e. $H' = G \setminus m(L \setminus l(I))$.*
2. *Add the non-interface elements of R into H, i.e. $H = H' \cup (R \setminus r(I))$.*

A *negative application condition* [12] is an extension of the LHS which prevents matches from being applied in a derivation step.

Definition 5 (Negative Application Condition (NAC)). *A NAC for a graph transformation rule $L \xleftarrow{l} I \xrightarrow{r} R$, is defined by a pair of injective graph morphisms: $L \xleftarrow{s} NI \xrightarrow{t} N$, where N is the negative graph, and NI defines the interface graph between L and N.*

A match $m : L \rightarrow G$ satisfies the NAC if and only if there does not exist an injective graph morphism $n : N \rightarrow G$ which preserves the NI interface mappings, i.e. for all nodes v in NI we have $n_N(t_N(v)) = m_N(s_N(v))$ and for all edges e in NI we have $n_E(t_E(v)) = m_E(s_E(e))$.

A rule can have an arbitrary number of NACs, and a derivation step can only be applied if a match satisfies all the NACs of the matched rule.

In addition to the above, we adopt the theory of *typed attributed graphs* [8], where graphs are extended by assigning types to nodes and edges, and by assigning a set of named attributes to each node type. A graph morphism must now also preserve the node and edge types, and the attribute values.

In the graph transformation rules throughout this paper we only explicitly display the LHS and the RHS graphs, while the interface graph is given by shared identifiers of elements in the LHS and the RHS.

3.1   Collection Operator

A collection operator [3] can be used in a rule to match and transform a set of similar subgraphs in one step. A dotted frame is used to visualize a collection operator, where all the contained nodes and edges are placed inside the frame. Shared identifiers between the LHS and the RHS denote interface collection operators and is together with a cardinality placed next to its frame. There can be multiple collection operators, but two collection operators must be specified such that they cannot match the same nodes or edges.

The set of all collection operators in a rule $p : L \xleftarrow{l} I \xrightarrow{r} R$ is referred to as $Coll_p$. We use ψ to denote a function that maps each collection operator, in a rule p, to a number within its cardinality range, i.e. $\psi : Coll_p \to (\mathbf{N} = \{0, 1, 2, \ldots\})$, where $\forall c \in Coll_p : \psi(c) \in [c.min, c.max]$.

We let $p^{\psi} : L^{\psi} \xleftarrow{l} I^{\psi} \xrightarrow{r} R^{\psi}$ denote the collection free rule where each collection operator c in p is replaced by $\psi(c)$ number of collection content copies. In these copies all the copied elements/attributes get fresh identifiers/variables respectively, while the interface elements between the pointcut and the advice are maintained.

The minimal configuration of ψ, denoted ψ^-, for which we can find a match for a rule is when $\forall c \in Coll_p : \psi(c) = c.min$. In the matching process we look for a match of the collection free rule p^{ψ^-}. Then, each collection operator match and the ψ is extended as much as possible to achieve a complete match. This results in a dynamically built rule p^{ψ} with a match upon which we can try to apply a derivation step according to Definition 4.

4   Our Transformation Rules Are Specified in the Concrete Syntax

The concrete syntax of a diagram type uses a tailored visualization with icons and rendering rules depending on the element types. To improve the usability for the graph transformation designer, we define the transformation rules upon concrete syntax. A clear benefit for the user is that the specification of the rules does not require knowledge of the often complicated metamodels of the involved source and target languages.

As with algebraic graph transformation, our rules use a LHS, a RHS, and an implicit interface model defined by identifiers which are displayed next to its corresponding element. The LHS and the RHS can both be a mix of sequence diagrams and state machines, and our transformation rules use an ordinary graph edge to link a lifeline to a state.

Our rules are automatically transformed into traditional abstract syntax rules, where we have a tailored support for (1) the parent state relation, (2) the ordering of occurrences on a lifeline, and (3) combined fragments.

All states and transitions in a state machine model, except the outermost state, have a parent state. Together with the dangling condition, this means that we cannot delete a state or a transition without also matching the parent state. Furthermore, new states and transitions must also get the proper parent state. For convenience, we include an implicit parent state around the whole LHS and the RHS state machine models.

Except for the implicit parent state, the state machine part of our rule models can basically use the same abstract syntax representation as ordinary state machine models. This makes the state machine support quite trivial in our approach, and due to limited space we omit many details about the state machine part of the rules.

For the sequence diagram part of our rules, however, we introduce a fragment operator and tailored matching and transformation definitions. This special treatment of sequence diagrams is incorporated into the mapping to abstract syntax rules, such that ultimately plain algebraic graph transformation is used.

5   Transformation of Sequence Diagrams

Figure 2 shows our simplified metamodel for UML 2 sequence diagrams. A sequence diagram is represented by a set of lifelines. A lifeline has a top-down ordered sequence of occurrences.

An occurrence can be one of five kinds (`event`, `combinedFragment`, `start`, `end`, `arbEvt`), where only events or combined fragments conceptually occur on an ordinary sequence diagram lifeline. The meta occurrence of kind `start` shall be the very first occurrence on a lifeline, and the meta occurrence of kind `end` shall be the very last occurrence on a lifeline. These meta occurrences enables us to easily specify the replacement of a subsequence of occurrences in an arbitrary position on a lifeline.

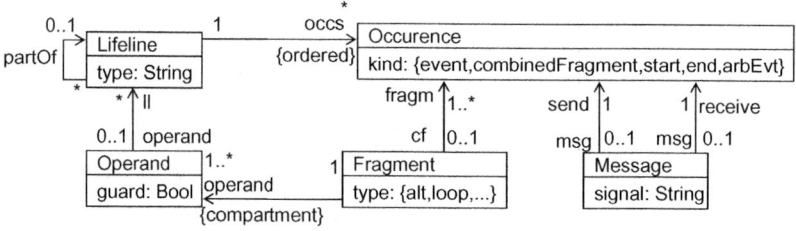

Fig. 2. A simplified metamodel for UML 2 sequence diagrams

Finally, an occurrence of kind `arbEvt` represents the lifeline symbol called *arbitrary events*, which was previously introduced in [5]. This symbol allows matches to have an arbitrary number of occurrences in the symbol's position. Generally, the symbol can be placed anywhere on a lifeline. In this paper we restrict the usage to at most one symbol per lifeline and if used it shall be placed as the very first occurrence on the lifeline. This restriction is sufficient for our transformation from sequence diagrams to state machines, and allows us to focus on the contributions of this paper.

A message consists of a send and a receive event, which are normally placed on two different lifelines. A combined fragment spans over many lifelines and it has one or more operands. A combined fragment with operator `opt`, `loop`, `break` or `neg` contains exactly one operand, while for other operators (e.g. `alt`, `par`) it contains an arbitrary number of operands.

Each operand has a guard attribute and spans over a subset of the lifelines which its combined fragment spans over. An operand lifeline has a `partOf` relation to indicate to which lifeline it belongs.

5.1 Fragment Operator

In the transformation rules (e.g. the `Alt` rule shown later) there is a need to match a combined fragment with an unknown number of operands, and to keep only the operand parts in the RHS of a rule. In the standard concrete syntax of sequence diagrams it is not straightforward to distinguish between the combined fragment operator itself and its operands. A similar challenge applies to state regions of state machines, which are also displayed in separate compartments of a state. We call such relations for a compartment relation and indicate this by the tag {compartment} in the metamodel (Figure 2).

For relations that are tagged as compartment in the metamodel, we provide a new graphical element in the rules. For sequence diagrams we call this element a *fragment operator*. It is displayed as an ordinary combined fragment rectangle with a set of rectangles labeled 'operand' inside to denote the fragment operands. The fragment operator has a clear border between itself and its operands, as opposed to the syntax of ordinary sequence diagrams.

Multiple operands are expressed by explicitly drawing several compartment operands, or by placing a collection operator around a compartment operand as illustrated by the rule in Figure 3a. Notice that the rule in concrete syntax is very concise compared to the relatively complicated corresponding rule in abstract syntax (Figure 3b).

The semantics of the rule can be explained as follows. A match shall have a combined fragment of type `alt` as the first occurrence on some lifeline identified by id=1. The abstract syntax rule ensures this by requiring that the combined fragment is the first occurrence after the meta-occurrence `start` on a lifeline with identifier 1. The NAC introduced in the abstract syntax requires that a lifeline specified in the concrete syntax is not part of an operand. Such a fixed NAC is introduced for all LHS lifelines so that we can only match a lifeline which is not part of another lifeline.

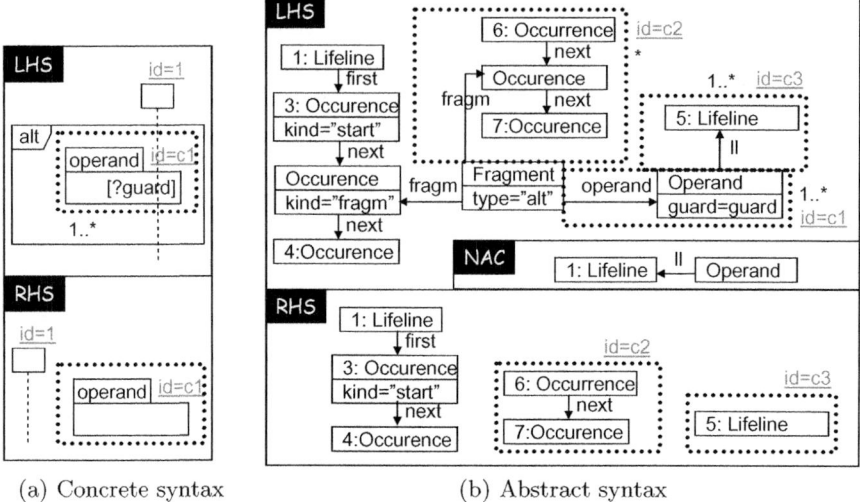

(a) Concrete syntax   (b) Abstract syntax

Fig. 3. Mapping a rule with the fragment operator from concrete to abstract syntax

The collection operators with ids c2 and c3 are introduced by the mapping to abstract syntax rule, and they allow a matching combined fragment to span across lifelines not specified by the concrete syntax rule. Furthermore, these collection operators enables us to delete the combined fragment even though some of its lifelines are not explicitly matched by the concrete syntax rule.

When the combined fragment operator is removed, and its operands are kept, the 11 edge to the part lifelines with identifier id=5 is removed, and these lifelines are no longer prevented from matches by the generated fixed NACs in the abstract syntax rules.

5.2 Transformation Rules

In this section we present the transformation rules, and we show how the rules gradually transform from a sequence diagram into state machines.

We use the term *source model* for the model to be transformed, and *target model* for the final result of the transformation. The source model in Figure 4d is a sequence diagram for a gas pump scenario. A user inserts a payment card (insertCard). The gas pump requests the pin code from the user (requestPin) and the user enters the pin code (pinCode). A bank validates the pin code (validate and result), and an alt operator models the two possible outcomes: 1) *valid pin code*: The user is informed to start fuel (startFuel) and the user indicates end of fueling by hanging up the gas pump (hangUp), or 2) *invalid pin code*: The user is informed that the entered pin code is invalid (invalidPin). In both cases, the scenario ends by ejecting the card (cardOut).

Each lifeline corresponds to a state machine. When producing a state machine, it is sufficient to look at the single corresponding lifeline with its events and how

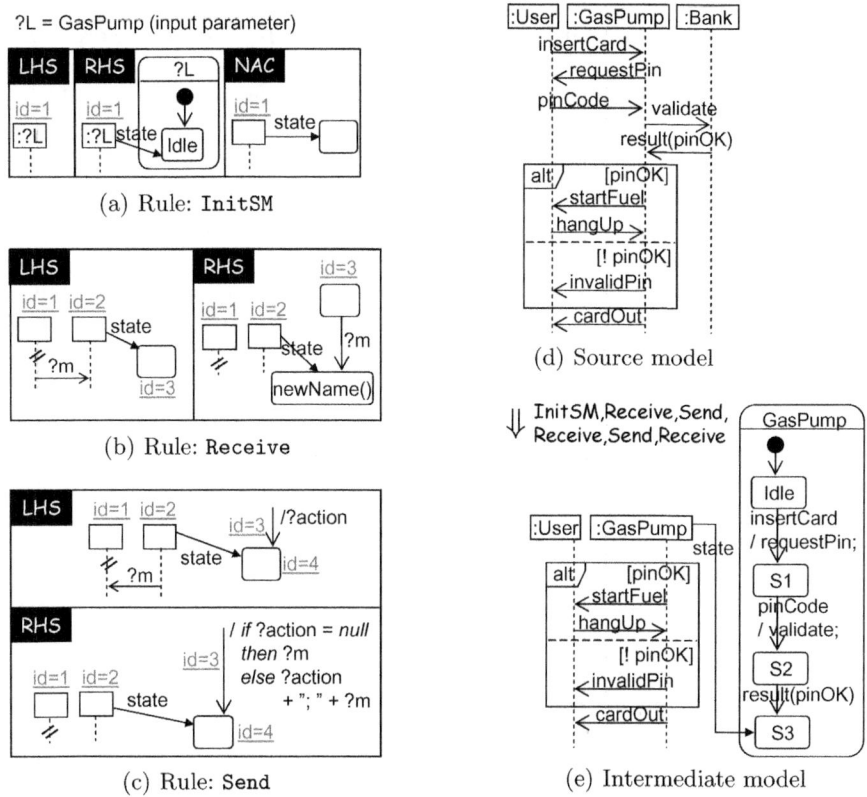

Fig. 4. GasPump: From SD to SM. From source model to intermediate model.

these events are structured within the combined fragments. A prerequisite to this claim is that each lifeline occurs only in one sequence diagram, which is ensured by introducing the combined fragments in step 2 of the method described in Section 2.

The intermediate models in the transformation process contains sequence diagrams, state machines and one helper edge (an abstract syntax edge) with type name **state** to link a lifeline to its current position in the corresponding state machine.

The transformation process takes a lifeline type as input so that we can produce a state machine for that lifeline. A rule called **InitSM** (Figure 4a) simply adds a new state machine with the same name as the given lifeline type and adds an initial state with a transition leading to a state called **Idle**. The rule adds the edge of type **state** from the lifeline to the **Idle** state. A NAC ensures that the **InitSM** rule is applied exactly once.

The transformation rules then proceed by matching the top-most occurrence on the lifeline, adding corresponding behavior to the state machine and removing the treated occurrence from the lifeline. Removing an occurrence normally means that we need to delete an occurrence also from another lifeline, e.g. removing the send event from a lifeline can only be done if we also remove the receive event of the message.

A top-most 'occurrence' is either a combined fragment or an event which is part of a message. The rule Receive (Figure 4b) pops a receive event (and its corresponding send event from another lifeline), adds a state which now becomes the current state, and adds a transition with trigger labeled by the message name. The transition goes from the previous current state to the new current state. We use an arbEvt symbol to indicate that the matched send event does not need to be the very first occurrence on its lifeline. The rule Send (Figure 4c) pops a send event (and its corresponding receive event from another lifeline) and adds a corresponding effect on the incoming transition to the current state.

The model in Figure 4e shows the result after applying the rule sequence <InitSM, Receive, Send, Receive, Send, Receive>. We have omitted the Bank lifeline from this model and the following models in this transformation, since it has no more events.

The rule Alt in Figure 5a pops an alt fragment, makes the current state into a composite state by adding internal behavior: initial, Idle and final states, an inner composite state for each alt operand.

We produce a transition from the Idle state to each inner composite state, where the transition guard is equal to the corresponding alt operand guard. For each alt operand we also produce a new lifeline with the alt operand content and where the lifeline has a current state edge to the Idle state of the inner composite state. Finally the original lifeline where we popped the alt operator, gets a new state as its current state, and the old current state gets a transition leading to the new current state. The model in Figure 5b shows the result after applying the Alt rule.

A rule called FinalState (not shown) deletes a lifeline with a top message, and its current state is replaced by a final state. Due to the dangling condition, such a deletion is only allowed when the sequence diagram has no other connecting messages than the top message.

The model in Figure 5c shows a part of the final target model, which is a state machine for the GasPump lifeline (the target model also contains state machines for the other lifelines). We have applied three flattening rules to produce a more readable and concise state machine. The flattening rules collapse composite states that have been produced by the Alt and Loop rules. A rule for messages having the same lifeline as sender and receiver, the flattening rules, and rules to handle combined fragments of types loop, par and opt are omitted due to space limitations. These rules can be found in [2].

The transformation produces one state machine per lifeline, and these state machines are each placed as a region within a combined outermost state machine. This means that all the state machines are started in parallel.

The transformation rules are implemented in the graph transformation tool AGG. The transformation is tested on some examples, including the GasPump example shown in this paper, with success. The AGG tool only supports abstract

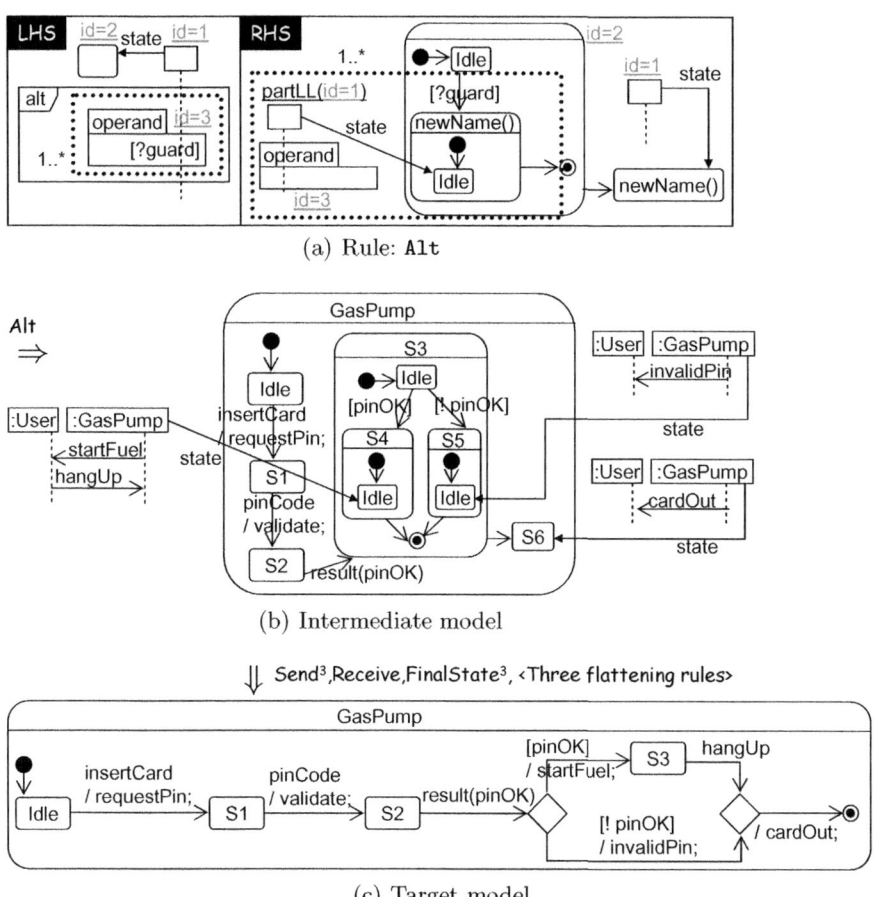

(a) Rule: Alt

(b) Intermediate model

(c) Target model

Fig. 5. GasPump: From SD to SM. Reaching the target model.

syntax rules, and we have manually translated from concrete syntax to abstract syntax rules. We have also used multiple collection free rules to simulate each rule with collection operators by following the algorithm defined in [3]. This paper defines semantics for concrete syntax based rules of sequence diagrams which can be used to automate the translation to abstract syntax rules, as we have implemented previously for activity models [4].

5.3 Transformation of Sequence Diagrams Formalized

This section formalizes the matching and transformation of sequence diagrams. The definitions use an injective mapping function, $\phi : L \to M$, to denote an injective mapping from the LHS elements in L to elements in the source model M. The ϕ mapping preserves the type of an element, and also all the attribute values that are specified for a LHS element.

In the definitions below a lifeline has a sequence of occurrences, where an occurrence is either an event or a combined fragment. Hence, we ignore the meta occurrences `start`, `end` and `arbEvt`, except for checking if the `arbEvt` symbol is present on a lifeline. First, we define a list of useful notation and helper definitions:

- $s \frown t$ denotes the concatenation of two (finite) sequences s and t
- $Occur^*$ denotes the set of all possible occurrence sequences
- $l.hasArbEvt$ denotes if a lifeline l has the `arbEvt` symbol on top
- $l.operand$ denotes the operand in which a lifeline l is a part and returns `null` if l is an ordinary lifeline that is not part of an operand
- $l.occs$ denotes the top-down sequence of occurrences of lifeline l
- $o.cf$ denotes the combined fragment of an occurrence o. If the occurrence is an event, then the value is `null`
- M_{LL} / M_F denotes the set of lifelines / combined fragments respectively of a sequence diagram M

The definition below defines a match for a lifeline without an `arbEvt` symbol.

Definition 6 (Lifeline match from top). *The mapping ϕ is a lifeline match from top if and only if ϕ maps the top-down occurrence sequence O_l of a LHS lifeline to a continuous beginning subsequence of the corresponding source lifeline's top-down occurrence sequence O_s. Formally,*

$$LLMatch_{\phi}^{1}(O_l, O_s) \stackrel{\text{def}}{=} \exists O \in Occur^* : O_s = \phi(O_l) \frown O$$

The definition below defines a match for a lifeline with an `arbEvt` symbol.

Definition 7 (Lifeline match in an arbitrary position). *This definition is equal to the previous except that the match does not have to start from the beginning of the source lifeline. Formally,*

$$LLMatch_{\phi}^{*}(O_l, O_s) \stackrel{\text{def}}{=} \exists O_{beg}, O_{end} \in Occur^* : O_s = O_{beg} \frown \phi(O_l) \frown O_{end}$$

Definition 8 (Sequence diagram match). *Given a LHS sequence diagram L and a source sequence diagram S. The mapping $\phi : L \to S$ is a sequence diagram match if and only if for all lifelines $l \in L_{LL}$ the following two conditions are satisfied: (1) l is not mapped to a lifeline which is part of an operand, and (2) l is mapped to a lifeline match. Formally,*

$$
\begin{aligned}
sdMatch_{\phi}(L, S) \stackrel{\text{def}}{=} \\
\forall l \in L_{LL} : \quad & \phi(l).operand = \textbf{null} \\
& \wedge \; \textbf{if } l.hasArbEvt \textbf{ then } LLMatch_{\phi}^{*}(l.occs, \phi(l).occs) \\
& \quad \textbf{else } LLMatch_{\phi}^{1}(l.occs, \phi(l).occs)
\end{aligned}
$$

As pointed out in the previous section, we are allowed to delete combined fragments even though all its spanning lifelines are not explicitly matched. Let Del denote the set of to-be-deleted combined fragments, i.e. $Del = \{\phi(f) \mid f \in (L_F \setminus l(I_F))\}$. The function $delCF(O, Del)$ returns the occurrence sequence O where all combined fragments in Del has been removed.

Definition 9 *(Sequence diagram transformation step). Given a rule $p :$ $L \xleftarrow{l} I \xrightarrow{r} R$, a source sequence diagram S, and a mapping $\phi : L \to S$, where $sdMatch_\phi(L, S)$. The rule p and the mapping ϕ define a transformation step from S to a target sequence diagram T, denoted $S \overset{p_\phi}{\Rightarrow} T$. The lifelines of T, T_{LL}, are the union of (1) the transformed L lifelines (the occurrences given in an L lifeline are replaced by the occurrences in the corresponding R lifeline (retrieved by the helper function getOccsR), (2) all the new R lifelines, and (3) all the unmapped lifelines in S. For each lifeline in the lifeline sets (1) and (3), we need to delete every occurrence that represents a to-be-deleted combined fragment by using the function delCF. Formally,*

$$\textbf{let } getOccsR(l_l) \overset{\text{def}}{=} \textbf{if } \exists l_i \in I_{LL} : l(l_i) = l_l \textbf{ then } r(l_i).occs \textbf{ else } \langle\rangle$$

$$\textbf{in } S \overset{p_\phi}{\Rightarrow} T \overset{\text{def}}{=} sdMatch_\phi(L, S) \quad \wedge$$
$$T_{LL} = \{l_t \mid l_l \in L_{LL} \wedge \exists O_{beg}, O_{end} \in Occur^* : \tag{1}$$
$$\phi(l_l).occs = O_{beg} \frown \phi(l_l.occs) \frown O_{end} \wedge$$
$$l_t.occs = delCF(O_{beg} \frown getOccsR(l_l) \frown O_{end}, Del)\}$$
$$\cup R_{LL} \setminus r(I_{LL}) \tag{2}$$
$$\cup \{l_s \mid l_s \in (S_{LL} \setminus \phi(L_{LL})) \wedge l_s.occs = delCF(l_s.occs, Del)\} \tag{3}$$

6   Related Work

Our methodology is quite similar to the one prescribed by Whittle and Schumann [17] and Ziadi et al. [18]. Whittle and Schumann need OCL expressions to express similar behavior across multiple diagrams, while we and Ziadi et al. take advantage of the combined fragments which were introduced in UML 2 after the work of Whittle and Schumann.

Ziadi et al. [18] define their transformation by pseudocode operating on algebraic definitions of sequence diagrams and state machines, while our transformation is based on graph transformation. Our support for guards in `alt/loop` and support for `par/opt/neg` is new compared to their approach.

Harel et al. [6] define a transformation from Live Sequence Charts to UML state charts, which are described by traditional algorithms. Their focus is on the transformation itself in contrast to our work that provide an improved way to specify such transformations.

Sun [14] specifies a transformation from state charts to state machines in the AToM tool which like our approach takes advantage of combined fragments (`alt` and `loop`). With our fragment operator and the collection operator, we can define the transformation rules completely by graphical models. Sun, on the other hand, needs to use relatively complicated textual pre- and post-conditions associated with the rules.

The MATA tool [16] and Klein et al. [10] are two promising sequence diagram aspect proposals where transformation on sequence diagrams can be specified based on the concrete syntax and where an occurrence sequence on a lifeline easily can be replaced another occurrence sequence.

The MATA tool also has a way to match combined fragments in a sequence diagram aspect language. However, it is too limited as a basis for the transformation from sequence diagrams to state machines, since there is no way to match a combined fragment with an unknown number of operands.

Klein et al. have no support for matching combined fragments. Furthermore, in Klein et al. all matches are identified and treated at once which is not appropriate for our transformation from sequence diagrams to state machines.

Hermann [9] uses algebraic graph transformation, restricted to abstract syntax, to specify transformation rules for sequence diagrams. Without the collection operator and the fragment operator, our transformation rules to state machines will be very difficult to express.

We have not seen other proposals where it is easy to specify that an event or a combined fragment has to be the very first occurrence on a lifeline. Although a bit cumbersome, it is expressible in other graph transformation approaches by using several NACs.

Our previously defined semantics-based aspect language [5] cannot be used as a basis for the transformation from sequence diagrams to state machines, since it is not structure preserving. The structure of combined fragments is utterly important in order to generate readable state machines.

7   Conclusions

We have shown how concrete syntax-based graph transformation rules can be used to specify a transformation from sequence diagrams to state machines. These rules are much more concise than traditional graph transformation rules which are specified in abstract syntax.

We introduced a novel fragment operator that allows us to graphically specify the matching and transformation of a combined fragment with an arbitrary number of operands. Furthermore, we formalized a suitable way to handle the order of occurrences on a lifeline, which is crucial when specifying transformations of sequence diagrams.

Acknowledgment. The work reported in this paper has been funded by The Research Council of Norway, grant no. 167172/V30 (the SWAT project), and by the DiVA project grant no. 215412 (EU FP7 STREP).

References

1. Brændshøi, B.: Consistency Checking UML Interactions and State Machines. Master's thesis, Department of Informatics, University of Oslo (2008)
2. Grønmo, R.: Using Concrete Syntax in Graph-based Model Transformations. PhD thesis, Dept. of Informatics, University of Oslo (2009)
3. Grønmo, R., Krogdahl, S., Møller-Pedersen, B.: A Collection Operator for Graph Transformation. In: Paige, R.F. (ed.) ICMT 2009. LNCS, vol. 5563, pp. 67–82. Springer, Heidelberg (2009)
4. Grønmo, R., Møller-Pedersen, B.: Aspect Diagrams for UML Activity Models. In: Schürr, A., Nagl, M., Zündorf, A. (eds.) AGTIVE 2007. LNCS, vol. 5088, pp. 329–344. Springer, Heidelberg (2008)
5. Grønmo, R., Sørensen, F., Møller-Pedersen, B., Krogdahl, S.: A Semantics-based Aspect Language for Interactions with the Arbitrary Events Symbol. In: Schieferdecker, I., Hartman, A. (eds.) ECMDA-FA 2008. LNCS, vol. 5095, pp. 262–277. Springer, Heidelberg (2008)
6. Harel, D., Kugler, H., Pnueli, A.: Synthesis Revisited: Generating Statechart Models from Scenario-Based Requirements. In: Kreowski, H.-J., Montanari, U., Orejas, F., Rozenberg, G., Taentzer, G. (eds.) Formal Methods in Software and Systems Modeling. LNCS, vol. 3393, pp. 309–324. Springer, Heidelberg (2005)
7. Haugen, Ø., Møller-Pedersen, B.: JavaFrame: Framework for Java-enabled modelling. In: Ericsson Conference on software Engineering, ECSE (2000)
8. Heckel, R., Küster, J.M., Taentzer, G.: Confluence of Typed Attributed Graph Transformation System. In: Corradini, A., Ehrig, H., Kreowski, H.-J., Rozenberg, G. (eds.) ICGT 2002. LNCS, vol. 2505, Springer, Heidelberg (2002)
9. Hermann, F.: Typed Attributed Graph Grammar for Syntax Directed Editing of UML Sequence Diagrams. Diploma thesis. Master's thesis, Technical University of Berlin, Department for Computer Science (2005)
10. Klein, J., Fleurey, F., Jézéquel, J.-M.: Weaving multiple aspects in sequence diagrams. Trans. on Aspect Oriented Software Development 3 (2007)
11. Krüger, I., Grosu, R., Scholz, P., Broy, M.: From MSCs to Statecharts. In: International Workshop on Distributed and Parallel Embedded Systems (1999)
12. Lambers, L., Ehrig, H., Orejas, F.: Conflict Detection for Graph Transformation with Negative Application Conditions. In: Corradini, A., Ehrig, H., Montanari, U., Ribeiro, L., Rozenberg, G. (eds.) ICGT 2006. LNCS, vol. 4178, pp. 61–76. Springer, Heidelberg (2006)
13. Runde, R.K., Haugen, Ø., Stølen, K.: Refining UML interactions with underspecification and nondeterminism. Nordic Journal of Computing 2(12) (2005)
14. Sun, X.: A Model-Driven Approach to Scenario-Based Requirements Engineering. Master's thesis, School of Comp. Science, McGill Univ., Montreal, Canada (2007)
15. Taentzer, G.: AGG: A graph transformation environment for modeling and validation of software. In: Pfaltz, J.L., Nagl, M., Böhlen, B. (eds.) AGTIVE 2003. LNCS, vol. 3062, pp. 446–453. Springer, Heidelberg (2004)
16. Whittle, J., Jayaraman, P., Elkhodary, A., Moreira, A., Araújo, J.: MATA: A Unified Approach for Composing UML Aspect Models based on Graph Transformation. In: Katz, S., Ossher, H., France, R., Jézéquel, J.-M. (eds.) Transactions on Aspect-Oriented Software Development VI. LNCS, vol. 5560, pp. 191–237. Springer, Heidelberg (2009)
17. Whittle, J., Schumann, J.: Generating statechart designs from scenarios. In: The 22nd international conference on Software engineering (ICSE) (2000)
18. Ziadi, T., Hélouët, L., Jézéquel, J.-M.: Revisiting statechart synthesis with an algebraic approach. In: 26th International Conference on Software Engineering (ICSE), IEEE Computer Society, Los Alamitos (2004)

Safe Composition of Transformations

Florian Heidenreich, Jan Kopcsek, and Uwe Aßmann

Institut für Software- und Multimediatechnik
Technische Universität Dresden
D-01062, Dresden, Germany
florian.heidenreich@tu-dresden.de

Abstract. Model transformations are at the heart of Model-Driven Software Development (MDSD) and, once composed in transformation chains to MDSD processes, allow for the development of complex systems and their automated derivation. While there already exist various approaches to specify and execute such MDSD processes, only few of them draw focus on ensuring the validity of the transformation chains, and thus, safe composition of transformations. In this paper, we present the TraCo composition system, which overcomes these limitations and evaluate and discuss the approach based on two case studies.

1 Introduction

Model-Driven Software Development (MDSD) [1,2] is an approach to software development that uses models as its main artefacts where different concerns of the desired software product are described at various levels of abstraction. The overall idea of MDSD is to transform these abstract models into more concrete models, which can then be used to generate implementation (i.e., source code) or related artefacts. What exactly the models describe and how they are processed by transformations is described in a transformation chain, an MDSD process. This process can for example describe the derivation of a dedicated software product for different platforms—similar to what has been proposed by the Object Management Group (OMG) in its Model-Driven Architecture (MDA) [3]. In Software Product Line Engineering (SPLE) [4,5], such processes can be used to describe how variability in models is resolved in possibly multiple stages and various transformation steps to create a dedicated product of the Software Product Line (SPL).

MDSD processes usually consist of multiple steps that range from loading and storing of models to performing transformations and generating artefacts. Many of those (e.g., loading models, performing transformations, . . .) are often reused between projects which requires modularisation of the steps into reusable units. Existing work in this direction, e.g. MWE [6] and UniTI [7], allows for defining and executing custom MDSD processes and reusing common parts across different of such processes.

Although these frameworks provide many benefits for defining MDSD processes, such as stepwise refinement, and are already widely used in industry and

L. Tratt and M. Gogolla (Eds.): ICMT 2010, LNCS 6142, pp. 108–122, 2010.
© Springer-Verlag Berlin Heidelberg 2010

academia, they also bear the difficulty of making those transformations work together correctly. The resulting models or implementation artefacts of an MDSD process are only valid if all input models and parameters are valid and each single transformation step receives valid input data and produces valid output data. Additionally, every transformation step needs to work as intended to ensure validity of the produced output. Because of the many intermediate models it can be very hard to trace a single error in the final product to the input model or the transformation that originally caused that error. Furthermore, there are many heterogenous transformation technologies that are used in combination, suit different use cases and behave differently. This causes additional difficulties when composing multiple steps in such an MDSD process. We observed that existing technologies to describe and execute those processes lack concepts and functionality to ensure the correct interaction between the different transformation steps.

In this paper we present TraCo, a *Transformation Composition* framework for safe composition of transformations. The goal is to allow the description, composition, and execution of heterogeneous transformation processes, while providing mechanisms for ensuring validity of these processes, which is checked both statically while developing MDSD processes and dynamically while executing them. By composition is meant, the chaining of transformation steps into complex transformation.

The remainder of the paper is structured as follows. Section 2 presents existing work in the area of model transformation and composition of transformation steps. Section 3 presents the conceptual basis for TraCo, introduces the underlying component model and describes the composition of transformation steps. The implementation of TraCo is outlined in Section 4. In Section 5, we present two case studies and discuss the applicability of the approach. Section 6 summarises the paper and presents directions for future work.

2   Background

In this section existing approaches to model transformation are presented. In the scope of this paper, we are interested in approaches that are used to define basic transformation steps (i.e., transformations that are not built by composing multiple, possibly heterogenous, transformations) and complex transformations that are the result of composing basic or complex transformations. First, a short overview of approaches to model transformation is given. Next, we present existing approaches for defining and executing MDSD processes and highlight important criteria that led to the solution presented in this paper.

2.1   Basic Transformation Approaches

In [8], Czarnecki and Helsen present an in-depth classification of various transformation approaches regarding multiple criteria. What is visible from this classification is, that there exist a plentitude of approaches, ranging from direct manipulation (e.g., with Java), operational (e.g., QVT Operational [9] or

Kermeta [10]), relational (e.g., QVT Relational [9], MTF [11], or AMW [12]), template-based (e.g., model templates [13] or FeatureMapper [14]), to approaches based on concepts of graph transformation (e.g., AGG [15] or Viatra [16]). All these approaches require specific input models and parameterisation for transformation and provide approach-specific means to constrain this input data. Furthermore, transformations specified using these approaches often lack a formally specified interface which would foster reuse and is key to safe composition of such transformations.

2.2   Complex Transformation Approaches

In the following, we present three approaches for composing basic transformations to complex transformations and highlight important properties of those approaches.

Modeling Workflow Engine. The Modeling Workflow Engine (MWE) [6] is the workflow engine of the widely-used generator framework openArchitectureWare (oAW) [17]. An XML-based workflow definition configures the MDSD process by sequentially listing the calls to WorkflowComponents that need to be executed including their parameterisation. oAW provides simple components for loading and saving models, but also exposes languages for certain tasks through specific components, like validating models using the *Check* language and performing model-to-text transformations using the *Xpand* template language. Each component in a workflow is implemented in a Java class, identified by its class name, and parameterised through one or more tags. The parameter tag names correspond to names of properties of the component class and use its accessor methods. That means that Java classes effectively form the specification and implementation of the components. Using an extended convention for accessor methods, it is easily to distinguish in, out, and inout parameters, work with collection types and perform typing of the parameters against Java types.

Slots that are parameterised by models are not explicitly specified and typed against metamodels. MWE does not provide means to specify constraints for input and output models—although this can be realised using the *Check* language which is similar to the Object Constraint Language (OCL). In order to provide the level of validation desired for safe composition of transformations, *Check* components need to be used before and after each component instantiation. This separates the contract from the component. Putting the constraints and the component into a separate workflow voids the specification of the component. Using a workflow as part of another workflow is also possible. This is done by including the workflow using a reference to the file in which the workflow is defined. It is possible to explicitly define parameter values or simply pass the complete state of the outer workflow to the inner. However, it is not possible to specify the parameters of a workflow explicitly. That means, that knowledge about parameter values given to the inner workflow are solely based on any documentation or comment bundled with the workflow.

UniTI. In [7], Vanhooff et al. present UniTI, a system specifically designed for defining and executing composed transformation processes. They identify the shortages of existing transformation systems, especially the lack of precise and complete specifications, and provide means to solve these shortcomings. The approach is based on a metamodel that is used to define transformation specifications that can contain multiple input and output parameters. Typing of parameters is done through `ModelingPlatforms` and parameter-specific constraints. Transformation specifications and `ModelingPlatforms` are stored in library elements (`TFLibrary`). In contrast to MWE workflows, UniTI follows a data-driven design. It introduces execution elements for specific transformation steps conforming to a transformation specification, actual parameters (`TFActualParameter`) for every formal parameter and connectors (`Connector`) that connect output and input parameters of different transformation steps. Using this structure it is possible to build non-sequential transformation processes. It is also possible to check whether connections between input and output parameters are valid, because both are typed. Every actual parameter directly links to a model. This model link can either be manually defined—in order to set the input and output models of the transformation chain—or will be automatically set for intermediate models.

Although UniTI provides mechanisms for ensuring the validity of transformation chains (including a precise specification of components, explicit model typing and additional constraints), it lacks an important element. It is not possible to define constraints ranging over multiple parameters, as it is required to express contract conditions (especially if cross-relationships between models exist). So although each single input model can be checked for consistency, the whole input including all models cannot be checked. Similarly, the output cannot be checked for consistency with the input.

MDA Control Center. In [18], Kleppe presents MDA Control Center (MCC), another approach that supports composition of transformation. Kleppe defines different components that form a composed transformation such as `Creators` (for reading input), `Finishers` (for storing output) and `Transformers`. MCC also provides `ModelTypes` as a means to describe the type of a model. Finally, different means for composing components are provided. First, sequences of two strictly ordered components are possible, where the output of the first is the input of the second. Secondly, parallel combination is allowed, where multiple components take the same input models and the output models are returned as a combined list containing them. Finally, a choice combination is offered that contains multiple components in an ordered list. Every component's condition in this list is tested using the input models and the first components, whose condition is met, is executed or none, if all conditions fail.

Although not further elaborated, MCC does not seem to put more than a reference to the concrete metamodel implementation into the `ModelType` concept. Also, the `ModelTypes` are not directly used in the definitions of the components. They are, however, used in the script language that is used to combine multiple components. This implies that typing of parameters of a component is only done against Java classes. The framework itself does not provide the possibility of defining further constraints on model types. Other conditions such as pre- or postconditions are not available in the specification as well.

2.3 Summary

The analysis of existing basic transformation approaches has shown, that many heterogeneous technologies exists and many of them only offer basic means for the specification of external interfaces, their typing, and pre- and postconditions. Only some technologies offer references to actual metamodels and additional constraints for model types. None of the technologies offer explicit contract constraints, that span all input and output parameters.

In the second part of this section, we presented and discussed three concrete approaches for defining and executing composed MDSD processes. In Table 1, we give an overview of important properties of these technologies. All of the technologies provide explicit specifications for the components used in a composed process, although MWE lacks specifications for sub-processes. UniTI, and to a lesser extent MCC, differ from MWE in that they concentrate solely on model transformations. The only parameter type in UniTI is the model parameter, and thus, it is not possible to parameterise components with native values (e.g., paths to input data). MCC allows this for the special components `Creator` and `Finisher` in a specific way. In contrast to that, MWE operates solely on non-model parameter values like strings, numbers, and class references. Models are only addressed through their respective slot name. Where UniTI components cannot receive native values required for parameters, MWE lacks any typing of

Table 1. Overview of the transformation composition technologies

	MWE	UniTI	MCC
Languages			
For Composition	XML	Model	Textual
For Specification	Java/None for workflows	Component Model	Eclipse Plugins
Type System			
Native Types	Yes	No	Only internal
Model Types	No	Yes	Yes
Additional Constraints	No	Yes	No
Parameters			
Supported Directions	All	In, Out	In, Out
Multi-Value	Yes	No	No
Additional Constraints	No	Yes	No
Validation and Verification			
Contracts for Components	No	No	No
Design-Time Validation	No	No	No

model parameters. Only UniTI allows more precise specifications using additional constraints, that can be defined to further restrict model types.

The properties of parameters of components used in a composed process also differs between the different technologies. Where UniTI and MCC only support input and output direction, MWE also supports the inout direction. Additionally, they allow multi-valued parameters (which must be supported by the actual transformation technology as well). Again, only UniTI allows to define additional constraints for parameters.

None of the technologies provides the possibility to define contracts for components to ensure the consistency and validity of their input and output data. Despite the fact, that UniTI's constraints for model types and parameters allow to precisely express what kind of model is required, they cannot be used to check consistency across different models. Also, none of the technologies provide additional tool support for design-time validation of MDSD processes in order to identify errors as early as possible in the development process. Besides the metamodel-based specification of components and MDSD processes, we consider contracts for components and extended means for validation as the main requirements for a system that ensures safe composition of transformations.

3   Approach

In this section we conceptualise the framework for safe composition of transformations as a *composition system*. According to [19], a composition system consists of a *component model*, a *composition language*, and a *composition technique*. The analysis of existing model transformation technologies in Section 2 showed that a key requirement for safe composition of transformation steps is a dedicated *component model*, which allows the complete and precise definition of transformation specifications. In addition, a *composition language* is required, which allows explicit definition of composition recipes and, thus, composed transformation processes. The *composition technique* expands on these concepts by defining how the composition is actually performed. To ensure safe composition, extensive checks for *validation* of those processes need to be performed statically and dynamically.

3.1   Component Model

The component model defines the concepts that can be used to describe arbitrary basic transformation steps that can be used in an MDSD process.

Figure 1 depicts the metamodel of our component model which is defined using Ecore [20]. It constitutes the actual language to specify components and model types. According to this metamodel, a Library consists of multiple ComponentSpecifications and ModelTypes. A Library collects reusable or project-specific ComponentSpecifications.

A ComponentSpecification has a name[1], multiple PortSpecifications, pre- and postconditions and its actual implementation definition.

---

[1] The metaclass Nameable was omitted from the metamodel figures to improve clarity.

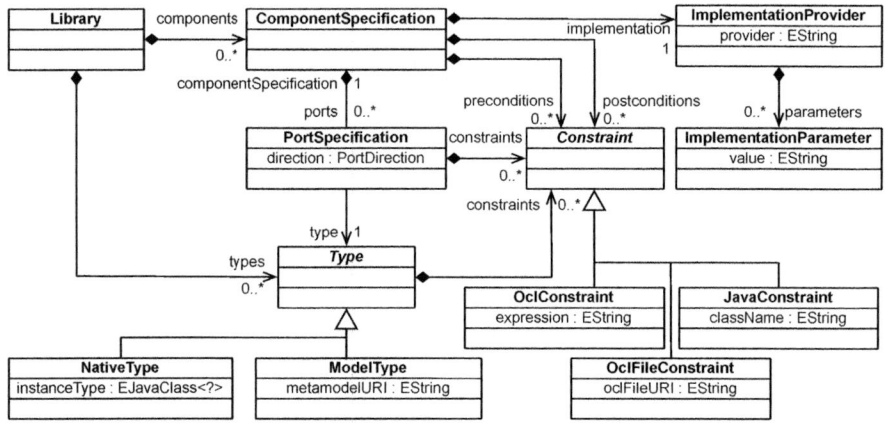

Fig. 1. Metamodel of the Component Model

PortSpecifications have a name, a type and multiple Constraints. The Type might have Constraints and is either a ModelType, which references an EMF-based metamodel declaration, or a NativeType, which references a Java type. Currently, no means for subtyping of ModelTypes are provided.

The pre- and postconditions of a component are realised using Constraints. The OclConstraint uses a user-defined OCL expression to check the input and output models for consistency. OclFileConstraint references a file containing OCL expressions. The JavaConstraint metaclass, represents constraints implemented in Java. This initial set of constraint types can be easily extended to support other constraint languages.

The ImplementationProvider of a component consists of the identifier of its implementation provider and ImplementationParameters. The implementation class is not referenced directly, but is made available using a registry of implementation providers. These implementations can be technology-specific adapters or custom component implementations. In contrast to the component implementations, this adapter may enforce a more strict and more well-defined interface on the target classes.

3.2   Composition Language

The presented component model describes the structure of single components. On top of this component model, a dedicated language is provided, which allows the description of composed transformations. This language introduces additional constructs necessary to use and connect components described using the component model.

Figure 2 depicts the metamodel of the composition language. Referenced parts of the component model are coloured grey. According to the metamodel, a Process consists of ComponentInstances, ExternalPortInstances and Connections. A ComponentInstance is an instance of a component specified using

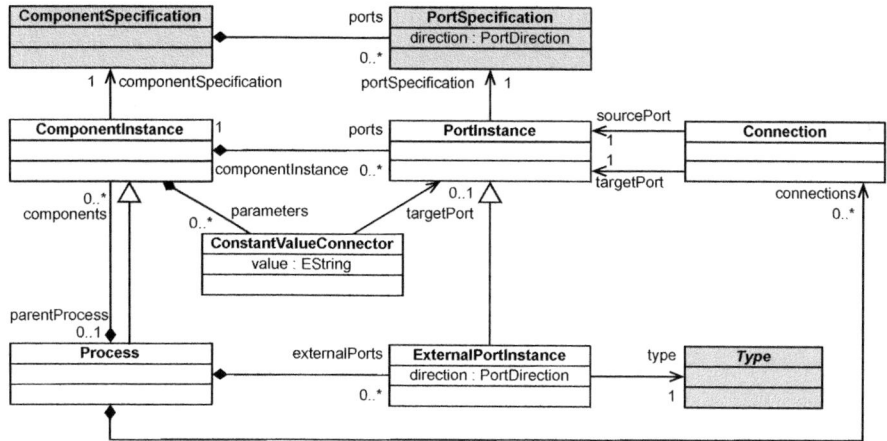

Fig. 2. Metamodel of the Composition Language

the component model. This instance references its ComponentSpecification. Additionally, it may contain ConstantValueConnectors to parameterise non-model ports. ComponentInstances have PortInstances that are instances of the ComponentSpecification's PortSpecifications. PortInstances and ExternalPortInstances can be connected using Connections. They may both be the source and target of a Connection, although it is not allowed to connect two ExternalPortInstances. ExternalPortInstances have a name by which they can be identified and parameterised. The type and direction of the port is inferred from the connection and the opposite port.

3.3   Composition Technique

The composition technique describes the mechanisms necessary to perform the composition of multiple components and execute them. For the developed composition system a black-box composition is used. That means that components only communicate with each other through their ports. The implementation, the implementation parameters and pre- and postconditions are hidden within the component itself and cannot be changed by the composition process.

The execution of a composed transformation process is data-flow based. Any transformation component is executed as soon as it has received all required data on its in-ports. In case the component does not have any in-ports, it is considered ready for execution. Any component is only executed once. If there are multiple components ready for execution they are executed in parallel. After a components execution is finished, its output models are transferred to other components via connections. If all components were run exactly once, the process is terminated.

The execution of a transformation component consists of the invocation of its implementation. This implementation may be a technology-specific adapter which initialises and invokes the actual transformation module. After that, the adapter will extract any generated output models from the transformation module and provide them as the components output models.

In case a components execution is aborted due to errors or in case it did not generate models for all output ports, the process is aborted. If a components implementation does not terminate after a certain time, this is considered an error as well.

3.4 Validation

Besides the specification and execution of MDSD processes, we want to ensure the consistency and validity of the constructed processes. This is done by performing validation checks for both *intra-component* and *inter-component* consistency.

Intra-Component Consistency covers consistency within a single component. This especially includes the implementation of a component, which can consist of a single Java class or an adapter and the actual transformation module. The pre- and postconditions can also be used to ensure internal consistency to a certain degree. In the following, we describe the various checks performed either statically or dynamically to ensure intra-component consistency.

Consistency of Component Specification. Component specifications must be valid and complete. This includes its naming, a reference to an existing component implementation and correct naming and typing of all its port specifications. Additionally, valid port directions have to be specified. This can be checked statically for a single component specification.

Consistency of Implementation Parameterisation. If a component implementation requires parameters (e.g., references to resources) to make the actual implementation work, the component implementation has to check the completeness and validity of those parameters. This can be checked statically for a single component specification by the component's implementation.

Consistency Between Specification and Adapted Transformation. If a transformation technology is adapted by the framework, the consistency between the component specification and the technology-dependent specification can be checked as well. The level of detail regarding consistency at this level depends on the implementation technology. The more complete and precise the provided specification is, the more checks can be performed. This can be checked statically for a single component specification by the components implementation.

Consistency of the Transformation Module. An adapter implementation can use arbitrary specific transformation technologies. Depending on the concrete technology, there may be means to check the actual implementation for consistency (e.g., checking a transformation script for errors). The level of detail again depends on the amount of information provided. This can be checked statically for a single component specification by the components implementation.

Ensuring Component Contracts. The contract of a component, consisting of pre- and postconditions, defines a specific behaviour of the component under certain preconditions. Whether or not this promise holds is hard to check statically against the transformation implementation, because it requires a formal algebra for the underlying implementation technology, which may be Java code and arbitrary transformation technology and may also depend on the concrete input provided. At runtime, however, these constraints can be checked against actual input and output models.

Ensuring Implicit Assumptions. Even if an MDSD process is completely specified, implicit assumptions on the behaviour of component implementations are drawn. In the given composition system we assume that a component always terminates, produces no errors and outputs data on all output ports. If any of these conditions fail, the process needs to be aborted. This can be checked dynamically on a single component instance by the framework.

Consistency of Type Specifications. Native types must have a name and must reference an existing Java type. Model types must also have a name and must reference a valid and existing metamodel. Additional constraints must be valid constraints. This can be checked statically for a single type definition.

Inter-Component Consistency covers consistency of the interactions between components within a composed transformation process. All elements including component instances, connectors, constant value connectors, and external ports need to be checked for consistency in different ways. We identified the following checks that ensure inter-component consistency of a composed transformation process.

All Ports Connected Check. A component instance must have all its ports connected either by connectors or constant value connectors. For in ports, there must be exactly one incoming connection or exactly one constant value. For out ports, one outgoing connection and for inout ports exactly one incoming connection or constant value and exactly one outgoing connection is required. This can be checked statically for each component instance. Optional ports are currently not supported.

Connection Structure Check. It has to be ensured that any connection has a valid port instance as source and as target. These port instances must refer to valid ports of a component specification and must have a valid direction. The source port must have a direction of out or inout, the target port of in or inout. This implies that source ports may not be in ports and target ports may not be out ports. This can be checked statically for each connection.

Connection Type Check. This ensures the correct typing between source and target ports of connections which can be checked statically for each connection.

No Cycles Check. A cycle is a connection between any of a components output ports to any of its input ports (also across multiple components). Although these compositions are structurally valid, they need to be avoided, as there is no way to invoke any component involved in the cycle due to missing inputs. This can be checked statically for each connection.

External Port Connection Check. External ports are the connection points of a composed transformation process to other components. They do not perform any action on their own. That is why an external port must be connected to exactly one port of one component. It is not possible to connect two different external ports, without any transformation component in between. Also, an external port must be connected to exactly one component. This can be checked statically for external ports and connections.

Constant Value Connectors Check. The constant value connectors are used to parameterise non-model input ports of a component. Similar to other connections, it has to be checked whether they are connected to a valid port of a component and whether they are correctly typed. This can be checked statically for each constant value connector.

Runtime Type Check. Types of all input and output models can be checked dynamically independent from the component implementation or transformation technology.

Runtime Constraint Check. Additional constraints may be defined with the type or port specification. These constraints are checked dynamically for each port when it receives or outputs data.

4   Implementation

Building upon the definition of the composition system, we implemented TraCo as a set of Eclipse plug-ins based on the Eclipse Modeling Framework [20]. The current implementation consists of tooling to visually build and maintain component libraries and composed transformation processes and an execution environment that performs the actual transformations. These tools also integrate the mechanisms for ensuring intra-component and inter-component consistency as described in Section 3.4. The checks are enforced by the metamodel structure, many of them by dedicated OCL constraints, or programmatic constraints implemented in the component implementations. All errors that are determined statically or dynamically are collected and reported to the developer.

Based on the component model presented in Section 3, an EMF-based editor has been generated and extended by means for easy creation of component specifications (based on wizards) and validation of such specifications. We have also defined a basic set of component specifications and types in the TraCo Standard Library (TSL), which includes components to load and store models and type definitions for common native types and model types.

A visual editor is provided, that allows for specifying MDSD processes by instantiating components from TraCo libraries. Again, this editor performs validation on all elements participating in such a process and reports possible errors to the developer.

A TraCo process can be executed via Eclipse's run configuration dialog. This dialog takes the actual TraCo process as input and the TraCo execution environment performs the invocation of the process and the execution of all referenced components.

Our current experience with TraCo is with using EMF-based models and we designed the tool to fit nicely in the EMF modelling landscape. However, neither the transformed models nor the adapted transformation techniques are limited to the Ecore technological space.

5 Evaluation

We evaluated TraCo based on two case studies performed as student projects, where the students specified transformation components and developed transformation chains for a given transformation problem.

5.1 Case Studies

The first project consisted of the de-facto standard of transformation examples, where a UML class model was transformed to a Relational model. While this project did not provide any new insights regarding the creativity in the field of model transformations, it gave enough motivation to develop the TSL and provided helpful information regarding usability of the tool (ranging from the demand for wizard-based component instantiation to the way how errors are reported to the developer).

The second project was a more complex MDSD scenario where a Java-based issue management system was developed. The students developed multiple EMF-based Domain-Specific Languages (DSLs) that were used to describe the domain model, the user interface, actions and navigation, and the internal application state. Furthermore, this issue management system was designed as an SPL where the focus was more on platform variability than on functional variability (although it also had three functional variation points). On platform level, variability between SWT and JSP for the presentation layer, Java and EJB3 on the business layer, and local storage and EJB3 on the persistence layer was required.

We developed a two-staged MDSD process, where platform variability was resolved on the first stage and the actual implementation was generated in various steps on the second stage. To express the variability regarding platform decision, we used our SPL tool FeatureMapper [14,21,22] and mapped features or combinations of such from a platform variability feature model to the respective transformation component instances and connections of a TraCo process. To actually perform the feature-based transformation of the TraCo process in TraCo, we developed a dedicated FeatureMapper component for TraCo which required a TraCo process, a mapping definition and a concrete feature selection as input and produced a TraCo process specific to a concrete platform selection.

This specific process model contained several component instances ranging from loading and storing of models, over feature-based transformation of DSL models and model-to-model transformations with ATL [23], to model-to-text transformations with MOFScript [24].

The feature-based transformation of models was performed on all DSL input models, hence, specifying this transformation as a reusable component was worthwhile. In the overall process, which consists of 32 component instances, this component was reused for each of the 5 DSL models.

In addition, this component was also reused for the process on stage one, where the TraCo process itself was transformed and after that executed via a dedicated TraCo component.

5.2 Discussion

The two case studies showed to a certain extent, that it is possible and feasible to create and manage multi-staged MDSD processes with the developed TraCo framework. This does not imply that this observation can be directly generalised to other development efforts. However, as we will see, a number of observations reflect the fact that improved means for validation of complex transformation processes result in safer transformation chains, so there is some tentative grounds for careful generalisation.

The composition system and its supplemental tools made it possible to incorporate heterogeneous transformation technologies including ATL, MOFScript, and feature-based transformation using FeatureMapper. The validation functionalities on component-specification level helped at identifying and fixing erroneous specifications. This also included the detection of component specifications that mismatch with their corresponding transformation modules (which was the case when transformation modules were refactored).

Equally, for the transformation processes, the extended means for validation proved to be helpful at identifying and fixing type errors, yet unconnected ports or ports that did no longer exist because of changes in the component specification. The definition of constraints and contracts using OCL enabled us to more precisely specify expected input and output data. As an example, the transformation for the SWT user interface required unique identifiers on model elements, but the DSL itself did not enforce this. By defining an additional transformation to augment model elements with generated identifiers and providing an additional precondition to the model transformation, we were able to create a reusable transformation component without putting more bloat to the original transformation—while still maintaining integrity of the whole transformation.

The preconditions also helped when working with multiple input models in transformations. For example, some transformations rely on the consistency between two given input models. Any state variable referenced in the first model (in this case the user interface model) must be declared in the second model (in this case the application state model). Similarly, the transformations of action models require consistency of references to state variables as well. Especially in the context of multiple possible variants of the source models—as a result of feature-based transformation—the preconditions help to quickly identify consistency errors. We observed, that the reasons for these errors were not always inconsistent models, but also incorrect mappings of features to DSL model elements. In addition, we also noticed another issue when working with multiple variants specified in one model. Some constraints can no longer be applied without taking the mapping information into account, e.g., when components have multiple incoming connections for the same port which is not allowed in a single-variant scenario and detected by TraCo's validation mechanisms. They can, however, be used to ensure consistency of a specific process variant.

6 Conclusion

In this paper, we presented TraCo, a framework for *safe* composition of transformations. First, we analysed existing work in this field and derived requirements for TraCo from our observations. In addition to metamodel-based specification of components and MDSD processes, we identified contracts for components and means for validation of component specifications and MDSD processes as the main requirements for a system that ensures safe composition of transformations. Second, we conceptualised a composition system (consisting of the modules component model, composition language and composition technique) for TraCo and presented a classification of checks that can be performed to ensure intra-component and and inter-component consistency, thus, resulting in a system that allows for safe composition of transformations. We outlined TraCo's implementation and presented two case studies, followed by a discussion of the applicability of the approach.

In the future, we want to further evaluate TraCo and possibly integrate the concepts developed in this work with existing approaches, preferably MWE. On implementation level, means for debugging TraCo processes are planned.

Acknowledgement

This research has been partly co-funded by the German Ministry of Education and Research within the project feasiPLe.

References

1. Völter, M., Stahl, T.: Model-Driven Software Development. John Wiley & Sons, Chichester (2006)
2. Ritsko, J.J., Seidman, D.I.: Preface. IBM Systems Journal – Special Issue on Model-Driven Software Development 45(3) (2006)
3. Object Management Group: MDA Guide Version 1.0.1. OMG Document (2003), http://www.omg.org/cgi-bin/doc?omg/03-06-01
4. Pohl, K., Böckle, G., van der Linden, F.: Software Product Line Engineering: Foundations, Principles, and Techniques. Springer, Heidelberg (2005)
5. Clements, P., Northrop, L.: Software Product Lines: Practices and Patterns. Addison-Wesley, Reading (2002)
6. The MWE Project Team: Modeling Workflow Engine (2010), http://www.eclipse.org/modeling/emft/?project=mwe

7. Vanhooff, B., Ayed, D., Baelen, S.V., Joosen, W., Berbers, Y.: UniTI: A Unified Transformation Infrastructure. In: Engels, G., Opdyke, B., Schmidt, D.C., Weil, F. (eds.) MODELS 2007. LNCS, vol. 4735, pp. 31–45. Springer, Heidelberg (2007)
8. Czarnecki, K., Helsen, S.: Classification of Model Transformation Approaches. In: OOPSLA 2003 Workshop on Generative Techniques in the Context of Model-Driven Architecture (2003)
9. Object Management Group: MOF QVT Specification, v1.0. OMG Document (2008), http://www.omg.org/spec/QVT/1.0/
10. The Kermeta Project Team: Kermeta (2010), http://www.kermeta.org/
11. IBM United Kingdom Labratories Ltd., IBM alphaWorks: Model Transformation Framework, MTF (2004), http://www.alphaworks.ibm.com/tech/mtf
12. ATLAS Group: Atlas Model Weaver (2010), http://eclipse.org/gmt/amw/
13. Czarnecki, K., Antkiewicz, M.: Mapping Features to Models: A Template Approach Based on Superimposed Variants. In: 4th International Conference on Generative Programming and Component Engineering, pp. 422–437 (2005)
14. Heidenreich, F., Kopcsek, J., Wende, C.: FeatureMapper: Mapping Features to Models. In: Companion Proc. 30th International Conference on Software Engineering, pp. 943–944. ACM, New York (2008)
15. Taentzer, G.: AGG: A Graph Transformation Environment for System Modeling and Validation. In: Tool Exhibition at Formal Methods (2003)
16. The VIATRA2 Project Team: Eclipse GMT VIATRA2 (2010), http://www.eclipse.org/gmt/VIATRA2/
17. The openArchitectureWare Project Team: openArchitectureWare (2010), http://www.openArchitectureWare.org
18. Kleppe, A.: MCC: A Model Transformation Environment. In: Rensink, A., Warmer, J. (eds.) ECMDA-FA 2006. LNCS, vol. 4066, pp. 173–187. Springer, Heidelberg (2006)
19. Aßmann, U.: Invasive Software Composition. Springer, Heidelberg (2003)
20. Steinberg, D., Budinsky, F., Paternostro, M., Merks, E.: Eclipse Modeling Framework, 2nd edn. Pearson Education, London (2008)
21. Heidenreich, F., Şavga, I., Wende, C.: On Controlled Visualisations in Software Product Line Engineering. In: 2nd Workshop on Visualisation in Software Product Line Engineering, collocated with the 12th International Software Product Line Conference, Limerick, Ireland (September 2008)
22. The FeatureMapper Project Team: FeatureMapper (2010), http://www.featuremapper.org
23. ATLAS Group: ATLAS Transformation Language (ATL) User Guide (2006), http://wiki.eclipse.org/ATL/User_Guide
24. Oldevik, J.: MOFScript User Guide (2006), http://www.eclipse.org/gmt/mofscript/doc/MOFScript-User-Guide.pdf

Towards Incremental Execution of ATL Transformations

Frédéric Jouault and Massimo Tisi

AtlanMod (INRIA & École des Mines de Nantes), France
`firstname.lastname@inria.fr`

Abstract. Up to now, the execution of ATL transformations has always followed a two-step algorithm: 1) matching all rules, 2) applying all matched rules. This algorithm does not support incremental execution. For instance, if a source model is updated, the whole transformation must be executed again to get the updated target model.

In this paper, we present an incremental execution algorithm for ATL, as well as a prototype. With it, changes in a source model are immediately propagated to the target model. Our approach leverages previous works of the community, notably on live transformations and incremental OCL. We achieve our goal on a subset of ATL, without requiring modifications to the language.

1 Introduction

Model transformations are used in many different kinds of scenarios nowadays. Some of these scenarios involve evolving source models for which updated target models need to be computed. There are two main kinds of solution to this problem: 1) the whole transformation is reexecuted, or 2) changes are propagated from source to target (e.g., if the name of a source element changes, only the name of the corresponding target element may need to be changed).

Solution 1 has three obvious deficiencies: a) it is generally less efficient than solution 2, b) because a new model is created, any entity holding references to the original target model elements (e.g., a graphical editor) will not see the changes, and c) because a new model is created, any change performed on the original target model will not be kept in the new target model. However, this is the only possibility in ATL (AtlanMod Transformation Language) with the current execution algorithm specified in [1].

Conversely solution 2 does not suffer from these deficiencies. Solution 2 is commonly referred to as incremental transformations (i.e., forward change propagation).

In this work, we aim at providing an incremental execution mode for ATL. As an additional requirement, this execution mode should integrate with existing model-driven tools (e.g., graphical model editors), and be able to propagate changes from one of them holding the source model to another holding the target model. This restricts the kind of solution that we can provide to live transformations. A *live* incremental transformation directly propagates events

L. Tratt and M. Gogolla (Eds.): ICMT 2010, LNCS 6142, pp. 123–137, 2010.
© Springer-Verlag Berlin Heidelberg 2010

between models already loaded in memory. It can generally rely and relatively precise change events emitted by the modeling framework holding the source model.

Conversely, an *offline* incremental transformation loads both a source and a target model before propagating the changes. For this purpose, it generally keeps track of the original unmodified source, which it compares to the new source in order to identify the changes that have occurred.

Note that live transformation techniques may be applied to offline scenarios (e.g., we get a new version of a .xmi file) with two modifications: 1) the two source models (original and updated) must be compared, and corresponding modification events synthesized, and 2) trace information must be persistable and reloadable in a way that makes it immune to the exchange of one .xmi file for another. However, offline solutions cannot be as efficiently applied to live scenarios because they generally reanalyze the all source models (they generally do not have change information, but need to recompute it).

As can be seen above, incremental and live transformations are two distinct concepts: live transformations are a special case of incremental transformations. However, in the context of this work we only consider live implementations of incrementality. Therefore, we can and will use these two words interchangeably in the rest of this paper.

Our approach consists in relying on the declarative constructs of ATL in order to propagate changes from source models to target models. We start by defining a declarative subset of ATL. Then, we develop a mechanism that automatically detects which parts of a transformation need to be reexecuted in order to bring the target models in sync with the source models.

We achieve our goal without changing ATL (apart from subsetting it): we keep its syntax and semantics, so that many existing transformations may benefit from the live execution mode. Only the expressions that are impacted by source changes are reexecuted. Only minimal changes to the ATL compiler [2] are required. The evaluation of navigation expressions is the only part of the OCL (Object Constraint Language) evaluation code that is impacted. No change to the ATL Virtual Machine (VM) is required. This VM can notably operate on EMF (Eclipse Modeling Framework) models. The incremental ATL prototype can therefore be used with models loaded in any EMF editor such as the tree-based reflective editor, or graphical editors based on GMF (the Graphical Modeling Framework of Eclipse [3]).

The remainder of this paper is organized as follows. Section 2 presents some related works. A running example is introduced in Section 3. Our approach is described in Section 4. Section 5 gives some details about implementation and tool support. Finally, Section 6 concludes.

2   Related Works

The most common approach to incremental transformations investigated in related works is offline incrementality. In this area, the work most related to our paper is [4], that proposes an automatic way to synchronize the source and target models of an ATL transformation offline. Incrementality is implemented by interfacing with existing differencing tools for calculating changes to the models and propagating them bidirectionally. With respect to their work, we propose a live approach that requires only limited changes to the ATL compiler and no change to the ATL Virtual Machine (VM), whereas they rely on several VM modifications.

Hearnden et al. [5] synchronize two models incrementally, by using a declarative logic-based transformation engine. The approach, alternative to ours, records a transformation execution and links each transformation step to the correspondent changes in the source model. This information is then used for change propagation.

Live and offline incrementality has been already implemented with Graph Transformations techniques, for example in [6]. Especially the work in [7] implements live incrementality, based on the Rete algorithm, a well-known technique in the field of rule-based systems. These graph transformation approaches focus on incremental pattern-matching to improve the performances of the transformation. In opposition to these graph-based systems, our proposal does not directly apply in-place transformations, but it could be extended for that purpose. In this sense our proposal is more similar to [8], that employs Triple Graph Grammars for incremental offline model synchronization in both directions.

The topic of evaluating OCL expression incrementally has been investigated by Cabot [9], especially for detecting if a modification to a UML model violates OCL constraints that were satisfied before. While Cabot considers only boolean constraints, we need to evaluate general OCL expressions for calculating any kind of output values. Apart from this, some ideas from [9] could be integrated in future versions of our prototype in order to improve its performance.

Finally, incremental transformations are often coupled with Retainment Rules. These rules make it possible to avoid overriding manual changes performed to the target model when the correspondent part of the source model has been updated. Retainment rules for model transformations have been investigated in [10], and would be an useful complement to our approach.

3   Running Example

To better describe the incrementality mechanism we introduce a short example transformation, that translates class diagrams into relational schemas. The ATL header of this transformation, *ClassDiagram2Relational*, defines the source and destination metamodels (see Listing 1).

Listing 1. *ClassDiagram* to *Relational* transformation header

```
1 module ClassDiagram2Relational ;
2 create OUT : Relational from IN : ClassDiagram ;
```

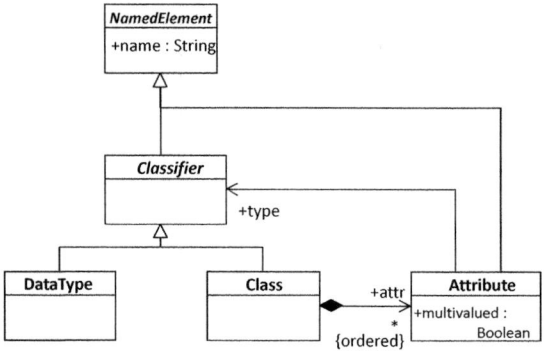

Fig. 1. Source metamodel: *ClassDiagram*

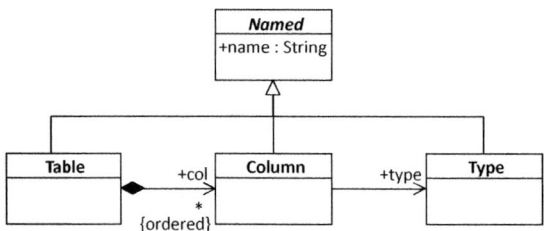

Fig. 2. Target metamodel: *Relational*

The two metamodels are shown in Figure 1 and Figure 2. The *ClassDiagram* metamodel describes a minimal class diagram, including classes, attributes and datatypes. Each *Class* contains an ordered set of *Attributes*, that can be associated to a referenced *Class* or *DataType*. *Attributes* can be *multivalued*, expressing that they are associated with an unbounded number of elements (equivalent to the * (star) multiplicity in UML).

The *Relational* metamodel comprises the basic elements of a relational schema: tables, columns, and types. A *Table* contains an ordered set of *Columns*, each one associated to a specific *Type*.

Our simplified *ClassDiagram2Relational* transformation is composed of three transformation rules. Each ATL rule associates elements in the source model: the *from* part (also called *InputPattern* or source pattern), with the target elements into which they will be translated: the *to* part (also called *OutputPattern* or target pattern). For instance, the *DataType2Type* rule (Listing 2) is responsible for the translation of class diagram datatypes into relational types. Precisely, each *DataType* of the *ClassDiagram* will be translated into a corresponding *Type* of the *Relational* model. A rule also specifies a set of *Bindings*, that assign values to the attributes of the generated elements. In this case, a single binding, at line 8 assigns to the name of the generated type the name of the matched datatype, referenced using variable *s*.

Listing 2. Sample rule: *DataType2Type*

```
3  rule DataType2Type {
4      from
5          s  :  ClassDiagram!DataType
6      to
7          t  :  Relational!Type (
8              name <- s.name
9          )
10 }
```

The *Attribute2Column* rule in Listing 3 transforms class diagram *Attributes* into relational *Columns*. The *InputPattern* in this case specifies also a *filter* (or guard) at line 14, that excludes from this translation every multivalued *Attribute*. For each single-valued attribute the rule creates a new *Column* in the output model, and copies the *Column* name from the matched *Attribute*. Finally, the binding at line 19 specifies how to set the *type* reference of the generated *Column*. To easily specify where to direct a reference, the ATL language allows the developer to point to a generated element by indicating the corresponding source element. In this example, the *type* reference should point to the translation of the class diagram *DataType* of the attribute in the relational world. The binding at line 19: 1) computes *s.type*, i.e. the class diagram *DataType* of matched element *s*, 2) looks for the corresponding relational *Type*, according to some transformation rule, and 3) binds the reference with that *Type*.

Listing 3. Sample rule: *Attribute2Column*

```
11 rule Attribute2Column {
12     from
13         s  :  ClassDiagram!Attribute (
14             not s.multiValued
15         )
16     to
17         t  :  Relational!Column (
18             name <- s.name,
19             type <- s.type
20         )
21 }
```

Listing 4. Sample rule: *Class2Table*

```
22 rule Class2Table {
23     from
24         s  :  ClassDiagram!Class
25     to
26         t  :  Relational!Table (
27             name <- s.name,
28             col <- s.attr->select(e | not e.multiValued)->prepend(key)
29         ),
30         key :  Relational!Column (
31             name <- s.name + 'objectId'
32         )
33 }
```

Finally the *Class2Table* rule in Listing 4 translates every *Class* into a corresponding *Table* with an associated *Column* as key. This rule has to generate two elements and associate them to each other. The binding at line 28 performs this connection by selecting, by means of an OCL expression [11], the set of class attributes that are not multivalued, and prepending to it the key column that has been just generated. Note that, in ATL, all expressions are expressed in OCL, although this is more specifically apparent at line 28 of our example.

After the first execution of the described transformation, incrementality should be usable in order to keep the target model in a synchronized state with the source model, without reexecuting all the rules at each change.

For instance, let us suppose that the name of a class in the class diagram model is changed. Since this name is only used in the binding at line 27, an optimal incremental approach requires only that binding to be reevaluated, and only using the updated class name. The binding execution would update accordingly the name of the table corresponding to the updated class.

As another example, a change in the multivalued attribute of a class diagram *Attribute* would trigger a similar process. In this case, however, the attribute does not only influence a binding (at line 28) but it is also used in a filter (line 14). For instance, a switch from *false* to *true* would invalidate the filter. Since in our examples multivalued attributes are not transformed, the incremental transformation would have to delete an element from the target model, in order to maintain the synchronization. Conversely, a switch from *true* to *false* would trigger a new matching of the *Attribute2Column* rule, with the creation of a new *Column* element.

Finally, moving an attribute from one class A to another class B, would change the evaluation of the binding at line 28. When the *Class2Table* rule matches B, the binding evaluation will count a column more, and the opposite will happen when it matches A. The net effect would be the movement of a column from one table to another. Only the binding at line 28 should be reexecuted: once for class A and once for class B.

4   Approach

In order to implement incrementality in ATL, we rely on two runtime mechanisms:

1. **Tracking dependencies of OCL expressions.** During the evaluation of OCL expressions, we collect dependency information. When a change takes place in the source model, we thus know which OCL expressions are impacted (i.e., may have a new value as a consequence of the change).
2. **Controlling individual rule execution.** The connection between source models and rules happens at the OCL expression level. Therefore, the information gathered in the first mechanism is used in order to control rule execution. In standard execution mode, all rules are matched and applied on whole source models. Instead, we enable precise control over the matching and application of each rule for each source element. Then, we just need to actually trigger the rules in response to changes in the source models.

Our approach could benefit from additional static analysis, but this is kept for future extensions of this work.

This presentation starts by defining (in Section 4.1) the subset of ATL that we consider in the present work. Then, Section 4.2 presents the mechanism that we use to track OCL expression dependencies. Before presenting control over individual rule execution in Section 4.4, we remind the reader about the standard execution algorithm of ATL in Section 4.3.

4.1 Considered ATL Subset

In this work, we consider a subset of ATL, which excludes some advanced constructs for three distinct reasons. The first reason is that some of them cannot be handled satisfactorily. There are three such categories of constructs:

- **Imperative statements**, because the exact impact of a change would be hard to pinpoint. Whole action blocks could be reexecuted, but this is not satisfactory.
- **Metamodel-specific operations**, which may for instance be defined in the Java implementation of a metamodel. This is sometimes done for EMF-based metamodel implementations such as for UML (Unified Modeling Language). The problem with these operations is that there is no easy way to get their dependencies, apart from analysing their Java code, or listening to individual navigation events over the source model (which EMF may not even provide).
- **Queries** are a special kind of ATL program, which correspond to the evaluation of a single OCL expression (possibly invoking helpers) over a set of source model. Because this is not an actual transformation, and cannot be invoked from a transformation, the kind of incrementality we are aiming at is not relevant for this construct.

Then, we also exclude **refining mode** from the considered subset. The reason is that supporting it would require deep changes to our approach. Because refining mode deals with in-place transformations, adding incrementality to it would lead to two main issues: 1) possible non-termination because of loops (e.g., two rules mutually depending on the output of each other), and 2) possible non-confluence. Coupled refining mode and incrementality in ATL would probably need to be handled using similar solutions than those used in graph transformation. These problem do not arise in the standard execution mode of ATL because the source and target models are kept isolated (i.e., no change to source models, and no navigation of target models is allowed). However, this is beyond the scope of this paper.

Finally, there are other constructs, which we do not consider here for the sake of simplicity. They could be handled by extending our approach, but: 1) there are many cases in which they are not strictly necessary[1], and 2) supporting them would only require extending our approach, not changing it. There are eight such constructs, which would need specific support:

---

[1] See the ATL transformation library at:
    http://eclipse.org/m2m/atl/atlTransformations/

- **Helpers** (i.e., user-defined operations or attributes) could either be inlined as part of the compilation process (unless they are recursive), or the OCL expression dependency tracking could be extended to take care of them.
- **Rule inheritance** could be flattened, or directly handled.
- **Lazy rules** could be flattened (not always as ATL code, but systematically in the bytecode), unless there is a recursion.
- **Multiple source elements** would need an extension of the format of the trace information we keep. This format would basically need to be extended in the similar way to what is done for standard execution mode (i.e., using tuples).
- **Rule variables** could be inlined, or explicitly handled (similarly to how helpers could be handled).
- **Reflection** (i.e., refGetValue(), refSetValue(), refImmediateComposite()) would need to report dependency information. This could be achieved by modifying the incremental ATL compiler so that it would identify their calls in a similar way to what is currently done for regular navigation: .refGetValue('name') is equivalent to .name, and could thus be treated similarly. Moreover, because this identification is performed at runtime, the fact that the property name (e.g., *name* in this example) may only be known during the execution of the transformation (e.g., because it is computed by a more complex expression than a String literal) is not an issue.
- **Resolution of specific target elements** instead of the default one. This would require some slight modifications to trace information format.
- **The allInstances() operation**, which make the expression using it dependant on a large part of the source models (i.e., all elements of a given type).

4.2   Tracking OCL Expression Dependencies

The purpose of OCL expression dependencies tracking is to know what expressions are impacted by a given source model change. For instance, if the name of a class changes in our running example, then the only OCL expression that is impacted is the value of the binding at line 27 in Listing 4. Moreover, it only needs to be reevaluated for the specific class on which the change occurred.

In order to achieve this purpose, we must know at any point which property of which model element is used in the evaluation of each OCL expression. Cabot has been confronted to a similar problem [9], but in the case of OCL constraints over UML models. In this context, all expressions are boolean expressions, and each constraint needs to be evaluated for all model elements of a given type. His solution relies on static analysis of the expression, and is able to compute which constraints need to be reevalued upon a given change in the model. For instance, he knows that a given expression depends on a given attribute of a given type. If any model element of that type has a change in the value of that attribute, the constraint need to be reevaluated on that model element.

We are in a slightly different situation than Cabot's. First, we have to handle expressions that return values of any type. Second, and more importantly, most of our expressions (i.e., the ones in the bindings) are connected to a specific context (i.e., a rule). Rules may not match all elements of a given type. Therefore, binding expressions are not impacted by changes to any element of a given type, but only by changes to elements that match a given rule. For instance, the expression at line 19 in Listing 3 is impacted by changes in the type of every *Attribute* that is not multivalued. Multivalued attributes are not relevant in the context of that rule (unless their multiplicity changes, of course).

Instead of relying on static analysis of the expressions, we build dependency information during their evaluation. This is done by means of a hook in navigation expressions evaluation code: in addition to navigating the model, it stores some information about which properties (attributes and references) of which elements (i.e., the source of the expression) have been navigated. Then, information about all navigations in a given expression is aggregated in order to get the full list of dependencies. For every expression, we thus obtain a list of pairs (*model element, property name*). The last step consists in reversing this mapping, and to associate the list of all impacted expressions to every one of these pairs. This is performed by aggregating the information from all expressions. A drawback of this approach is that we need more trace information than Cabot, because our trace information needs to be more detailed (element level instead of type level).

Our approach is not optimal, but rather makes a conservative estimate of which are the impacted OCL expressions. For instance, a given attribute may change its value but the overall value of the expression may not actually change. Therefore, we will sometimes reevaluate expressions that would not actually need to. In the future, we could use Cabot's approach, which is more optimal, for boolean guards. Indeed, these guards apply to every element of a given type, and they are boolean expressions, much like constraints.

4.3   Standard Execution Algorithm

The standard algorithm for the execution of declarative ATL rules (the imperative part is not considered in this work) has been initially published in [1] and it is shown in Listing 5. We provide a brief description here, focusing on elements relevant in the context of this paper. A more detailed description is notably available in [1] The algorithm is structured in two phases. First, a matching phase evaluates the input pattern of each matched rule and detects in the input model the candidate patterns that, according to their types, could match the input pattern. The guard expression (i.e., the filter) of the rule is evaluated on each candidate pattern. Whenever the condition evaluates to *true*, the rule is matched, and the corresponding target elements are instantiated in the target models. Moreover a traceability link is created, that connects the rule, the candidate pattern, and the target elements just instantiated.

In the second phase, the algorithm iterates over the traceability links created at the previous step. For each target element associated with the trace link, the algorithm proceeds with evaluating and setting its bindings. For each binding the following steps are performed: the initialization OCL expression is read from the transformation (line 27), then it is evaluated (line 28), references to other elements are resolved (line 29), and the resulting value is set to the target feature (line 30).

The resolution step at line 29 is particularly interesting when the evaluation step (line 28) returns an element of the source model. In this case ATL looks for a traceability link connected to this source element. Since ATL imposes as a constraint that every source element can be matched at most once, this link, if it exists, is unique. The resolution step returns the corresponding target element (the first one in case of multiple target elements). This target element is finally used to set the binding at line 30.

Listing 5. Original ATL execution algorithm (excluding imperative part)

```
1  -- Match standard matched rules:
2  ForEach standard rule R {
3      ForEach candidate pattern C of R {
4          -- a candidate pattern is a set of elements matching the
5          -- types of the source pattern of a rule
6
7          G := Evaluate the guard of R on C
8          If G is true Then
9              Create target elements in target pattern of R
10             Create TraceLink for R, C, and target elements
11         Else
12             Discard C
13         EndIf
14     }
15 }
16
17 -- Apply standard matched rules:
18 ForEach TraceLink T {
19     R := the rule associated to T
20     C := the matched source pattern of T
21     P := the created target pattern of T
22
23     -- Initialize elements in the target pattern:
24     ForEach target element E of P {
25         -- Initialize each feature of E:
26         ForEach binding B declared for E {
27             expression := Get initialization expression of B
28             value := Evaluate expression in the context of C
29             featureValue := Resolve value
30             Set featureValue to corresponding feature of B
31         }
32     }
33 }
```

4.4 Controlling Individual Rule Execution

Now that the standard execution algorithm of ATL is fresh in our minds, we can have a second look at Listing 5. Our objective is now to identify the parts that are impacted by incrementality, and the parts that are not.

OCL expressions are found at two different places in an ATL transformation[2]:

---

[2] Note that we only mention the elements included in the considered subset of ATL. More generally, in standard ATL, OCL expressions are also found in imperative statements, helpers, and query bodies.

- **In a guard**, an OCL expression evaluates to a boolean value. If this value is *true*, then the enclosing rule is matched, otherwise it is not. A source change that switches the value of a guard from *false* to *true* or from *true* to *false* will impact the matching of a rule.
- **In a binding**, an OCL expression evaluates to any value (i.e., primitive, source element, target element from the same rule). This value is used to initialise a property of a target element. A source change that makes the value of a binding OCL expression will impact the value of the corresponding property of the target element.

Individual matching (i.e., the matching of a single candidate pattern against a single rule) happens between lines 7 and 13. In incremental mode, individual matching is unchanged from what it is in standard mode. However, instead of performing all individual matchings at once, we perform them upon receiving change events. Therefore, we need to be able to execute this part of the algorithm on demand (i.e., not within the two nested loops starting at lines 2 and 3).

Individual rule application happens between lines 24 and 32. When a rule is applied for the first time after a match (or after a rematch[3]), we need to execute this part of the algorithm.

Actual binding application happens between lines 27 and 30. Once an element has been created and initialized, individual properties may change. Therefore, some changes over the source models will trigger reexecution of individual bindings. We also need to be able to perform this operation.

There are three different kinds of source model change event, each having a specific impact on the transformation:

- **Element creation** has an impact over rule matching. If the created element is also added to a specific property (e.g., an *Attribute*) that is created and added to a *Class* separate property change events will be received. Therefore, element creation only impacts rule matching.
- **Element deletion** has an impact over rule matching. Similarly to element creation, related changes in specific property values will trigger property changes.
- **Property change** is sent each time a property of an element is changed. Depending on which OCL expression depends on the specific property for the specific source element, the impact may be on: 1) rule matching if a filter expression depends on it, or 2) a binding if a binding expression depends on it. Actually, several bindings or rules, or both bindings or rules may be impacted by the change of a single property on a single element. This is notably the case for changes of the multivalued property of an attribute in our example (at lines 14, and 28).

As can be seen, we require detailed events (as those generated by EMF): for instance, deletion of an element should be accompanied by property changes

---

[3] A rematch of a rule can happen in incremental mode. For instance: in the initial state of the source model, rule R is matched for element E. Then, the source model changes, and R does not match E any more. Finally, a second change occurs, and R matches element E again (i.e., rematches it).

for property values that refer to this element. If these events are not available from the modeling framework, then we must synthesize them as part of the transformation controller. This is not especially hard, but requires some more trace information. However, this is beyond the scope of this paper.

5   Tool Support

Support for live transformations impacts both the ATL compiler, and the transformation controller. These are respectively presented in Sections 5.1, and 5.2 below. Furthermore, the live execution engine must be integrated with some concrete tools (like model editors) in order to be useful. This is presented in Section 5.3.

5.1   Compiler

The ATL compiler consists of a set of bytecode generation rules. There are notably rules for every element of the model that corresponds to an OCL expression. We can reuse all of these OCL-related rules except for navigation expressions (i.e., expressions of the kind: *someExpression.someProperty*). Navigation expressions have to build dependency information, and we had to implement a new incremental-specific compilation rule for them.

There are also rules for ATL constructs like rules, patterns, and bindings. These rules cannot be reused because their implementation strongly relies on the batch processing (i.e., the nested loops of Listing 5) that is part of the ATL standard execution algorithm. Instead, specific rules have been written in order to support incrementality. For instance, event listeners are created for rules (in case their guard is impacted, or an element gets created or deleted), and bindings (in case their value is impacted, and a target property needs to be set to a new value). These event listeners are simply specific operations created in the bytecode. There are three kinds of event listeners that are generated, that correspond to the three kinds of events described in Section 4.4.

- *sourceType*.elementCreated().
- *sourceType*.elementDeleted().
- *sourceType*.propertyChanged(propertyName : String).

These listeners are created for every source metamodel type appearing in the source pattern of transformation rules.

Specific actions are performed depending on the event on its depending OCL expressions:

- *sourceType*.__applyRule_*ruleName*() For instance in the case of rule DataType2Type of Listing 2, the corresponding operation is: Class Diagram!DataType.__applyRule_DataType2Type(). This action is triggered when an element is created, deleted, or when the guard of a rule is impacted by a property change.

- ***targetType*.set_*ruleName_targetElementName_bindingName*** **(sourceElement : *sourceType*)** For instance, the following operation is generated for binding *name* in Listing 2 at line 8: Relational!Type. set_DataType2Type_t_name(sourceElement : ClassDiagram!DataType). We declare this operation in the context of the target type instead of the source type because each binding is specific to a given target element. This action is triggered when a binding is impacted by a property change.

Another difference between the standard compiler and the incremental compiler is related to context handling. In standard mode, rule context (i.e., variables holding source and target elements) is maintained at rule level. Because bindings are handled within the rule context, nothing specific is required at binding level. However, in incremental mode, a specific binding may need to be reexecuted independtly of its owning rule. Therefore, in the case of live transformations, we need to retrieve the rule context at binding level from the trace information.

5.2 Transformation Controller

The transformation controller is the element responsible for forwarding source model changes to the event listeners generated by the compiler. In this section, we focus on the specific Eclipse implementation of our prototype.

The current implementation listens to events sent by EMF. For this purpose, it registers an *EContentAdapter* on the source *Resources*. Once our adapter is registered, we are notified of every change that occurs on the source models.

Forwarding the events to the transformation is a relatively simple matter. We only have to call the appropriate operation among those generated by the compiler (see Section 5.1). For instance, when EMF notifies us of the deletion of an element of type A, we only need to call operation `A.elementDeleted()` on the deleted element (i.e., the deleted element is passed as the *self* argument to the operation).

In standard mode, the transformation controller only calls the *main* operation. The only specific support required from the ATL VM in order to implement our incremental approach is for calling any operation (i.e., not only *main*). This was already possible in the ATL VM available from *Eclipse.org*.

5.3 Integration to EMF-Based Tools

Integration with editors notably means being able to access the EMF *Resources* that they use to manipulate the models. To this end, we implemented specific actions that currently work with both the EMF default editor, as well as GMF editors. Specific support for any editor is inexpensive to add. For instance, in the case of GMF, the plugin we implemented allows the developer to select two models currently opened in a GMF editor. It is then able to keep them synchronized by monitoring the events on the GMF editor corresponding to the source model.

Any change to the source model (the first selected model) will be propagated to the target model almost instantaneously. Apart from the specific bindings that are triggered by our incremental algorithm upon a given set of change, no other rule is reexecuted. Hence, manual changes on the target model are only overwritten when they conflict with changes on the source model. We do not presently support retainment rules [10], but our prototype could be extended in this direction.

6 Conclusions

This paper has presented a concrete solution for supporting live transformations in the ATL engine. A corresponding prototype has been implemented and described. Moreover, the OCL expression dependencies approach which we extended from Cabot's work [9] may be reused with other transformation languages. However, control flow adaptations are generally dependent on the language.

The three contributions of this work are:

1. **Live transformation support for ATL.** We provide a working solution for ATL, which could only be executed in standard mode up to now.
2. **A corresponding prototype.** In addition to designing a solution, we have implemented it, and started experimenting with it. Our prototype[4] is implemented on Eclipse, and more specifically relies on the Eclipse Modeling Framework [12] (EMF). It is notably able to transform models that are being edited in GMF-based editors.
3. **Element-level OCL expression dependencies** as an improvement to previous works [9] that is especially useful in the case of live transformations. This may notably be applied to other OCL execution problems, including for the purpose of implementing live transformation support in other languages.

Some possible extensions of the work presented here include:

- **More optimal dependencies estimate** using a more detailed trace, or by reusing more advanced features of Cabot's approach [9] (e.g., OCL expression rewriting).
- **Support for retainment rules** [10] would increase the numbers of scenarios in which the solution presented here is applicable. There do not seem to be any specific technical issue preventing this.
- **Exploring live transformation chaining** by applying a second live transformation to the output of a first one. Thus, both transformations execute in parallel in order to propagate changes from a source model to a target model (possibly via possibly several intermediate steps in more complex scenarios). This is especially useful because many complex transformations are split into several steps.

---

[4] We currently plan to publish this prototype on *Eclipse.org* as part of the ATL Research initiative. It should become available from
http://www.eclipse.org/m2m/atl/ shortly (i.e., in the coming weeks).

The performance issues (especially about the size of trace information) need to be more closely studied. Use of a weaving model [13] to persist trace information could also be useful. This information is currently only kept in memory.

Acknowledgements

The present work has been partially supported by the EDONA project.

References

1. Jouault, F., Kurtev, I.: Transforming models with atl. In: Bruel, J.-M. (ed.) MoDELS 2005. LNCS, vol. 3844, pp. 128–138. Springer, Heidelberg (2006)
2. Jouault, F., Allilaire, F., Bézivin, J., Kurtev, I.: Atl: a model transformation tool. Science of Computer Programming, Special Issue on Second issue of experimental software and toolkits (EST) 72(3), 31–39 (2008)
3. Gronback, R.C.: Eclipse Modeling Project: A Domain-Specific Language (DSL) Toolkit. Addison-Wesley Professional, Reading (2009)
4. Xiong, Y., Liu, D., Hu, Z., Zhao, H., Takeichi, M., Mei, H.: Towards automatic model synchronization from model transformations. In: Proc. of ASE 2007, p. 164 (2007)
5. Hearnden, D., Lawley, M., Raymond, K.: Incremental model transformation for the evolution of model-driven systems. In: Nierstrasz, O., Whittle, J., Harel, D., Reggio, G. (eds.) MoDELS 2006. LNCS, vol. 4199, pp. 321–335. Springer, Heidelberg (2006)
6. Bergmann, G., Ráth, I., Varró, D.: Parallelization of graph transformation based on incremental pattern matching. Electronic Communications of EASST 18 (2009)
7. Ráth, I., Bergmann, G., Ökrös, A., Varró, D.: Live model transformations driven by incremental pattern matching. In: Vallecillo, A., Gray, J., Pierantonio, A. (eds.) ICMT 2008. LNCS, vol. 5063, pp. 107–121. Springer, Heidelberg (2008)
8. Giese, H., Wagner, R.: From model transformation to incremental bidirectional model synchronization. Software & Systems Modeling 8(1), 21–43 (2008)
9. Cabot, J., Teniente, E.: Incremental evaluation of OCL constraints. In: Dubois, E., Pohl, K. (eds.) CAiSE 2006. LNCS, vol. 4001, p. 81. Springer, Heidelberg (2006)
10. Goldschmidt, T., Uhl, A.: Retainment Rules for Model Transformations. In: 1st International Workshop on Model Co-Evolution and Consistency Management at Models (2008)
11. OMG: 2.0 OCL specification. Adopted Specification, ptc/03-10-14 (2003)
12. Budinsky, F., Brodsky, S.A., Merks, E.: Eclipse Modeling Framework. Pearson Education, London (2003)
13. Valduriez, P., Didonet Del Fabro, M.: Towards the efficient development of model transformations using model weaving and matching transformations. Software and Systems Modeling 8(3), 305–324 (2009)

Constructing and Navigating
Non-invasive Model Decorations

Dimitrios S. Kolovos[1], Louis M. Rose[1], Nikolaos Drivalos Matragkas[1,2],
Richard F. Paige[1], Fiona A.C. Polack[1], and Kiran J. Fernandes[2]

[1] Department of Computer Science, University of York
{dkolovos,louis,nikos,paige,fiona}@cs.york.ac.uk
[2] The York Management School, University of York
kf501@york.ac.uk

Abstract. Model-Driven Engineering tasks, such as simulation or transformation, often cannot be carried out directly on the models at hand; models often need to be *decorated* with additional information, and this information is in some cases not accounted for by existing metamodels. Moreover, engineers often need to experiment with alternative and complementary types of model decorations, particularly when carrying out more exploratory styles of development. Heavyweight approaches to decoration are not convenient in such situations. In this paper we demonstrate the limitations of existing model decoration mechanisms and tools, and present a novel approach that enables engineers to capture decoration information in the form of separate interchangeable models. The approach allows engineers to transparently and programmatically navigate decorations as if they were embedded in the decorated model.

1 Introduction

When engineers design a modelling language, they try to anticipate scenarios of use, and thereby equip the language with necessary constructs, properties and relationships. In practice, languages often need to be used outside of the scope for which they were originally designed. For example, UML activity diagrams can be used beyond their original scope of specifying the activities and control flows of a process, to actually *simulate* the process. Similarly, object-oriented models such as UML class models or Ecore metamodels are often used as input for generating artefacts such as user interfaces or database schemas/queries.

In such cases, engineers often need to be able to capture additional information related to usage-specific properties. For example, to be able to simulate a UML activity model, engineers need to be able to annotate model elements with appropriate information (e.g. delays for activities and probabilities in control flows). Similarly, object-oriented models need to be decorated with UI or database-specific information so that they can be used to generate fully-functional user interfaces and complete database schemas and queries.

In this paper we provide an overview of the existing approaches to decorating models with information needed for specific tasks, and discuss their advantages and shortcomings. We then introduce a novel approach for capturing additional information in the

L. Tratt and M. Gogolla (Eds.): ICMT 2010, LNCS 6142, pp. 138–152, 2010.

form of separate *decorator* models, and demonstrate how those decorator models can be constructed within the very same editors that support the decorated languages. We also show how they can then be seamlessly navigated in model management operations such as model validation, transformation and code generation, using languages of the Epsilon model management platform.

The remainder of the paper is organized as follows. Section 2 provides an overview of existing approaches to model decoration and discusses their advantages and short-comings. Then, section 3 distils the findings of this review and presents the main open problems in the establishment and programmatic navigation of decorator models. Section 4 outlines a technique for specifying decorator models within the graphical editors that support the decorated languages and section 5 demonstrates how decorator models can be seamlessly navigated programmatically in languages provided by the Epsilon platform. Finally, section 6 provides a case study that outlines the application of this approach for refactoring an existing tool, and section 7 concludes the paper.

2 Existing Approaches to Model Decoration

In this section we provide an overview of existing approaches to decorating models with additional information which is not explicitly accommodated for by their respective metamodels, and discuss the advantages and shortcomings of each approach.

2.1 Metamodel Adaptation

In this approach, when a requirement for capturing additional information is identified, the metamodel is adapted accordingly to include direct support for accommodating this information. This may involve adding new task-specific properties to existing meta-classes or even also adding new meta-classes, depending on the extent and the nature of the additional information that needs to be captured.

The main advantage of this approach is that it is straightforward to implement and does not require additional tool support. However, it also demonstrates significant short-comings. Firstly, this approach does not apply to cases where engineers do not have control over the metamodel (e.g., in case a standard metamodel - such as UML2 - is used). Moreover, even if engineers have control over the metamodel, extending the metamodel with support for capturing information related to different tasks can quickly lead to metamodel-, and effectively model *pollution* [1] and as such has significant shortcomings. Also, in this case modellers embed the additional information inside the models and this reduces their flexibility to experiment with different sets of decorations. Finally, model evolution can cause inconsistency with existing instance models when, for example, a mandatory feature (one whose lower bound is non-zero) is introduced to capture additional information. While there are several approaches for managing and reconciling model and metamodel inconsistency [2,3,4,5], none of these is cost-free.

2.2 Metamodel Extensibility Mechanisms

This is a proactive approach in which the metamodel engineers recognize that in the future users may need to attach additional information to model elements - which cannot be predicted at the time of designing the metamodel. Therefore, they design the meta-model in such a way so that it provides built-in support for attaching arbitrary key-value pairs of information to any element of the model. This approach was followed in UML 1.x where *stereotypes* holding an arbitrary number of *tagged values* could be attached to any element (the *profiles* mechanism of UML 2.x is technically more elaborated but essentially builds on a very similar principle). Similarly Ecore (the metamodelling language of EMF[6]) allows users to attach *annotations* on any element of a metamodel to capture additional information. While this approach addresses most of the problems demonstrated by the metamodel adaptation approach, decoration information relating to different aspects/tasks still needs to be hard-coded in the same model, effectively leading to model pollution.

2.3   Model Weaving

In the *model weaving* approach [7], decorations are stored externally to the decorated model; in separate models that conform to a separate metamodel. This approach enables users to keep core models disentangled from task-specific decorations and can be applied to any language as it is not an invasive technique. The main disadvantage of this approach is that weaving models are counter-intuitive to construct with the currently available tools (e.g. Modelink[1], AMW[2]), and cumbersome to navigate in model management programs. For example, consider the simple weaving metamodel presented in Figure 1, models of which can capture decoration information relevant to performance simulation for UML activity models.

The *ExecutableNodePerformance* class can be used to add a *delay* decoration to an instance of the *ExecutableNode* class (from the UML metamodel). The delay indicates the time the node takes to execute. The instance to which the *delay* value is added is stored in the *node* feature of *ExecutableNodePerformance*. Similarly, *DecisionNode-Cost* and *ControlFlowProbability* can be used to add a *cost* to a *DecsionNode* and a *probability* to a *ControlFlow*, respectively. The *probability* decoration of a control flow represents the probability with which this control flow will be selected during simulation when a choice needs to be made over alternative possible control flows. Finally, the *cost* of a decision node represents the cost of the infrastructure that determines the probabilities of its outgoing control flows. This is further elaborated in Section 4.1 on a concrete example.

To construct a decorator model that conforms to the decorator metamodel, and in order to weave it with the decorated elements in a UML model, developers need to use one of the *tree-based* model weaving tools that are currently available. While several tools are currently available for this task, using different tools to specify the core model and its decorations is counter-intuitive. Figure 2 demonstrates using the tree-based Modelink tool to construct a decoration model that conforms to the metamodel of Figure 1 and weave it with the decorated UML model.

In terms of programmatic navigation, since references from the decorator model to the UML model are unidirectional, finding the *delay* of an *ExecutableNode* in the UML

---

[1] http://www.eclipse.org/gmt/epsilon/doc/modelink
[2] http://www.eclipse.org/gmt/amw

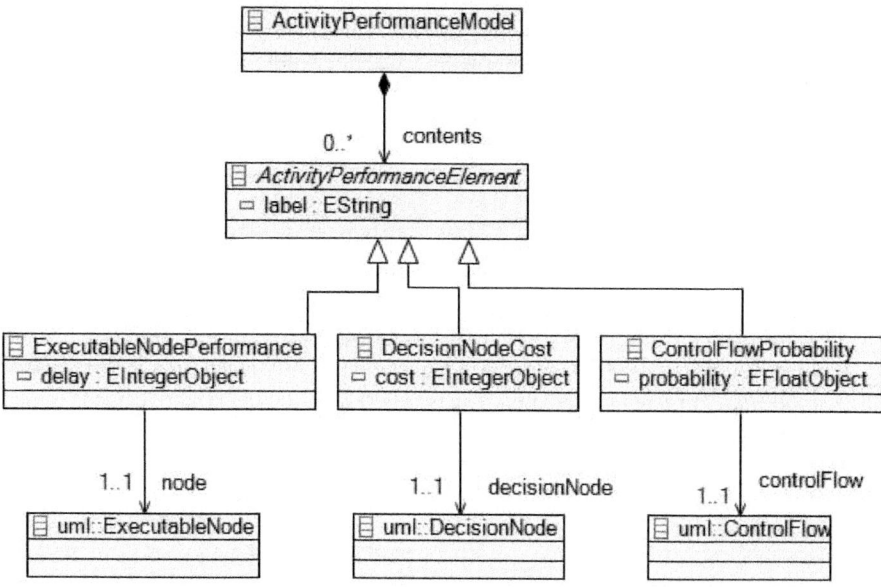

Fig. 1. Weaving metamodel for decorating UML activity models

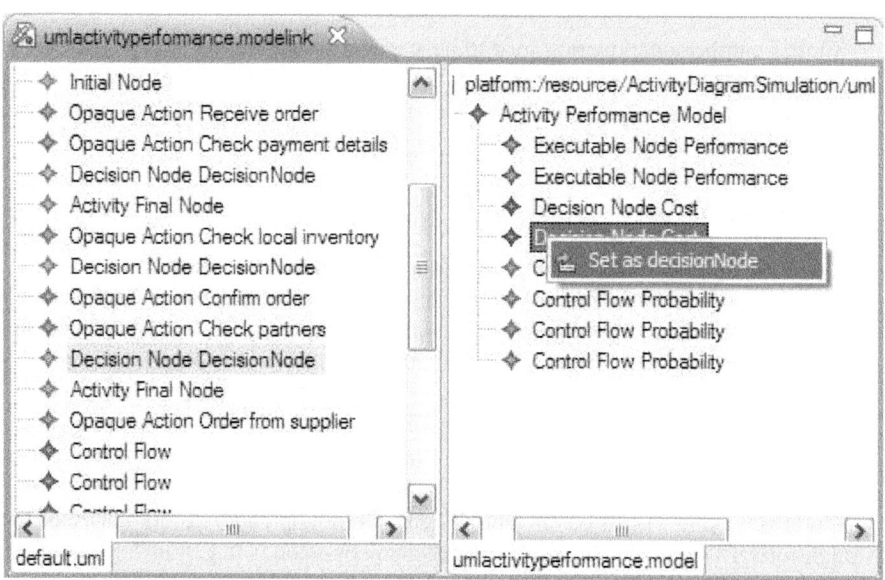

Fig. 2. Constructing a weaving model that conforms to the metamodel of Figure 1 with the tree-based Modelink tool

model requires developers to write code that iterates through all the instances of *ExecutableNodePerformance*, finds the one that references the *ExecutableNode* in question and returns its *delay* value. For example, in EOL one would need to express this using the following statement, where *self* is a variable that refers to the *ExecutableNode* in question.

Listing 1. Finding the delay of an ExecutableNode

```
var delay = ActivityPerformance!ExecutableNodePerformance.allInstances().
  selectOne(enp|enp.node = self).delay;
```

Moreover, since some *ExecutableNodes* may not have corresponding *ExecutableNodePerformance* decorators, the call to *selectOne* may return a null value. Consequently, developers need to be more defensive and actually check that a corresponding *ExecuableNodePerformance* element exists. Therefore, the query above needs to be reworked as follows.

Listing 2. Finding the delay of an ExecutableNode

```
var delay = 0;
var executableNodePerformance : ActivityPerformance!ExecutableNodePerformance;
executableNodePerformance = ActivityPerformance!ExecutableNodePerformance.
  allInstances().selectOne(enp|enp.node = self);
if (executableNodePerformance.isDefined()) {
  delay = executableNodePerformance.delay;
}
```

Similar cumbersome queries need to be specified manually for every type of decoration provided by the decorator metamodel. As well as being cumbersome, iterating through all elements every time the value of a decoration needs to be retrieved can lead to performance problems, particularly for large models.

3   Motivation

Through the review of existing approaches we have identified two desirable characteristics for a model decoration approach. First, as demonstrated in the model weaving approach, a model decoration approach should be *non-invasive*; decorations should be stored externally to the decorated model so that they can be interchangeable, and do not pollute it.

However, like in the metamodel adaptation approach, decorations should be easy to specify within the same editors (graphical or textual) that support the decorated language in order for the approach to be acceptable to practitioners.

Moreover, again like in the metamodel adaptation approach, decorations should be straightforward to navigate in model management operations (e.g. transformation, validation) and not require developers to write lookup code to locate and access. For example, in terms of the UML2 activity performance decoration example illustrated in the previous section, performance decoration information for executable nodes and control flows should be kept in a separate model but users should still be able to retrieve the *delay* of an ExecutableNode (*exNode*) using a syntax as simple as *exNode.delay* in a model-to-model transformation or in validation constraints.

4 Decoration Extraction and Injection

To provide a more usable and scalable alternative to the use of tree-based weaving tools for model decoration, we now demonstrate how in-place model transformation can be used to enable users to construct, inspect and modify decorator models within the same graphical editors that support the decorated models. More specifically we propose two operations: *decorator extraction* in which a decorator model is extracted from a model and its corresponding diagram and *decoration injection* in which a decorator model is injected on the diagram of the model it decorates.

4.1 Decorator Extraction

In this operation, a decorator model is extracted from a model and its supporting diagram. This approach exploits generic annotation mechanisms provided by the diagram notation (e.g. the Notes mechanism provided by all GMF-based editors). In our example, we have used GMF notes to specify the annotation values in the GMF-based UML2 activity diagram editor for our UML2 model as demonstrated in Figure 3[3].

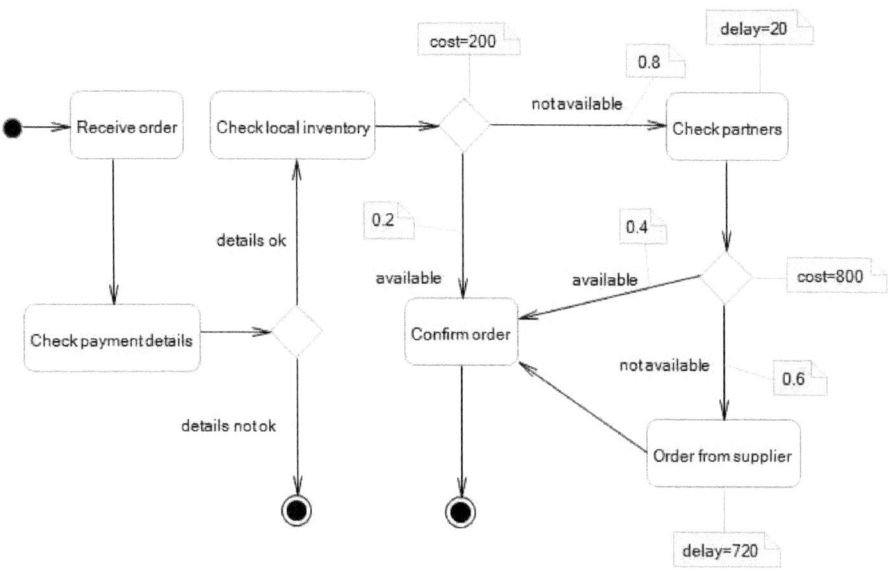

Fig. 3. Annotated UML activity diagram

---

[3] On the semantics of *cost* decoration of decision nodes, in this example by choosing to allocate limited storage space that costs 200 units, the probability of not having a particular item in stock is rather high (0.8). A solution that would allow for more storage space would decrease this probability, but at a higher cost. The values of cost/probability used in this example are ad-hoc; in a real context they are estimated by domain experts.

Listing 3. An excerpt of the decoration extraction transformation in EOL

```
1   var activityPerformanceModel = new Decorator!ActivityPerformanceModel;
2
3   for (executableNode in Model!ExecutableNode.all) {
4     var decorations = executableNode.getNoteDecorations();
5     if (not decorations.isEmpty()) {
6       var executableNodePerformance =
7         new Decorator!ExecutableNodePerformance;
8       executableNodePerformance.node = executableNode;
9       var delay = decorations.get('delay');
10      if (delay.isDefined()) {
11        executableNodePerformance.delay = delay.asInteger();
12      }
13      activityPerformanceModel.contents.add(executableNodePerformance);
14    }
15  }
16
17  // Similarly for instances of ControlFlow and DecisionNode (omitted)
18
19  operation Any getNotes() {
20    var incoming = Diagram!Edge.all.select
21      (e|e.target.element = self and e.source.isNote());
22    var outgoing = Diagram!Edge.all.select
23      (e|e.target.isNote() and e.source.element = self);
24    return incoming.collect(e|e.source) + outgoing.collect(e|e.target);
25  }
26
27  operation Diagram!Node getNoteText() : String {
28    var shapeStyle = self.styles.selectOne
29      (s|s.isTypeOf(Diagram!ShapeStyle));
30    if (shapeStyle.isDefined()) {return shapeStyle.description;}
31    else {
32      return '';
33    }
34  }
35
36  operation Any getNoteDecorations() : Map {
37    var map : Map;
38    for (note in self.getNotes()) {
39      var text = note.getNoteText();
40
41      var lines = text.split('\n');
42
43      for (line in lines) {
44        var parts = line.split('=');
45        if (parts.size() = 2) {
46          map.put(parts.at(0).trim(), parts.at(1).trim());
47        }
48      }
49    }
50    return map;
51  }
52
53  operation Diagram!View isNote() {
54    return self.isTypeOf(Diagram!Node) and self.type = 'Note';
55  }
```

We have implemented a model-to-model transformation, using the Epsilon Object Language [8][4], that identifies the element to which each note is attached, parses the contents of the notes, constructs the respective elements in the decorator model, and populates their values. An excerpt of this transformation is demonstrated in Listing 3.

This approach addresses the main shortcomings of tree-based weaving tools; It is far more usable to specify annotations within a familiar graphical editor instead of a non-intuitive tree-based editor and also this approach scales to the same extent with the graphical editor itself.

4.2 Decorator Injection

This operation is the reverse of the decorator extraction operation discussed above. In this operation, an in-place transformation is used to inject information in the decorator model on a *clean* diagram. Depending on the case-specific requirements and on whether multiple decorators can be projected on the same diagram concurrently, *cleaning* the diagram from existing annotations can be performed either within the injection transformation, or in a separate step.

When the extraction and injection operations have been implemented, end users can decorate the diagram with additional information in a usable manner and then use the extract operation to store decorations in the form of a separate decorator model. Then, when they need to inspect or modify the decoration information, they can invoke the decorator injection operation to reconstruct an annotated version of the diagram.

Regarding our example, we have implemented a injection transformation that reversely to the transformation of Listing 3, injects a decorator model on the diagram by creating notes attached to the decorated elements. The specification of the transformation is not provided in this paper for brevity purposes.

4.3 Remarks

Decorator extraction and injection transformations vary significantly according to the decorated modelling language, the structure of the decorator metamodel and the diagram annotation features provided by the graphical editor that supports the decorated language. In any case however, to implement this approach the following requirements need to be satisfied: the diagram needs to be a model itself so that it can be queried/modified by the model transformation language, the model transformation language of choice should support in-place transformation to avoid expensive copy transformations, and be able to access more than two models - all of different metamodels - (model, diagram and decorator) concurrently.

5   Seamless Decoration Navigation in Epsilon

In the previous section we demonstrated an approach for constructing, inspecting and modifying non-invasive decorator models in a usable and scalable manner. While we

---

[4] In principle any other model transformation language that satisfies the requirements set in Section 4.3 could have been used instead.

used EOL to implement the extraction and injection transformations, as stressed in Section 4.1, there is nothing specific to it about EOL or Epsilon and it can be realized with any appropriate model transformation language. By contrast, in this section we present a technical solution for achieving seamless navigation of non-invasive decorator models – as envisioned in Section 3 – in languages of the Epsilon [9] platform.

This section provides a brief overview of Epsilon and a more detailed discussion of its underlying model connectivity layer before introducing the core contribution in Section 5.4.

5.1 A Brief Overview of Epsilon

Epsilon [9] is a family of integrated languages for model management and a component of the Eclipse GMT research project. The core of Epsilon is an OCL-based model navigation and modification language (EOL). Atop EOL several task-specific languages have been designed and implemented, each tailored to a task such as model transformation, validation, comparison, merging, code generation and in-place model transformation. The main characteristic of Epsilon is that, by building atop EOL, all languages of the platform are consistent and interoperable with each other. As such, code can be reused across programs written in different Epsilon languages, and different programs can be tightly integrated to form complex workflows.

5.2 The Epsilon Model Connectivity (EMC) Layer

Another important characteristic of Epsilon is the ability of its languages to manage (e.g. transform, validate) models of diverse modelling technologies. This is achieved through a model connectivity layer (EMC) that provides a generic interface for loading, storing, querying and updating models, and support for pluggable drivers that implement the generic interface for diverse modelling technologies such as EMF [6] and MDR. This rationale behind EMC is very similar to that of the database connectivity layers provided by many contemporary languages and frameworks to abstract away from the implementation differences of relational databases. The following sections provide a detailed insight into the operation of EMC and demonstrates how it is used to support seamless navigation of non-invasive model decorations, as envisioned in Section 3.

5.3 Getting and Setting Values of Model Element Properties in EMC

At runtime all Epsilon programs (e.g. validation constraints, M2M and M2T transformations, in-place transformations) are associated with a runtime context. The context contains a model repository which, as shown in Figure 4, contains a collection of named models that implement the *IModel* interface, and which are available to the program at runtime for querying and modification.

Of particular interest is the *knowsAboutProperty(Object instance, String property)* method of *IModel* which returns *true* if the model can get/set the value of the property of a specific instance. If a model responds positively to this method call, it must also provide an instance of *IPropertyGetter/Setter* to which this task can be delegated.

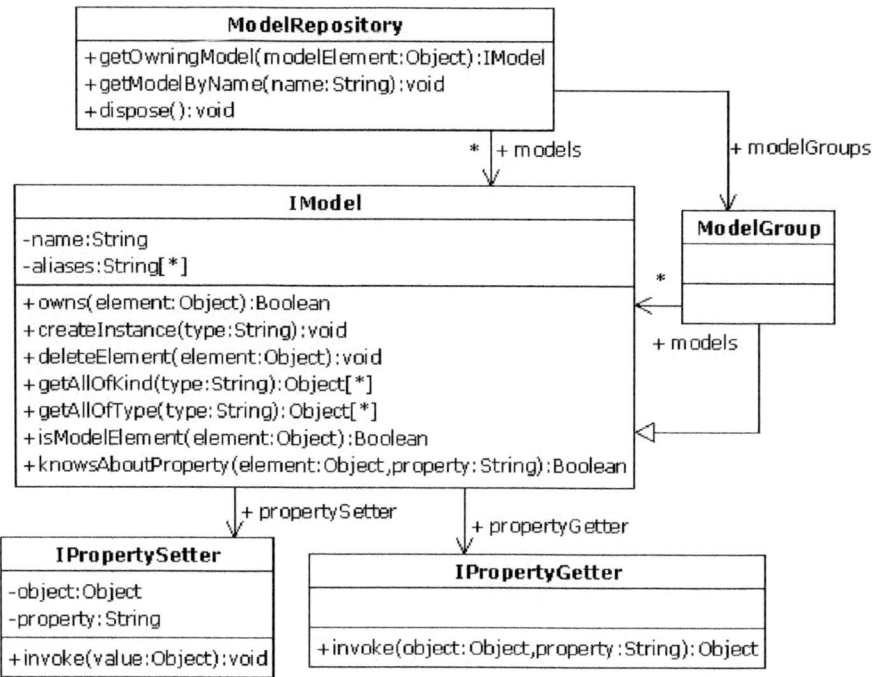

Fig. 4. Simplified view of the Model Connectivity layer of Epsilon

Therefore, when the runtime needs to access the value of a property *p* of an object *o*, it iterates over all models in the model repository, calling *knowsAboutProperty(o, p)* for each model. If a model responds positively, the runtime then retrieves and invokes the respective *IPropertyGetter/Setter* for that combination of object *o* and property *p*.

This lightweight approach to getting/setting property values delivers a number of benefits. In terms of memory usage, it avoids using wrappers around native model elements (*EObjects* in EMF, *RefObjects* in MDR, etc) thus keeping the memory footprint low. In terms of flexibility, elements of the same native type (e.g. *EObject*) can be treated in very different ways according to the model in which they are contained. This has been demonstrated in [10] where an implementation of *IModel* is used to enable accessing M0-level *models* in EMF.

EmfModel is an implementation of *IModel* that can handle EMF models. *EmfModel.knowsAboutProperty(Object instance, String property)* returns true if all of the following are satisfied:

- *instance* is an EMF model element (i.e. *instance* is an *EObject*).
- *instance* belongs to the EMF model that underpins this instance of *EmfModel* (i.e *instance* is a member of *getAllContents()* collection of the underlying EMF *Resource*).
- the metaclass of *instance* (*instance.eClass()*) has a structural feature with name equal to *property*.

Recall our example from Section 2. A *Performance* metamodel was used to decorate a *UML* model. In particular, the *Performance* metamodel contained a class called *ExecutableNodePerformance*, used to decorate instances of the *UML* class, *ExecutableNode* with a *delay* attribute. We wish to access the *delay* of an *ExecutableNode*, *exNode*, using the EOL expression *exNode.delay*.

Suppose now the implementation of *EmfModel*, described above, is used to manipulate the *UML* model. To execute the EOL expression, the *knowsAboutProperty(Object instance, String property)* method of *EmfModel* would be called with arguments, *exNode* and *'delay'*. Because the *ExexutableNode* metaclass in the UML2 metamodel does not have a feature called *delay*, the method returns *false*.

Consequently, the model connectivity layer continues to seek a model that knows about the property in question, inspecting the next model in the context, an instance of *EmfModel* that represents our *Performance* model. Again, *knowsAboutProperty(Object instance, String property)* returns false, this time because *exNode* does not belong to the *Performance* model.

5.4   Specifying and Navigating Decorations

To achieve the proposed concise syntax (*exNode.delay*) we have implemented a specialization of *EmfModel*, called *EmfDecoratorModel*. The metamodel of an *EmfDecoratorModel* can use the *decorator* and *decorator.hook* annotations for *EClasses* and *EReferences* respectively, to denote that particular *EClasses* and *EReferences* should be treated as decorators and hooks respectively.

Figure 5 demonstrates the annotated version of the *UMLActivityPerformance* metamodel[5] originally displayed in Figure 1. In this annotated version *ExecutableNodePerformance* and *ControlFlowProbability* have been annotated with the *decorator* annotation while *executableNode* and *controlFlow* have been annotated with the *decorator.hook* annotation.

The implementation of *EmfDecoratorModel* overrides the behaviour of *knowsAboutProperty(Object instance, String property)*, making use of the decorator and hook annotations described above. In *EmfDecoratorModel* the *knowsAboutProperty(Object instance, String property)* method returns true if:

- *instance* is an EMF model element (i.e. *instance* is an *EObject*).
- *instance* belongs to the EMF model being manipulated by this instance of *EmfModel* (i.e *instance* is a member of *getAllContents()* collection of the underlying EMF *Resource*).
- **or** there exists an *EClass* in the metamodel that is annotated as bridge, and which has the following properties
    - it contains an *EReference* annotated as *decorator.hook* and its type is compatible with the *EClass* of *instance*
    - it has an *EStructuralFeature* with name equal to *property*

---

[5] In this diagram, annotations are visualised as notes. This has been necessary to present a readable diagram as the current version of the Ecore graphical editor does not show annotations on EReferences on the diagram.

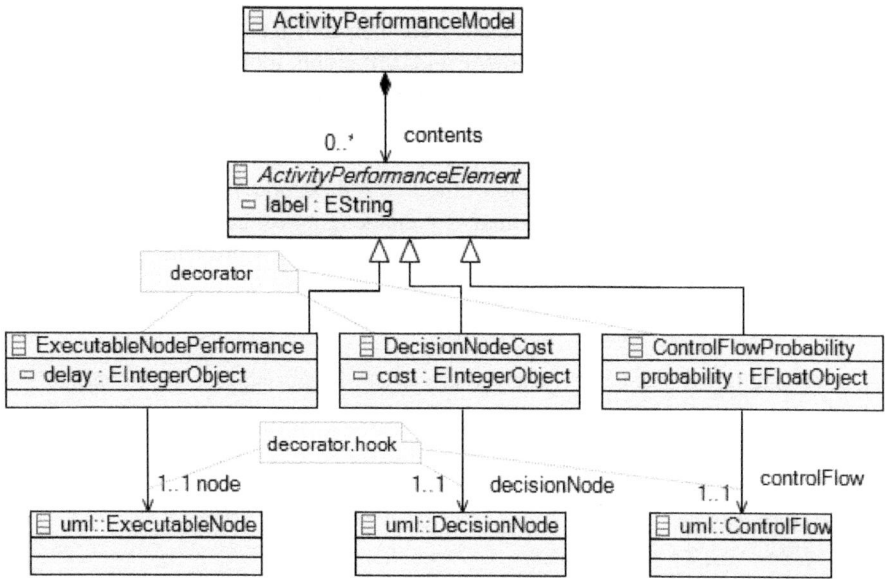

Fig. 5. The metamodel of Figure 5 annotated with decorator and decorator.hook annotations

Therefore, when the EOL expression, *exNode.delay* (where *exNode* is an instance of the *UML* class, *ExecutableNode*), is now evaluated, the runtime first calls *knowsAbout-Property(exNode, 'delay')* on the *UML* model and – for the reasons discussed earlier – it responds negatively.

However, when *knowsAboutProperty(exNode, 'delay')* is called on the *Performance* model, it inspects the *UmlActivityPerformance* EPackage and discovers that the *ExecutableNodePerformance* EClass is annotated as *decorator* and also contains a *decorator.hook* EReference (*executableNode*) typed as *uml.ExecutableNode*, as well as an attribute that matches the required name (*delay*) and therefore it responds positively. An instance of PropertyGetter (PropertySetter) can then be retrieved and used to read (write) the *node.delay* value.

By using the *EmfDecoratorModel* driver for EMC, decorating values can be accessed in EOL using convenient and familiar notation of the form *object.value*. It is worth mentioning again that due to the hierarchical organization of languages in Epsilon, discussed in section 5.1, *EmfDecoratorModel* can be used automatically by all of the other Epsilon languages without additional effort. Therefore, it can be used in model management tasks such as model validation, transformation and text generation without any additional effort.

6   Case Study

In this section we illustrate how we applied the proposed approach for re-engineering EuGENia. EuGENia [11] is a tool that simplifies the development of GMF-based graphical editors by allowing developers to decorate Ecore metamodels with graphical syntax information. Annotated metamodels are then comsumed by a model transformation to automatically generate the low-level GMF graph, tooling and mapping models which GMF needs in order to generate the editor code. In the version of EuGENia that is currently publicly available, decorations are stored within the Ecore model itself in the form of annotations (*EAnnotation*). As discussed in section [11] this approach enhances usability but on the other hand pollutes the Ecore metamodels and entangles abstract syntax with graphical syntax. This makes it challenging for developers to experiment with different graphical syntaxes for a metamodel. Listing 4 presents an example of a minimal annotated Ecore metamodel.

Listing 4. Exemplar Ecore metamodel annotated with graphical syntax information

```
1  package graph;
2
3  @gmf.diagram
4  class Graph {
5    val Node[*] nodes;
6    val Edge[*] edges;
7  }
8
9  @gmf.node(label="name")
10 class Node {
11   attr String name;
12 }
13
14 @gmf.link(source="source", target="target", label="label")
15 class Edge {
16   attr String label;
17   ref Node source;
18   ref Node target;
19 }
```

To overcome these issues we are in the process of refactoring EuGENia according to the approach illustrated in this paper. More specifically, we have defined a dedicated meta-model for capturing information related to graphical syntax, a small excerpt of which is displayed in Figure 6. In addition, we have defined two transformations: an extraction transformation that takes an annotated Ecore metamodel as input, cleans it up from annotations and produces a graphical syntax model, and an injection transformation that merges a graphical syntax model with a clean Ecore metamodel. Therefore, developers can still specify graphical syntax information in the form of embedded annotations (for usability reasons) but when done, this information can be extracted in a separate model (and when needed again it can be re-injected) automatically.

Adopting this approach has also simplified the transformation that produces the low-level GMF models from the Ecore metamodel and the decorator graphical syntax model as it has eliminated all reverse lookups and defensive code, as explained in section 5, resulting to code that is more concise, and easier to understand and maintain.

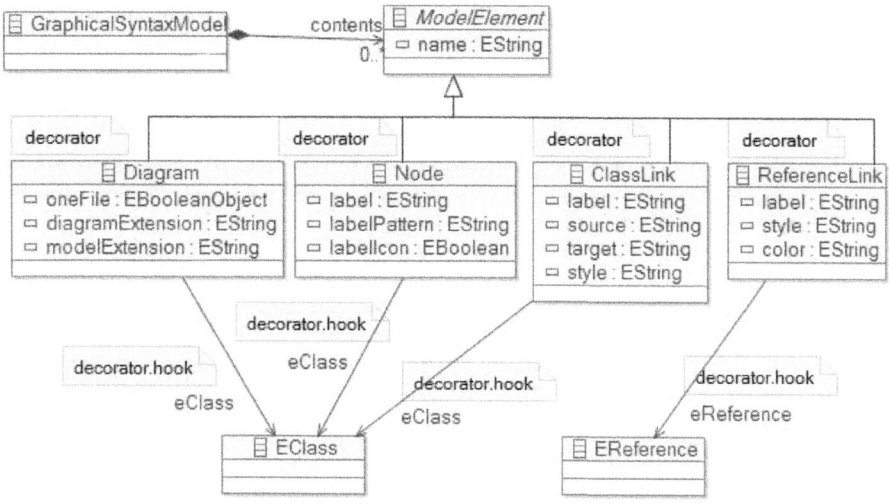

Fig. 6. A small exceprt of the Graphical Syntax Metamodel

7 Conclusions and Further Work

We have presented a non-invasive approach for decorating EMF models in Epsilon that achieves separation of the decoration information from the decorated models while still preserving the same degree of usability in the construction and programmatical navigation offered by invasive approaches such as metamodel evolution. This approach is particularly useful when developers do not have control over the metamodel they wish to extend, when they need to capture multiple alternative decorations for the same model, and/or to prevent model pollution. On the other hand adopting this approach introduces the additional overhead of needing to specify the injection and extraction transformations, which may not pay-off in cases of developer-controlled metamodels which require only minor extensions; in such cases direct metamodel adaptation may be deemed as more appropriate.

An area for further development and enhancement is the performance of the lookup algorithm discussed in Section 5. To this end, we are working on integrating the implementation of the *EmfDecoratorModel* driver with Concordance[6], a framework that monitors the Eclipse workspace and captures cross-model references in EMF models and stores them in an scalable and fast-to-query index. It is anticipated that integration with Concordance will significantly speed up the lookup process.

References

1. Kolovos, D.S., Paige, R.F., Polack, F.A.C.: On-Demand Merging of Traceability Links with Models. In: Proc. 2nd EC-MDA Workshop on Traceability, Bilbao, Spain (July 2006)
2. Sprinkle, J.: Metamodel Driven Model Migration. PhD thesis, Vanderbilt University, TN, USA (2003)

---

[6] http://www.eclipse.org/gmt/epsilon/doc/concordance/

3. Wachsmuth, G.: Metamodel adaptation and model co-adaptation. In: Ernst, E. (ed.) ECOOP 2007. LNCS, vol. 4609, pp. 600–624. Springer, Heidelberg (2007)
4. Cicchetti, A., Di Ruscio, D., Eramo, R., Pierantonio, A.: Automating co-evolution in Model-Driven Engineering. In: Proc. International Enterprise Distributed Object Computing Conference, IEEE Computer Society, Los Alamitos (2008)
5. Herrmannsdoerfer, M., Benz, S., Juergens, E.: COPE: A language for the coupled evolution of metamodels and models. In: Proc. Workshop on Model Co-Evolution and Consistency Management (2008)
6. Steinberg, D., Budinsky, F., Paternostro, M., Merks, E.: EMF: Eclipse Modelling Framework, Eclipse Series, 2nd edn. Addison-Wesley Professional, Reading (2008)
7. Del Fabro, M.D., Bezivin, J., Jouault, F., Breton, E., Gueltas, G.: AMW: A Generic Model Weaver. In: Proceedings of IDM 2005 (2005)
8. Kolovos, D.S., Paige, R.F., Polack, F.A.C.: The Epsilon Object Language. In: Rensink, A., Warmer, J. (eds.) ECMDA-FA 2006. LNCS, vol. 4066, pp. 128–142. Springer, Heidelberg (2006)
9. Extensible Platform for Specification of Integrated Languages for mOdel maNagement (Epsilon), http://www.eclipse.org/gmt/epsilon
10. Kolovos, D.S., Paige, R.F., Polack, F.A.C.: Aligning OCL with Domain-Specific Languages to Support Intance-Level Model Queries. Electronic Communications of the EASST (2007)
11. Kolovos, D.S., Rose, L.M., Paige, R.F., Polack, F.A.C.: Raising the Level of Abstraction in the Development of GMF-based Graphical Model Editors. In: Proc. 3rd Workshop on Modeling in Software Engineering (MISE), ACM/IEEE International Conference on Software Engineering (ICSE), Vancouver, Canada (May 2009)

Model-to-Model Transformations
By Demonstration*

Philip Langer[1], Manuel Wimmer[2], and Gerti Kappel[2]

[1] Department of Telecooperation, Johannes Kepler University Linz, Austria
philip.langer@jku.ac.at
[2] Business Informatics Group, Vienna University of Technology, Austria
{wimmer,gerti}@big.tuwien.ac.at

Abstract. During the last decade several approaches have been proposed for easing the burden of writing model transformation rules manually. Among them are Model Transformation By-Demonstration (MTBD) approaches which record actions performed on example models to derive general operations. A current restriction of MTBD is that until now they are only available for in-place transformations, but not for model-to-model (M2M) transformations.

In this paper, we extend our MTBD approach, which is designed for in-place transformations, to also support M2M transformations. In particular, we propose to demonstrate each transformation rule by modeling a source model fragment and a corresponding target model fragment. From these example pairs, the applied edit operations are computed which are input for a semi-automatic process for deriving the general transformation rules. For showing the applicability of the approach, we developed an Eclipse-based prototype supporting the generation of ATL code out of EMF-based example models.

Keywords: model transformations, by-example, by-demonstration.

1 Introduction

Model transformations are an essential constituent in Model-driven Engineering (MDE) [6]. Therefore, several approaches have been proposed for easing the burden of writing model transformation rules by hand. One of the most prominent approaches is Model Transformation By-Example (MTBE) [12,14] which tries to generalize model transformation rules from aligned example models by comparing the structure and the content of the example models. A similar idea is followed by Model Transformation By-Demonstration (MTBD) approaches [3,13]. MTBD exploits edit operations performed on an example model to gain transformation specifications which are executable on arbitrary models.

---

* This work has been partly funded by the Austrian Federal Ministry of Transport, Innovation and Technology (BMVIT) and FFG under grant FIT-IT-819584 and by the Austrian Science Fund (FWF) under grant P21374-N13.

L. Tratt and M. Gogolla (Eds.): ICMT 2010, LNCS 6142, pp. 153–167, 2010.

Until now, MTBD approaches are only available for in-place transformations like refactorings. An open challenge is how to adapt MTBD to be applicable for model-to-model (M2M) transformations due to the following hitherto unsolved issues. First, when using MTBD for in-place transformations, the trace model between the initial model (before transformation execution) and the revised model (after transformation execution) comes nearly for free. That trace may either be achieved using an ID-based comparison [3] or by directly recording all performed actions [13]. Unfortunately, these methods cannot be used for M2M transformation examples, because the corresponding elements in the source and target model are independently created and, consequently, have different IDs. Additionally, they are in most cases structurally heterogeneous. Second, state-of-the-art MTBD approaches for in-place transformations allow to specify one composite operation, e.g., a refactoring, performed on the initial model. After generalization, the resulting composite operation is executed on arbitrary models separately from other composite operations. However, in M2M scenarios, the whole target model has to be established based on the source model from scratch by applying a set of different, strongly interdependent transformation rules.

In this paper we tackle the mentioned challenges with a novel MTBD approach for developing M2M transformations. In particular, we elaborate on how the approach presented in [3] for developing in-place transformations is adapted for M2M transformations. To specify a M2M transformation, the user iteratively demonstrates each transformation rule by specifying an example using her preferred editor. Subsequently, the example models are automatically generalized to templates which the user may configure and customize by following a well-defined annotation process. Finally, model transformation rules are automatically derived from these annotated templates. Since the user only gets in touch with templates representing the user-specified examples, she is able to develop general model transformations without requiring in-depth knowledge of the underlying transformation language. Please note that our approach is orthogonal to existing high-level transformation approaches, such as Triple Graph Grammars and QVT Relations, because instead of directly developing the generalized templates, the user first develops concrete examples which are then systematically generalized. For showing the applicability of the approach, we developed an Eclipse-based prototype which supports the generation of ATL code out of EMF-based example models.

The paper is organized as follows. Starting with a motivating example in Section 2, we outline the process of developing M2M transformations by-demonstration in Section 3. Section 4 provides a by-example presentation of the by-demonstration approach. Section 5 discusses related work, and finally, we conclude with an outlook on future work in Section 6.

2   Motivating Example

To emphasize our motivation for developing a by-demonstration approach for M2M transformations, we introduce a well-known M2M transformation scenario,

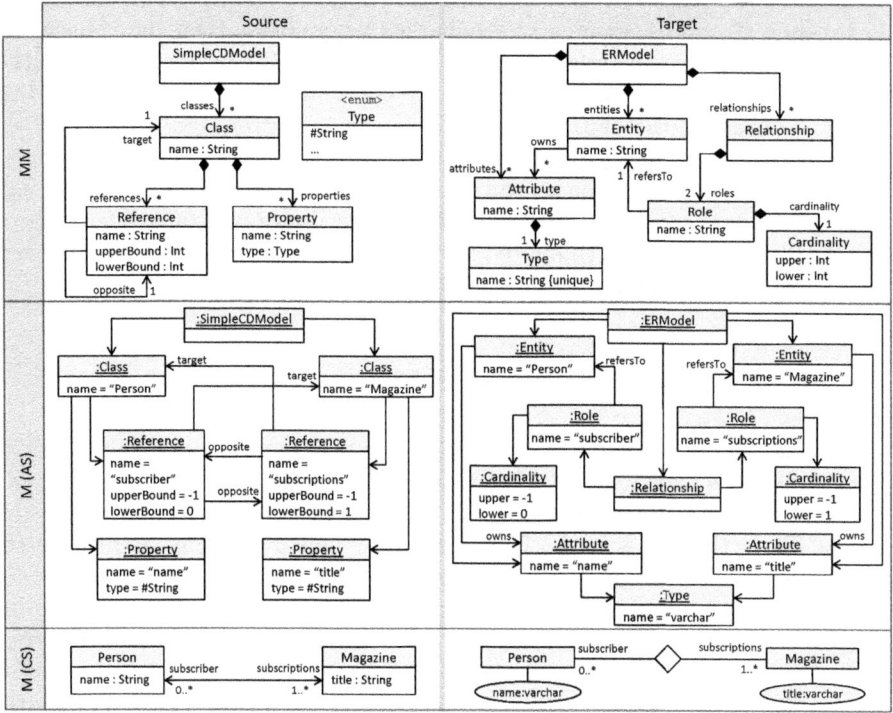

Fig. 1. Motivating example: Source metamodel, target metamodel, source model (abstract syntax), target model (abstract syntax), source model (concrete syntax), and target model (concrete syntax)

namely the transformation from UML Class Diagrams to Entity Relationship (ER) Diagrams. Fig. 1 illustrates the scenario which serves as a running example throughout the rest of the paper. Although the involved modeling languages provide semantically similar modeling concepts, this scenario also exhibits challenging correspondences between metamodel elements.

In the following, the main correspondences between the UML Class Diagram and the ER Diagram are shortly described. Simple one-to-one correspondences exist between the root containers SimpleCDModel and ERModel as well as between Class and Entity. However, the example also contains more complex correspondences. In particular, these are the correspondences between (1) the class Property and the classes Attribute and Type as well as (2) between the class Reference and the classes Relationship, Role, and Cardinality. In the first case, for each property, an attribute has to be generated. However, only for each distinct value of Property.type a type should be generated. When a type already exists with the same name, it should be reused. In the second case, for *every unique pair* of References that are marked as opposite of each other a corresponding Relationship has to be established containing two Roles, which again contain their Cardinalities. With *every unique pair*, we mean that the order in which the references are matched does not matter. For example, if `Reference` r1 and `Reference` r2 are marked as opposite, then the transformation should produce *one* relationship for the match <r1, r2>, instead of creating another one for <r2, r1>. Therefore, we speak about the matching strategy *Set* if the order of the matched elements does not matter, and *Sequence* if the order does matter. On the attribute level, only simple one-to-one correspondences occur. On the reference level, some references can easily be mapped, e.g., `SimpleCDModel.classes` to `ERModel.entities`. However, some references on the target side have to be computed from the context of the source side, because they miss a direct counterpart, e.g., `ERModel.relationship`.

3 M2M Transformation By-Demonstration at a Glance

The design rationale for our by-demonstration approach is as follows. M2M transformations may be seen as a set of operations that are applied to the target model for each occurrence of a pattern of model elements in the source model. Thus, the target model is incrementally built by finding patterns in the source model and by applying the appropriate operations to the target model. Target elements created by these operations might need to be added to and refer to already existing elements, which had been created in prior transformation steps. Therefore, operations mostly have to be applied within a context. To enable the derivation of a transformation rule from examples, we apply the *by-demonstration process* depicted in Fig. 2.

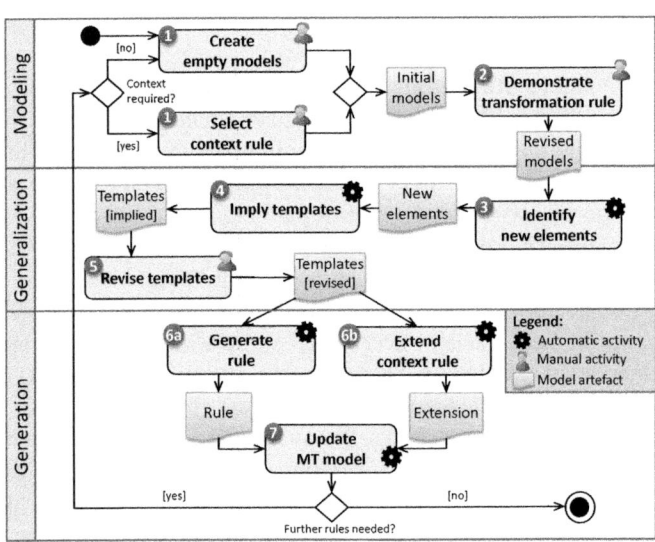

Fig. 2. By-Demonstration Process

Phase 1: Modeling. The user demonstrates a single transformation rule by adding model elements to the source model and by modeling the desired outcome in the target model. A transformation usually consists of several transformation rules. If a rule does not depend on other rules, no context elements are necessary to illustrate the rule, thus the user creates empty models. But usually, rules depend on other rules, which must have been previously applied forming the context. Thus, they are called *context rules*. Therefore, the user might select a context in which a new rule is demonstrated. If a context rule is selected, the source and target example model contained by the context rule is extended by the user to demonstrate the new context-dependent rule. For ensuring a high reusability of rules as context rules, they should be as small as possible.

Phase 2: Generalization. Added elements are identified and the illustrated transformation scenario is generalized. To determine the new elements if the demonstrated rule is context-dependent, we conduct a comparison between the revised models (source and target) to the respective models of the selected context rules. If the rule is context-free, all elements are considered as new. The new elements in the source model act as "trigger elements" which trigger to create the detected new elements in the target model. The most obvious way to identify the new elements is to record user interactions within the modeling environment. However, this would demand an intervention in the modeling environment, and due to the multitude of modeling environments, we refrain from this possibility. Instead, we apply a state-based comparison to determine the executed operations after modeling the context models and the extended models. This allows the use of any editor without depending on editor-specific extensions. After the new elements are identified, we automatically imply templates for each model element in the respective models. A template is a generalized description of a model element. It contains conditions, which have to be fulfilled to identify an arbitrary model element as a valid match for a template. The automatic, metamodel-agnostic condition generation is done by creating a new condition for each feature and its value of a specific model element. After an automatic default configuration like the deactivation of conditions restricting to empty feature values is applied, the user may refine templates by adding or modifying certain conditions during the REMA process.

Attribute values in the target model usually depend on values in the source model. Therefore, we search for similar values in the source and the target model's elements and, for each detected similarity, automatically derive suggestions for the user to create attribute value correspondences. Accepted correspondences are incorporated by adding them to the condition in the target template. Attribute correspondence conditions bind a feature value or a combination of feature values in the source template model to a feature in the target template model. Unambiguous correspondences are automatically added, but the user might adjust the conditions using the semi-automatic REMA process by relaxing, enforcing, modifying or augmenting templates.

We distinguish between usual templates and inherited templates. Usual templates represent model elements that have been newly created in the current demonstration. Inherited templates represent context elements that have either been already introduced in a context rule, or that conform to a template in a context rule, i.e., they are processed by the context rule.

Phase 3: Generation. After the revision of the templates, transformation rules are generated by a higher-order transformation. In particular, for the demonstrated scenario, a new rule has to be generated and attached to the transformation model. Furthermore, in case a context-dependent scenarios has been illustrated, the context rules have to be extended with further reference bindings to the newly introduced elements referenced by the context elements.

4 M2M Transformation By-Demonstration in Action

In the previous section, we illustrated the by-demonstration process from a generic point of view. In this section, we show how this process is adopted from a user's point of view. In particular, we discuss each iteration necessary to solve the motivating example of Section 2. To support the user in the demonstration process, we implemented a prototype presented on our project homepage[1].

4.1 Iteration 1: Class Diagram to Entity Relationship Diagram

In Iteration 1, a context-free object-to-object correspondence is illustrated to create for each SimpleCDModel instance an ERModel instance.

Step 1: Create empty models. The user creates a context-free rule by specifying an empty source model and an empty target model. These models are extended in the following steps.

Step 2: Demonstrate transformation rule. To illustrate the transformation of SimpleCDModels to ERModels, the user just has to add these elements to the empty models as shown in Fig. 3(a).

Step 3: Identifying new elements. Since the demonstrated rule is context-free, all model elements are considered as new.

Step 4: Imply templates. The example models are generalized by automatically implying templates for each model element. The goal of creating these templates is to generically describe model elements. With the help of source templates, we are able to verify if arbitrary model elements should be transformed equally to the illustrated model elements. Target templates indicate which properties and values should be set in the target elements according to the source model. In this example the templates Template_L_1_1 and Template_R_1_1 (cf. *specific templates* in Fig. 3(a)) are implied for the respective elements in the example models. The L in the template name indicates the *left* side and R the right side. The first digit in the template name indicates the rule it has been introduced. The second digit enumerates the templates. Since both elements do not contain any classes or entities, for both templates a condition is created which constrains these features to be empty, e.g., cf. classes = {}. After all templates are initially generated, they are automatically pre-configured and generalized.

---

[1] http://www.modelversioning.org/m2m-operations

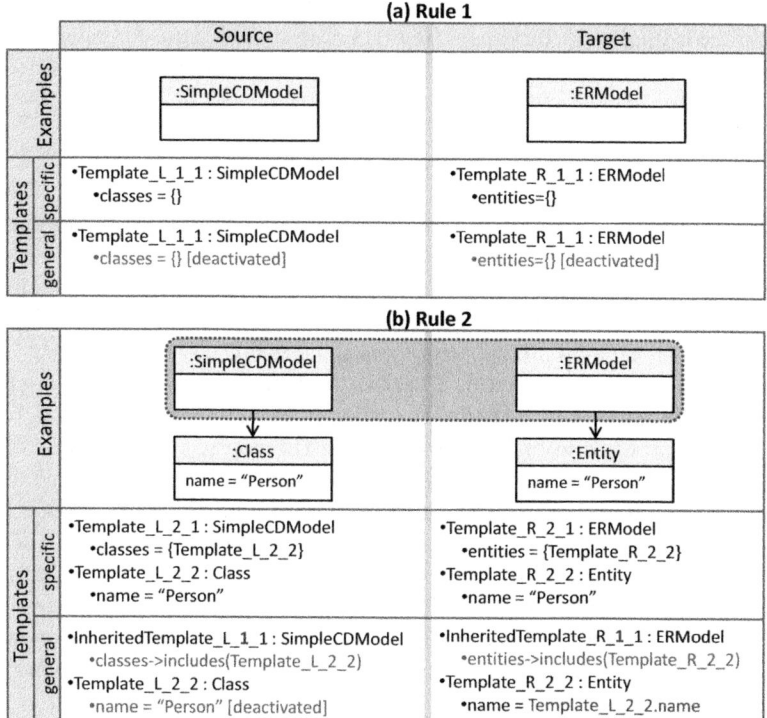

Fig. 3. (a) Rule 1: Class Diagram to ER Diagram. (b) Rule 2: Class to Entity.

This is done by deactivating all conditions in the source templates by default. Solely, source template conditions referring to object values that are represented by other source templates are left to be active. Consequently, source templates only restrict the type of the elements and their dependencies to other source templates. Additionally, conditions in the target templates are deactivated if the features are not set (cf. *general templates* in Fig. 3(a)). This reflects an open world assumption. Only aspects are restricted which are explicitly modeled.

Step 5: Revise templates. Since the templates and their contained conditions are automatically implied, they might not always reflect the user's intention. Therefore, the user may adjust the generated templates and conditions using the *REMA* process. She may **relax** currently active conditions, **enforce** currently inactive conditions, or **modify** existing conditions. Additionally, templates may be **augmented** by adding annotations. Using these techniques, the user might for instance tighten source templates by enforcing (reactivating) or modifying certain conditions to restrict the execution of a transformation rule. However, in this iteration none of these is necessary.

Step 6-7: Generation. The revised templates are transformed into ATL transformations. Basically, the source templates are transformed into the `from` block and the target templates into the `to` block of an ATL rule. Additional conditions in source templates are used as *guards* and attribute correspondences are set accordingly via bindings. The generated ATL rule for this iteration is shown in List. 1 (line 4-6, 11). Step 6b is not applicable for context-free rules, since no context rule has to be extended.

4.2   Iteration 2: Class to Entity

In this iteration, the transformation of Classes to Entities is demonstrated. This rule requires a one-to-one object correspondence, a value-to-value correspondence, and a context—the created target elements have to be added to an ERModel instantiated in the previous iteration. The example models, the implied templates, and the generalized templates are depicted in Fig. 3(b).

Step 1: Select context rule. Classes and Entities are always contained by SimpleCDModels and ERModels, respectively. Thus, the user has to select the transformation rule of Iteration 1 to be the context of the rule created in this iteration. When a context is selected, a copy of the context rule's example models is created and opened in diagram editors in order to be extended.

Step 2: Demonstrate transformation rule. The user extends the loaded context models to illustrate the transformation of a Class to an Entity. An instance of both model elements have to be added in the respective models. To allow a subsequent automatic detection of attribute value correspondences, the user should use exactly the same values for which a correspondence exists. Consequently, the class is named equally to the entity (cf. Fig. 3(b)).

Step 3: Identifying new elements. New elements are identified automatically by comparing the current source model to the source model of the context rule as well as the current target model to the context rule's target model. Thus, the class and the entity are marked as new elements.

Step 4: Imply templates. Like in the previous iteration, for each element in the example models, a template is implied and a condition for each feature is added to the template (cf. *specific templates* in Fig. 3(b)). In contrast to the previous iteration, the current rule depends on a context, i.e., it includes context elements to be processed by the context rule. For that reason, templates which represent a context model element are replaced during the generalization mechanism with *InheritedTemplates* pointing to the respective template contained by the context rule (cf. *general templates* in Fig. 3(b)). The first digit of the template name indicates the context rule in which the elements have been introduced, e.g., InheritedTemplate_R_1_1 represents the ERModel introduced in Iteration 1. Note that this inherited template is refined in this iteration by an additional condition (entities->includes(Template_R_2_2)). This condition indicates that the created entity has to be added to the feature ERModel.entitites. The conditions of the source templates are again deactivated by default. Additionally, for setting attribute correspondences, for each value in the target model, a corresponding value in the source model is searched. If an unambiguous correspondence is detected, the target value is automatically restricted to be the value of the source element's attribute by replacing the value assignment (name = ''Person'') with a template reference (name = Template_L_2_2.name).

Step 5: Revise templates. Like in Iteration 1, no user adjustments are necessary due to the accurate default implications.

Step 6-7: Generation. After the generalization phase, the current rule is transformed into an ATL rule as shown in List. 1 (line 13-16, 18). As mentioned in Step 4, we refined `InheritedTemplate_R_1_1` with a new condition. This condition preserves the relationship of the context element `ERModel` to the newly added `Entity`. Hence, an assignment of generated `Entities` to the feature `entities` is added to the context rule (cf. line 7 in List. 1).

4.3   Iteration 3: Property to Attribute

Now the transformation of `Properties` to `Attributes` is demonstrated. Properties are contained by classes whereas attributes are directly contained by the root model element. Entities only incorporate a reference to the attributes they own. Moreover, in class diagrams, the property type is expressed using an attribute. In contrast, the type of an attribute in `ERModels` is represented by an additional instance. Thus, we need to specify a one-to-many object correspondence as well as two value-to-value correspondences.

Step 1: Select context rule. This transformation rule has to be illustrated within the context of Rule 1 and Rule 2, because Attributes are referenced by ERModels as well as by Entities.

Step 2: Demonstrate transformation rule. In the source model the user adds a property to the class created in Iteration 2. Correspondingly, an attribute with the same name is appended to the entity (cf. Fig. 4(a)). Corresponding to the type of the property, an instance of `Type` has to be created in the target model and linked to the attribute.

Step 3: Identifying new elements. As in the previous iterations, the new elements are identified properly using the state-based comparison.

Step 4: Imply templates. For each model element, a template is implied. Model elements which have already been created in previous iterations are represented by inherited templates. As in the previous iteration, the both inherited templates in the target template model are refined by additional conditions (e.g., `attributes->includes(Template_R_3_3)`), because the attribute is referenced by the entity and contained by the ERModel. The value-to-value correspondence regarding the attribute `name` is detected and annotated automatically (`name = Template_L_3_3.name`).

Step 5: Revise templates. In contrast to the previous iterations, the user now has to apply two augmentations in the REMA process. First, type has to be reused since it is not intended to add a new type each time an attribute is created. Instead, `Type` instances have to be reused whenever a type already exists with the same name. This is done by annotating the corresponding template with the *reuseObject* operator and providing the `name` feature as discriminator for reuse. Second, the literals of the `Type` enumeration of the Class Diagram have to be converted to String values in ER Diagrams. To enable such static value-to-value conversions, the user may set up a mapping table. In the template conditions, this table is used by calling its name (cf. `name = MapTypes(Template_L_3_3)`).

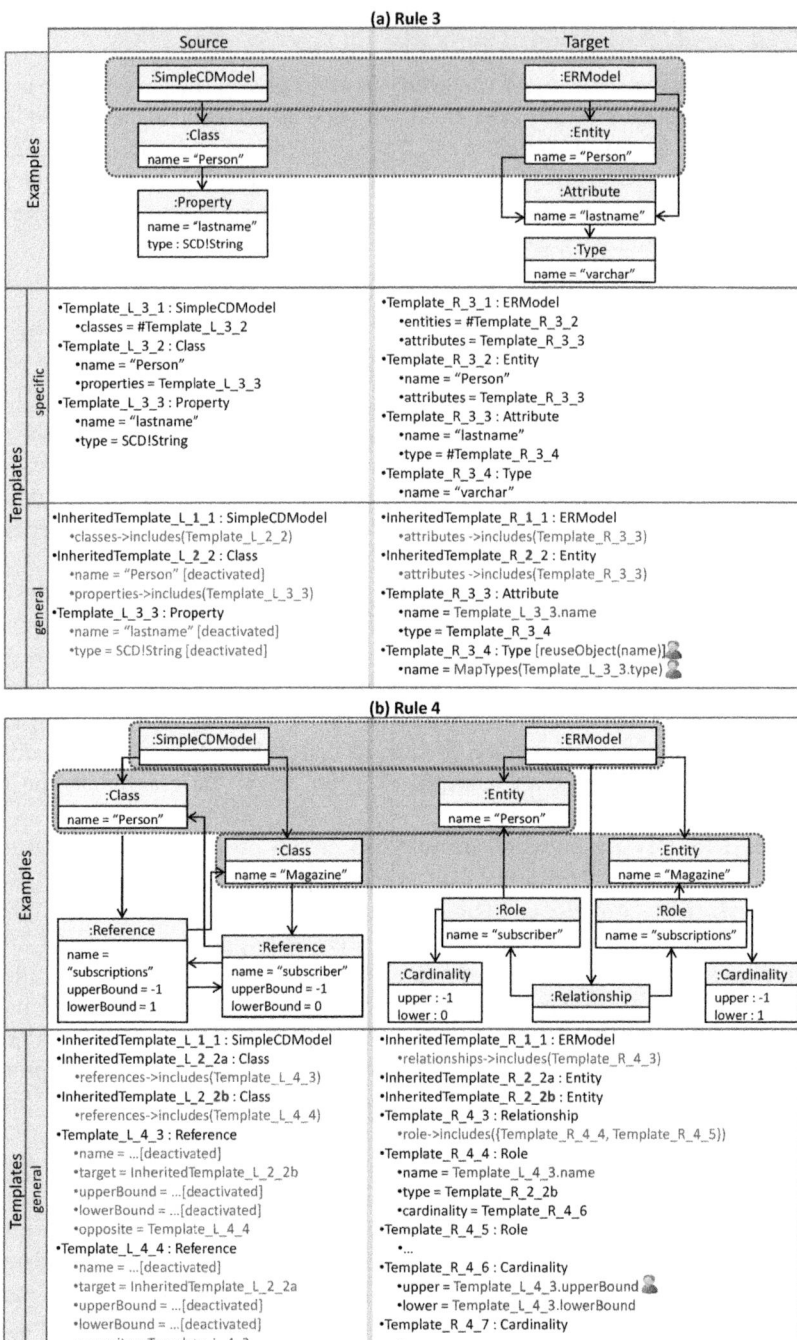

Fig. 4. (a) Rule 3: Property to Attribute. (b) Rule 4: Reference to Relationship.

Step 6-7: Generation. A matched rule is created to generate attributes from properties (cf. line 25-33 in List. 1). A lazy rule and a helper is generated for creating types if necessary (cf. line 35-40, 23). Furthermore, a helper for the mapping table is generated (cf. line 20-21). Both ATL rules created for the used context rules are extended by new feature bindings (cf. line 8, 17).

4.4   Iteration 4: Reference to Relationship

The last iteration demonstrates the transformation of References to Relationships. For this, a many-to-many object correspondence is needed, since two references marked as opposite are transformed into a relationship with two Roles comprising Cardinalities (cf. Fig. 4(b)). As in the previous iteration, the context rule 2 has to be used. Furthermore, tuples of reference instances have to be processed only once by applying the *Set* matching strategy (cf. Section 2). In our experience, this is the intuitive matching strategy for multiple query patterns matching for the same type, thus it is used as default.

Step 1: Select context rule. The transformation of References into Relationships is in the context of Rule 1 and of Rule 2.

Step 2: Demonstrate transformation rule. A new class named "Magazine" and two new references ("subscriber" and "subscriptions") are added to the source model. In the target model, the user adds an Entity "Magazine", a relationship, two roles, and cardinalities for each role. All values in the target are consciously set according to the corresponding values in the source model.

Step 3: Identifying new elements. Beside the Class and Entity "Person", which has been directly added in the context rule, the user also added a second Class and correspondingly a second Entity named "Magazine". To correctly identify these two "Magazine" elements to be context elements and not new elements, we match each added element in the example against all context templates. Since the left and right "Magazine" elements are matching the corresponding context templates, they are considered as context elements.

Step 4: Imply templates. For each model element, a template or an inherited template is created. Since there are now two instances of Class and of Entity we enumerate the corresponding inherited templates with a letter (a and b). The InheritedTemplate_R_1_1 (representing a ERModel) is extended for this rule by an additional condition specifying the reference to the added relationship. All attribute value correspondences are detected and annotated automatically. Solely, for the upper bounds of the Cardinalities only suggestions can be made since the values of these features cannot be unambiguously mapped.

Step 5: Revise templates. The current transformation rule should only be executed for reference pairs which are marked as opposite of each other. As already mentioned before, all source template conditions are deactivated, except for those, which refer to an object value that is represented by another template. Consequently, also the two conditions restricting the two references to be opposite of each other remains active which is the intended configuration. Also the aforementioned difficulty regarding the matching strategy of these two instances of Reference is solved by using the matching strategy *Set* which is adopted by default. With this strategy, every combination of the reference instances irrespectively of their order is "consumed" during the transformation. Consequently, two references that refer to each other are only processed once by the resulting rule. If this is not intended, the user may annotate the templates to use the matching strategy *Sequence*.

Step 6-7: Generation. To realize the aforementioned *Set* matching strategy we generate a *unique lazy rule* with a guard expression (cf. line 42-56 in List. 1) which is called by the root rule to create and to add the relationships to the feature ERModel.relationships (cf. line 9-10).

5   Related Work

Varró [14] and Wimmer et al. [15] have been the first proposing to develop M2M transformation by-example. Both used input models, corresponding output models, and the alignments between them to derive general transformation rules. In [1], Balogh and Varró extended their MTBE approach by leveraging the power of inductive logic programming. As before, the input of their approach are one or more aligned source and target model pairs which are translated to Prolog clauses. These clauses are fed into an inductive logic programming engine that induces inference rules which are translated into model transformation rules. If these rules do not entirely represent the intended transformation, the user has to refine either the generated rules directly or she has to specify additional model pairs and start another induction iteration. That approach might require less user interaction compared to our approach, but we follow a different conceptual aim. By our demonstration approach we are aiming at a very interactive approach. In particular, the user is guided to demonstrate and configure each transformation rule iteratively. To ease that interaction for the user, in each iteration the user may focus only on one part of the potentially huge transformation until the current rule is correctly specified. We believe, this is a natural way of dividing and conquering the whole transformation.

For omitting to manually define alignments between source and target models, two further by-example approaches have been proposed. (1) García-Magariño et al. [7] propose to develop M2M transformations by annotating the source metamodel and the target metamodel with additional information, which is required to derive transformations based on given example models. Because the approach of García-Magariño et al. uses a predefined algorithm to derive the transformations purely automatically, the user has no possibility to influence the generalization process, which is in our point of view a must for developing model transformation in practice. The implication of this limitation is that most attribute correspondences cannot be detected as well as configurations such as reusing existing objects for aggregation or determining the matching strategy such as Sequence or Set cannot be considered during the generalization process. The only possibility for the user is to adapt and extend the generated ATL code, which is more difficult compared to providing such configurations in our proposed template language. (2) Kessentini et al. [10] interpret M2M transformations as an optimization problem. Therefore, Kessentini et al. propose to apply

Listing 1. Generated ATL Code

```
1  module CD2ER;
2  create OUT : ER from IN : CD;
3
4  rule GenerateERModel {
5    from cdmodel : CD!SimpleCDModel
6    to ermodel : ER!ERModel (
7      entities <- cdmodel.classes,
8      attributes <- cdmodel.classes ->
9        collect(e| e.properties) -> flatten(),
10     relationships <- cdmodel.classes -> collect(x| x.references) ->
11       flatten() -> collect(x| thisModule.GenerateRelationship(
12       x, x.opposite )))
13 }
14 -----------------------------------------------------------------
15 rule GenerateEntity {
16   from class : CD!Class
17   to entity : ER!Entity (
18     name <- class.name,
19     attributes <- class.properties)
20 }
21 -----------------------------------------------------------------
22 helper def : mapTypes(x : CD!Types) : ER!Types =
23   Map{(#String,'varchar'), ...)}.get(x);
24
25 helper def : seenERTypes : Set(ER!Type) = Set{};
26
27 rule GenerateAttribute {
28   from property : CD!Property
29   to attribute : ER!Attribute (
30     name <- property.name,
31     type <-
32       if(thisModule.seenERTypes -> exists(e|
33               e.name = thisModule.mapTypes(property.type)))
34       then thisModule.seenERTypes -> any(e|
35               e.name = thisModule.mapTypes(property.type))
36       else thisModule.CreateType(property.type) endif)
37 }
38
39 lazy rule CreateType {
40   from cdType : CD!Types
41   to erType : ER!Type (
42     name <- thisModule.mapTypes(cdType))
43   do{thisModule.seenERTypes <- thisModule.seenERTypes ->
44         including(erType);}
45 }
46 -----------------------------------------------------------------
47 unique lazy rule GenerateRelationship {
48   from reference1 : CD!Reference,
49     reference2 : CD!Reference (reference1.opposite = reference2)
50   to relationship1 : ER!Relationship (
51     roles <- Set{role1, role2}),
52     role1 : ER!Role(
53       name <- reference1.name,
54       refersTo <- reference1.target,
55       cardinality <- cardinality1),
56     role2 : ER!Role(...),
57     cardinality1 : ER!Cardinality(
58       upper <- reference1.upperBound,
59       lower <- reference1.lowerBound,
60     cardinality2 : ER!Cardinality(...)
61 }
```

an adapted version of a particle swarm optimization algorithm to find an optimal solution for the transformation problem, which is described by multiple source and target model pairs. However, as it is the case with most artificial intelligence approaches, only an approximation of the optimal solution can be found. This may be enough for some scenarios, e.g., searching for model elements in a model repository where the user has to select one of the best matches, for others, e.g., model exchange between different modeling tools, carefully-engineered model transformations are necessary [2]. Such scenarios are not supported by Kessentini et al., because the transformation logic is only implicitly available in the trained optimization algorithm, which is not adaptable.

Finally, a complementary approach for generating model transformations automatically is metamodel matching. Two dedicated approaches [4,5] have been proposed for computing correspondences between metamodels which are input for generating model transformations. We have experimented with technologies for ontology matching by transforming metamodels into ontologies [9]. However, we have experienced [8] that in a setting where (1) metamodels use different terminology for naming metamodel elements and (2) the structures of metamodels are very heterogeneous, it is sometimes impossible for the matching algorithms to find the correct correspondences. However, we have to mention that a hybrid approach, i.e., combining a matching approach with a by-example approach, seems to be very promising for gaining the benefits of both worlds. We consider this topic as subject to future work.

6   Conclusions and Future Work

The presented by-demonstration approach provides a novel contribution to the field of MTBD for developing carefully-engineered M2M transformations. Our approach is metamodel-independent and does not rely on the editors used to illustrate the transformation scenarios. The automatic generalization technique uses default implications which are proven useful in most of the cases. However, the user may still fine-tune the derived rules using the REMA process without touching the automatically generated ATL code.

Up to now, we support four operators that may be used to annotate templates, namely *reuseObject*, *MapTypes*, as well as two different matching strategies *Set* and *Sequence*. In future work, we will evaluate our approach in further scenarios to determine if further operators are required. For instance, we will elaborate on *selector templates* to support complex user-defined selections of source elements, e.g., a recursive selection of elements. Negative application conditions (NAC) as well as many-to-one attribute correspondences are currently only supported by manually editing conditions. In future work, we plan to imply NACs from user-specified examples and incorporate techniques from instance-based ontology matching [11] to allow automatic detection of many-to-one attribute correspondences. Furthermore, we intend to add features easing large transformation development like rule inheritance and debugging support. By employing user-specified test scenarios and comparing their transformation result to the desired result, we can backtrack the differences to the relevant rule and directly point the user to the template specification causing the difference. Finally, we will elaborate if it is possible to derive Triple Graph Grammar definitions from example models by using our REMA process. By this, we want to conduct if the approach is generic enough to generate also transformation rules for other transformation languages which might follow different trace models and execution semantics.

References

1. Balogh, Z., Varró, D.: Model transformation by example using inductive logic programming. Software and Systems Modeling 8(3), 347–364 (2009)
2. Bernstein, P.A., Melnik, S.: Model Management 2.0: Manipulating Richer Mappings. In: SIGMOD 2007, pp. 1–12 (2007)
3. Brosch, P., Langer, P., Seidl, M., Wieland, K., Wimmer, M., Kappel, G., Retschitzegger, W., Schwinger, W.: An Example Is Worth a Thousand Words: Composite Operation Modeling By-Example. In: Schürr, A., Selic, B. (eds.) MODELS 2009. LNCS, vol. 5795, pp. 271–285. Springer, Heidelberg (2009)
4. Fabro, M.D.D., Valduriez, P.: Semi-automatic model integration using matching transformations and weaving models. In: SAC 2007, pp. 963–970 (2007)
5. Falleri, J.-R., Huchard, M., Lafourcade, M., Nebut, C.: Metamodel matching for automatic model transformation generation. In: Czarnecki, K., Ober, I., Bruel, J.-M., Uhl, A., Völter, M. (eds.) MODELS 2008. LNCS, vol. 5301, pp. 326–340. Springer, Heidelberg (2008)
6. France, R., Rumpe, B.: Model-driven Development of Complex Software: A Research Roadmap. In: FOSE 2007, pp. 37–54 (2007)
7. García-Magariño, I., Gómez-Sanz, J.J., Fuentes-Fernández, R.: Model Transformation By-Example: An Algorithm for Generating Many-to-Many Transformation Rules in Several Model Transformation Languages. In: Paige, R.F. (ed.) ICMT 2009. LNCS, vol. 5563, pp. 52–66. Springer, Heidelberg (2009)
8. Kappel, G., Kargl, H., Kramler, G., Schauerhuber, A., Seidl, M., Strommer, M., Wimmer, M.: Matching metamodels with semantic systems - an experience report. In: Workshop Proceedings of BTW 2007, pp. 38–52 (2007)
9. Kappel, G., Reiter, T., Kargl, H., Kramler, G., Kapsammer, E., Retschitzegger, W., Schwinger, W., Wimmer, M.: Lifting metamodels to ontologies - a step to the semantic integration of modeling languages. In: Nierstrasz, O., Whittle, J., Harel, D., Reggio, G. (eds.) MoDELS 2006. LNCS, vol. 4199, pp. 528–542. Springer, Heidelberg (2006)
10. Kessentini, M., Sahraoui, H., Boukadoum, M.: Model Transformation as an Optimization Problem. In: Czarnecki, K., Ober, I., Bruel, J.-M., Uhl, A., Völter, M. (eds.) MODELS 2008. LNCS, vol. 5301, pp. 159–173. Springer, Heidelberg (2008)
11. Rahm, E., Bernstein, P.A.: A Survey of Approaches to Automatic Schema Matching. The VLDB Journal 10(4), 334–350 (2001)
12. Strommer, M., Wimmer, M.: A Framework for Model Transformation By-Example: Concepts and Tool Support. In: TOOLS 2008, pp. 372–391 (2008)
13. Sun, Y., White, J., Gray, J.: Model transformation by demonstration. In: Schürr, A., Selic, B. (eds.) MODELS 2009. LNCS, vol. 5795, pp. 712–726. Springer, Heidelberg (2009)
14. Varró, D.: Model Transformation by Example. In: Nierstrasz, O., Whittle, J., Harel, D., Reggio, G. (eds.) MoDELS 2006. LNCS, vol. 4199, pp. 410–424. Springer, Heidelberg (2006)
15. Wimmer, M., Strommer, M., Kargl, H., Kramler, G.: Towards Model Transformation Generation By-Example. In: HICSS 2007, pp. 285–286 (2007)

Implementing Business Process Recovery Patterns through QVT Transformations

Ricardo Pérez-Castillo, Ignacio García-Rodríguez de Guzmán, and Mario Piattini

Alarcos Research Group, University of Castilla-La Mancha
Paseo de la Universidad, 4 13071, Ciudad Real, Spain
{ricardo.pdelcastillo,ignacio.grodriguez,mario.piattini}@uclm.es

Abstract. Traditionally, software maintenance takes only technical information into account to evolve legacy systems. However, business knowledge, which could help to improve the comprehension of legacy systems, is rarely recovered. Probably, that knowledge is not considered due to the fact that business knowledge recovery is a problem with a non trivial solution. This paper contributes to the solution of this problem through the use of a set of patterns and the implementation through QVT transformations, which takes KDM (Knowledge Discovery Metamodel) models concerning the system and obtains BPMN (Business Processes Model and Notation) models to represent the embedded business knowledge. A case study reports that the transformation obtains cohesive and loosely-coupling business processes diagrams; and it is scalable to large systems. As a consequence, the business processes recovery can enhance the maintenance since they provide the business concept location in legacy systems, among other improvements.

Keywords: Maintenance, legacy system, KDM, business process, case study.

1 Introduction

Software is an intangible thing that ages in similar way to any material object, thus it must be maintained, which can produce more ageing. This is known in software engineering as software erosion problem [23]. The difference between software and material things is that software cannot be replaced from scratch, since (i) the entire replacement of an information system is very expensive, which (ii) also stops the achievement of ROI (Return Of Investment) [21]; and finally (iii) the software embeds a lot of business knowledge over time that would be lost if it is replaced [15].

In order to deal with software erosion problem, the evolutionary maintenance is the most appropriate kind of maintenance because it preserves the legacy business knowledge and makes it possible to evolve the systems with an acceptable budget [19]. Nowadays, the software modernization, and specifically the Architecture-Driven Modernization (ADM) proposed by the Object Management Group (OMG) [11], became one of the most successful practice for carrying out evolutionary maintenance. ADM is based on traditional reengineering process but it treats the involved software artifacts as models and establishes model transformations between them according to the Model-Driven Architecture (MDA) principles. In addition, the OMG

L. Tratt and M. Gogolla (Eds.): ICMT 2010, LNCS 6142, pp. 168–183, 2010.
© Springer-Verlag Berlin Heidelberg 2010

has defined Knowledge Discovery Metamodel (KDM) [14] together with ADM. KDM allows ADM-based processes to represent as models all the different artifacts involved in a legacy system such as source code, databases, user interfaces.

The reverse engineering stage of any ADM-based process obtains the models that represent the legacy system. The reverse engineering stage can reach three different abstraction levels, which lead to three kinds of ADM-based processes [9]: (i) technical level, which is related to migration to another language, where a physical model of the systems is obtained; (ii) application/data architecture level, which focuses on obtaining a model of the system design at intermediate abstraction level; and (iii) business level, which increases the degree of abstraction since a business architecture model is obtained.

The first and second levels have been addressed in traditional maintenance processes for many years in order to recover technical information about how the computation is done. However, besides that technical information there is a lot of business knowledge like concepts from the business domains and their relations, business rules and constraints, etc. that is rarely recovered to maintain legacy systems reaching the third level. When modernization process reaches the business level, the additional business knowledge helps to comprehend and maintain the system as well as to locate the business logics in the source code and other software artifacts [3].

Recovery business knowledge from legacy systems is a challenge that is addressed frequently in literature but it is still a latent problem since its solution is not trivial. This paper shows MARBLE [16], an ADM-based framework to obtain business knowledge, through a set of business processes, embedded in legacy information systems. MARBLE uses the KDM metamodel to represent a model of the legacy system, and the BPMN (Business Processes Model and Notation) metamodel to represent a business process model. This paper proposes, within MARBLE, a declarative model transformation in order to transform KDM models into BPMN models. The proposed transformation is based on a set of business patterns [17], thus it is implemented in declarative way. The transformation is implemented by means of QVT-Relations, the declarative language of QVT (Query/View/Transformation) [13].

In addition, this paper presents a case study that involves a CRM (Customer Relationship Management) system, which was used to apply the proposed transformation. The case study reports that the transformation is efficient and enables to obtain business process models with specific quality characteristics. The case study is conducted according to the case study protocol proposed by *Brereton el al.* [2] in order to ensure the greatest rigor and validity of the case study.

The remainder of this paper is organized as follows. Section 2 summarizes the background of business process as well as ADM and KDM standard. Section 3 presents MARBLE, the framework where the proposed transformation is applied. Section 4 presents the proposed declarative model transformation in detail. Section 5 reports the case study conducting to validate the proposal. Section 6 shows the work related to business knowledge recovery. Finally, Section 7 draws the conclusions of this paper.

2   Background

This section presents the background of this paper: firstly, it shows the business process concept; secondly, it introduces ADM and KDM standard.

2.1 Business Process

A *business process* is a sequence of coordinated activities performed in an organizational environment, which aims at a certain business goal [24]. Interest inside organizations in knowing their business processes has increased because they consider them to be a key asset (i) for their performance since the business processes depict the operations of the organization; (ii) in order to improve their competitiveness, because the business processes can be adapted in order to increase customer satisfaction, reduce costs, distinguish products or services, and so on; and finally, (iii) understanding business processes is an important step for the comprehension and maintenance of the source code, and in general of the information systems.

In order to achieve optimal business process management, it is necessary to represent explicitly the business processes by means of a notation understandable by the different roles involved in its management [8]. The most important notations are the Activity Diagrams of UML 2.0 and the Business Processes Model and Notation (BPMN) [12]. The Business Process Diagram (BPD) of BPMN is the notation used in this work since it is a well-known graphical notation and is easily understood by both system and business analysts.

2.2 ADM and KDM

ADM is the mechanism proposed by OMG to deal with software modernization. ADM is a process for understanding and evolving existing software assets in order to restore the value of existing applications. ADM provides several benefits such as ROI improvement on existing information systems, reducing development and maintenance costs, extending the life cycle of legacy systems and easy integration with other systems [11].

ADM is the concept of modernizing existing systems with a focus on all aspects of the current system architecture and the ability to transform current architectures to target architectures [11]. For this purpose, ADM advocates carrying out reengineering processes that treat any involved artifact as a model at specific abstraction level. Moreover, ADM makes it possible to refine models throughout different abstraction levels transforming the models by means of deterministic model transformations.

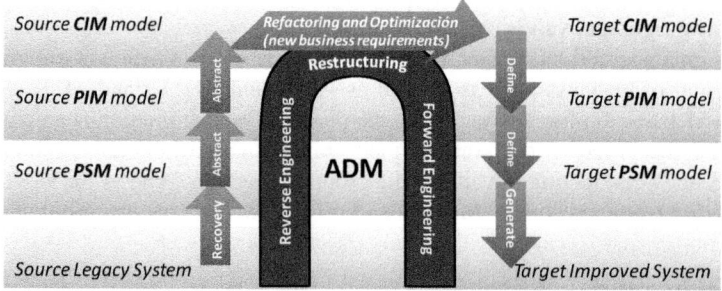

Fig. 1. Horseshoe modernization model

The horseshoe reengineering model has been adapted to ADM and it is known as the horseshoe modernization model [9] (see Fig. 1). The model consists of three stages: (i) reverse engineering identifies the components of the system and their inter-relationships, and it builds one or more abstract representations of the legacy system; (ii) restructuring transforms the abstract representation into another system representation at the same abstraction level, which improves the source legacy system but preserving the external behavior of the system; finally (iii) forward engineering generates physical implementations of the target system at a low abstraction level.

In addition, the horseshoe modernization model uses MDA nomenclature to refer to different abstraction levels (see Fig. 1): (i) CIM (Computation Independent Model) is a business view of the system from the computation independent viewpoint at a high abstraction level; (ii) (PIM) Platform Independent Model is a view of a system from the platform independent viewpoint at an intermediate abstraction level, thus a PIM models abstract all implementation details related to the platform; and finally (iii) PSM (Platform Specific Model) is a technological view of a system from the platform specific viewpoint at a low abstraction level.

Moreover, ADM spearheads the definition of several standards related to software modernization. KDM is the cornerstone within this set of standards and has been recognized as standard ISO 19506 [6]. KDM provides a metamodel to represent and exchange information about software artifacts in legacy systems. KDM enables the representation, at different abstraction levels, of all software artifacts like source code, user interfaces, database, business rules, and so on.

KDM can be compared with the *Unified Modeling Language* (UML) standard; while UML is used to generate new code in a *top-down* manner, the ADM processes involving KDM start from the existing code and build a higher level model in a *bottom-up* manner [10]. Despite this fact, KDM is not only used in reverse engineering stage. It is also used in restructuring and forward engineering stages since provides a common knowledge repository for the whole modernization process.

3 Marble

MARBLE (Modernization Approach for Recovering Business Processes from Legacy Systems) is an ADM-based framework for recovering business processes [16]. MARBLE focuses on the reverse engineering stage of the horseshoe modernization model to rebuild the business process embedded in legacy systems. MARBLE defines four abstraction levels (from L0 to L3) that represent four different kinds of models as well as three model transformations between the levels (see Fig. 2).

Firstly, the L0 level represents the legacy information system in the real world as a set of physical artifacts, that is: source code, databases, documentation and so on. Secondly, the L1 level represents a set of PSM models that can depict all the different software artifacts at L0 level according to different metamodels. For instance, a code model according to a Java metamodel, a user interface model according to a UIDL (User Interface Description Language) metamodel, a database model according to the SQL (Structure Query Language) metamodel, and so on. Thirdly, the L2 level integrates all knowledge about legacy software artifacts in a single PIM model

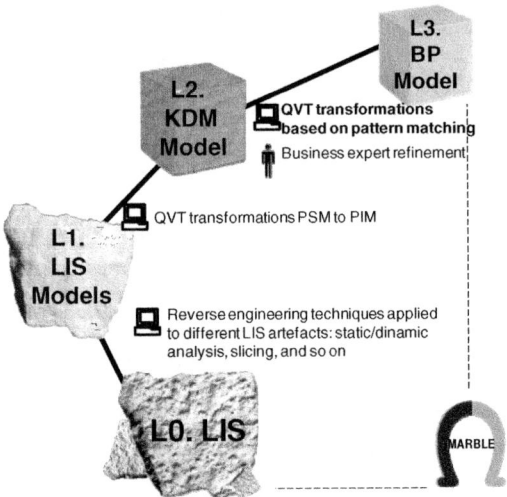

Fig. 2. MARBLE overview

represented in standardized way by means of the KDM metamodel. Finally, the L3 level represents the target model of the framework, a business model that represents the underlying business processes embedded in the legacy system. The business model is modeled according to the BPMN metamodel.

L0-to-L1 transformation. This transformation analyzes the legacy software artifacts at L0 level and build the PSM models according to the specific metamodels. The analysis can be done by means of different reverse engineering techniques like static analysis which examines the source code files, the dynamic analysis which analyzes the source code in run time, the program slicing that studies the code dividing it into different fragments, among other techniques. Currently, MARBLE supports static analysis of source code of Java-based legacy systems.

L1-to-L2 transformation. In order to obtain a KDM model, this transformation consists of a model transformation implemented in *QVT-Relation*. The transformation defines a set of declarative relations to transform instances of meta-classes related to different software artifacts into more abstract elements according to the KDM metamodel. Fig. 3 shows as example a QVT relation within the L1-to-L2 transformation. This relation transforms all instances of the *Class* meta-class in the Java code model (L1) into instances of *CompilationUnit*, a more generic meta-class of the KDM model (L2). The relation also examines instances of the *Method* meta-class that belong to the *Class* meta-class in order to the *method2CallableUnit* relation be also triggered.

L2-to-L3 transformation. The last transformation of MARBLE has a hybrid nature, since it consists of a model transformation as well as a manual transformation by business experts. Firstly, the model transformation obtains a BPMN model (L3) from the KDM model (L2) according to a set of business patterns that is implemented by means of QVT-Relation. The obtained business process models are preliminary since many of the recovered business process elements are business-independent, which including most of the utilities, input/output, and other auxiliary code. Secondly, manual interventions are done by the business experts in order to refine the preliminary business processes. Business experts could add or remove new business elements in a business process model; join or split a business process model; or even, they could discard a whole model. The next section presents the main contribution of this paper in detail: the declarative model transformation.

```
relation class2compilationUnit {
  className : String;
  checkonly domain java jc : java::classifiers::Class {
    name = className   ;
  enforce domain kdm kp : KDM::code::Package {
    codeElement = kcu : KDM::code::CompilationUnit {
      name = className
    }
  };
  where {
    jc.members->forAll (jm:java::members::Method |
    jm.oclIsKindOf(java::members::Method) implies method2callableUnit
      (jm.oclAsType(Method), kcu));
  }
}
```

Fig. 3. Example of QVT relation to transform Java code models into KDM models

4 KDM-to-BPMN Transformation

The KDM-to-BPMN transformation is a model transformation which is part of the L2-to-L3 transformation of MARBLE. The model transformation takes, as input, a KDM code model and produces, as output, a business process model according to the BPMN metamodel. Basically, the transformation carries out a business pattern matching that is implemented using the QVT-Relation language.

Firstly, this section explain briefly the metamodels used in both kinds of models, the input and output model. Secondly, it presents the set of patterns, which is used to carry out the pattern matching through the model transformation. Finally, it shows the most important implementation details of the model transformation using QVT.

4.1 Involved Metamodels

The KDM metamodel is divided into several packages organized in different abstraction layers. The transformation takes a KDM model that considers only the *code* and *action packages* at the *program element layer* of KDM. The *code* package enables the representation of code elements of legacy systems and their associations in a technological-independent manner. The *action* package extends the *code* package to represent behavior descriptions and control- and data-flow relationships between code elements. Fig. 4 shows the KDM metamodel concerning *code* and *action* packages. A legacy system is represented as a *CodeModel* element, the root meta-class. A *Code-Model* is composed of *AbstractCodeElements*, a meta-class that represents an abstract class for all KDM entities that can be used as *CallableUnit, StorableUnit,* etc. The *CodeElements* are also interrelated by means of *AbstractCode-Relationships,* a meta-class to represent an abstract class for all KDM relationships that can be used to represent the code such as *Flow, Calls, Reads, Writes*.

The BPMN metamodel is used to represent the target models obtained after the model transformation. Fig. 5 presents the BPMN metamodel, which enables the representation of business process diagrams. A business process diagram involves four kinds of meta-classes: (i) flow object classes such as *Events, Activities* and *Gateways*; (ii) connecting object classes like *SequenceFlows, MessageFlows* and *Associations*; (iii) artifact classes such as *DataObjects, Groups* and *Annotations*; and (iv) swimlane classes for grouping other elements such as *Pools* and *Lanes*.

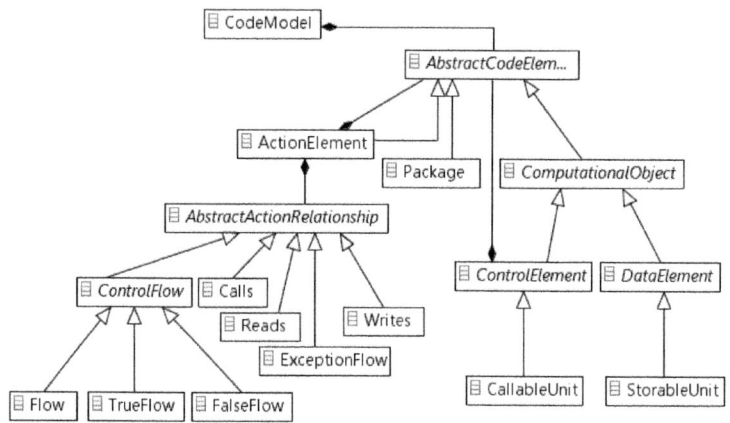

Fig. 4. KDM metamodel (the metamodel fragment related to the code and action packages)

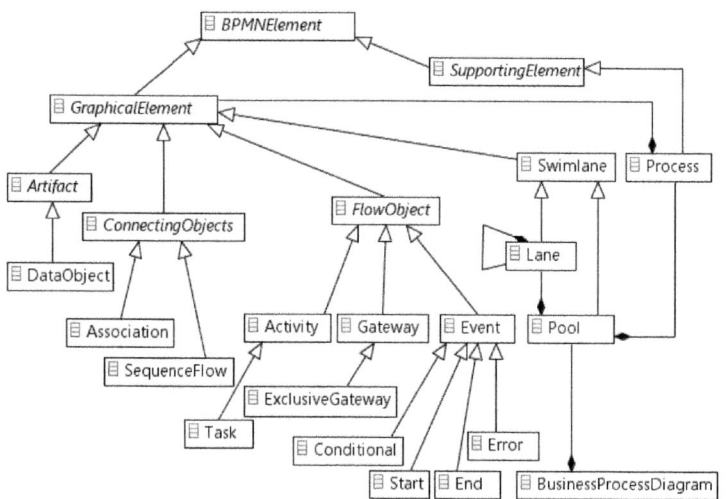

Fig. 5. BPMN metamodel

4.2   Pattern Matching to Detect Business Elements in KDM Models

The L2-to-L3 transformation is based on ten business patterns, which identify specific structures of meta-classes in the KDM models and establishes other specific structures of business meta-classes in output models. The patterns are built taking into account business patterns that are usually used by business experts for modeling business processes [1, 25]. The patterns proposed in this paper specify additionally those structures of source code elements (defined through KDM elements) that originate the specific business structures in BPMN models.

Table 1. Business patterns implemented in the model transformation

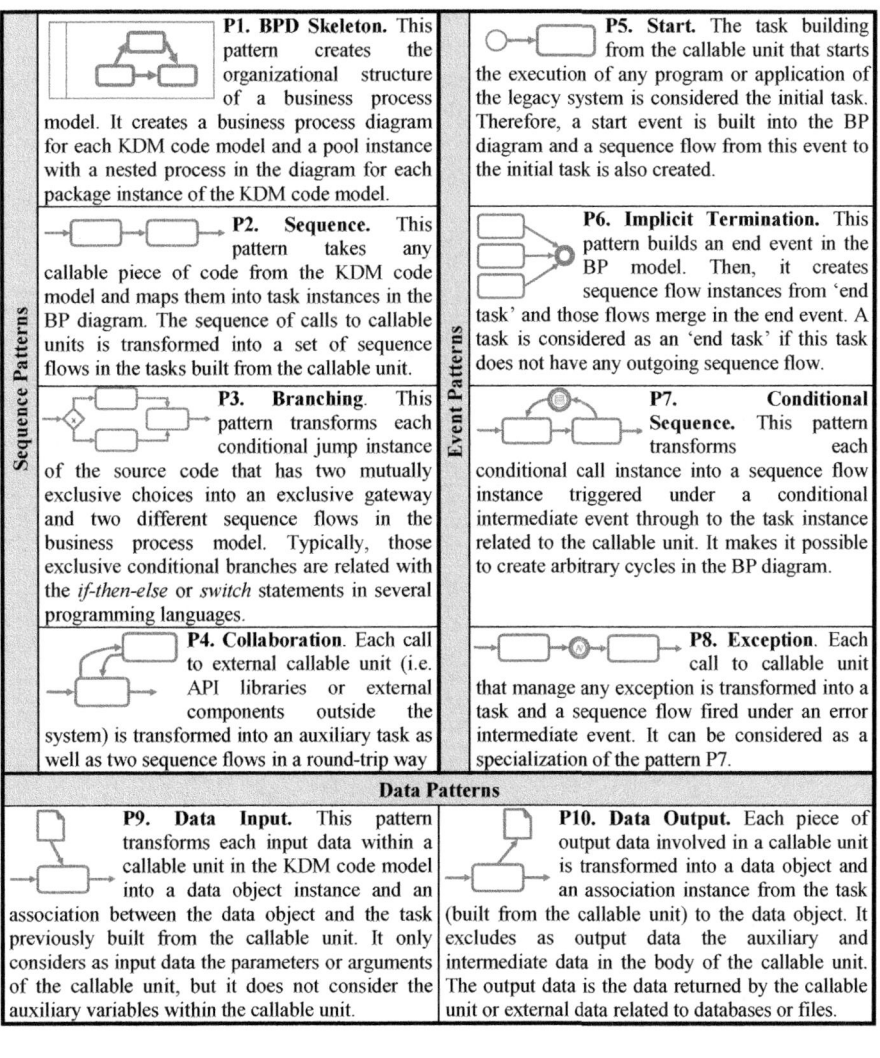

P1. BPD Skeleton. This pattern creates the organizational structure of a business process model. It creates a business process diagram for each KDM code model and a pool instance with a nested process in the diagram for each package instance of the KDM code model.	**P5. Start.** The task building from the callable unit that starts the execution of any program or application of the legacy system is considered the initial task. Therefore, a start event is built into the BP diagram and a sequence flow from this event to the initial task is also created.
P2. Sequence. This pattern takes any callable piece of code from the KDM code model and maps them into task instances in the BP diagram. The sequence of calls to callable units is transformed into a set of sequence flows in the tasks built from the callable unit.	**P6. Implicit Termination.** This pattern builds an end event in the BP model. Then, it creates sequence flow instances from 'end task' and those flows merge in the end event. A task is considered as an 'end task' if this task does not have any outgoing sequence flow.
P3. Branching. This pattern transforms each conditional jump instance of the source code that has two mutually exclusive choices into an exclusive gateway and two different sequence flows in the business process model. Typically, those exclusive conditional branches are related with the *if-then-else* or *switch* statements in several programming languages.	**P7. Conditional Sequence.** This pattern transforms each conditional call instance into a sequence flow instance triggered under a conditional intermediate event through to the task instance related to the callable unit. It makes it possible to create arbitrary cycles in the BP diagram.
P4. Collaboration. Each call to external callable unit (i.e. API libraries or external components outside the system) is transformed into an auxiliary task as well as two sequence flows in a round-trip way	**P8. Exception.** Each call to callable unit that manage any exception is transformed into a task and a sequence flow fired under an error intermediate event. It can be considered as a specialization of the pattern P7.
Data Patterns	
P9. Data Input. This pattern transforms each input data within a callable unit in the KDM code model into a data object instance and an association between the data object and the task previously built from the callable unit. It only considers as input data the parameters or arguments of the callable unit, but it does not consider the auxiliary variables within the callable unit.	**P10. Data Output.** Each piece of output data involved in a callable unit is transformed into a data object and an association instance from the task (built from the callable unit) to the data object. It excludes as output data the auxiliary and intermediate data in the body of the callable unit. The output data is the data returned by the callable unit or external data related to databases or files.

The left column groups are labeled **Sequence Patterns** (P1–P4) and **Event Patterns** (P5–P8).

Table 1 depicts the ten patterns grouped by category. There are three categories of patterns according to the type of elements managed by the pattern: (i) sequence patterns, (ii) event patterns, and (iii) data patterns.

4.3   Implementation of the L2-to-L3 Transformation

The model transformation is implemented by means of QVT-Relation. QVT-Relation is the selected language to implement the proposed patterns due to the fact that it is a declarative language, and therefore it facilitates the definition of declarative constraints that must be satisfied by the meta-class instances of the input and output models.

A model transformation defined through QVT-Relation language consists of a set of relations that specify two (or more) domains. A domain is a distinguished typed variable that can be matched in the type of a given model element. Input domains define a set of meta-classes of the input metamodel and a set of constraint bounded to those meta-classes that must be satisfied. These domains are usually tagged with the *checkonly* keyword. Moreover, outputs domains define a template of meta-classes and their properties that must be located, modified, or created in the output model to satisfy the relation. These domains are tagged with the *enforce* keyword.

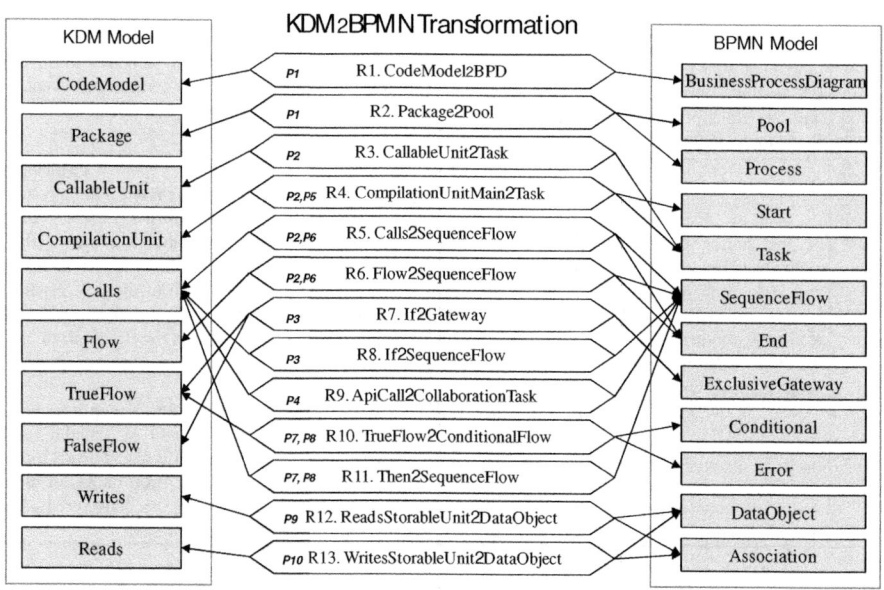

Fig. 6. Model transformation overview, relations and supported patterns

The model transformation consists of thirteen relations. Fig. 6 shows an overview depicting: (i) each relation and its involved elements, as well as (ii) the patterns supported for each relation.

Due to the space limitation, this paper does not show all the relations, but the most significant ones in charge of model the sequence flows in the target business

```
top relation CodeModel2BPD {
  xName : String;
  checkonly domain kdm cm : code::CodeModel {
    name = xName
  };
  enforce domain bpmn bpd : BusinessProcessDiagram  {
    Name = xName
  };
  where {
    cm.codeElement->forAll (pk:code::AbstractCodeElement | pk.oclIsKindOf(code::Package)
      implies Package2Pool(pk,bpd));
  }
}
```

Fig. 7. Relation R2.CodeModel2BPD to support partially the P1 pattern

```
relation Package2Pool {
  xName : String;
  checkonly domain kdm pk : code::Package  {
    name = xName
  };
  enforce domain bpmn bpd: BusinessProcessDiagram  {
    Pools = p : Pool {
      name = xName,
      ProcessRef = pr : bpmn::Process {
        Name = xName
      }
    }
  };
  where {
    pk.codeElement->forAll (c:code::AbstractCodeElement | c.oclAsType(code::CompilationUnit)
      .codeElement>forAll(m:code::AbstractCodeElement |(m.oclIsKindOf(code::CallableUnit)
      and m.oclAsType (code::CallableUnit).name='main') implies CompilationUnitMain2Task(c,m, pr)));
    pk.codeElement->forAll (c:code::AbstractCodeElement |c.oclAsType(code::
      CompilationUnit).codeElement->forAll(m:code::AbstractCodeElement|( m.oclIsKindOf
      (code::CallableUnit) and m.oclAsType (code::CallableUnit).name<>'main')
      implies  CallableUnit2Task (m, pr)));
  }
}
```

Fig. 8. Relation R2.Package2Pool to support partially the P1 pattern

```
relation MethodUnit2Task {
  xName : String;
  checkonly domain kdm m : code::CallableUnit {
    name = xName
  };
  enforce domain bpmn pr : bpmn::Process {
    GraphicalElements = t : Task {
      Name = xName,
      Status = StatusType::Ready
    }
  };
  where {
    ...
    m.codeElement->forAll (a:code::AbstractCodeElement | a.oclIsKindOf(action::
      ActionElement) and a.oclIsUndefined() implies ApiCall2CollaborationTask(a, t, pr));
    ...
    m.codeElement->forAll (a:code::AbstractCodeElement | a.oclAsType(action::
      ActionElement).actionRelation->forAll (w:action::AbstractActionRelationship |
      (w.oclIsKindOf(action::Writes)) and w.oclAsType(action::Writes).to.oclIsKindOf
      (code::StorableUnit) implies WritesStorableUnit2DataObject (w, t, pr)));
    ...
  }
}
```

Fig. 9. Relation R4.CallableUnit2Task to support partially the P2 pattern

processes: relations R1, R2 and R4. Fig. 7 shows the relations R1 that implements the P1 pattern. R1 takes any instance of the *CodeModel* meta-class and generates a *BusinessProcessDiagram* with the same name. In addition, it triggers the R2 relation in the *where* clause for each *Package* element belonging to the input domain.

The R2 relation defines the set of *Package* instances as input domain and instances of the *BusinessProcessDiagram* meta-class as output domain (see Fig. 8). R2 enforces the creation of a *Pool* and a nested *Process* instance, which will contain the remaining of business elements obtained through the proposed transformation. Also, R2 triggers the relations R3 and R4 that will define the *Task* instances of the business process.

Another important relation is *R4.CallableUnit2Task* (see Fig. 9). It defines the set of *CallableUnit* instances as input domain and enforces the creation of a *Task* instance in the process according to the argument in the call to this relation. In addition, the *where* clause (that can be understood as post-conditions of the relation) triggers the remaining of relations in order to fill the business process with elements obtained from another elements within callable units. Moreover, the R4 relation shows the calls to relations *R9.ApiCall2CollaborationTask* and *R13.WritesStorableUnit2DataObject*.

5   Case Study

The presented case study applies the KDM2BPMN transformation to a legacy system, which is based on the case study protocol of *Brereton et al.* [2]. Next subsections show the case study details according to the protocol: design, case selection, case study procedure, data collection and analysis.

Design

This case study applies the proposed model transformation to a legacy system. Data related to transformation is registered and then analyzed. The unit of analysis of the study is the code packages of legacy system, thus it considers multiple units of analysis. In addition, the case study establishes the following research questions to analyze the obtained results:

Q1. *Are the obtained business process models cohesive?*
Q2. *What is the degree of coupling of the business process models?*
Q3. *Is the execution of the transformation efficient?*

Questions Q1 and Q2 are related to the quality of the obtained business process diagram, which is measured by means of cohesion (1) and coupling (2) metrics proposed by *Rolón et al.* [20]. Moreover, question *Q3* is related to the time spent on executing the transformation that is analyzed with respect to the total number of elements built into the business process model.

$$COHESION = \frac{Number\ of\ tasks}{Number\ of\ sequence\ flows\ between\ tasks} \tag{1}$$

$$COUPLING = \frac{Number\ of\ output\ data\ objects}{Number\ of\ tasks} \tag{2}$$

Case selection

In order to select an appropriate case under study, the most suitable legacy system, the following criteria are defined: (i) the system should be a real-life system; and (ii) it should be an enterprise system.

After the application of those criteria, the selected case was an open source CRM system: *Source Tap CRM* [22]. It provides a powerful sales management system to improve a sales organization's productivity, allowing management to plan ahead of economic changes in order to effectively manage any market condition. This system, written in Java, consists of 170 source code files divided into 27 packages, and the size of the system is 49.6 *KLOC*.

Case study procedure

The execution procedure of the case study consists of four stages: firstly, (i) the source code is analyzed and the KDM code models are generated (the first and second MARBLE transformation); secondly (ii) the KDM code models are transformed into BPMN models by the proposed transformation that is executed through *MediniQVT*, a

Table 2. Results obtained in the case study

Package	# KDM models	# BPMN models	# Tasks	# Seq. Flows between Tasks	# Output Data Objects	COHESION	COUPLING	# Elements	Transf. time (ms)
account	4	1	31	48	7	0,65	0,23	163	1292
activity	6	1	34	56	9	0,61	0,26	210	959
address	2	1	8	12	4	0,67	0,50	59	276
attachment	3	1	13	18	2	0,72	0,15	76	300
chart	1	1	26	48	9	0,54	0,35	164	2899
code	5	1	13	18	1	0,72	0,08	66	604
contact	6	1	20	26	1	0,77	0,05	109	337
customization	14	1	18	44	7	0,41	0,39	237	1948
event	1	1	13	6	1	2,17	0,08	50	293
forecast	2	1	7	8	3	0,88	0,43	33	194
issue	4	1	15	26	1	0,58	0,07	95	450
lead	11	1	32	54	12	0,59	0,38	195	679
note	2	1	9	14	1	0,64	0,11	50	314
opportunity	10	1	40	76	19	0,53	0,48	289	1167
party	3	1	15	18	2	0,83	0,13	65	252
product	1	1	6	16	0	0,38	0,00	41	172
replication	14	1	17	28	1	0,61	0,06	105	545
report	1	1	7	12	9	0,58	1,29	111	4572
role	0	1	-	-	-	-	-	0	98
security	6	1	18	20	11	0,90	0,61	126	627
sql	1	1	5	6	3	0,83	0,60	30	168
ui	19	1	100	210	41	0,48	0,41	667	5841
user	3	1	20	42	1	0,48	0,05	115	1222
util	9	1	66	48	17	1,38	0,26	261	1088
view	0	1	-	-	-	-	-	0	95
multipartrequest	2	1	2	0	0	0	0,00	8	129
entity	1	1	5	0	0	0	0,00	10	129
Total	131	27	540	854	162	16,92	6,95	3335	26650
Mean	4,85	1,0	21,60	34,16	6,48	0,74	0,28	123,5	987,04
Std Deviation	4,94	0,0	21,54	41,71	8,98	0,38	0,29	135,4	1385,9

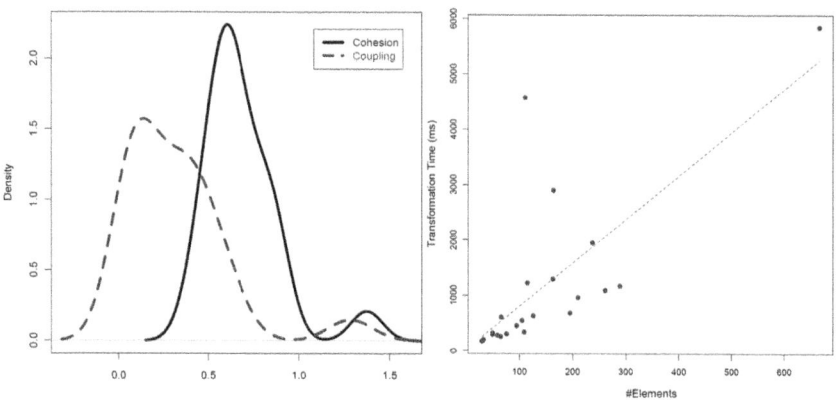

Fig. 10. Density chart cohesion/coupling (left side) and the scatter chart size/time (right side)

model transformation engine for *QVT Relation*; thirdly, (iii) the BPMN models are inspected and several measures are taken; and finally, (iv) the conclusions of the case study are obtained by means of the analysis of the measured values.

Data Collection

Table 2 summarizes the data collected after the execution of the transformation: the *package* column represents the source code package which is transformed into a business process model; *#KDM models* and *#BPMN models* represent the number of those models obtained; *#Tasks, #Seq. Flows between Tasks* and *#Output Data Objects* are the three base metrics to calculate *COHESION* (1) and *COUPLING* (2) metrics; *#Elements* represents the total number of elements; and finally *Transf. time (ms)* represents the milliseconds spent to obtain each BPMN model.

Analysis

A set of 27 BPMN models was obtained after the execution. Then, the collected data is analyzed in order to draw conclusions. In order to respond to questions *Q1* and *Q2*, Fig. 10 (left side) shows the density charts of the *Coupling* and *Cohesion*. Both density functions follow a normal distribution, approximately. *Cohesion* has a mean of 0.74 that is more close to 1.0. *Coupling* has a mean of 0.28 that is close to zero. Thus, the transformation can obtain cohesive and loosely coupled BPMN models.

Additionally, the transformation time is analyzed in order to answer question *Q3*. The 27 BPMN models were obtained with an average size of 21.6 tasks per diagram and an average time of 0.99 seconds. In addition, the feasibility of the time values for systems that are larger than *Source Tap CRM* must be evaluated. Fig. 10 (right side) shows the scatter chart of size/time which reports a linear relationship between the size and time spent on the execution. Due to the fact that the size/time relationship is not exponential, the time increase for large systems will be predictable.

6   Related Work

There are a lot of works in literature related to the recovery of business knowledge from legacy information systems. *Cai et al.* [3] propose an hybrid approach that combines the requirement reacquisition with dynamic and static analysis technique in order to extract complex business processes that are triggered by external actors. Firstly, a set of use cases are recovered by means of interviewing the users of the legacy system. Secondly, according to those use cases, the system is dynamically traced. Finally, the traces are statically analyzed to recover business processes.

Zou et al [26] developed a framework based on the MDA approach that uses the static analysis of source code as technique for extracting business processes by means of a set of heuristic rules to transform code entities into business entities. Moreover, the legacy source code is not the only artefact analyzed to obtain business processes. *Di Francescomarino et al* consider user interfaces [4]; this work proposes a technique for recovering Business Processes by means of a dynamic analysis of the GUI-forms of the Web applications that are exercised throughout the user navigation. The database is another artefact used to recover business knowledge. *Paradauskas et al.* [15] present a framework to recover business logic through the analysis of the data stored in databases. Also, *Perez-Castillo et al.* [18] propose a reengineering framework to extract business logic from relational database schemas. In other cases, documentation is also used to recover process. *Ghose et al* [5] propose a set of text-based queries in source code and documentation for extracting business knowledge from systems.

Despite the fact that business process recovery or business knowledge has been widely studied for many years, the proposals lack of the model-based formalization, standardization and interchange common format that provide ADM and KDM. *Izquierdo, J. L. C. and J. G. Molina* [7] propose a domain specific language for extracting models in ADM-based processes using Gra2MoL. In addition, *Perez-Castillo et al.* propose MARBLE [16], the ADM-based framework using KDM presented in this paper.

7 Conclusion

This paper proposes the KDM2BPMN model transformation within MARBLE, an ADM-based framework to rebuilt business processes embedded in legacy systems in order to facilitate and improve the evolutionary maintenance. For instance, when a new modification is requested, MARBLE facilitates the source code location of those business process concepts related to the required modification.

The KDM2BPMN transformation focuses on transform KDM code model into BPMN models that represents the business processes. The transformation is implemented by means of QVT-Relation, since it facilitates the implementation of the set of business patterns. The patterns define what parts of legacy code are transformed into specific business elements. The obtained business processes are undoubtedly preliminary, since there is a lot of business knowledge that is not embedded in source code. In a desirable scenario, the obtained business processes should be refined by the business experts as proposed in MARBLE. Despite this fact, the business processes obtained through the transformation help maintainers and business experts to comprehend the system in the business environment.

In addition, the case study reported that the proposed transformation can obtain BPMN models in a cohesive and non-coupling manner. Also, it reports that the transformation can be scalable to large legacy systems, since the business process models were obtained in linear time with respect to the size of the models.

The future extensions of this work will focus on addressing case studies with enterprise legacy systems, where system and business experts will assess the extent to which business processes represent faithfully the company's operation. Moreover, these case studies may also help to detect new business structure needs that will provide the definition of more refined patterns.

Acknowledgement

This work was supported by the FPU Spanish Program; by the R&D projects funded by *JCCM*: ALTAMIRA (PII2I09-0106-2463), INGENIO (PAC08-0154-9262) and PRALIN (PAC08-0121-1374); and the PEGASO/MAGO project (TIN2009-13718-C02-01) funded by MICINN and FEDER.

References

[1] Aalst, W.M.P.v.d., Hofstede, A.H.M.t., Kiepuszewski, B., Barros, A.P.: Workflow Patterns. Distributed and Parallel Databases 14(3), 5–51 (2003)

[2] Brereton, P., Kitchenham, B., Budgen, D., Li, Z.: Using a protocol template for case study planning. In: Evaluation and Assessment in Software Engineering (EASE 2008), Bari, Italia, pp. 1–8 (2008)

[3] Cai, Z., Yang, X., Wang, W.: Business Process Recovery for System Maintenance - An Empirical Approach. In: 25 th International Conference on Software Maintenance (ICSM 2009), pp. 399–402. IEEE CS, Edmonton (2009)

[4] Di Francescomarino, C., Marchetto, A., Tonella, P.: Reverse Engineering of Business Processes exposed as Web Applications. In: 13th European Conference on Software Maintenance and Reengineering (CSMR 2009), pp. 139–148. IEEE Computer Society, Germany (2009)

[5] Ghose, A., Koliadis, G., Chueng, A.: Process Discovery from Model and Text Artefacts. In: IEEE Congress on Services (Services 2007), pp. 167–174 (2007)

[6] ISO/IEC, ISO/IEC DIS 19506. Knowledge Discovery Meta-model (KDM), v1.1 (Architecture-Driven Modernization), ISO/IEC. p. 302 (2009),
http://www.iso.org/iso/catalogue_detail.htm?csnumber=32625

[7] Izquierdo, J.L.C., Molina, J.G.: A Domain Specific Language for Extracting Models in Software Modernization. In: Paige, R.F., Hartman, A., Rensink, A. (eds.) ECMDA-FA 2009. LNCS, vol. 5562, pp. 82–97. Springer, Heidelberg (2009)

[8] Jeston, J., Nelis, J., Davenport, T.: Business Process Management: Practical Guidelines to Successful Implementations. Butterworth-Heinemann (Elsevier Ltd.), NV (2008)

[9] Khusidman, V., Ulrich, W.: Architecture-Driven Modernization: Transforming the Enterprise. DRAFT V.5. OMG (2007),
http://www.omg.org/docs/admtf/07-12-01.pdf

[10] Moyer, B.: Software Archeology. Modernizing Old Systems. Embedded Technology Journal (2009), http://adm.omg.org/docs/Software_Archeology_4-Mar-2009.pdf

[11] OMG. ADM Task Force by OMG (2007), 9/06/2009 [cited 2008 15/06/2009]; http://www.omg.org/

[12] OMG, Business Process Model and Notation (BPMN) 2.0, p. 34 Object Management Group: Needham, MA 02494 USA (2008)

[13] OMG, QVT. Meta Object Facility (MOF) 2.0 Query/View/Transformation Specification. OMG (2008), http://www.omg.org/spec/QVT/1.0/PDF
[14] OMG, Architecture-Driven Modernization (ADM): Knowledge Discovery Meta-Model (KDM), v1.1. OMG. p. 308 (2009), http://www.omg.org/spec/KDM/1.1/PDF/
[15] Paradauskas, B., Laurikaitis, A.: Business Knowledge Extraction from Legacy Information Systems. Journal of Inf. Tech. and Control 35(3), 214–221 (2006)
[16] Pérez-Castillo, R., García-Rodríguez de Guzmán, I., Ávila-García, O., Piattini, M.: MARBLE: A Modernization Approach for Recovering Business Processes from Legacy Systems. In: International Workshop on Reverse Engineering Models from Software Artifacts (REM 2009), pp. 17–20. Simula Research Laboratory Reports, Lille (2009)
[17] Pérez-Castillo, R., García-Rodríguez de Guzmán, I., Ávila-García, O., Piattini, M.: Business Process Patterns for Software Archeology. In: 25th Annual ACM Symposium on Applied Computing (SAC 2010), pp. 165–166. ACM, New York (2010)
[18] Pérez-Castillo, R., García-Rodríguez de Guzmán, I., Caballero, I., Polo, M., Piattini, M.: PRECISO: A Reengineering Process and a Tool for Database Modernisation through Web Services. In: 24th ACM Symposium on Applied Computing, pp. 2126–2133 (2009)
[19] Polo, M., Piattini, M., Ruiz, F.: Advances in software maintenance management: technologies and solutions. Idea Group Publishing (2003)
[20] Rolón, E., Ruiz, F., García, F., Piattini, M.: Evaluation measures for business process models. In: 21th ACM Symposium on Applied Computing, pp. 1567–1568 (2006)
[21] Sneed, H.M.: Estimating the Costs of a Reengineering Project. In: Proceedings of the 12th Working Conference on Reverse Engineering, IEEE Computer Society, Los Alamitos (2005)
[22] Source Tap, Source Tap CRM (2009), http://sourcetapcrm.sourceforge.net/
[23] Visaggio, G.: Ageing of a data-intensive legacy system: symptoms and remedies. Journal of Software Maintenance 13(5), 281–308 (2001)
[24] Weske, M.: Business Process Management: Concepts, Languages, Architectures, Leipzig, Alemania. Springer, Heidelberg (2007)
[25] Zdun, U., Hentrich, C., Dustdar, S.: Modeling process-driven and service-oriented architectures using patterns and pattern primitives. ACM Trans. Web 1(3), 14 (2007)
[26] Zou, Y., Lau, T.C., Kontogiannis, K., Tong, T., McKegney, R.: Model-Driven Business Process Recovery. In: Proceedings of the 11th Working Conference on Reverse Engineering (WCRE 2004), pp. 224–233. IEEE Computer Society, Los Alamitos (2004)

Model Migration with Epsilon Flock

Louis M. Rose, Dimitrios S. Kolovos, Richard F. Paige, and Fiona A.C. Polack

Department of Computer Science, University of York, UK
{louis,dkolovos,paige,fiona}@cs.york.ac.uk

Abstract. In their recent book, Mens and Demeyer state that Model-Driven Engineering introduces additional challenges for controlling and managing software evolution. Today, tools exist for generating model editors and for managing models with transformation, validation, merging and weaving. There is limited support, however, for *model migration* - a development activity in which instance models are updated in response to metamodel evolution. In this paper, we describe Epsilon Flock, a model-to-model transformation language tailored for model migration that contributes a novel algorithm for relating source and target model elements. To demonstrate its conciseness, we compare Flock to other approaches.

1 Introduction

Today, metamodel developers can automatically generate tools [18] and graphical editors [6] for manipulating models. Models can be *managed* using a variety of operations, such as: transformation to other models [9], transformation to text [14], and validation against a set of constraints. There is limited support, however, for *model migration* - a development activity in which instance models are updated in response to metamodel evolution. More generally, MDE introduces additional challenges for controlling and managing software evolution [13].

When a metamodel evolves, instance models might no longer conform to the structures and rules defined by the metamodel. When an instance model does not conform to its metamodel, it cannot be manipulated with metamodel-specific editors, cannot be managed with model management operations and, in some cases, cannot be loaded by modelling tools.

In this paper, we compare existing approaches to model migration and perform a gap analysis in Section 3. From this analysis, we have derived Epsilon Flock, a model-to-model transformation language tailored for model migration (Section 4). Epsilon Flock contributes several novel features including: a hybrid approach to relating source and target model elements, migration between models specified in heterogenous modelling technologies, and a more concise syntax than existing approaches. In Section 5, we apply Epsilon Flock to two examples of co-evolution for comparison with existing model migration languages.

2 Background

Before introducing existing approaches, a more thorough definition of model migration is presented in this section, along with a discussion of some of the

L. Tratt and M. Gogolla (Eds.): ICMT 2010, LNCS 6142, pp. 184–198, 2010.
© Springer-Verlag Berlin Heidelberg 2010

characteristics of MDE modelling frameworks that affect the way in which model migration can be performed.

2.1 Conformance

A model *conforms to* a metamodel when the metamodel specifies every concept used in the model definition, and the model uses the metamodel concepts according to the rules specified by the metamodel. Conformance can be described by a set of constraints between models and metamodels [15]. When all constraints are satisfied, a model conforms to a metamodel. For example, a conformance constraint might state that every object in the model has a corresponding non-abstract class in the metamodel.

Metamodel changes can affect conformance. For example, when a concept is removed from a metamodel, any models using that concept no longer conform to the metamodel. *Model and metamodel co-evolution* (subsequently referred to as *co-evolution*) is the process of evolving model and metamodel such that conformance is preserved. *Model migration* is a development activity in which models are updated in response to metamodel evolution to re-establish conformance.

2.2 Relevant Characteristics of MDE Modelling Frameworks

Model and Metamodel Separation. In modern MDE development environments, models and metamodels are kept separate. Metamodels are developed and distributed to users. Metamodels are installed, configured and combined to form a customised MDE development environment. Metamodel developers have no programmatic access to downstream instance models.

Because of this, metamodel evolution occurs independently to model migration. First, the metamodel is evolved. Subsequently, the users of the metamodel find that their models are out-of-date and migrate their models. This process is facilitated when, during metamodel evolution, the metamodel developer devises and codifies a *migration strategy*, which is distributed with the evolved metamodel. Later, the metamodel user executes the migration strategy to migrate models that no longer conform to the metamodel. When no migration strategy is included with an evolved metamodel, model migration is a tedious and error-prone process, as we discuss in [17].

Implicit Conformance. MDE modelling frameworks implicitly enforce conformance. A model is *bound* to its metamodel, typically by constructing a representation in the underlying programming language (e.g. Java) for each model element and data value. Frequently, binding is strongly typed: each metamodel type is mapped to a corresponding type in the underlying programming language using mappings defined by the metamodel. Consequently, MDE modelling frameworks do not permit changes to a model that would cause it to no longer conform to its metamodel. Loading a model that does not conform to its metamodel causes an error. In short, MDE modelling frameworks cannot be used to manage any model that does not conform to its metamodel.

3   Existing Approaches

We now compare existing approaches to managing co-evolution, using the example of metamodel evolution given in Section 3.1. From this comparison, we derive requirements for a domain-specific language for specifying and executing model migration strategies in Section 3.5.

In [16], we propose three categories of co-evolution approaches: *manual specification*, *operator-based* and *metamodel matching*.

To date, only prototypical metamodel matching approaches exist [1,5] and, technical limitations of the prototypes prevented their application to the example described in this section. In general, metamodel matching approaches cannot always automatically infer an appropriate migration strategy [16]. For these reasons, metamodel matching approaches are not considered further in this paper.

Instead, we discuss co-evolution approaches that have been used in projects employing MDE. Model-to-model transformation (Section 3.2) and use of an Ecore2Ecore mapping (Section 3.3) are manual specification approaches. The former has been used in the Eclipse GMF project [6] and the latter in the Eclipse MDT UML2 project [4]. Section 3.4 discusses COPE, an operator-based approach, which has been applied to real world projects [7].

3.1   Co-evolution Example

In this paper, we use the example of an evolution of a Petri net metamodel, previously used in [1,5,19] to discuss co-evolution and model migration.

In Figure 1(a), a Petri Net comprises Places and Transitions. A Place has any number of src or dst Transitions. Similarly, a Transition has at least one src and dst Place. In this example, the metamodel in Figure 1(a) is to be evolved so as to support weighted connections between Places and Transitions and between Transitions and Places.

The evolved metamodel is shown in Figure 1(b). Places are connected to Transitions via instances of PTArc. Likewise, Transitions are connected

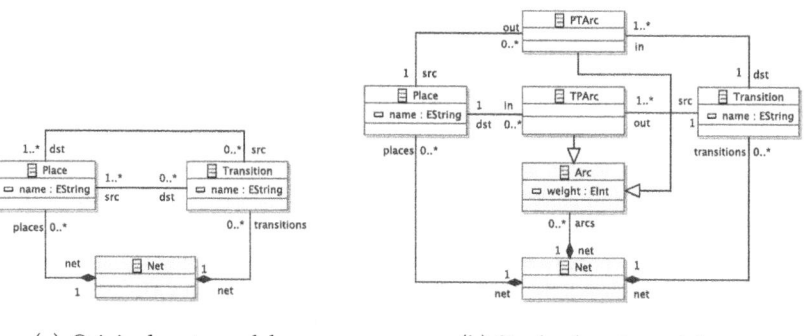

(a) Original metamodel.   (b) Evolved metamodel.

Fig. 1. Exemplar metamodel evolution. (Shading is irrelevant).

to Places via TPArc. Both PTArc and TPArc inherit from Arc, and therefore can be used to specify a weight.

Models that conformed to the original metamodel might not conform to the evolved metamodel. The following strategy can be used to migrate models from the original to the evolved metamodel:

1. For every instance, t, of Transition:
   - For every Place, s, referenced by the src feature of t:
   -- Create a new instance, arc, of PTArc.
   -- Set s as the src of arc.
   -- Set t as the dst of arc.
   -- Add arc to the arcs reference of the Net referenced by t.
   - For every Place, d, referenced by the dst feature of t:
   -- Create a new instance, arc, of TPArc.
   -- Set t as the src of arc.
   -- Set d as the dst of arc.
   -- Add arc to the arcs reference of the Net referenced by t.
2. And nothing else changes.

Using the above example, the existing approaches for specifying and executing model migration strategies are now compared.

3.2   Manual Specification with Model-to-Model Transformation

A model-to-model transformation specified between original and evolved meta-model can be used for performing model migration. This section briefly discusses two styles of model-to-model transformation and presents an example of a migrating model-to-model transformation.

In model transformation, [2] identifies two categories of relationship between source and target model, *new-target* and *existing-target*. In the former, the target model is constructed entirely by the transformation. In the latter, the target model is initialised as a copy of the source model before the transformation.

In model migration, source and target metamodels differ, and hence existing-target transformations cannot be used. Consequently, model migration strategies are specified with new-target model-to-model transformation languages, and often contain sections for copying from original to migrated model those model elements that have not been affected by metamodel evolution.

Part of the Petri nets model migration is codified with the Atlas Transformation Language (ATL) [9] in Listing 1.1. Rules for migrating Places and TPArcs have been omitted for brevity, but are similar to the Nets and PTArcs rules.

In ATL, *rules* transform source model elements (specified using the from keyword) to target model elements (specified using to keyword). For example, the Nets rule on line 1 of Listing 1 transforms an instance of Net from the original (source) model to an instance of Net in the evolved (target) model. The source model element (the variable o in the Net rule) is used to populate the target model element (the variable m). ATL allows rules to be specified as *lazy* (applied only when called by other rules).

The `Transitions` rule in Listing 1 codifies in ATL the migration strategy described previously. The rule is executed for each `Transition` in the original model, o, and constructs a `PTArc` (`TPArc`) for each reference to a `Place` in `o.src` (`o.dst`). Lazy rules must be used to produce the arcs to prevent circular dependencies with the `Transitions` and `Places` rules. On line 10, the feature `in` is escaped because `in` is an ATL keyword.

```
1   rule Nets {
2       from o : Before!Net
3       to m : After!Net ( places <- o.places, transitions <- o.transitions )
4   }
5
6   rule Transitions {
7       from o : Before!Transition
8       to m : After!Transition (
9           name <- o.name,
10          "in" <- o.src->collect(p | thisModule.PTArcs(p,o)),
11          out <- o.dst->collect(p | thisModule.TPArcs(o,p))
12          )
13  }
14
15  unique lazy rule PTArcs {
16      from place : Before!Place, destination : Before!Transition
17      to ptarcs : After!PTArc (
18          src <- place, dst <- destination, net <- destination.net
19          )
20  }
```

Listing 1. Fragment of the Petri nets model migration in ATL

As discussed above, a new-target transformation must be used to specify migration because the source and target metamodels differ. For the Petri nets example, the `Nets` rule (in Listing 1) and the `Places` rule (not shown) exist only to copy data from the original to the migrated model.

Here, we have considered ATL, which is a typical rule-based transformation language. Model migration would be similar in QVT. With Kermeta, migration would be specified in an imperative style using statements for copying `Nets`, `Places` and `Transitions`, and for creating `PTArcs` and `TPArcs`.

3.3   Manual Specification with Ecore2Ecore Mapping

Hussey and Paternostro [8] explain the way in which integration with the model loading mechanisms of the Eclipse Modeling Framework (EMF) [18] can be used to perform model migration. In this approach, the default metamodel loading strategy is augmented with model migration code.

Because EMF binds models to their metamodel (discussed in Section 2.2), EMF cannot use an evolved metamodel to load an instance of the original metamodel. Therefore, Hussey and Paternostro's approach requires the metamodel developer to provide a mapping between the metamodelling language of EMF, Ecore, and the concrete syntax used to persist models, XMI. Mappings are specified using a tool that can suggest relationships between source and target metamodel elements by comparing names and types.

Model migration is specified on the XMI representation of the model and hence presumes some knowledge of the XMI standard. For example, in XMI, references to other model elements are serialised as a space delimited collection of URI fragments [18]. For the Petri net example presented above, the Ecore2Ecore migration strategy must access the `src` and `dst` features of `Transition`, which no longer exist in the evolved metamodel and hence are not loaded automatically by EMF. To do this, the Ecore2Ecore migration strategy must convert a `String` containing URI fragments to a `Collection` of `Places`. In other words, to specify the migration strategy for the Petri nets example, the metamodel developer must know the way in which the `src` and `dst` features are represented in XMI. The complete Ecore2Ecore migration strategy for the Petri nets example, not shown here, exceeds 200 lines of code.

3.4 Operator-Based Co-evolution with COPE

Operator-based approaches to managing co-evolution, such as COPE [7], provide a library of *co-evolutionary operators*. Each co-evolutionary operator specifies both a metamodel evolution and a corresponding model migration strategy. For example, the "Make Reference Containment" operator from COPE [7] evolves the metamodel such that a non-containment reference becomes a containment reference and migrates models such that the values of the evolved reference are replaced by copies. By composing co-evolutionary operators, metamodel evolution can be performed and a migration strategy can be generated without writing any code.

To perform metamodel evolution using an operator-based approach, the library of co-evolutionary operators must be integrated with tools for editing metamodels. COPE provides integration with the EMF tree-based metamodel editor. Operators may be applied to an EMF metamodel, and a record of changes tracks their application. Once metamodel evolution is complete, a migration strategy can be generated automatically from the record of changes. The migration strategy is distributed along with the updated metamodel, and metamodel users choose when to execute the migration strategy on their models.

To be effective, operator-based approaches must provide a rich yet navigable library of co-evolutionary operators, as we discuss in [16]. To this end, COPE allows model migration strategies to be specified manually when no co-evolutionary operator is appropriate. Rather than use either of the two manual specification approaches discussed above (model-to-model transformation and Ecore2Ecore mapping), COPE employs a fundamentally different approach for manually specifying migration strategies using an existing-target transformation. Because this paper focuses on model migration languages, subsequent discussion of COPE concentrates on manually-specified migration.

As discussed above, existing-target transformations cannot be used for specifying model migration strategies as the source (original) and target (evolved) metamodels differ. However, models can be structured independently of their metamodel using a *metamodel-independent representation*. By using a metamodel-independent representation of models as an intermediary, an existing-target transformation can be used for performing model migration when the migration strategy is specified in terms of the metamodel-independent representation. Further details of this technique are given in [7].

Listing 2 shows the COPE model migration strategy for the Petri net example given above[1]. Most notably, slots for features that no longer exist must be explicitly unset. In Listing 2, slots are unset on four occasions, once for each feature that exists in the original metamodel but not the evolved metamodel. Namely, these features are: src and dst of Transition and of Place. Failing to unset slots that do not conform with the evolved metamodel causes migration to fail with an error.

```
1   for (transition in Transition.allInstances) {
2     for (source in transition.unset('src')) {
3       def arc = petrinets.PTArc.newInstance()
4       arc.src = source; arc.dst = transition;
5       arc.net = transition.net
6     }
7
8     for (destination in transition.unset('dst')) {
9       def arc = petrinets.TPArc.newInstance()
10      arc.src = transition; arc.dst = destination;
11      arc.net = transition.net
12    }
13  }
14
15  for (place in Place.allInstances) {
16    place.unset('src'); place.unset('dst');
17  }
```

Listing 2. Petri nets model migration in COPE

3.5   Analysis

By analysing the above approaches to managing co-evolution, requirements were derived for Epsilon Flock, a domain-specific language for specifying and executing model migration. The derivation of the requirements for Epsilon Flock is now summarised, by considering the way in which languages used for specifying migration strategies relate source and target elements and represent models.

Source-Target Relationship. New target transformation languages (Section 3.2) require code for explicitly copying from the original to the evolved metamodel those model elements that are unaffected by the metamodel evolution. In contrast, model migration strategies written in COPE (Section 3.4) must explicitly unset any data that is not to be copied from the original to the migrated model. The Ecore2Ecore approach (Section 3.3) does not require explicit copying or unsetting code. Instead, the relationship between original and evolved metamodel elements is captured in a mapping model specified by the metamodel developer. The mapping model can be configured by hand or, in some cases, automatically derived.

In each case, extra effort is required when defining a migration strategy due to the way in which the co-evolution approach relates source (original) and target

---

[1] In Listing 2, some of the concrete syntax has been changed in the interest of brevity.

(migrated) model elements. This observation led to the following requirement: *Epsilon Flock must **automatically** copy every model element that conforms to the evolved metamodel from original to migrated model, and must not automatically copy any model element that does not conform to the evolved metamodel from original to migrated model.*

Model Representation. When using the Ecore2Ecore approach, model elements that do not conform to the evolved metamodel are accessed via XMI. Consequently, the metamodel developer must be familiar with XMI and must perform tasks such as dereferencing URI fragments and type conversion. With COPE and the Atlas Transformation Language, models are loaded using a modelling framework (and so migration strategies need not be concerned with the representation used to store models). Consequently, the following requirement was identified: *Epsilon Flock must not expose the underlying representation of original or migrated models.*

To apply co-evolution operators, COPE requires the metamodel developer to use a specialised metamodel editor, which can manipulate only metamodels defined with EMF. Like, the Ecore2Ecore approach, COPE can be used only to manage co-evolution for models and metamodels specified with EMF. Tight coupling to EMF allows the Ecore2Ecore approach to schedule migration automatically, during model loading. To better support integration with modelling frameworks other than EMF, the following requirement was derived: *Epsilon Flock must be loosely coupled with modelling frameworks and must not assume that models and metamodels will be represented in EMF.*

4   Epsilon Flock

Driven by the analysis presented in Section 3, we have designed and implemented Epsilon Flock (subsequently referred to as Flock). Flock is a domain-specific language for specifying and executing model migration strategies. Flock uses a model connectivity framework, which decouples migration from the representation of models and provides compatibility with several modelling frameworks (Section 4.1). Flock automatically maps each element of the original model to an equivalent element of the migrated model using a novel conservative copying algorithm and user-defined migration rules (Section 4.2).

4.1   The Epsilon Platform

Before presenting Flock, it is necessary to introduce the underlying Epsilon [10] platform. Epsilon, a component of the Eclipse GMT project [3], provides infrastructure for implementing uniform and interoperable model management languages, for performing tasks such as model merging, model transformation and inter-model consistency checking.

The core of the platform is the Epsilon Object Language (EOL) [11], a reworking and extension of OCL that includes the ability to update models, conditional and loop statements, statement sequencing, and access to standard I/O streams. EOL provides mechanisms for reusing sections of code, such as user-defined operators along with modules and import statements. The Epsilon task-specific languages are built atop EOL, giving highly efficient inheritance and reuse of features.

4.2   Flock

Flock is a rule-based transformation language that mixes declarative and imperative parts. Its style is inspired by hybrid model-to-model transformation languages such as the Atlas Transformation Language [9] and the Epsilon Transformation Language [12]. Flock has a compact syntax. Much of its design and implementation is focused on the runtime. The way in which Flock relates source to target elements is novel; it is neither a new- nor an existing-target relationship.

Abstract Syntax. As illustrated by Figure 2, Flock migration strategies are organised into modules (`FlockModule`), which inherit from EOL modules (`EolModule`), which provides support for module reuse with import statements and user-defined operations. Modules comprise any number of rules (`Rule`). Each rule has an original metamodel type (`originalType`) and can optionally specify a `guard`, which is either an EOL statement or a block of EOL statements. `MigrateRules` must specify an evolved metamodel type (`evolvedType`) and/or a `body` comprising a block of EOL statements.

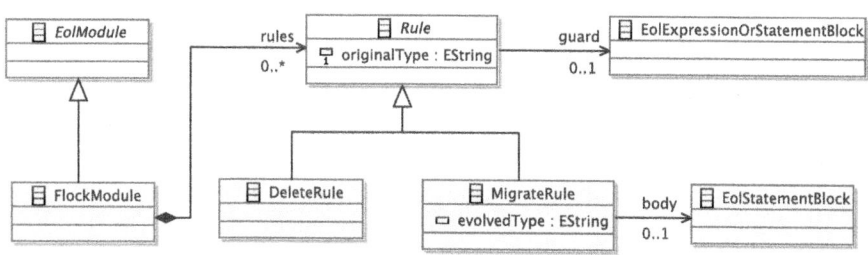

Fig. 2. The abstract syntax of Flock

Concrete Syntax. Listing 3 shows the concrete syntax of migrate and delete rules. All rules begin with a keyword indicating their type (either `migrate` or `delete`), followed by the original metamodel type. Guards are specified using the `when` keywords. Migrate rules may also specify an evolved metamodel type using the `to` keyword and a `body` as a (possibly empty) sequence of EOL statements.

Note there is presently no create rule. In Flock, the creation of new model elements is usually encoded in the imperative part of a migrate rule specified on the containing type.

```
1  migrate <originalType> (to <evolvedType>)?
2  (when (:<eolExpression>)|({<eolStatement>+})))? {
3      <eolStatement>*
4  }
5
6  delete <originalType>
7  (when (:<eolExpression>)|({<eolStatement>+})))?
```

Listing 3. Concrete syntax of migrate and delete rules

Execution Semantics. A Flock module has the following behaviour when executed:

1. For each original model element, e:
   - Identify an applicable rule, r. To be applicable for e, a rule must have as its original type the metaclass (or a supertype of the metaclass) of e and the guard part of the rule must be satisfied by e.
   - When no rule can be applied, a default rule is used, which has the metaclass of e as its original type, and an empty body.
   - When more than one rule could be applied, the first to appear in the Flock source file is selected.
2. For each mapping between original model element, e, and applicable delete rule, r:
   - Do nothing.
3. For each mapping between original model element, e, and applicable migrate rule, r:
   - Create an equivalent model element, e′ in the migrated model. The metaclass of e′ is determined from the evolvedType (or the originalType when no evolvedType has been specified) of r.
   - Copy the data contained in e to e′ (using the *conservative copy* algorithm described in the sequel).
4. For each mapping between original model element, e, applicable migrate rule, r, and equivalent model element, e′:
   - Execute the body of r binding: e and e′ to variables named original and migrated, respectively.

These semantics allow the two variables defined in Step 4, original and migrated to be used in the body of any migration rule. In addition, Flock defines an equivalent() operation which can be called on any original model element and returns the equivalent migrated model element.

Conservative Copying. Flock contributes an algorithm, termed *conservative copy*, that copies model elements from original to migrated model only when those model elements conform to the evolved metamodel. Because of its conservative copy algorithm, Flock is a hybrid of new- and existing-target transformation languages. This section discusses the conservative copying algorithm in more detail.

The algorithm operates on an original model element, o, and its equivalent model element in the migrated model, e. When o has no equivalent in the migrated model (for example, when a metaclass has been removed and the migration strategy specifies no alternative metaclass), o is not copied to the migrated model. Otherwise, conservative copy is invoked for o and e, proceeding as follows:

- For each metafeature, f for which o has specified a value
  - Locate a metafeature in the evolved metamodel with the same name as f for which e may specify a value.
  -- When no equivalent metafeature can be found, do nothing.
  -- Otherwise, copy to the migrated model the original value (o.f) only when it conforms to the equivalent metafeature

The definition of conformance varies over modelling frameworks. Typically, conformance between a value, v, and a feature, f, specifies at least the following constraints:

- The size of v must be greater than or equal to the lowerbound of f.
- The size of v must be less than or equal to the upperbound of f.
- The type of v must be the same as or a subtype of the type of f.

Epsilon includes a model connectivity layer (EMC), which provides a common interface for accessing and persisting models. Currently, EMC provides drivers for several modelling frameworks, permitting management of models defined with EMF, the Metadata Repository (MDR), Z or XML. To support migration between metamodels defined in heterogenous modelling frameworks, EMC was extended during the development of Flock. The connectivity layer now provides a conformance checking service. Each EMC driver was extended to include conformance checking semantics specific to its modelling framework. Flock implements conservative copy by delegate conformance checking responsibilities to EMC.

Finally, some categories of model value must be converted before being copied from the original to the migrated model. Again, the need for and semantics of this conversion varies over modelling frameworks. Reference values typically require conversion before copying. In this case, the mappings between original and migrated model elements maintained by the Flock runtime can be used to perform the conversion. In other cases, the target modelling framework must be used to perform the conversion, such as when EMF enumeration literals are to be copied.

5   Example

Flock is now demonstrated using two examples of model migration. Listing 4 illustrates the Flock migration strategy for the Petri net example introduced in Section 3, which is included for direct comparison with other approaches. In addition, we present a larger example, based on changes between versions 1.5 and 2.0 of the UML specification.

5.1 Petri Nets in Flock

In Listing 4, `Nets` and `Places` are migrated automatically. Unlike the ATL migration strategy (Listing 1), no explicit copying rules are required. Compared to the COPE migration strategy (Listing 2), the Flock migration strategy does not explicitly unset the original `src` and `dst` features of `Transition`.

```
1  migrate Transition {
2    for (source in original.src) {
3      var arc := new Migrated!PTArc;
4      arc.src := source.equivalent(); arc.dst := migrated;
5      arc.net := original.net.equivalent();
6    }
7
8    for (destination in original.dst) {
9      var arc := new Migrated!TPArc;
10     arc.src := migrated; arc.dst := destination.equivalent();
11     arc.net := original.net.equivalent();
12   }
13 }
```

Listing 4. Petri nets model migration in Flock

```
1  migrate Association {
2      migrated.memberEnds := original.connections.equivalent();
3  }
4
5  migrate Class {
6      var fs := original.features.equivalent();
7      migrated.operations := fs.select(f|f.isKindOf(Operation));
8      migrated.attributes := fs.select(f|f.isKindOf(Property));
9      migrated.attributes.addAll(original.associations.equivalent())
10 }
11
12 delete StructuralFeature when: original.targetScope <> #instance
13
14 migrate Attribute to Property {
15     if (original.ownerScope = #classifier) {
16        migrated.isStatic = true;
17     }
18 }
19 migrate Operation {
20     if (original.ownerScope = #classifier) {
21        migrated.isStatic = true;
22     }
23 }
24
25 migrate AssociationEnd to Property {
26     if (original.isNavigable) {
27        original.association.equivalent().navigableEnds.add(migrated)
28     }
29 }
```

Listing 5. UML model migration in Flock

5.2 UML 1.5 to UML 2.0 in Flock

Figure 3 illustrates a subset of the changes made between UML 1.5 and UML 2.0. Only class diagrams are considered, and features that did not change are omitted. In Figure 3(a), association ends and attributes are specified explicitly and separately. In Figure 3(b), the `Property` class is used instead. The Flock migration strategy (Listing 5) for Figure 3 is now discussed.

Firstly, `Attributes` and `AssociationEnds` are now modelled as `Prope-`
`rties` (lines 16 and 28). In addition, the `Association#navigableEnds`
reference replaces the `AssociationEnd#isNavigable` attribute; following
migration, each navigable `AssociationEnd` must be referenced via the na-
vigableEnds feature of its `Association` (lines 29-31).

In UML 2.0, `StructuralFeature#ownerScope` has been replaced by `#i-`
`sStatic` (lines 17-19 and 23-25). The UML 2.0 specification states that `Scop-`
`eKind#classifier` should be mapped to true, and `#instance` to false.

The UML 1.5 `StructuralFeature#targetScope` feature is no longer
supported in UML 2.0, and no migration path is provided. Consequently, line
14 deletes any model element whose `targetScope` is not the default value.

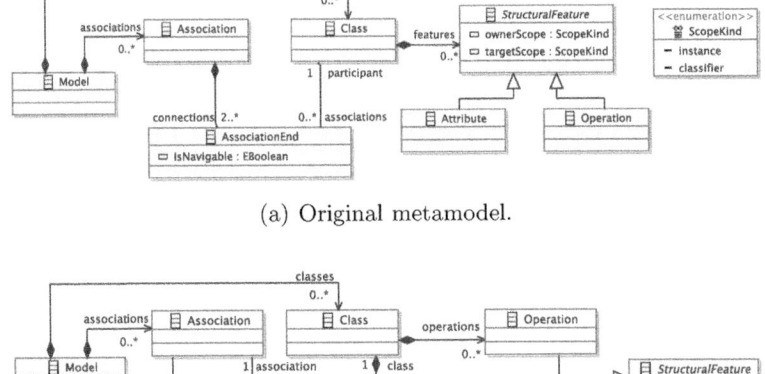

(a) Original metamodel.

(b) Evolved metamodel.

Fig. 3. Exemplar UML metamodel evolution. (Shading is irrelevant).

Finally, `Class#features` has been split to form `Class#operations` and
`#attributes`. Lines 8 and 10 partition features on the original `Class`. `Cl-`
`ass#associations` has been removed in UML 2.0, and `AssociationEnds`
are instead stored in `Class#attributes` (line 11).

5.3   Comparison

Table 1 illustrates several characterising differences between Flock and the
related approaches presented in Section 3. Due to its conservative copying algorithm, Flock is the only approach to provide both automatic copying and unsetting. Automatic copying is significant for metamodel evolutions with a large
number of unchanging features, such as those observed for UML.

Table 1. Properties of model migration approaches

	Automatic copy	Automatic unset	Modelling technologies
Ecore2Ecore	✓	✗	XMI
ATL	✗	✓	EMF, MDR, KM3, XML
COPE	✓	✗	EMF
Flock	✓	✓	EMF, MDR, XML, Z

All of the approaches considered in Table 1 support EMF, arguably the most widely used modelling framework. The Ecore2Ecore approach, however, requires migration to be encoded at the level of the underlying model representation XMI. Both Flock and ATL support other modelling technologies, such as MDR and XML. However, ATL does not automatically copy model elements that have not been affected by metamodel changes. Therefore, migration between models of different technologies with ATL requires extra statements in the migration strategy to ensure that the conformance constraints of the target technology are satisfied. Because it delegates conformance checking to an EMC driver, Flock requires no such checks.

6   Conclusions and Further Work

Existing approaches for managing model and metamodel co-evolution in the context of model-driven engineering have been reviewed. The way in which existing approaches either require the copying of model elements from the original to the migrated model or the deletion of model elements from the migrated model has been discussed. To this end, the design and implementation of Epsilon Flock, a model-to-model transformation language tailored for model migration, has been presented. Flock treats the relationship between source (original) and target (migrated) model elements novelly, using a conservative copying algorithm that has been designed to minimise the need for explicitly copying or unsetting model elements.

Initial experiments suggest that Flock is more concise than the approaches discussed in Section 3. We intend to more thoroughly test this hypothesis by measuring, for example, cyclomatic complexity and to compare Flock with other co-evolution approaches in a case study. Other future work will involve studying the way in which Flock should be expanded to capture further concepts specific to the domain of model migration. In particular, we intend to explore the need for rule inheritance.

Acknowledgement. The work in this paper was supported by the European Commission via the MODELPLEX project, co-funded by the European Commission under the "Information Society Technologies" Sixth Framework Programme (2006-2009).

References

1. Cicchetti, A., Di Ruscio, D., Eramo, R., Pierantonio, A.: Automating co-evolution in MDE. In: Proc. EDOC, pp. 222–231. IEEE Computer Society, Los Alamitos (2008)
2. Czarnecki, K., Helsen, S.: Feature-based survey of model transformation approaches. IBM Systems Journal 45(3), 621–646 (2006)
3. Eclipse. Generative Modelling Technologies project (2008), http://www.eclipse.org/gmt (accessed June 30, 2008)
4. Eclipse. UML2 Model Development Tools project (2009), http://www.eclipse.org/modeling/mdt/uml2 (accessed September 7, 2009)
5. Garcés, K., Jouault, F., Cointe, P., Bézivin, J.: Managing model adaptation by precise detection of metamodel changes. In: Paige, R.F., Hartman, A., Rensink, A. (eds.) ECMDA-FA 2009. LNCS, vol. 5562, pp. 34–49. Springer, Heidelberg (2009)
6. Gronback, R.: Introduction to the Eclipse Graphical Modeling Framework. In: Proc. EclipseCon, Santa Clara, California (2006)
7. Herrmannsdoerfer, M., Benz, S., Juergens, E.: COPE - automating coupled evolution of metamodels and models. In: Drossopoulou, S. (ed.) ECOOP 2009 – Object-Oriented Programming. LNCS, vol. 5653, pp. 52–76. Springer, Heidelberg (2009)
8. Hussey, K., Paternostro, M.: Advanced features of EMF. Tutorial at EclipseCon 2006, California, USA (2006), http://www.eclipsecon.org/2006/Sub.do?id=171 (accessed September 07, 2009)
9. Jouault, F., Kurtev, I.: Transforming models with ATL. In: Bruel, J.-M. (ed.) MoDELS 2005. LNCS, vol. 3844, pp. 128–138. Springer, Heidelberg (2006)
10. Kolovos, D.S.: An Extensible Platform for Specification of Integrated Languages for Model Management. PhD thesis, University of York, United Kingdom (2009)
11. Kolovos, D.S., Paige, R.F., Polack, F.A.C.: The Epsilon Object Language (EOL). In: Rensink, A., Warmer, J. (eds.) ECMDA-FA 2006. LNCS, vol. 4066, pp. 128–142. Springer, Heidelberg (2006)
12. Kolovos, D.S., Paige, R.F., Polack, F.A.C.: The Epsilon Transformation Language. In: Vallecillo, A., Gray, J., Pierantonio, A. (eds.) ICMT 2008. LNCS, vol. 5063, pp. 46–60. Springer, Heidelberg (2008)
13. Mens, T., Demeyer, S.: Software Evolution. Springer, Heidelberg (2007)
14. Oldevik, J., Neple, T., Grønmo, R., Øyvind Aagedal, J., Berre, A.: Toward standardised model to text transformations. In: Hartman, A., Kreische, D. (eds.) ECMDA-FA 2005. LNCS, vol. 3748, pp. 239–253. Springer, Heidelberg (2005)
15. Paige, R.F., Brooke, P.J., Ostroff, J.S.: Metamodel-based model conformance and multiview consistency checking. ACM Transactions on Software Engineering and Methodology 16(3) (2007)
16. Rose, L.M., Kolovos, D.S., Paige, R.F., Polack, F.A.C.: An analysis of approaches to model migration. In: Proc. Joint MoDSE-MCCM Workshop (2009)
17. Rose, L.M., Kolovos, D.S., Paige, R.F., Polack, F.A.C.: Enhanced automation for managing model and metamodel inconsistency. In: Proc. ASE 2009, pp. 545–549. IEEE Computer Society, Los Alamitos (2009)
18. Steinberg, D., Budinsky, F., Paternostro, M., Merks, E.: EMF: Eclipse Modeling Framework. Addison-Wesley Professional, Reading (2008)
19. Wachsmuth, G.: Metamodel adaptation and model co-adaptation. In: Ernst, E. (ed.) ECOOP 2007. LNCS, vol. 4609, pp. 600–624. Springer, Heidelberg (2007)

Exceptional Transformations

Eugene Syriani[1], Jörg Kienzle[1], and Hans Vangheluwe[1,2]

[1] McGill University, Montréal, Canada
[2] University of Antwerp, B-2020 Antwerp, Belgium

Abstract. As model transformations are increasingly used in model-driven engineering, the dependability of model transformation systems becomes crucial to model-driven development deliverables. As any other software, model transformations can contain design faults, be used in inappropriate ways, or may be affected by problems arising in the transformation execution environment at run-time. We propose in this paper to introduce exception handling into model transformation languages to increase the dependability of model transformations. We first introduce a classification of different kinds of exceptions that can occur in the context of model transformations. We present an approach in which exceptions are modelled in the transformation language and the transformation designer is given constructs to define exception handlers to recover from exceptional situations. This facilitates the debugging of transformations at design time. It also enables the design of fault-tolerant transformations that continue to work reliably even in the context of design faults, misuse, or faults in the execution environment.

1 Introduction

Model transformation is at the heart of model-driven engineering approaches, and it is therefore crucial to ensure that the transformations are safe to use: when a model transformation is requested to execute, any exceptional situations that prevent the transformation from executing successfully must be detected and the requester must be made aware of the problem. Informing the requester about the situation allows for possible reactions. What exactly needs to be done depends highly depends on the context in which the model transformation has been requested.

A model transformation can be seen as an operation on models, taking a model as input and producing a (possibly implicit) model as output. This is similar to operations in a programming language, which can have input and output parameters and in addition can affect the application state stored in objects or variables. In order to address exceptional situations that prevent the normal execution of an operation, modern programming languages introduced *exception handling* [1].

A programming language or system with support for exception handling allows users to signal exceptions and to define handlers [1]. To signal an exception amounts to detecting the exceptional situation, interrupting the usual processing sequence, looking for a relevant handler, and then invoking it. Handlers are defined on (or attached to) entities, such as data structures or contexts for one or several exceptions. Depending on the language, a context may be a program, a process, a procedure, a statement, an expression, etc. Handlers are invoked when an exception is signalled during the execution or the use of the associated or nested context. Exception *handling* means to put

L. Tratt and M. Gogolla (Eds.): ICMT 2010, LNCS 6142, pp. 199–214, 2010.
© Springer-Verlag Berlin Heidelberg 2010

the system into a coherent state, *i.e.*, to carry out forward error recovery and then to take one of these steps: transfer control to the statement following the signalling one (resumption model [2]); or discard the context between the signalling statement and the one to which the handler is attached (termination model [2]); or signal a new exception to the enclosing context.

In model transformation, the transformation units (or *rules* in rule-based transformations) that compose a transformation have the notion of *applicability* (of a rule). In contrast to an operation at the programming language level, the model transformation may or may not be applied depending on the applicability of its constituting rules. We must from the beginning clearly distinguish *transformation failure* from *transformation inapplicability*, as we consider these as two distinct outcomes. In graph transformation for example, a rule r is said to be *applicable* if and only if an occurrence of its left-hand side (LHS) is found in the model (encoded as a typed attributed graph). When r also specifies a negative application condition (NAC), such a pattern shall *not* be found given the LHS match. In case of a successful match, the match is replaced by the right-hand side (RHS) of r. Thus the result of a *successfully applied rule* is the (possible) modification of the graph it received. If no occurrences of the LHS were found in the input model, the rule is said to be *inapplicable* and the resulting graph is identical to the input graph. Both a successfully applied rule and a rule that did not match (inapplicable) describe the regular execution of a transformation rule. However, as in the case of the execution of an operation in a program, it is possible that during a model transformation an exceptional situation is encountered in which it is impossible to continue normal execution. At run-time, there are situations in which neither an output model can be produced by applying the transformation in its entirety nor is it possible to determine the non-applicability of the transformation. In this case the rule is said to have *failed*. The definition of applicability, inapplicability, and failure of rules can also be extended to the level of the transformation. That is respectively, the transformation has at least one rule that was successfully applied, no rule in the transformation has been applied, and the last rule to be applied has failed.

Currently, no model transformation language offers means to reason about such exceptional situations encountered during model transformations (see related work section). This paper is a first attempt to motivate and define the notion of exception and exception handling in model transformations. Some may argue that it is not needed in a transformation language and that it is a tool or system issue instead. This contribution claims however that there are many kinds of exceptional situations that can arise while transforming a model, and that these should be modelled in the transformation language to give the modeller control over how such a situation is to be handled. If applied rigorously, exception handling leads to the design of safe model transformations.

The remainder of the paper is structured as follows. In Section 2, we analyse what kind of exceptions can occur in model transformations. Then, in Section 3, we elaborate on possibilities for handling such exceptions. We also outline the implementation of transformation exceptions and their handling in our transformation language. Finally, we put the presented work in perspective in Section 4 and conclude in Section 5.

2 Classification of Exceptions in Model Transformations

Similar to exception class hierarchies used in object-oriented programming languages to distinguish between different kinds of exceptions, we propose in this paper a classification of the exceptions that may arise during a model transformation. In a transformation model, faults may originate from (1) the transformation design, (2) the model on which a transformation is applied, (3) or the context in which the transformation is executed. This section provides a non-exhaustive classification of potential exceptions that may arise during a transformation.

2.1 Terminology

In this subsection we define the terms *failure*, *error*, and *fault* that are used in fault-tolerant computing, in the context of model transformation. A *failure* is an observable deviation from the specification of a transformation. In other words, a failed transformation either produced a result that, according to the specification, is not a valid output model for the specified input, or produced no result at all. An *error* is a part of the transformation state that leads to a failure. The transformation state includes the input and output models, as well as potentially created temporary models and auxiliary variables. A *fault* is a defect or flaw that affects the execution of the transformation. A fault is thus typically present before the transformation execution, *e.g.,* when there is a flaw in the design of the transformation, or the fault arises from the fact that a transformation is applied to a model that it was not designed to work on, or finally the fault resides in the execution environment. At run-time, a fault can be activated and lead to an error, *i.e.,* an erroneous state in the transformation, which in turn may be detected if the transformation language supports it. If it is not handled, however, an error propagates through the system until the transformation fails.

We define an *exception* in the context of model transformation as a description of a situation that, if encountered, requires something exceptional to be done in order to resolve it. An *exception occurrence* at run-time signals that such an exception was encountered.

2.2 Execution Environment Exceptions

Execution Environment Exceptions (EEE) represent exceptional situations that typically originate from the transformation's virtual machine.

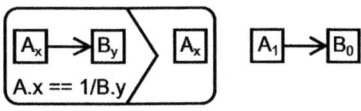

Fig. 1. A rule with attribute constraints written in an action language (on the left) applied to a specific input model (on the right). The rule is specified in **MoTif** [3] syntax where the left and right compartments represent the LHS and RHS respectively.

Action Language Exceptions

When the transformation language allows the use of an action language (which can contain a constraint language such as OCL), a complete exception tree may be provided for types of exceptions specific to the action language itself. Depending on the capabilities of the action language, these exceptions can come from arithmetic manipulations, list manipulations, de-referencing null references, etc. For example, Fig. 1 illustrates a specific Action Language Exception (ALE), namely the case of a division by 0.

System Exceptions

During the execution of a transformation, the virtual machine executing the transformation can encounter exceptional situations, *e.g.*, it can run out of memory. There are many reasons that could lead to such a problem, one of which is a design fault in the transformation itself. Consider a transformation that contains an iteration over a monotonically increasing rule (that never deletes an element nor disables itself) as depicted in Fig. 2. A memory overflow will eventually occur if an infinite loop or recursion (like a recursive rule as described in [4]) is executed.

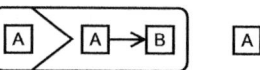

Fig. 2. A monotonically increasing rule (on the left) applied to a specific input model (on the right)

Other kinds of System Exceptions (SE) may arise, *e.g.*, I/O Exception when logging is used and the logging device is not writeable. Also, if the access to the model is provided via web-service functions, for example, the server may be down leading to communication or access errors.

2.3   Transformation Language-Specific Exceptions (TLSE)

Features specific to a particular transformation language can also be the source of exceptional situations. For example, **ProGReS** [5], **QVT** [6], and to a certain extent, **Fujaba** [7] allow rules to be parametrized by specific model elements that may be bound to matches from previous rules. In these languages, executing a rule with unbound parameters results in an exceptional situation that needs to be resolved. A similar exceptional situation arises when a pivot node is passed from one rule to another by connecting input and output ports in **GreAT** [8] or even through nesting in **MoTif**, if the rules are not appropriately connected.

But there are other kinds of exceptional situations that can arise due to a specific transformation language design. In languages such as **QVT-R**, for example, the creation of duplicate elements is semantically avoided by the concept of *key* properties. Two elements are logically the same if and only if their key properties are equal. The *key* is used to locate a matched element of the model and a new element is created (with a new *key*) when a matched element does not exist. However, if multiple keys with the same value are found in a model, this indicates that the model is faulty[1].

Moreover, exceptions proper to the implementation of the scheduling language can also be considered. In **MoTif**, for instance, since the underlying execution engine allows for timed transformations by specifying the duration of an application of a rule, bad timing synchronization may arise when *e.g.*, rules are evaluated at the same time (through conditional branching or parallel application). This typically happens due to the numerical error of floating point operations.

2.4   Rule Design Exceptions

Rule Design Exceptions (RDE) represent errors that stem from a fault in the design of the transformation model itself.

---

[1] We assume in this paper that the transformation engines are fault-free.

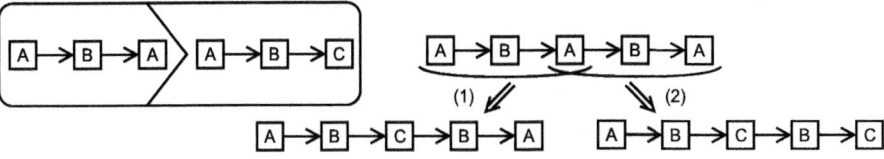

Fig. 3. An inconsistent use of an *iterated rule* (on the left) with respect to a specific input model (on the right)

Inconsistent Use Exception

One class of design faults that may happen in a transformation is when rules are conflicting with one another. We distinguish the case when a rule conflicts with itself from when several rules conflict with each other. The former occurs when a rule finds multiple matches on a given input model and is executed several times in a row. This typically happens during an iteration; *e.g.*, a rule executed in a `loop` in **ProGReS**, iterated in a for-loop or a while-loop in **QVT-OM** [6], or in case the rule is an FRule or an SRule in **MoTif**. This is the case in the example of Fig. 3, where the rule matches the input model twice, but depending on the order in which the matches are processed, two different output models are produced. Although the transformation itself is a valid transformation, the application of the transformation to this particular input model results in a non-deterministic result and as such is very likely to be incorrect. We consider such a situation as an *inconsistent use* of a transformation and propose that in these cases the transformation should be notified with an `Inconsistent Use Exception` (IUE).

Synchronization Exceptions

Another class of design fault can happen in the context of parallel execution of model transformations, a technique often used for efficiency reasons. Semantically, if a transformation designer specifies that two rules should be executed in parallel, this implies that the order of execution of the transformation rules is irrelevant. This optimization can, however, only work if the two rules are independent from one another. For example, the two rules in Fig. 4 are clearly not independent, as

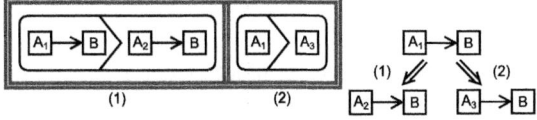

Fig. 4. Two conflicting rules to be applied in parallel (on the left) with respect to a specific input model (on the right). The two rules are specified in a PRule depicting that they will be executed concurrently.

the application of one disables the application of the other. In fact, executing both rules in parallel yields two different models that cannot be trivially merged without knowledge of the application domain. We propose to signal such situations by raising a `Synchronization Exception` (YE).

2.5 Transformation-Specific Exceptions

Finally, we believe that a dependable transformation language should also support user-defined exceptions. Almost all programming languages with support for exception handling support user-defined exceptions that allow the programmer to signal application-specific exceptional conditions to a calling context. Similarly, a transformation language that supports user-defined `Transformation-Specific Exceptions` (TSE) makes it possible for the transformation designer to check desired properties of the model being transformed at specific points during the transformation execution. These property checks can take the form of *assertions* as pre-/post-conditions on a (sub-)transformation by specifying a constraint on the current state of the model. In case the assertion fails, the corresponding TSE can be explicitly raised by the transformation model and signalled to the calling context.

2.6   Using Exceptions in Model Transformations

Fig. 5 summarizes the classification of potential exceptions that may arise during the execution of a transformation. Some classes of exceptions like ALEs and TLSEs can be empty for certain model transformation environments, if the design of the transformation language and action language allows the corresponding problems to be detected statically. In the domain of programming languages, for example, dynamically typed languages such as Python define certain types of exceptions (*e.g.,* NoSuchField Exception) that strongly typed languages do not need to provide. In C++, for instance, a compiler can always statically determine that the programmer was erroneously trying to access a field of a class that has not been declared.

We foresee that exceptions are going to be used in two different ways in the context of model transformation: during transformation development to help eliminate design faults (*debug mode*) and when the transformation is applied to different models in order to increase dependability of the transformation at run-time (*release mode*). Some exceptions are more likely to occur in debug mode while others are relevant only in release mode.

Debug Mode.   When running a transformation in debug mode, the goal of applying the transformation to an input model is not so much to obtain an output model that is subsequently used for other purposes, but to validate that the transformation design is correct. Debugging a transformation is not trivial and exceptions are very helpful for *debugging*, namely to detect logical errors in the design of a transformation.

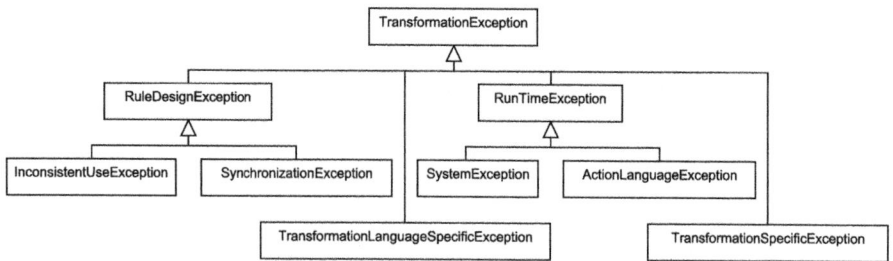

Fig. 5. The proposed classification of model transformation exceptions in UML class diagrams

If the generated output model does not correspond to what the transformation designer expects, then there must be a flaw in the transformation design that has to be found. In this case, the modeller can debug the transformation by adding "assertion" rules at intermediate points in the transformation that check that the previous rule achieved the desired effect. If not, a user-defined TSE is thrown.

If unhandled, the exception halts the transformation execution and the transformation modelling environment informs the modeller of the exception kind and point of occurrence. Using this information, the modeller can more easily locate the rules that contain design faults.

When transformation rules are run distributed or in parallel to increase performance, a YE indicates a merging problem of the different output models. The problem occurs if the rules that are executed concurrently are not independent, *i.e.*, the intersection of the model elements modified by the rules is not empty. No transformation tool can provide an automated general merge operation, not only because general graph merging is undecidable, but also because the correct merging algorithm depends on the specifics of the transformation and its domain(s). Most likely a YE indicates that the modeller incorrectly assumed rule independence when he decided to instruct the transformation engine to use parallel execution.

The occurrence of an IUE on an input model, that the transformation under development should be able to handle, indicates that the iterated rule in which the exception was detected was incorrectly specified. The modeller needs to inspect the information carried with the exception such as the faulty matched model elements as well as the context of execution to then correct the faulty rule or revise the transformation design.

An EEE in debug mode can signal various problems to the modeller. It can signal design flaws, including flaws that are due to the incorrect use of a specific action language feature (*e.g.,* UnboundParameter Exception), incorrect expressions specified by the modeller using the action language (DivisionByZero Exception), or faulty transformation designs that result in infinite recursion or loops (MemoryOverflow Exception).

Release Mode. In release mode, a transformation that is assumed to work correctly is applied to an input model with the goal of producing an output model that is used for a specific purpose. Most likely it is essential that the transformation was applied successfully and did indeed produce the expected result, otherwise the output model is unusable. It is therefore important to design reliable transformations that can recover from exceptional situations and still provide a useful output.

In release mode, a SE such as `IOException` could signal that the device used for logging transformation related information is currently not writeable, for instance because the communication link broke down. Instead of immediately halting the transformation process, a reliable transformation could try to handle this situation. For instance, if the fault is assumed to be transient, the exception could be handled simply by waiting for some time and restarting the failed transformation. Alternatively, a different device could be used to store the log information.

The occurrence of an IUE in release mode signals that the transformation is being applied to an input model that the transformation was not designed to handle. An example of such a situation is given in Fig. 3. This does not mean, however, that the rule cannot produce a correct output model. Both possible outputs shown in Fig. 3 might be correct, or maybe only one of them is. The problem is that the transformation system cannot guess what the correct behaviour of the transformation should be. One way of handling the exception could be to obtain *user (or external) input* from the transformation environment, *i.e.,* halt the transformation, prompt the user to designate the correct match or output, and continue with the transformation. Another transparent way of handling could be to apply a different set of rules instead that can produce an appropriate output model using different rules.

3   Exception Handling in Model Transformation

The previous classification identifies the exceptional situations that can occur during a model transformation. In order for a transformation to be dependable, the transformation designer should think of potential exceptions that could occur at run-time and design a way of addressing them in order to recover. We must therefore define a way that allows a modeller to reason about exceptions and express exception handling behaviour at the same level of abstraction as the model transformation itself.

3.1   Modelling Exceptions

In order to be able to reason about exceptions at the transformation level, exceptions should be treated as first-class entities, *i.e.,* just like any other model element that can itself be used as an input to a transformation. From a transformation language design point of view, a transformation exception can be considered as a model conforming to a distinct meta-model as shown in Fig. 6. An exception is identified by a name and has a status which can be: `active` (*i.e.,* the exception instance has not been addressed yet), `handling` (*i.e.,* it is currently being handled), or `handled` (*i.e.,* it has been addressed by a handler).

In order to enable proper handling, an exception must hold relevant information regarding its activation point context: where it happened, what happened, and when it happened.

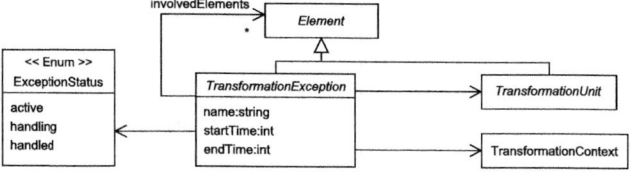

Fig. 6. The transformation exception meta-model

The transformation exception therefore references the transformation unit (the rule) that triggered its activation. The transformation context depicted in Fig. 6 contains all the information needed to effectively investigate the origin of the exception occurrence and allow the designer to model an appropriate handler. In our implementation, for instance, the context contains the stack frame and the state of the packet (see Section 3.3) at the activation of the exception. In compositional or hierarchical transformation languages such as **MoTif**, **GReAT**, or **QVT**, knowing the exact path to the rule helps locating the fault in the transformation design, especially if the handler is not in the same scope as the activation point. The activation point can be specified at the level of primitive transformation operations supported by the virtual machine instruction set (*e.g.,* CRUD[2]) or at the transformation rule that triggered the exception. If the modelling language makes it possible to isolate the transformation operators (match, rewrite, iterate, etc.) from the virtual machine operations, such as in [9], then the activation point can be specified in terms of these operations. In addition to the point of activation, the transformation context should also indicate the state of the transformed (input) model at the time when the exception was thrown. For instance, in order to handle an RDE effectively, the input model elements involved in the matcher of the current rule should certainly be accessible to the handler.

In our proposed meta-model of an exception we also included timing information, such as the timestamp at which the exception was generated (active) and has been handled (handled). This can be useful for profiling the transformation and gathering statistical measures on the handling policy. Moreover, in timed transformations such as in **MoTif**, the global (simulated) transformation time as well as the local time of the transformation rule operator may be useful.

3.2   Detection of Exceptions

When a transformation executes, the transformation run-time and the underlying virtual machine must monitor the transformation steps to detect the different kinds of exceptions presented in Section 2 and signal them appropriately.

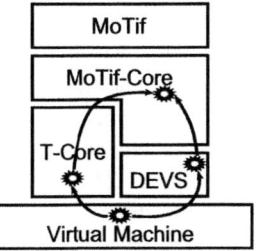

Fig. 7. The **MoTif** framework and the propagation of exceptions across different layers

For example, the transformation run-time of the **MoTif** framework is depicted in Fig. 7. It consists of several layers. **MoTif**, the language that a modeller uses to express transformations is a shortcut language of **MoTif-Core**, which consists of the core elements of the language. The former language simply defines a more user-friendly syntax encapsulating the different transformation operators provided in the latter language. **MoTif-Core** combines **T-Core** [9] and the *Discrete EVent system Specification* (a.k.a. DEVS), both running on a model-aware virtual machine. The different classes of exceptions relevant to the modeller presented in Section 2 are detected at different layers, but must all be propagated to the **MoTif-Core** layer (and conceptually to the **MoTif** layer) in order to allow the modeller to handle them explicitly within the transformation, if unhandled in the meantime.

Detection of ALEs, such as *null de-reference* or *division by zero*, are typically detected at the level of the virtual machine in the **MoTif** framework. Depending on whether the action language is interpreted or compiled, certain design faults can even be detected at compile-time, in which case the corresponding exception never occurs at run-time. Similarly, the transformation language may prevent the action language from accessing model elements that are not explicitly part of the LHS, RHS, or NAC patterns, in which case null de-referencing can never occur. This may, however, be considered as a restriction on the expressiveness of the transformation language used and may lead to excessively large rules.

---

[2] The commonly known Create, Read, Update, and Delete operations on model elements.

SEs are typically detected by the underlying operating system and the implementation language which is a Python interpreter in the **MoTif** case. To properly propagate the detected exception to the modeller, the exception needs to be caught at the virtual machine interface and transformed into the corresponding exception model instance shown in the previous section.

TLSEs are detectable at the level of **T-Core**, typically by checking pre-conditions before executing any language constructs. TLSEs are again an example of exceptions that can be rendered obsolete if the transformation language is compiled and strongly typed, in which case the compiler should be able to detect unbound parameters and similar situations. Bad timing synchronization of events can also be detected at the level of DEVS.

RDEs are also detected at the transformation language level. In algebraic graph transformation approaches, some RDEs can be detected statically. In grammar-like languages (a.k.a. unordered graph transformation), rule non-confluence can be detected through critical pair analysis [10]: verifying if a rule can disable another, *i.e.,* making it inapplicable. In such languages, this technique can assert parallel and sequential independence of the rules. Tools such as **AGG** detect these conflicts by overlapping the rules (all possible combination of the LHSs, taking NACs into consideration). However, their current approach is sometimes too conservative leading to false positives as it does not take into consideration the meta-model constraints (an example is given in [11]). Moreover, although containing critical pairs of rules, a transformation may still be semantically correct and avoid the conflicts depending on the matches selected at runtime. The occurrence of an IUE can usually also not be checked statically since, most of the time, the input model to which a transformation is applied is not known at compile time.

Controlled graph transformation languages—which are more general than algebraic graph transformation approaches—consist of (partially) ordered rules, where rule scheduling is not implicit but modelled explicitly by the transformation designer. In this case, critical pair analysis is not directly applicable. It must first be adapted to controlled transformations as it may consider a pair of rules in conflict although the conflict does not occur at run-time because of a particular rule scheduling. For instance, let r_1, r_2, r_3 be a sequence of rules to be applied in this order such that the critical pair analysis test fails on (r_1, r_3) because r_1 deletes an element that can be matched by r_3. If r_2 re-creates those deleted elements, r_3 may still be applicable. In our framework, **T-Core** primitives such as a `resolver` or a `synchronizer` can be customized to detect IUEs and YEs [9].

Detection of TSEs cannot be done by the transformation framework automatically, since those situations depend on the semantics of the specific transformation. As mentioned in Section 2, they represent user-defined exceptions. Just like in programming languages that support user-defined exceptions where the programmer is responsible for detecting the exceptional situation using `if` statements or assertions, TSEs have to be detected by the transformation modeller. Fortunately, expressing a condition that needs to be satisfied by a model (or a condition that should never be satisfied by a model) is trivial in a transformation language: the condition can simply be expressed as a query on the input model. In graph transformation systems, this query can be modelled by a transformation rule consisting solely of a LHS. Depending on the query, either a match being found or the fact that no matches are found depicts a violation of a constraint. To signal that, the rule must have the ability to throw an exception, which is described in the following subsection.

3.3   Extending Rules with Exceptions

In order to allow rules to signal exceptions to the enclosing transformation, we propose to add exceptional outcomes to rules. Therefore, such an *exceptional rule* receives a model as input and has three possible outcomes: a successfully transformed model (in case of a successful match and execution of the transformation), an unmodified model (in case the rule is inapplicable on the model), or an exception (when an exceptional situation occurred). If the rule outputs an exception, there are two possibilities: either (1) if the error took place in the matching phase, then the input model is not modified, or (2) if the error took place during the application phase of the rule, then the input model may have been partially modified. The latter outcome seems to defeat the *atomicity* property of a rule. However, as expressed in [12], a partial output may sometimes be desirable. This feature is certainly very helpful in debugging mode, as the modeller would like to see a partial result even if not complete to understand at what point the transformation execution failed in terms of the input model. Nevertheless, if backward recovery is desired, the transformation language should offer a mechanism to roll-back to the previous "safe" state of the model, *i.e.,* to the state that was valid before the rule was applied.

We have integrated the notion of exception in **MoTif** following the ideas mentioned above. **MoTif** is a graph transformation language whose semantic domain is the **DEVS** formalism. Among the elements composing the language, **MoTif** *rule blocks* represent transformation rules. They exchange *packets*[3] through *input* and *output ports* connected via *channels*. Upon receiving a packet from the *packet inport*, an ARule (atomic rule block as illustrated by **Faulty** in Fig. 8) finds the potential matches and then applies the transformation depicted by the rule it encodes. If the rule is applicable, the transformed graph is output through the *success outport* (depicted by a tick); otherwise the input graph is output through the *inapplicable outport* (depicted by a cross). Being an event-based system, we model exceptions as events since they allow interruption. Transformation exceptions are output through an *exception outport* (depicted by a zigzag line). Therefore a rule has three possible outcomes: a new graph when the transformation is successful, the unmodified graph when the rule is not applicable, or an exception (modelled as in Section 3.1) if an exceptional situation is detected. In the latter case, the packet may have been partially modified. On the one hand in the matching phase, information concerning the matched elements may have already been stored in the packet. On the other hand, if the rewriting phase was already initiated, the input model may have been modified. In any case, the packet is in an *inconsistent state* with respect to the atomicity property of graph transformation rules application. The modeller can choose to output either the recovered packet or the packet as is in the exception. This is done if the exceptional rule is an XRule, supporting backward recovery of the packet through checkpointing.

---

[3] A packet consists of the graph to be transformed as well as matching information from previous rules, all embedded in DEVS events.

3.4   Modeling the Handler

Unlike current transformation tools such as **ATL** [13] or **Fujaba** where exception handling is available only at the level of the code of the implementation of the transformation language, we believe again that the most appropriate level of abstraction at which exception handling behaviour should be expressed is at the transformation language level. This is similar to what is done in programming languages, *e.g.*, in Python, where exception constructs are provided in Python and not in C (the language in which Python is implemented). This could be achieved by specifying exception handlers either (1) at the level of transformation rules (in which case an exception handler would take the form of a transformation rule that is only applied in exceptional situations), (2) at the level of the transformation operators (*e.g.*, at the level of **T-Core** primitives such as the matcher or the rewriter), (3) or at the level of the primitive model manipulation implementation provided by the virtual machine level (CRUD). For the same reasons that we detailed in Section 3.1, we consider specifying exception handlers at the same level of abstraction as the transformation rules themselves as the optimal choice.

We propose two alternatives for how transformation exception handlers can be specified in a model transformation language. From a pure model transformation point of view, an exception can be seen as an ordinary model, although its semantics distinguishes it from a "normal" model. Hence when a rule emits an exception (model), this model can serve as input for other rules whose pre-condition looks for a specific exception type. Given an appropriate meta-model for modelling an exception (such as partly given in Fig. 6), the meta-model of the LHS pattern of an exception handling rule (*i.e.*, its domain) would need to involve multiple meta-models: the meta-model of the input model to transform as well as the meta-model of the transformation exception. This can be easily accomplished if the transformation language is itself meta-modelled as in [14].

Although this solution is elegant, our experience showed that it is not very practical to let the modeller specify rules that match elements from the transformation domain and simultaneously from the domain of exceptions. A more pragmatic solution is to let the exception produced by a rule be used to influence the control flow of the transformation, redirecting it to rules designed for handling specific exceptions. To support this, **MoTif** introduces an explicit *handler block* where the modeller may access the information of the exception model and specify subsequent rules to pursue the exception flow. The handler block acts as a dispatcher sending the packet contained in the transformation context of the exception through the outport corresponding to the exception name. Fig. 8 shows the use of the handler block. The handler block associates the packet with the appropriate exception outport given a predefined exception tree. Since it is possible that not all the exceptions that can occur during a model transformation execution have a specific handler rule designed

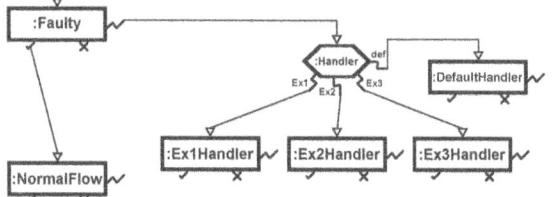

Fig. 8. Handling exceptions in the transformation model

to address them, a default exception port is provided with the handler block (which is linked to the top-most exception class in the classification tree presented in Fig. 5, *e.g.,* TransformationException).

Note that in both models the handling part may itself produce an exception which can be in turn handled. For example, since the handling process involves further pattern matching, memory overflows are likely to occur and hence it is necessary to properly handle such exceptions.

3.5   Control Flow Concerns

When a rule emits an exception, the control flow is redirected to a handler component which, in release mode at least, handles the exception with the goal of continuing the transformation. After the exception is handled, there are three options: the enclosing transformation may *resume, restart,* or *terminate.*

Resuming the transformation means to return the flow of control to the place where it was interrupted by the exception. As depicted by channel (1) in Fig. 9, the transformation continues in the "normal" flow *after* the rule that activated the exception. Such a resumption model allows to express an alternative execution of the transformation. However, care should be taken if the input model (or even the packet) was modified. As outlined in Section 3.3, the modeller may choose to recover the model to a state that was valid before the rule started applying its modifications, if desired.

Restarting the transformation means to re-run the enclosing transformation from the beginning. As depicted by channel (2) in Fig. 9, the transformation restarts the "normal" flow *before* the rule that activated the exception. This is certainly an interesting way to tolerate transient faults. However, restarting the transformation induces a loop in the control flow which may lead to dead-locks, in case the fault is of a permanent nature.

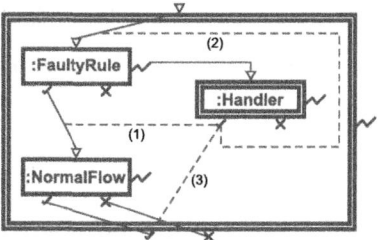

Fig. 9. Modelling possible control flows after handling an exception locally at a sub-transformation level: (1) resume after the activation point, (2) restart at the beginning of the enclosing context, and (3) terminate enclosing context

Terminating the transformation means to skip the entire flow of the transformation in which a rule raised the exception. As depicted by channel (3) in Fig. 9, the enclosing transformation exits the scope of the occurrence of the exception seamlessly. It ends in a "normal" flow, *i.e.,* in success or not applied mode, and not in generating an exception. As a result, the outer scope is not aware that an exception occurred.

Exception Propagation

Up to now, we have considered that it is at the level of a transformation rule that an exception is generated and subsequently handled at the level of the enclosing transformation. As mentioned previously, **MoTif** transformation models are hierarchical, in the sense that transformations can be nested. Constructs such as a CRule modularly define scoped sub-transformations, allowing to compose transformations models.

Just like in programming languages, it is recommended to handle exceptions in a scope that is as close as possible to the point of activation. In other words, local exception handling is preferred. However, it is possible that handling an exception locally is not possible, because the necessary context information that is needed to define a useful handler is only available in a more global context.

Therefore, unhandled exceptions must be propagated up the transformation hierarchy as long as no corresponding handler can be found. Only if an exception propagates unhandled out of the topmost CRule, the transformation execution must be halted and debugging information displayed. Nevertheless, at each level, a handler could be specified to "clean up" any local state before the exception is propagated outside. Note that once an exception is handled, it can no longer be propagated. If propagation is needed, the handler must create a new user-defined exception which can refer to the previously handled exception in its `TransformationContext`.

4 Related Work

The concept of exceptions exists in programming languages since the 1970s [2]. Several approaches have been proposed for modelling exceptions in workflow languages [15] and event-driven languages [16]. However, there has not been any work on modelling exceptions in model transformation languages. Current tools mostly rely on exceptions triggered from the underlying virtual machine. As a matter of fact, debugging in tools such as ATL [17], Fujaba [7], GReAT [8], QVTo [18], SmartQVT [19], or VIATRA [20] is specific to their respective integrated development editors (IDE).

QVT Operational Mappings (**QVT-OM**) supports exception handling at the action language level, an imperative extension of OCL 2.0 [6]. The language allows to handle exceptions in a *try … except* statement in the same way as in modern programming languages such as Java, It is however unclear where, when, or how an exception occurs in **QVT-OM**. User-defined exceptions can be declared and raised arbitrarily[4] in the *main* operation of a transformation. Moreover, an exception is also raised when a *fatal assertion* is not satisfied. However, it is unclear what information exceptions carry and whether they can be propagated outside the scope of the transformation. Implementations of **QVT-OM** such as SmartQVT and QVTo (an Eclipse plug-in into EMF) have different interpretations from the standard, *e.g.,* allowing *map* to raise an exception if the pre-condition is not fulfilled. The advantage of our approach is to (1) explicitly model the raising of exceptions and (2) explicitly model the control flow subsequent to the handling of an exception.

Fujaba is a model transformation tool based on graph transformation combined with Story diagrams [7]. There, exceptions are also not modelled, although present at the code level. The *maybe* statements in Story diagrams can be used to handle exceptions in the transformation, but they are only available for statement activities (*i.e.,* Java code). The same argument can be used as for the choice of allowing exception handling at the level of **T-Core**.

More elaborate details of the presented approach can be found in [21].

---

[4] This fits in the *Action Language Exceptions* category according to our classification.

5   Conclusion

In this paper, we have motivated the need for providing the concepts of exception and exception handling at the level of transformations. We have outlined a classification of potential exceptions that can occur in the context of model transformation. Though having different uses at different steps of the development of a transformation model, these transformation exception must be handled by the transformation model itself. We have discussed the different issues related to the handling of these exceptions.

We have implemented the main concepts of this approach in **MoTif**. As the prototype is still in an early stage, we are working on a system which will allow for user friendly debugging of model transformation.

The same exercise this paper presented for the **MoTif** framework can be done for the **ATL** or **QVT-OM** languages. We are confident that it is also applicable to transformation languages at different levels of abstraction such as relational transformations (*e.g.*, **QVT-Relational** or **Triple Graph Grammars**).

Exception handling can become handy when designing a higher-order transformation. For example in **ATL**, static verification of well-formed higher-order transformation rules is quite limited [14]. In this case, with an exception handling mechanism at the transformation level, the designer may safely rely on the engine to design arbitrarily complex higher-order transformations.

References

1. Dony, C.: Exception handling and object-oriented programming: Towards a synthesis. In: ECOOP. SIGPLAN, vol. 25, pp. 322–330. ACM Press, New York (1990)
2. Goodenough, J.B.: Exception handling: Issues and a proposed notation. Communications of the ACM 18, 683–696 (1975)
3. Syriani, E., Vangheluwe, H.: DEVS as a Semantic Domain for Programmed Graph Transformation. In: Discrete-Event Modeling and Simulation: Theory and Applications, CRC Press, Boca Raton (2009)
4. Guerra, E., de Lara, J.: Adding recursion to graph transformation. In: GT-VMT 2007, ECEASST, Braga, vol. 6 (2007)
5. Zündorf, A., Schürr, A.: Nondeterministic control structures for graph rewriting systems. In: Schmidt, G., Berghammer, R. (eds.) WG 1991. LNCS, vol. 570, pp. 48–62. Springer, Heidelberg (1992)
6. Object Management Group: Meta Object Facility 2.0 QVT Specification (2008)
7. Fischer, T., Niere, J., Turunski, L., Zündorf, A.: Story diagrams: A new graph rewrite language based on UML and Java. In: Ehrig, H., Engels, G., Kreowski, H.-J., Rozenberg, G. (eds.) TAGT 1998. LNCS, vol. 1764, pp. 296–309. Springer, Heidelberg (2000)
8. Agrawal, A., Karsai, G., Kalmar, Z., Neema, S., Shi, F., Vizhanyo, A.: The design of a language for model transformations. SoSym 5, 261–288 (2006)
9. Syriani, E., Vangheluwe, H.: De-/re-constructing model transformation languages. In: GT-VMT, ECEASST, Paphos (2010)
10. Heckel, R., Küster, J.M., Taentzer, G.: Confluence of typed attributed graph transformation systems. In: Corradini, A., Ehrig, H., Kreowski, H.-J., Rozenberg, G. (eds.) ICGT 2002. LNCS, vol. 2505, pp. 161–176. Springer, Heidelberg (2002)
11. Hausmann, J.H., Heckel, R., Taentzer, G.: Detection of conflicting functional requirements in a use case-driven approach. In: ICSE 2002, pp. 105–115. ACM, Orlando (2002)

12. Gardner, T., Griffin, C., Koehler, J., Hauser, R.: A review of QVT submissions and recommendations towards the final standard. In: MetaModelling for MDA, pp. 178–197 (2003)
13. Jouault, F., Kurtev, I.: Transforming models with ATL. In: Bruel, J.-M. (ed.) MoDELS 2005. LNCS, vol. 3844, pp. 128–138. Springer, Heidelberg (2006)
14. Kühne, T., Mezei, G., Syriani, E., Vangheluwe, H., Wimmer, M.: Systematic transformation development. In: ECEASST, vol. 21 (2009)
15. Brambilla, M., Ceri, S., Comai, S., Tziviskou, C.: Exception handling in workflow-driven web applications. In: WWW 2005, Chiba, pp. 170–180 (2005)
16. Pintér, G., Majzik, I.: Modeling and analysis of exception handling by using UML statecharts. In: Guelfi, N., Reggio, G., Romanovsky, A. (eds.) FIDJI 2004. LNCS, vol. 3409, pp. 58–67. Springer, Heidelberg (2005)
17. Jouault, F., Allilaire, F., Bézivin, J., Kurtev, I.: ATL: A model transformation tool. Science of Computer Programming, Special Issue on EST 72, 31–39 (2008)
18. Dvorak, R.: Model transformation with operational QVT. In: EclipseCon 2008 (2008)
19. France Telecom R&D: SmartQVT (2008)
20. Varró, D., Balogh, A.: The model transformation language of the VIATRA2 framework. Science of Computer Programming 68, 214–234 (2007)
21. Syriani, E., Kienzle, J., Vangheluwe, H.: Exceptional transformations. Technical Report SOCS-TR-2010.2, McGill University, School of Computer Science (2010)

Improving Higher-Order Transformations Support in ATL

Massimo Tisi, Jordi Cabot, and Frédéric Jouault

AtlanMod, INRIA & École des Mines de Nantes, France
{massimo.tisi,jordi.cabot,frederic.jouault}@inria.fr

Abstract. In Model-Driven Engineering (MDE), Higher-Order Transformations (HOTs) are model transformations that analyze, produce or manipulate other model transformations. In a previous survey we classified them, and showed their usefulness in different MDE scenarios. However, writing HOTs is generally considered a time-consuming and error-prone task, and often results in verbose code.

In this paper we present several proposals to facilitate the definition of HOTs in ATL. Each proposal focuses on a specific kind of scenario. We validate our proposals by assessing their impact over the full list of HOTs described in the survey.

1 Introduction

With the continuous growing in the popularity of the transformational approach in Model Driven Engineering (MDE), a vast number of model transformations is being developed and organized in complex patterns. Model transformations are becoming a common technological means to handle models both at development time and at runtime.

In complex environments, where transformations are a central artifact of the software production and structure, the idea of transformation manipulation naturally arises to automatically generate, adapt or analyze transformation rules. While transformation manipulation can already be performed by means of an independent methodology (e.g., program transformation, aspect orientation), the elegance of the model-driven paradigm allows again the reuse of the same transformation infrastructure, by defining model transformations as models [3]. The transformation is represented by a transformation model that has to conform to a transformation metamodel. Just as a normal model can be created, modified, augmented through a transformation, a transformation model can itself be instantiated, modified and so on, by a so-called Higher Order Transformation (HOT). This uniformity is beneficial in several ways: especially it allows reusing tools and methods, and it creates a framework that can in theory be applied recursively (since transformations of transformations can be transformed themselves).

In previous work [16], we investigated how developers have used HOTs to build applications. We detected four wide usage classes, Transformation Analysis, Synthesis, Modification and Composition, and for each class we described

L. Tratt and M. Gogolla (Eds.): ICMT 2010, LNCS 6142, pp. 215–229, 2010.

how HOTs were integrated in the application structure. To perform this analysis we gathered a set of 41 HOTs in different transformation languages, comprising all the ATL HOT applications published at that date, to our knowledge.

A preliminary analysis of this dataset confirmed an intuitive perception about HOT programming: while HOTs are becoming more and more necessary for complex transformational scenarios, HOT programming tends to be perceived as a tedious activity. HOTs are generally very verbose, even in simple cases. This seemingly unnecessary verbosity could strongly hamper the diffusion of the HOT paradigm. It makes HOTs less readable and the whole development activity more time-consuming and error-prone.

It is important to remark that the reasons for the verbosity of HOTs are not to ascribe to a fault in the transformation language design. The manipulation of transformation models is made complex by the fact that metamodels of programming languages (such as ATL) are inherently complex. For the sake of uniformity, model transformations deal with these complex metamodels in the same way as they deal with any other metamodel, without providing any specific facility. This paper represents a first step in the direction of improving the definition of this special kind of transformation.

In this sense, the contribution of the paper is a set of proposals for increasing the productivity of HOT programming in ATL, by providing both a support library and directly extending the ATL language syntax and semantics. The paper provides an assessment of the impact of these proposals on the length of real-world HOTs. While we focus our discussion on ATL, the results of this paper can be easily generalized to other transformation environments.

The rest of the paper is organized as follows: Section 2 introduces the basic concept of HOT; Section 3 suggests a set of practical enhancements to improve HOT programming in ATL; Section 4 evaluates the outcome of applying the previous proposals to a set of real-world HOTs; Section 5 compares our approach to HOTs with related work; Section 6 draws the conclusions.

2   Higher-Order Transformations

An essential prerequisite for fully exploiting the power of transformations is the ability to treat them as subjects of other transformations. In an MDE context, this demands the representation of the transformation as a model conforming to a transformation metamodel.

Not all transformation frameworks provide a transformation metamodel. In this work we will refer to the AmmA framework [12] that contains a mature implementation of the ATL transformation language. Within AmmA an ATL transformation is itself a model, conforming to the ATL metamodel. Besides the central classes of *Rule*, *Helper*, *InPattern*, and *OutPattern* the ATL metamodel also incorporates the whole OCL metamodel to write expressions to filter and manipulate models.

Once the representation of a transformation as a transformation model is available, a HOT can be defined as follows:

Definition 1 (Higher-order transformation). *A higher-order transformation is a model transformation such that its input and/or output models are themselves transformation models.*

According to this definition HOTs either take a transformation model as input, produce a transformation model as output, or both.

The typical schema of a HOT, particularized for the AmmA framework, is shown in Figure 1. This example reads and writes a transformation, e.g. with the purpose of performing a refactoring. The three operations shown as large arrows at level M1 (Models) are:

- *Transformation injection.* The textual representation of the transformation rules is read and translated into a model representation. This translation in AmmA is performed using TCS [10]. The generated model is conforming to the ATL metamodel.
- *Higher-order transformation.* The transformation model is the input of a model transformation that produces another transformation model. The input, output and HOT transformation models are all conforming to the same ATL metamodel.
- *Transformation extraction.* Finally an extraction is performed to serialize back the output transformation model into a textual transformation specification.

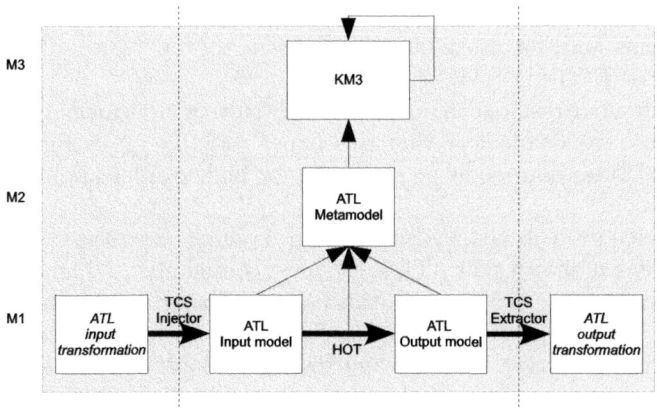

Fig. 1. A typical Higher-Order Transformation

Note that the injection and extraction operations are not always involved in a HOT. For instance, the source transformation model may come from a previous transformation, and already be in the form of a model. Similarly, the target transformation model is sometimes reused as a model without need to serialize it.

3 Facilitating HOT Development

To approach the problem of facilitating HOT development we started, in [16], by identifying four groups of similar HOT applications and gathering real-world examples for each one of them. The transformation classes can be characterized by their input and output models, in a schema that we briefly summarize here:

Transformation analysis: HOTs that process other transformations to extract meaningful data. They have at least one transformation as input model, no transformations as output models.
Transformation synthesis: HOTs that create new transformations from data modeled in other forms. They have no transformations as input models, at least one transformation as output model.
Transformation modification: HOTs that manipulate the logic of an input transformation. They have one transformation as input model, one transformation as output model.
Transformation (de)composition: HOTs that merge or split other transformations, according to a (de)composition criterion. They have at least one transformation as input model, at least one as output model, and the input and/or the output models contain more than one transformation.

Inspection of previous work on HOTs and our experience with HOT development in ATL, has highlighted that the development of transformations in each one of these classes shows peculiar and recurrent problems. In this section we describe the problems and, for every class, we present a proposal to allow simpler and more concise HOTs in ATL.

We believe our results can be generalized to other transformation frameworks. In this sense we also believe that this paper could be an useful working example of transformation language extension for higher-order applications in every framework.

The choice to focus the analysis on ATL is justified by the fact that previous work in [16] has shown that ATL is the most commonly used language for HOTs development to date. The ideas of this paper are based on the analysis of a set of 42 freely available transformations in ATL, that constitute an up-to-date sample of HOT applications in industry and research. Moreover, this significant set of examples are leveraged for validating our proposals in Section 4.

When possible we base our proposals on the built-in extension mechanisms of ATL. ATL provides three ways to reuse transformation modules.

Libraries. Collections of helpers, i.e. query operations whose body is defined by OCL expressions.
Module superimposition. A *Module A* can be *superimposed* to a *Module B*, obtaining a *Module C*, by a simple kind of internal composition such that: 1) *C* contains the union of the sets of transformation rules and helpers of *A* and *B*; 2) *C* does not contain any rule or helper of *B*, for which *A* contains a rule or helper with the same *name* and the same *context*.

Transformation composition. ATL *Modules* can be composed by executing them sequentially or in articulated patterns, usually using ANT scripts (this kind of composition is usually called *external composition*).

In this paper we will make use of libraries and transformation composition. Especially the second technique is particularly powerful, thanks to the uniformity of the transformational paradigm. For instance, HOT composition allows us to extend the ATL language without even touching the language implementation. In fact, it is possible in principle to add a higher-order preprocessing phase before the transformation execution, to have it translated in an equivalent version compatible with the standard environment.

When the extension mechanisms are not sufficient for our purposes we suggest extensions to the ATL language implementation and show the outcome of these extensions. Depending on the case, it will be more convenient to extend the ATL virtual machine or the compiler.

3.1   Transformation Analysis

HOTs in the transformation analysis class share a single aspect, i.e. being applied to transformation models conforming to the ATL metamodel. They need to navigate the ATL metamodel and return elements by defining filtering conditions on it.

In ATL, the logic for input navigation and filtering is scattered in several places: filters inside input patterns, variable definitions in the *using* part of rules, imperative sections. The navigation and filtering logic contained in these parts is composed by *OclExpressions* that can be very complex. ATL provides an ad-hoc means to modularize this logic, i.e. libraries of *Helpers*.

To facilitate the development of analysis HOTs we propose a HOT library, composed by those helpers that we found to be recurrently used within our set of HOTs. The helpers that we propose can be roughly divided in the following categories.

– Helpers that execute a query over all instances of a metaclass in the input metamodel. Our proposal includes:
  • helpers to retrieve ATL rules depending on the type of their matched or generated elements (*generatingRules, matchingRules, copyRules*),
  • a HOT helper to retrieve the calls to operations and helpers by providing their name (*callsByName()*),
  • a helper to check if the contextual element belongs to one of the input transformations (*belongsTo()*).
– Helpers that implement a recursive logic, when some associations between metaclasses can be navigated recursively. We provide the following helpers.
  • Within the OCL Package a *PropertyCallExpression* in the OCL metamodel has a *source* association with another *OclExpression*. This expression can have a source too, and so on. A *navigationRootExpression()* helper can navigate recursively the source relations to return the root of the chain.

- Another important example is given by the *reflmmediateComposite()* operation, that returns the immediate container of the contextual element. We provide several recursive versions: *firstContainerOfType()* to get a container of a given generic type, *rootExpression()* to get the root of a complex OclExpression, *knownVariables()* and *containedVariables()* to get the variables defined within or before the contextual element.

Distributing the previous helpers in a standard HOT-specific library for ATL allows HOT developers to simply import them in any HOT. This would allow for shorter HOTs but also, in our opinion, it would foster a general improvement of the transformation design and reusability.

Table 1 lists all the helpers showing for each one the context type, the result type and a short description. This library of helpers is publicly available at [15].

Table 1. A library for HOTs

Name	Context	Returns
Description.		
belongsTo(modelName: String)	ATL!OclAny	Boolean
return true if the element belongs to the specified model.		
firstContainerOfType(ATL!OclType)	ATL!OclAny	ATL!OclAny
compute the ATL element of the specified type in which the contextual element is declared		
rootExpression	ATL!OclExpression	ATL!OclExpression
navigationRootExpression	ATL!PropertyCallExp	ATL!OclExpression
return the root OCL element of the containment or navigation tree that includes the contextual element.		
knownVariables	ATL!OclAny	OrderedSet(ATL!VariableDeclaration)
containedVariables	ATL!OclAny	OrderedSet(ATL!VariableDeclaration)
computes an ordered set containing the VariableDeclarations that are defined higher or lower than the contextual ATL element in its namespace tree.		
generatingRules	ATL!OclModelElement	OrderedSet(ATL!Rule)
matchingRules	ATL!OclModelElement	OrderedSet(ATL!Rule)
copyRules	ATL!OclModelElement	OrderedSet(ATL!Rule)
computes an ordered set containing all the rules that can generate, match or copy the contextual element type.		
callsByName(name: String)	thisModule	OrderedSet(ATL!NavigationExp)
computes an ordered set containing the calls to operations with the given name.		

3.2 Transformation Synthesis

HOTs in the transformation synthesis group are characterized by the task of producing new ATL code, as an output model conforming to the ATL metamodel. The production of ATL code is usually parametrized using one or more input models, but no assumption can be done on the structure of the input metamodels.

In ATL, new output elements are created by specifying them inside the *OutputPatterns* of transformation rules. An *OutputPattern* has to fully describe all the elements to create, with their attributes and associations. Usually "normal" transformation rules have simple output patterns and interact with each other to create complex models. In synthesis HOTs, instead, a single transformation rule is often in charge of creating several elements at once, leading to the development of complex *OutputPatterns*.

In our HOT dataset, typical examples of complex output patterns are related to the creation of:

- the root of a new transformation module, including references to its input and output metamodels;
- a new transformation rule or helper, together with its complete input and output patterns;
- complex OCL expressions.

These output patterns are generally very verbose. For example the second one, depending on the complexity of the generated transformation rule, can contain a large number of output elements and feature assignments. This results in a high percentage of LOC spent for building the output part of HOT rules.

Our experience has shown that the impact of output patterns in HOT verbosity is remarkable. For instance, Listing 1 shows the example of a HOT rule that synthetizes a new ATL rule. The example is taken from the KM32ATLCopier HOT [8] that, given a metamodel as input (in the KM3 format), generates a copier for that metamodel, i.e. a transformation that makes a copy of any input model conforming to that metamodel. The rule shown in Listing 1, generates a copier for each KM3 class.

As it can be seen in the example, the output pattern has to create an element for each metaclass of the abstract syntax, and fill the features of these elements with 1) constant values, 2) references among the elements, 3) variables calculated from the input model.

We propose to extend ATL, by allowing the production of ATL rules directly using an adapted version of the ATL concrete syntax when defining output patterns. Since ATL has an unambiguous concrete syntax, it is possible to parse it and derive which model elements have to be created and which constant values and inter-element references are needed.

Listing 2 shows the same rule as Listing 1, using the proposed syntax. Output pattens can be directly specified with an embedded concrete syntax by delimiting it using special sequences of characters, i.e. '|[' and ']|'. In the example the output pattern contains the whole rule that has to be generated (i.e. a simple copier). The embedded concrete syntax substitutes the long list of model elements and bindings in Listing 1. Inside of the concrete-syntax output patterns, it is possible to include strings obtained dynamically from the input models. As it is shown in Listing 2, a special notation is introduced for variables in the concrete syntax, denoted by the '%' character. The variables can be declared and defined in the *using* part of the transforamation rule, as any other variable. They are ideally computed and expanded inside the output pattern at runtime, after the rule has being matched.

This extension to ATL can be easily implemented using the above-mentioned technique of HOT composition: a HOT pre-processor can take as input the transformation in Listing 2 and rewrite it as in Listing 1, to make it executable on the default ATL environment. In this way, we can simplify the specification of synthesis HOTs, without changing the ATL compiler.

Listing 1. Original ATL rule

```
rule Class {
  from s : KM3!Class [...]
  to
    t : ATL!MatchedRule (
      isAbstract <- false ,
      isRefining <- false ,
      name <- 'Copy' + s.name ,
      inPattern <- ip ,
      outPattern <- op
    ),
      ip : ATL!InPattern (
        elements <- Sequence{ipe},
        filter <- f
      ),
        ipe :
          ATL!SimpleInPatternElement (
          varName <- 's',
          type <- ipet
        ),
          ipet : ATL!OclModelElement (
            name <- s.name ,
            model <- thisModule.metamodel
          ),
          f : ATL!OperationCallExp (
            operationName <- 'oclIsTypeOf',
            source <- fv ,
            arguments <- Sequence{ft}
          ),
          fv : ATL!VariableExp (
            name <- 's',
            referredVariable <- ipe
          ),
          ft : ATL!OclModelElement (
            name <- s.name ,
            model <- thisModule.metamodel
          ),
        op : ATL!OutPattern (
          elements <- Sequence{ope}
        ),
          ope :
            ATL!SimpleOutPatternElement (
            varName <- 't',
            type <- opet ,
            bindings <- b
          ),
            opet : ATL!OclModelElement (
              name <- s.name ,
              model <- thisModule.metamodel
            )
}
```

Listing 2. Equivalent ATL rule

```
rule Class {
  from s : KM3!Class [...]
  using {
    name : String = 'Copy' + s.name ;
    metamodel : String = thisModule.metamodel ;
    meName : String = s.name ;
  }
  to
    t : ATL!MatchedRule |[
      rule %name {
        from
```

```
     s : %metamodel!%meName (
       s.oclIsTypeOf(%metamodel!%meName)
     )
    to
       t : %metamodel!%meName
   }
  ]|
}
```

Our proposal can be generalized outside HOTs, to the concrete-syntax of any output model. In this case, the ATL launch configuration should allow the developer to specify any concrete syntax for output models, as a TCS file. The pre-processor we propose would parse the provided TCS file and use it into the pre-processing phase.

3.3   Transformation Modification and (De)Composition

Applications that modify ATL transformations and compose (or decompose) them, generally need to parse one or more input transformations and generate one or more output transformations. Hence, they contain both the aspects of input filtering and output creation that characterize transformation analysis and transformation synthesis. For this reason their development can benefit from both the proposals in Sections 3.1 and 3.2.

Moreover, while the transformation logic for modification and composition is generally strongly dependent on the application domain, all the transformations of this class share a further important aspect, i.e. the need to select and transport chunks of unchanged transformation code from the input to the output.

The ATL language provides an ad-hoc execution mode for transformations that perform little changes on the input model, i.e. ATL refining mode. In this mode, model elements that are not matched by an explicit transformation rule are copied, with all their features, to the output model.

However, HOT developers in previous work have sometimes preferred alternatives to the built-in ATL refining mode:

- in some cases developers use superimposition to base their transformation on *ATLModuleCopier*, a verbose HOT that simply performs a copy of the whole input transformation, and they override only a small set of rules;
- other cases make use of several element copier rules, i.e. transformation rules that copy a single ATL element from the input transformation to the output transformation, with all its features and sometimes only slight modifications;

The choice to rely on these alternatives was probably related to limitations in the implementation of refining mode in ATL2004 (e.g., the copying was performed implicitly only for contained elements of copied elements and it was mandatory to specify all bindings). The effort of copying some elements of a transformation, while modifying others, have been reduced by the latest version of the ATL language (ATL2006), that introduces *in-place refining mode*. In this mode every element stays unchanged if it is not explicitly matched by a transformation rule.

Our experience has shown that migrating to ATL2006 refining mode has already a big impact on the length of several HOTs, and we recommend the developers to consider in-place refining mode for every transformation modification and (de)composition.

However, a few HOTs that do not present a general semantics of refinement, need simply to copy a set of elements from the input to the output. In these cases a fine-graned refining mode could be beneficial, allowing the user to choose exactly which subset of the input model is subject to refinement. *Refining rules* are our proposal to give the developer the possibility to specify with minimal effort that a single element has to be copied to the output, together with all its contained and associated elements.

To describe our proposal, we show an excerpt from the MergeHOT transformation, that creates a new transformation by the simple union of transformation rules given in input. In this case, even the ATL2006 version of the refining mode is not optimal, because it is able to refine only a single input module. Listing 3 is a solution in normal execution mode, where the developer is forced to include a long list of copying rules for all the elements of the two models to merge (e.g., Binding, NavigationOrAttributeCallExp, VariableExp). Refining rules allow the substitution of all this code (more than 100 LOCs) with the excerpt in Listing 4. The refining rule states that the *MatchingRule* have to be copied to the output with a different name, and implicitly triggers the recursive copy of all the elements contained in the *MatchingRule*, making the other HOT rules superfluous.

Listing 3. Original ATL excerpt

```
rule matchedRule {
    from
        lr : ATL!MatchedRule (
            lr.isLeft or lr.isRight
        )
    to
        m : ATL!MatchedRule (
            name <- lr.fromLeftOrRight + '_' + lr.name,
            children <- lr.children,
            superRule <- lr.superRule,
            isAbstract <- lr.isAbstract,
            isRefining <- lr.isRefining,

            inPattern <- lr.inPattern,
            outPattern <- lr.outPattern
        )
}
rule inPattern {
    from
        lr : ATL!InPattern (
            lr.isLeft or lr.isRight
        )
    to
        m : ATL!InPattern (
            elements <- lr.elements
        )
}
...[100 lines]
```

Listing 4. Equivalent ATL excerpt

```
refining rule matchedRule {
    from
        lr : ATL!MatchedRule (
            lr.isLeft or lr.isRight
        )
    to
        m : ATL!MatchedRule (
            name <- lr.fromLeftOrRight + '_' + lr.name
        )
}
```

Similarly to the previous proposal, refining rules could provide a noticeable gain in HOT conciseness, but also a general impact on ATL productivity outside HOT development.

4 Experimentation

To assess the impact of our proposals on real-world transformations we evaluate a set of HOTs taken from industry and research publications. The set, shown in Table 2, comprises all publicly available HOTs written in ATL, to our knowledge. Most of the transformations in the dataset are already included in the survey from [16] (or they are updated versions of those transformations). We have chosen to remove from the dataset HOTs that are not hand-written but automatically generated, such as ATLCopier[16] because they can't be considered representative of HOT development. The set has also a few additions comprising HOTs for: detecting constraints for chaining transformations [4], generating transformations from matching models [6] or reconstructing matching models from transformations [11]. Moreover Table 2 comprises the HOT we have built in this paper, for the purpose of deriving structural data about our transformation dataset shown in the table. This HOT is executed iteratively over the experimentation set using an ANT script [7]. The Analysis HOT is a second-order HOT, since it expects another HOT as the input model. It generates an Analysis Model, conforming to an Analysis metamodel, whose content is then shown in tabular format. The complete code of the analysis tool can be found in [15].

For each HOT in the dataset Table 2 shows:

- the classification of the HOT inside one of the four classes proposed in [16]
- the execution mode of the transformation, i.e. normal or refining;
- the input and output metamodels of the HOT;
- size metrics for the transformations (number of rules, number of helpers, lines of code);
- experimentation results after individually applying each proposal: HOT-library (1), concrete syntax in output patterns (2) and improved refining mode (3); for each proposal we show:
  - the number of times the specific proposal can be applied on the HOT,
  - the new number of LOCs after applying the proposal,

- the percentage of improvement;
- global experimentation results from the application of the three proposals at once, comprising:
  - the final number of LOCs,
  - the percentage of improvement with respect to the original code.

The experimentation results were obtained by manually rewriting the HOTs in Table 2 by means of: 1) substituting OCL expressions with calls to our HOT Library, 2) substituting complex output patterns with their resulting concrete syntax, 3) substituting copying rules with in-place rules (in ATL2006) or refining rules. Each one of the substitutions has the effect of decreasing the global length of the HOT.

Results in Table 2 show the optimizations have a clear impact on the simplification of HOTs specification. On average, we can observe a decrease of the LOCs by 35% (up to a 42% when considering the size of the transformations in the computation). Note that LOC as a software size metric counts as well comments and blank lines. Therefore, the real percentage of improvement on the transformation code length is in fact higher.

As expected, the impact of a optimization type on a specific HOT depends on the class the HOT belongs to. Therefore, to get the most of our optimizations with the minimal effort, HOT designers should first classify the HOT in one of the four categories and focus on applying the optimization described for that category.

Even if difficult to numerically quantify, this reduction in the HOT length could bring some additional benefits: it could improve the modularity and reusability of HOTs, reduce the possibility of errors and facilitate their extensibility and maintanibility. We will conduct more experiments in the future to try to validate these assumptions as well.

5   Related Work

This paper can be placed among proposals to speed-up transformation development with pre-existing transformation languages. The main work in this area focuses on transformations by example [2],[14], model transformation patterns [9], transformation generation [17]. Our work is the first to introduce specific extensions for HOTs.

In the MDE community there is no previous work in evaluating the extension of a model transformation language for specific transformation classes. This is also due to the fact that, apart from the HOT class, a widely recognized categorization of model transformations, independent of the transformation language, is not available. Some transformation languages, such as RubyTL [5], are designed with extensibility as one of the main requirements, but the potential of this extensibility has yet to be investigated.

Extension mechanisms are instead deeply leveraged in more mature languages in other technical spaces. For example, user communities develop around XSLT extensions [1]. Using the XSLT extension mechanism, [13] propose a library for

Table 2. Semantic features of HOTs

Name	Class	Mode	Source Mms	Target Mms	# rules	# helpers	LOCs	Applications (1)	LOCs (1)	Improvement % (1)	Applications (2)	LOCs (2)	Improvement % (2)	Applications (3)	LOCs (3)	Improvement % (3)	Final LOCs	Improvement %	Weighted Improvement %
1 AnalyzeTransformation	Analysis	normal	ATL_MOF	TA	2	12	263	4	222	15.59	0	263	0	0	263	0	222	15.59	
2 ATL2AMW	Analysis	normal	ATL,MOF	EqualMM	6	19	259	2	229	11.58	0	259	0	0	259	0	229	11.58	
3 ATL2Problem	Analysis	normal	ATL	Problem	18	20	923	14	470	49.08	0	923	0	0	923	0	470	49.08	
4 HOTAnalysis	Analysis	normal	ATL	Analysis	2	3	50	1	31	38	0	50	0	0	50	0	31	38	
TOTAL Analysis					28	54	1495	21	952		0	1495		0	1495		952		
AVERAGE Analysis					7	13.5	373.75	5.25	238	28.56	0	373.75	0	0	373.75	0	238	28.56	36.32
5 AMW2ATL_DoDAF	Synthesis	normal	AMW,MOF,MOF,XML	ATL	24	18	631	0	631	0	15	526	16.64	0	631	0	526	16.64	
6 AMWtoATL	Synthesis	normal	AMW	ATL	17	1	388	0	388	0	11	283	27.06	0	388	0	283	27.06	
7 AMWtoATL_Key2Nested	Synthesis	normal	AMW, MOF	ATL	17	2	373	0	373	0	9	294	21.18	0	373	0	294	21.18	
8 AMWtoATL_KM2SQL	Synthesis	normal	AMW	ATL	40	8	1149	0	1149	0	26	744	35.25	0	1149	0	744	35.25	
9 AMWtoATL_MantisBug	Synthesis	normal	AMW	ATL	22	3	489	0	489	0	11	380	22.29	0	489	0	380	22.29	
10 DUALLyLeft2Right	Synthesis	normal	AMW, MOF, MOF	ATL	30	42	1707	0	1707	0	12	1348	21.03	0	1707	0	1348	21.03	
11 GenDiff	Synthesis	normal	MOF	ATL	9	0	1056	0	1056	0	6	209	80.21	0	1056	0	209	80.21	
12 GenMatchBottomUp	Synthesis	normal	MOF,MMParams	ATL	11	0	944	0	944	0	9	285	69.81	0	944	0	285	69.81	
13 GenMatchFilter	Synthesis	normal	MOF,MMParams	ATL	5	0	709	0	709	0	4	157	77.86	0	709	0	157	77.86	
14 GenMatchTopDown	Synthesis	normal	MOF,MMParams	ATL	10	0	1086	0	1086	0	7	311	71.36	0	1086	0	311	71.36	
15 GenPatch	Synthesis	normal	DiffMM,MOF,LMM,RMM,MatchMM	ATL	6	6	499	0	499	0	8	425	14.83	0	499	0	425	14.83	
16 HOT_match	Synthesis	normal	EqualMM,MOF,MOF	ATL	7	1	157	0	157	0	3	132	15.92	0	157	0	132	15.92	
17 inverseAMWtoATL	Synthesis	normal	AMW, MOF, MOF	ATL	18	2	466	0	466	0	10	334	28.33	0	466	0	334	28.33	
18 KM32ATLCopier	Synthesis	normal	KM3	ATL	2	4	144	0	144	0	2	110	23.61	0	144	0	110	23.61	
19 KM32CONFATL	Synthesis	normal	KM3	ATL	7	1	1057	0	1057	0	7	225	78.71	0	1057	0	225	78.71	
20 meo2atl4model2rdf	Synthesis	normal	MOF, OWL, MEO	ATL	66	19	1018	0	1018	0	10	362	64.44	0	1018	0	362	64.44	
21 meo2atl4rdf2model	Synthesis	normal	MOF, OWL, MEO	ATL	63	17	802	0	802	0	7	725	9.6	0	802	0	725	9.6	
22 MM2Profile	Synthesis	normal	AMW, MOF, MOF, Profile	ATL	23	16	959	0	959	0	7	861	10.22	0	959	0	861	10.22	
23 MMD2ATL	Synthesis	normal	KM3	ATL	8	4	1484	0	1484	0	8	494	66.71	0	1484	0	494	66.71	
24 Profile2MM	Synthesis	normal	AMW, MOF, MOF, Profile	ATL	30	12	1117	0	1117	0	13	799	28.47	0	1117	0	799	28.47	
25 SimpleATLtoATL	Synthesis	normal	AMW, MOF, MOF	ATL	14	8	277	0	277	0	7	274	1.08	0	277	0	274	1.08	
TOTAL Synthesis					429	164	16512	0	16512		186	9278		0	16512		9278		
AVERAGE Synthesis					20.43	7.81	786.29	0	786.29	0	8.86	441.81	37.36	0	786.29	0	441.81	37.36	43.81
26 ATL2BindingDebugger	Modification	refining	ATL	ATL	2	0	41	0	41	0	3	24	41.46	0	41	0	24	41.46	
27 ATL2Tracer	Modification	refining	ATL	ATL	2	0	96	0	96	0	3	58	39.58	1	84	12.5	46	52.08	
28 ATL2WTracer	Modification	refining	ATL	ATL	8	2	333	1	328	1.5	3	166	50.15	1	324	2.7	152	54.35	
29 CACA	Modification	refining	ATL	ATL, Trace	6	2	178	0	178	0	0	178	0	3	133	25.28	133	25.28	
30 CACD	Modification	refining	ATL	ATL, Trace	6	5	224	2	210	6.25	0	210	0	3	154	31.25	140	37.5	
31 CCCR	Modification	refining	ATL	ATL, Trace	6	2	178	0	178	0	0	178	0	3	133	25.28	133	25.28	
32 CFCA	Modification	refining	ATL	ATL, Trace	6	2	180	0	180	0	0	180	0	3	130	27.78	130	27.78	
33 CFCD	Modification	refining	ATL	ATL, Trace	6	2	122	0	122	0	0	122	0	3	98	19.67	98	19.67	
34 CFCP	Modification	refining	ATL	ATL, Trace	6	2	178	0	178	0	0	178	0	3	131	26.4	131	26.4	
35 MergeHOT	Composition	normal	ATL,ATL	ATL	11	3	185	1	175	5.41	0	175	0	2	70	62.16	60	67.57	
36 MMTtoMT	Modification	normal	ATL,MOF	ATL	4	0	260	0	260	0	4	93	64.23	1	249	4.23	82	68.46	
37 RefactorATL	Modification	refining	ATL	ATL	1	1	37	0	37	0	0	37	0	1	37	0	37	0	
38 ROCC	Modification	refining	ATL	ATL, Trace	6	2	158	0	158	0	0	158	0	3	110	30.38	110	30.38	
39 RSCC	Modification	refining	ATL	ATL, Trace	6	2	179	0	179	0	0	179	0	3	132	26.26	132	26.26	
40 RSMA	Modification	refining	ATL	ATL, Trace	6	5	228	2	214	6.14	0	214	0	3	147	35.53	133	41.67	
41 RSMD	Modification	refining	ATL	ATL, Trace	6	4	171	0	171	0	0	171	0	3	123	28.07	123	28.07	
42 Superimpose	Composition	normal	ATL, ATL	ATL, Trace	6	16	267	1	264	1.12	0	264	0	5	217	18.73	214	19.85	
TOTAL Modification + Composition					94	50	3015	7	2969		13	2626		41	2313		1878		
AVERAGE Modification + Composition					5.53	2.94	177.35	0.41	174.65	1.2	0.76	154.47	11.5	2.41	136.06	13.33	110.47	34.83	37.71
TOTAL					551	268	21022	28	20433		199	13399		41	20320		12108		
AVERAGE					13.12	6.38	500.52	0.67	486.5	3.21	4.74	319.02	23.33	0.98	483.81	8.96	288.29	35.5	42.4

Higher Order Functions (HOFs). The authors implement in XSLT a set of HOFs, classical in the functional programming paradigm (e.g. *map, fold*), accepting XSLT templates as arguments. Our work is instead focused on facilitating the development of new, user-defined HOTs in the transformational paradigm.

6   Conclusions and Future Work

HOTs are a relatively novel topic in MDE and specialized tools are not yet available for them. In this paper we show how some modifications to a well-known transformation language could facilitate HOT development by allowing more concise transformations. We support experimentally our proposals, by measuring their impact on a set of real-world HOTs.

The proposals we introduce have also a wider contribution scope, since they could have a positive outcome also outside HOT classes.

There are several possible directions for future work. We plan to further exploit the homogeneity of HOT classes by defining transformation patterns and introducing a pattern-based design methodology for them. We want to embed a deeper support of HOTs in the AmmA environment, allowing the user to easily define composite HOT patterns and to execute them seamlessly at compilation time. Finally we plan to generalize our results to the other transformation languages, and create cross-environment tools for HOTs.

Acknowledgments. The present work has been supported by the ITEA2 OPEES European project.

References

1. EXSLT, http://www.exslt.org (2006)
2. Balogh, Z., Varró, D.: Model transformation by example using inductive logic programming. Software and Systems Modeling 8(3), 347–364 (2009)
3. Bézivin, J., et al.: Model Transformations? Transformation Models! In: Nierstrasz, O., et al. (eds.) MoDELS 2006. LNCS, vol. 4199, pp. 440–453. Springer, Heidelberg (2006)
4. Chenouard, R., Jouault, F.: Automatically Discovering Hidden Transformation Chaining Constraints. In: Schürr, A., Selic, B. (eds.) MODELS 2009. LNCS, vol. 5795, p. 92. Springer, Heidelberg (2009)
5. Cuadrado, J.S., Molina, J.G., Tortosa, M.M.: RubyTL: A practical, extensible transformation language. In: Rensink, A., Warmer, J. (eds.) ECMDA-FA 2006. LNCS, vol. 4066, pp. 158–172. Springer, Heidelberg (2006)
6. Garcés, K., Jouault, F., Cointe, P., Bézivin, J.: Managing model adaptation by precise detection of metamodel changes. Evolution 2, 2 (2009)
7. Apache Group. The Apache ANT Project (2010), http://ant.apache.org/
8. ATLAS INRIA Research Group. KM3 to ATL Copier (2005), http://www.eclipse.org/m2m/atl/atlTransformations/#KM32ATLCopier
9. Iacob, M.E., Steen, M.W.A., Heerink, L.: Reusable Model Transformation Patterns. In: Workshop on Models and Model-driven Methods for Enterprise Computing (3M4EC 2008), vol. 1 (2008)

10. Jouault, F., Bézivin, J., Kurtev, I.: TCS: a DSL for the specification of textual concrete syntaxes in model engineering. In: Proceedings of the 5th international conference on Generative programming and component engineering, p. 254. ACM, New York (2006)
11. Jouault, F., Garces, K., Kling, W.: Automatizing the Evaluation of Model Matching Systems. In: Workshop on Matching and Meaning: Automated development, evolution and interpretation of ontologies, in AISB'10 Convention, Leicester, UK (2010) (submitted)
12. Kurtev, I., Bézivin, J., Jouault, F., Valduriez, P.: Model-based DSL frameworks. In: Companion to the 21st ACM SIGPLAN symposium on Object-oriented programming systems, languages, and applications, Portland, Oregon, USA, p. 616. ACM, New York (2006)
13. Novatchev, D.: Higher-order functional programming with XSLT 2.0 and FXSL. In: Extreme Markup Languages, vol. 7, vol. 7, Citeseer (2006)
14. Strommer, M., Wimmer, M.: A framework for model transformation by-example: Concepts and tool support. In: Proceedings of the 46th International Conference on Technology of Object-Oriented Languages and Systems, Zurich, Switzerland, pp. 372–391. Springer, Heidelberg (2008)
15. Tisi, M., Jouault, F.: ATL HOT Library (2010), http://docatlanmod.emn.fr/HOT-library/
16. Tisi, M., Jouault, F., Fraternali, P., Ceri, S., Bézivin, J.: On the Use of Higher-Order Model Transformations. In: Proceedings of the Fifth European Conference on Model-Driven Architecture Foundations and Applications (ECMDA), pp. 18–33. Springer, Heidelberg (2009)
17. Valduriez, P., Didonet Del Fabro, M.: Towards the efficient development of model transformations using model weaving and matching transformations. Software and Systems Modeling 8(3), 305–324 (2009)

Towards a Rewriting Logic Semantics for ATL

Javier Troya and Antonio Vallecillo

GISUM/Atenea Research Group, Universidad de Málaga, Spain
{javiertc,av}@lcc.uma.es

Abstract. As the complexity of model transformation (MT) grows, the need to count on formal semantics of MT languages also increases. Firstly, formal semantics provide precise specifications of the expected behavior of transformations, which are crucial for both MT users (to be able to understand them and to use them properly) and MT tool builders (to develop correct MT engines, optimizers, etc.). Secondly, we need to be able to reason about the MTs to prove their correctness. This is specially important in case of large and complex MTs (with, e.g., hundreds or thousands of rules) for which manual debugging is no longer possible. In this paper we present a formal semantics to the ATL model transformation language using rewriting logic and Maude, which allows addressing these issues. This formalization provides additional benefits, such as enabling the simulation of the specifications or giving access to the Maude toolkit to reason about them.

1 Introduction

Model transformations (MT) are at the heart of Model-Driven Engineering, and provide the essential mechanisms for manipulating and transforming models. As the complexity of model transformations grows, the need to count on formal semantics of MT languages also increases. Formal semantics provide precise specifications of the expected behavior of the transformations, which are crucial for all MT stakeholders: users need to be able to understand and use model transformations properly; tool builders need formal and precise specifications to develop correct model transformation engines, optimizers, debuggers, etc.; and MT programmers need to know the expected behavior of the rules and transformations they write, in order to reason about them and prove their correctness. This is specially important in case of large and complex MTs (with, e.g., hundreds or thousands of rules) for which manual debugging is no longer possible. For instance, in the case of rule-based model transformation languages, proving that the specifications are confluent and terminating is required. Also, looking for non-triggered rules may help detecting potential design problems in large MT systems.

ATL [1] is one of the most popular and widely used model transformation languages. The ATL language has been normally described in an intuitive and informal manner, by means of definitions of its main features in natural language. However, this lack of rigorous description can easily lead to imprecisions and misunderstandings that might hinder the proper usage and analysis of the language, and the development of correct and interoperable tools.

In this paper we investigate the use of rewriting logic [2] and its implementation in Maude [3], for giving semantics to ATL. The use of Maude as a target semantic domain

L. Tratt and M. Gogolla (Eds.): ICMT 2010, LNCS 6142, pp. 230–244, 2010.

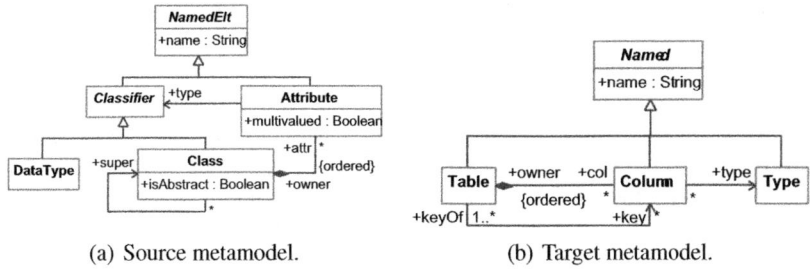

(a) Source metamodel.   (b) Target metamodel.

Fig. 1. Transformation metamodels

brings interesting benefits, because it enables the simulation of the ATL specifications and its formal analysis. In particular, we show how our specifications can make use of the Maude toolkit to reason about some properties of the ATL rules.

2   Transformations with ATL

ATL is a hybrid model transformation domain specific language containing a mixture of declarative and imperative constructs. ATL transformations are unidirectional, operating on read-only source models and producing write-only target models. During the execution of a transformation, source models may be navigated but changes are not allowed. Target models cannot be navigated.

ATL modules define the transformations. A module contains a mandatory header section, an import section, and a number of helpers and transformation rules. The header section provides the name of the transformation module and declares the source and target models (which are typed by their metamodels). Helpers and transformation rules are the constructs used to specify the transformation functionality.

Declarative ATL rules are called **matched rules** and **lazy rules**. Lazy rules are like matched rules, but are only applied when called by another rule. They both specify relations between source patterns and target patterns. The source pattern of a rule specifies a set of source types and an optional guard given as a Boolean expression in OCL. A source pattern is evaluated to a set of matches in source models. The target pattern is composed of a set of elements. Each of these elements specifies a target type from the target metamodel and a set of bindings. A *binding* refers to a feature of the type (i.e., an attribute, a reference or an association end) and specifies an expression whose value is used to initialize the feature. Lazy rules can be called several times using a collect construct. **Unique lazy rules** are a special kind of lazy rules that always return the same target element for a given source element. The target element is retrieved by navigating the internal traceability links, as in normal rules. Non-unique lazy rules do not navigate the traceability links but create new target elements in each execution.

In some cases, complex transformation algorithms may be required, and it may be difficult to specify them in a declarative way. For this reason ATL provides two imperative constructs: **called rules** and **action blocks**. A called rule is a rule called by others like a procedure. An action block is a sequence of imperative statements and can be used instead of or in combination with a target pattern in matched or called rules. The imperative statements in ATL are the usual constructs for attribute assignment and control flow: conditions and loops.

ATL also provides the **resolveTemp** operation for dealing with complex transformations. This operation allows to refer to any of the target model elements generated from a given source model element: resolveTemp(srcObj,targetPatternName). The first argument is the source model element, and the second is a string with the name of the target pattern element. This operation can be called from the target pattern and imperative sections of any matched or called rule.

In order to illustrate our proposal we will use the typical example of Class-to-Relational model transformation. This example and many others can be found in [4]. The two metamodels involved in this transformation are shown in Fig. 1. Our input model contains two classes: Family and Person. It is shown below, written in KM3 [5]:

```
datatype String;
datatype Integer;
class Family {
    attribute name : String;
    attribute members[*] : Person; }
class Person {
    attribute firstName : String;
    attribute closestFriend : Person;
    attribute emailAddresses[*] : String; }
```

An example of an output model is the following:

```
table Person {
    primary column objectId : Integer;
    column firstName : String;
    column closestFriendId : Integer; }
table Family_members {
    column familyId : Integer;
    column membersId : Integer; }
table Person_emailAddresses {
    column personId : Integer;
    column emailAddresses : String; }
table Family {
    primary column objectId : Integer;
    column name : String; }
```

An ATL transformation that takes the first model as input and produces the second is shown below. It has 6 rules, each one showing a particular ATL feature. The complete description of this example and its encoding in Maude can be found in [6]. Although the ATL rules are mostly self-explanatory, readers not fluent in ATL can consult [1,6] for all the details.

```
module Class2Relation; -- Module Template
create OUT : RelationMM from IN : ClassMM;
helper def: objectIdType : Relational!Type =
      Class!DataType.allInstances() ->select(e | e.name = 'Integer')->first();
rule DataType2Type {
  from dt : Class!DataType
  to    t : Relational!Type ( name <- dt.name ) }
rule SingleValuedDataTypeAttribute2Column {
  from at : Class!Attribute (
          at.type.oclIsKindOf(Class!DataType) and not at.multiValued )
  to    co : Relational!Column ( name <- at.name, type <- at.type ) }
rule MultiValuedDataTypeAttribute2Column {
  from at : Class!Attribute ( at.type.oclIsKindOf(Class!DataType)
                    and at.multiValued )
  to    tb : Relational!Table (name <- at.owner.name + '_' + at.name,
```

```
                                col  <- Sequence {co, coo}),
        co : Relational!Column (
            name <- at.owner.name + 'Id', type <- thisModule.objectIdType),
        coo : Relational!Column ( name <- at.name, type <- at.type ) }
rule SingleValuedClassAttribute2Column {
  from at : Class!Attribute (
            at.type.oclIsKindOf(Class!Class) and not at.multiValued )
  to    co : Relational!Column ( name <- at.name + 'Id',
                                 type <- thisModule.objectIdType ) }
rule MultiValuedClassAttribute2Column {
  from at : Class!Attribute (
            at.type.oclIsKindOf(Class!Class) and at.multiValued )
  to    tb : Relational!Table ( name <- at.owner.name + '_' + at.name,
                                col <- Sequence {id, k} ),
        id : Relational!Column ( name <- at.owner.name.firstToLower() + 'Id',
                                 type <- thisModule.objectIdType ),
        k  : Relational!Column (
             name <- at.name + 'Id', type <- thisModule.objectIdType ) }
rule Class2Table {
  from c  : Class!Class
  to    tb : Relational!Table ( name <- c.name,
             col <- Sequence {k}->union(c.attr->select(iter | not iter.multiValued)),
             key <- Set {k} ),
        k  : Relational!Column(name <- 'objectId', type <-thisModule.objectIdType)}
```

3   Rewriting Logic and Maude

Maude [3] is a high-level language and a high-performance interpreter in the OBJ algebraic specification family that supports membership equational logic [7] and rewriting logic [2] specification and programming of systems. Thus, Maude integrates an equational style of functional programming with rewriting logic computation. We informally describe in this section those Maude's features necessary for understanding the paper; the interested reader is referred to [3] for more details.

Rewriting logic is a logic of change that can naturally deal with state and with highly nondeterministic concurrent computations. A distributed system is axiomatized in rewriting logic by a *rewrite theory* $\mathcal{R} = (\Sigma, E, R)$, where (Σ, E) is an equational theory describing its set of *states* as the algebraic data type $T_{\Sigma/E}$ associated to the initial algebra (Σ, E), and R is a collection of rewrite rules. Maude's underlying equational logic is membership equational logic [7], a Horn logic whose atomic sentences are equalities $t = t'$ and *membership assertions* of the form $t : S$, stating that a term t has sort S. Such a logic extends order-sorted equational logic, and supports sorts, subsort relations, subsort overloading of operators, and definition of partial functions with equationally defined domains.

Rewrite rules, which are written crl [l] : $t \Rightarrow t'$ if *Cond*, with l the rule label, t and t' terms, and *Cond* a condition, describe the local, concurrent transitions that are possible in the system, i.e., when a part of the system state fits the pattern t, then it can be replaced by the corresponding instantiation of t'. The guard *Cond* acts as a blocking precondition, in the sense that a conditional rule can be fired only if its condition holds.

The form of conditions is $EqCond_1 / \backslash \ldots / \backslash EqCond_n$ where each of the $EqCond_i$ is either an ordinary equation $t = t'$, a *matching equation* $t := t'$, a sort constraint $t : s$, or a term t of sort Bool, abbreviating the equation $t = $ true. In the execution of a matching equation $t := t'$, the variables of the term t, which may not appear in the lefthand side of the corresponding conditional equation, become instantiated by *matching* the term t against the canonical form of the bounded subject term t'.

4   Encoding ATL in Maude

To give a formal semantics to ATL using rewriting logic, we provide a representation of ATL constructs and behavior in Maude. We start by defining how the models and metamodels handled by ATL can be encoded in Maude, and then provide the semantics of matched rules, lazy rules, unique lazy rules, helpers and imperative sections. One of the benefits of such an encoding is that it is systematic and can be automated, something we are currently implementing using ATL transformations (between the ATL and Maude metamodels).

4.1   Characterizing Model Transformations

In our view, a model transformation is just an algorithmic specification (let it be declarative or operational) associated to a relation $R \subseteq MM \times MN$ defined between two metamodels which allows to obtain a target model N conforming to MN from a source model M that conforms to metamodel MM [8].

The idea supporting our proposal considers that model transformations comprise two different aspects: *structure* and *behavior*. The former aspect defines the structural relation R that should hold between source and target models, whilst the latter describes how the specific source model elements are transformed into target model elements. This separation allows differentiating between the relation that the model transformation ensures from the algorithm it actually uses to compute the target model.

Thus, to represent the structural aspects of a transformation we will use three models: the source model M, the target model N that the transformation builds, and the relation $R(M, N)$ between the two. $R(M, N)$ is also called the *trace* model, that specifies how the elements of M and N are consistently related by R. Please note that each element r_i of $R(M, N) = \{r_1, ..., r_k\} \subseteq \mathbb{P}(M) \times \mathbb{P}(N)$ relates a set of elements of M with a set of elements of N.

The behavioral aspects of an ATL transformation (i.e., how the transformation progressively builds the target model elements from the source model, and the traces between them) is defined using the different kinds of rules (matched, lazy, unique lazy); their possible combinations and direct invocation from other rules, and the final imperative algorithms that can be invoked after each rule.

4.2   Encoding Models and Metamodels in Maude

We will follow the representation of models and metamodels introduced in [9], which is inspired in the Maude representation of object-oriented systems mentioned. We represent models in Maude as structures of sort @Model of the form $mm\{obj_1\ obj_2\ ...\ obj_N\}$, where mm is the name of the metamodel and obj_i are the objects of the model. An object is a record-like structure $< o : c \mid a_1 : v_1, ..., a_n : v_n >$ (of sort @Object), where o is the object identifier (of sort Oid), c is the class the object belongs to (of sort @Class), and $a_i : v_i$ are attribute-value pairs (of sort @StructuralFeatureInstance).

Given the appropriate definitions for all classes, attributes and references in its corresponding metamodel (as we shall see below), the following Maude term describes the input model shown in Sect. 2.

```
@ClassMm@ {
  < 'd1 : DataType@ClassMm | name@NamedElt@ClassMm : "Integer" >
  < 'd2 : DataType@ClassMm | name@NamedElt@ClassMm : "String" >
  < 'a1 : Attribute@ClassMm | multivalued@Attribute@ClassMm : false #
    name@NamedElt@ClassMm : "name" # type@Attribute@ClassMm : 'd2 #
    owner@Attribute@ClassMm : 'c1 >
  < 'a2 : Attribute@ClassMm | multivalued@Attribute@ClassMm : true #
    name@NamedElt@ClassMm : "members" # type@Attribute@ClassMm : 'c2 #
    owner@Attribute@ClassMm : 'c1 >
  < 'a3 : Attribute@ClassMm | multivalued@Attribute@ClassMm : false #
    name@NamedElt@ClassMm : "firstName" # type@Attribute@ClassMm : 'd2 #
    owner@Attribute@ClassMm : 'c2 >
  < 'a4 : Attribute@ClassMm | multivalued@Attribute@ClassMm : false #
    name@NamedElt@ClassMm : "closestFriend" # type@Attribute@ClassMm : 'c2 #
    owner@Attribute@ClassMm : 'c2 >
  < 'a5 : Attribute@ClassMm | multivalued@Attribute@ClassMm : true #
    name@NamedElt@ClassMm : "emailAddresses" # type@Attribute@ClassMm : 'd2 #
    owner@Attribute@ClassMm : 'c2 >
  < 'c1 : Class@ClassMm | isAbstract@Class@ClassMm : false #
    name@NamedElt@ClassMm : "Family" # att@Class@ClassMm : Sequence['a1 ; 'a2] #
    super@Class@ClassMm : null >
  < 'c2 : Class@ClassMm | isAbstract@Class@ClassMm : false #
    name@NamedElt@ClassMm : "Person" # att@Class@ClassMm :
    Sequence['a3 ; 'a4 ; 'a5]# super@Class@ClassMm : null >  }
```

Note that quoted identifiers are used as object identifiers; references are encoded as object attributes by means of object identifiers; and OCL collections (Set, OrderedSet, Sequence, and Bag) are supported by means of mOdCL [10].

Metamodels are encoded using a sort for every metamodel element: sort @Class for classes, sort @Attribute for attributes, sort @Reference for references, etc. Thus, a metamodel is represented by declaring a constant of the corresponding sort for each metamodel element. More precisely, each class is represented by a constant of a sort named after the class. This sort, which will be declared as subsort of sort @Class, is defined to support class inheritance through Maude's order-sorted type structure. Other properties of metamodel elements, such as whether a class is abstract or not, the opposite of a reference (to represent bidirectional associations), or attributes and reference types, are expressed by means of Maude equations defined over the constant that represents the corresponding metamodel element. Classes, attributes and references are qualified with their containers' names, so that classes with the same name belonging to different packages, as well as attributes and references of different classes, are distinguished. See [9] for further details.

4.3 Modeling ATL Rules

Matched rules. Each ATL matched rule is represented by a Maude rewrite rule that describes how the target model elements are created from the source model elements identified in the left-hand side of the rule (that represents the "to" pattern of the ATL rule). The general form of such rewrite rules is as follows:

```
crl [rulename] :
  Sequence[
    (@SourceMm@ { ... OBJSET@ }) ;
    (@TraceMm@ { ... OBJSETT@ }) ;
```

```
      (@TargetMm@ { OBJSETTT@ }) ]
=> Sequence[
        (@SourceMm@ { ... OBJSET@ }) ;
        (@TraceMm@ { ... OBJSETT@}) ;
        (@TargetMm@ { ... OBJSETTT@ }) ]
   if ...
        /\ not alreadyExecuted(..., "rulename", @TraceMm@ { OBJSETT@ }) .
```

The two sides of the Maude rule contain the three models that capture the state of the transformation (see 4.1): the source, the trace and the target models.[1] The rule specifies how the state of the ATL model transformation changes as result of such rule.

The triggering of Maude and ATL rules is similar: a rule is triggered if the pattern specified by the rule is found, and the guard condition holds. In addition to the specific rule conditions, in the Maude representation we also check (alreadyExecuted) that the same ATL rule has not been triggered with the same elements.

An additional Maude rule, called Init, starts the transformation. It creates the initial state of the model transformation, and initializes the target and trace models:

```
rl [Init] :
   Sequence[ (@ClassMm@ { OBJSET@ }) ]
   => Sequence[
       (@ClassMm@ { OBJSET@ }) ;
       (@TraceMm@ { < 'CNT : Counter@CounterMm | value@Counter@CounterMm : 1 > }) ;
       (@RelationalMm@ { none }) ] .
```

The traces stored in the trace model are also objects, of class Trace@TraceMm, whose attributes are: two sequences (srcEl@TraceMm and trgEl@TraceMm) with the sets of identifiers of the elements of the source and target models related by the trace; the rule name (rlName@TraceMm); and a reference to the source and target metamodels: srcMdl@TraceMm and trgMdl@TraceMm.

The trace model also contains a special object, of class Counter@CounterMm, whose integer attribute is used as a counter for assigning fresh identifiers to the newly created elements and traces. As an example, consider the first of the rules of Class2Relation transformation described in Sect. 2:

```
rule DataType2Type {
  from dt : Class!DataType
  to   t : Relational!Type ( name <- dt.name ) }
```

The encoding in Maude of such a rule is as follows:

```
crl[DataType2Type] :
  Sequence[
    (@ClassMm@ { < DT@ : DataType@ClassMm | SFS > OBJSET@ }) ;
    (@TraceMm@ {
      < CNT@ : Counter@CounterMm | value@Counter@CounterMm : VALUE@CNT@ >
      OBJSETT@ }) ;
    (@RelationalMm@ { OBJSETTT@ }) ]
  => Sequence[
    (@ClassMm@ { < DT@ : DataType@ClassMm | SFS > OBJSET@ }) ;
    (@TraceMm@ {
      < CNT@ : Counter@CounterMm | value@Counter@CounterMm : VALUE@CNT@ + 2 >
      < TR@ : Trace@TraceMm | srcEl@TraceMm : Sequence[ DT@ ] #
      trgEl@TraceMm : Sequence[ T@ ] # rlName@TraceMm : "DataType2Type" #
      srcMdl@TraceMm : "Class" # trgMdl@TraceMm : "Relation" > OBJSETT@}) ;
```

---

[1] For simplicity, in this paper we will show examples where the transformation deals with only one input model. ATL can handle more than one, but the treatment in Maude is analogous—it is just a matter of including more models in the specification of the relation.

```
    (@RelationalMm@ { <  T@ : Type@RelationalMm |
       name@Named@RelationalMm : << DT@ . name@NamedElt@ClassMm ; CLASSMODEL@ >> >
       OBJSETTT@ }) ]
 if CLASSMODEL@ := @ClassMm@ { < DT@ : DataType@ClassMm | SFS > OBJSET@ }
    /\ TR@ := newId(VALUE@CNT@) /\ T@ := newId(VALUE@CNT@ + 1)
    /\ not alreadyExecuted(Sequence[DT@],"DataType2Type",@TraceMm@ { OBJSETT@ }) .
```

This rule is applied over instances of class DataType, as specified in the left hand side of the Maude rule. The rule guard guarantees that the rule has not been already applied over the same elements. The guard is also used to define some variables used by the rule (CLASSMODEL@, TR@ and T@).

After the application of the rule, the state of the system is changed: the source model is left unmodified (ATL does not allow modifying the source models); a new trace (TR@) is added to the trace model; the value of the counter object is updated; and a new element (T@) is created in the target model. We allow the evaluation of OCL expressions using mOdCL [10] by enclosing them in double angle brackets (<< ... >>).

The encoding of the rest of the ATL matched rules in the example of Sect. 2 follow the same schema and can be found in [6].

Lazy rules. While matched rules are executed in non-deterministic order (as soon as their "to:" patterns are matched in the source model), lazy rules are executed only when they are explicitly called by other rules. Thus, we have modeled lazy rules as Maude operations, whose arguments are the parameters of the corresponding rule, and return the set of elements that have changed or need to be created. In this way the operations can model the calling of ATL rules in a natural way.

Maude operations representing ATL lazy rules do not modify the trace model, this is the responsibility of the Maude calling rule. For every invoked lazy rule a trace is created. The name of the ATL rule recorded in the trace is not the name of the lazy rule, but the name of the matched rule concatenated with "_" and with the name of the lazy rule. We represent them in this way because a lazy rule can be invoked by different calling rules, and in this way we know which matched rule called it.

Special care should be taken when lazy rules are called from a collect construct. When lazy rules are not called from a collect, it is only necessary to write, in the target model, the identifier of the first object created by the lazy rule when we want to reference the objects it creates. But with lazy rules called from a collect we need to reference the sequence of objects created by the lazy rule. To do this, we use an auxiliary function, getOidsCollect, whose arguments are the ones of the lazy rule, the identifier of the first element created by the lazy rule, and the number of objects created in each iteration by the lazy rule. It returns a sequence with the identifiers of the objects created by the lazy rule, in the same order.

Unique lazy rules. This kind of rules deserve a special encoding in Maude, because their behavior is quite different from normal lazy rules. Now we need to check if the element created by the lazy rule is already there, or if it has to be created. If it was already there, we need to get its identifier. We also have to be careful with the traces, since only one trace has to be added for the elements created by a unique lazy rule.

Helpers. Helpers are side-effect free functions that can be used by the transformation rules for realizing the functionality. Helpers are normally described in OCL. Thus, their representation is direct as Maude operations that make use of mOdCL for evaluating the OCL expression of their body. For instance, the following Maude operation represents the obejctIdType helper shown in the ATL example in Sect. 2:

```
op objectIdType : @Model @Model -> Oid .
  eq objectIdType(@ClassMm@{OBJSET}, @TraceMm@{OBJSETT})
    = getTarget(<< DataType@ClassMm . allInstances -> select( ITER | ITER .
      name@NamedElt@ClassMm .=. "Integer" ) -> asSequence() -> first() ;
      @ClassMm@{OBJSET} >> , @TraceMm@{OBJSETT}) .
```

This helper receives the class and trace models as arguments. It returns the first Type whose name is Integer by looking for it in the trace model with the getTarget operation. OCL expressions allInstances, select, asSequence and first are encoded as such.

The imperative section. We represent the imperative section of rules using a data type called Instr that we have defined for representing the different *instructions* that are possible within a do block. Currently we implement three types of instructions: *assignments* (=), *conditional* branches (if) and *called rules*. In the following piece of code we show how type Instr and the sequence of instructions (instrSeq) are defined:

```
sort Instr instrSeq .
subsort Instr < instrSeq .
op none : -> instrSeq [ctor] .
op _^_ : Instr instrSeq -> instrSeq [ctor id: none] .
op Assign : Oid @StructuralFeature OCL-Exp -> Instr [ctor] .
op If : Bool instrSeq instrSeq -> Instr [ctor] .
---Instruction for our called rule
op AddColumn : Int String -> Instr [ctor] .
```

Thus, the same instruction is used for assignments and conditional instructions. A new instruction is needed for each called rule (AddColumn in this case).

The ATL imperative section, which is within a do block, is encapsulated in Maude by a function called do which receives as arguments the set of objects created by the declarative part of the rule, and the sequence of instructions to be applied over those objects. It returns the sequence of objects resulting from applying the instructions:

```
op do : Set{@Object} InstrSequ -> Set{@Object} .
  eq do(OBJSET@, none) = OBJSET@ .
  eq do(OBJSET@, Assign(O@, SF@, EXP@) ^ INSTR@) =
    do(doAssign(OBJSET@, O@, SF@, EXP@), INSTR@) .
  eq do(OBJSET@, If(COND@, INSTR1@, INSTR2@) ^ INSTR@) =
    if COND@ then do(OBJSET@, INSTR1@ ^ INSTR@)
    else do(OBJSET@, INSTR2@ ^ INSTR@)
    fi .
  ---For each called rule, AddColumn in this case
  eq do(OBJSET@, AddColumn(VALUE@CNT@, NAME) ^ INSTR@) =
    do(doAddColumn(OBJSET@, VALUE@CNT@, NAME), INSTR@) .
```

We see that the function is recursive, so it applies the instructions one by one, in the same order as they appear in the ATL do block. When the function finds an Assign instruction, it applies the doAssign operation. When it finds an If instruction, it checks wether the condition is satisfied or not, applying a different sequence of instructions in each case. With regard to called rule instructions, the Maude do operation applies them as they appear. The two operations mentioned are the following:

```
op doAssign : Set{@Object} Oid @StructuralFeature OCL-Exp -> Set{@Object} .
  eq doAssign(< O@ : CL@ | SF@ : TYPE@ # SFS > OBJSET@, O@, SF@, EXP@) =
     < O@ : CL@ | SF@ : EXP@ # SFS > OBJSET@ .

op doAddColumn : Set{@Object} Int String -> Set{@Object} .
  eq doAddColumn(OBJSET@, VALUE@CNT@, NAME) =
     < newId(VALUE@CNT@) : Column@RelationalMm | name@Named@RelationalMm : NAME >
     OBJSET@ .
```

Function **doAssign** assigns an OCL expression to an attribute of an object. It receives the set of objects created in the declarative part, the identifier of the object and its attribute, and the OCL expression that will be assigned to the attribute of the object. The function replaces the old value of the attribute with the result of the evaluation of the OCL expression. Function **doAddColumn** creates a new **Column** instance. It receives the set of objects created by the declarative part of the rule, the counter for giving an identifier to the new object, and the String that will be the name of the **Column**.

For example, consider the following ATL rule, that contains an imperative part to modify the elements that have been created by the rule:

```
rule MultiValuedClassAttribute2Column {
  from at : Class!Attribute(at.type.oclIsKindOf(Class!Class) and at.multiValued)
  to   tb : Relational!Table (
             name <- at.owner.name + '_' + at.name,
             col <- Sequence {id, k} ),
       id : Relational!Column (
             name <- at.owner.name.firstToLower() + 'Id',
             type <- thisModule.objectIdType ),
       k :  Relational!Column (name <- at.name + 'Id',
             type <- thisModule.objectIdType )
  do { tb.name <- tb.name + '_Multi';
       if (tb.col->size() = 2) { k.name <- 'key'; }
       else { k.name <- 'key_else'; }
       thisModule.AddColumn( New_Column ) ; }
}
```

The corresponding encoding in Maude is as follows:

```
crl[MultiValuedClassAttribute2Column] :
  Sequence [...]
  => Sequence [...
     (@RelationalMm@ { do(
        < TB@ : Table@RelationalMm | name@Named@RelationalMm : << AT@ .
          owner@Attribute@ClassMm . name@NamedElt@ClassMm + "_" + AT@ .
          name@NamedElt@ClassMm ; CLASSMODEL@ >> #
          col@Table@RelationalMm : Sequence[ID@ ; K@] #
          key@Table@RelationalMm : Set{K@} >
        < ID@ : Column@RelationalMm | name@Named@RelationalMm : << AT@ .
          owner@Attribute@ClassMm . name@NamedElt@ClassMm + "Id" ; CLASSMODEL@ >> #
          type@Column@RelationalMm:objectIdType(CLASSMODEL@,@TraceMm@{OBJSETT@})>
        < K@ : Column@RelationalMm | name@Named@RelationalMm : << AT@ .
          name@NamedElt@ClassMm + "Id" ; CLASSMODEL@ >> #
          type@Column@RelationalMm:objectIdType(CLASSMODEL@,@TraceMm@{OBJSETT@})>,
        Assign(TB@, name@Named@RelationalMm, << AT@ . owner@Attribute@ClassMm .
        name@NamedElt@ClassMm + "_" + AT@ . name@NamedElt@ClassMm ;
        CLASSMODEL@ >> + "_Multi") ^
        If(<< Sequence[ID@ ; K@] -> size() ; CLASSMODEL@ >> == 3,
        Assign(K@,name@Named@RelationalMm, "key"),
        Assign(K@, name@Named@RelationalMm, "key_else")) ^
        AddColumn(VALUE@CNT@, "New_Column") ) OBJSETTT@ }) ]
  if ...
```

The first argument of the function **do** is the set of objects created in the declarative part of the rule. Consequently, we make the declarative part of the rule to be executed before the imperative part. This reproduces the way in which ATL works. The second argument is a sequence of instructions which contains, in this case, three instructions. The first instruction executed is the Assign, then the If, and, finally, the instruction that represents the called rule, AddColumn, is executed.

ResolveTemp. The function looks for the trace which contains the source element passed as first argument and returns the identifier of the element from the sequence of elements created from the source element. It can be implemented in Maude as follows:

```
op resolveTemp : Oid Nat @Model @Model -> Oid .
 eq resolveTemp(O@ , N@ , @TraceMm@{ < TR@ : Trace@TraceMm | srcEl@TraceMm :
    Sequence[O@] # trgEl@TraceMm : SEQ # SFS > OBJSET} , CLASSMODEL@ ) =
    if (<< SEQ -> size ( ) < N@ ; CLASSMODEL@ >>) then null
    else << SEQ -> at(N@) ; CLASSMODEL@ >>
    fi .
```

It has four arguments: the identifier of the source model element from which the searched target model element is produced; the position of the target object identifier in the sequence trgEl@TraceMm; and the trace and class models, respectively. It returns the identifier of the element to be retrieved. The major difference with the ATL function is that here we receive as second argument the position that the searched target model element has among the ones created by the corresponding rule. In ATL, instead, the argument received is the name of the variable that was given to the target model element when it was created. This difference is not important since it is easy to retrieve the position that the element has among the elements created by the ATL rule.

5   Simulation and Formal Analysis

Once the ATL model transformation specifications are encoded in Maude, what we get is a rewriting logic specification for it. Maude offers tool support for interesting possibilities such as model simulation, reachability analysis and model checking [3].

5.1   Simulating the Transformations

Because the rewriting logic specifications produced are executable, this specification can be used as a prototype of the transformation, which allows us to simulate it. Maude offers different possibilities for realizing the simulation, including step-by-step execution, several execution strategies, etc. In particular, Maude provides two different rewrite commands, namely rewrite and frewrite, which implement two different execution strategies, a top-down rule-fair strategy, and a depth-first position-fair strategy, respectively [3]. The result of the process is the final configuration of objects reached after the rewriting steps, which is nothing but a model.

For example, the result of the ATL model transformation described in Section 2, when applied to the source Class model, is a sequence of three models: the source, the trace and the target Relational model. This last one is shown below.

```
@RelationalMm@{
    < '2 : Type@RelationalMm | name@Named@RelationalMm : "Integer" >
    < '10 : Type@RelationalMm | name@Named@RelationalMm : "String" >
    < '23 : Table@RelationalMm | name@Named@RelationalMm : "Person",
      col@Table@RelationalMm : Sequence ['24 ; '4 ; '21],
```

```
    key@Table@RelationalMm : Set {'24} >
< '24 : Column@RelationalMm | name@Named@RelationalMm : "objectId",
   type@Column@RelationalMm : '2 >
< '21 : Column@RelationalMm | name@Named@RelationalMm : "firstName",
   type@Column@RelationalMm : '10 >
< '4 : Column@RelationalMm | name@Named@RelationalMm : "closestFriendId",
   type@Column@RelationalMm : '2 >
< '6 : Table@RelationalMm | name@Named@RelationalMm : "Family_members",
   col@Table@RelationalMm : Sequence ['7 ;'8],key@Table@RelationalMm : Set {'8}>
< '7 : Column@RelationalMm | name@Named@RelationalMm : "FamilyId",
   type@Column@RelationalMm : '2 >
< '8 : Column@RelationalMm | name@Named@RelationalMm : "membersId",
   type@Column@RelationalMm : '2 >
< '14 : Table@RelationalMm | name@Named@RelationalMm : "Person_emailAddresses",
   col@Table@RelationalMm : Sequence ['15 ; '16] >
< '15 : Column@RelationalMm | name@Named@RelationalMm : "PersonId",
   type@Column@RelationalMm : '2 >
< '16 : Column@RelationalMm | name@Named@RelationalMm : "emailAddresses",
   type@Column@RelationalMm : '10 >
< '18 : Table@RelationalMm | name@Named@RelationalMm : "Family",
   col@Table@RelationalMm : Sequence ['19 ; '12],key@Table@RelationalMm :
   Set {'19} >
< '19 : Column@RelationalMm | name@Named@RelationalMm : "objectId",
   type@Column@RelationalMm : '2 >
< '12 : Column@RelationalMm | name@Named@RelationalMm : "name",
   type@Column@RelationalMm : '10 >
}
```

After the simulation is complete we can also analyze the trace model, looking for instance for rules that have not been executed, or for obtaining the traces (and source model elements) related to a particular target model element (or viceversa). Although this could also be done in any transformation language that makes the trace model explicit, the advantages of using our encoding in Maude is that these operations become easy because of Maude's facilities for manipulating sets:

```
op getSourceElements : @Model Oid -> Sequence .
   eq getSourceElements(@TraceMm@{< TR@ : Trace@TraceMm | srcEl@TraceMm :
      SEQ # trgEl@TraceMm : Sequence[O@ ; LO] # SFS > OBJSET}, O@) = SEQ .
   eq getSourceElements(@TraceMm@{< TR@ : Trace@TraceMm | srcEl@TraceMm :
      SEQ # trgEl@TraceMm : Sequence[T@ ; LO] # SFS > OBJSET}, O@)
      = getSourceElements(@TraceMm@{< TR@ : Trace@TraceMm | srcEl@TraceMm :
      SEQ # trgEl@TraceMm : Sequence[LO] # SFS > OBJSET}, O@) .
   eq getSourceElements(@TraceMm@{OBJSET} , O@) = Sequence[mt-ord] [owise] .
```

5.2 Reachability Analysis

Executing the system using the rewrite and frewrite commands means exploring just one possible behavior of the system. However, a rewrite system does not need to be Church-Rosser and terminating,[2] and there might be many different execution paths. Although these commands are enough in many practical situations where an execution path is sufficient for testing executability, the user might be interested in exploring all possible execution paths from the starting model, a subset of these, or a specific one.

Maude search command allows us to explore (following a breadthfirst strategy up to a specified bound) the reachable state space in different ways, looking for certain states

---

[2] For membership equational logic specifications, being Church-Rosser and terminating means not only confluence (a unique normal form will be reached) but also a sort decreasingness property, namely that the normal form will have the least possible sort among those of all other equivalent terms.

of special interest. Other possibilities would include searching for any state (given by a model) in the execution tree, let it be final or not. For example, we could be interested in knowing the partial order in which two ATL matched rules are executed, checking that one always occurs before the other. This can be proved by searching for states that contain the second one in the trace model, but not the first.

6   Related Work

The definition of a formal semantics for ATL has received attention by different groups, using different approaches. For example, in [11] the authors propose an extension of AMMA, the ATLAS Model Management Architecture, to specify the dynamic semantics of a wide range of Domain Specific Languages by means of Abstract State Machines (ASMs), and present a case study where the semantics of part of ATL (namely, matched rules) are formalized. Although ASMs are very expressive, the declarative nature of ATL does not help providing formal semantics to the complete ATL language in this formalism, hindering the complete formalization of the language—something that we were pursuing with our approach.

Other works [12,13] have proposed the use of Alloy to formalize and analyze graph transformation systems, and in particular ATL. The analyses include checking the reachability of given configurations of the host graph through a finite sequence of steps (invocations of rules), and verifying whether given sequences of rules can be applied on an initial graph. These analyses are also possible with our approach, and we also obtain significant gains in expressiveness and completeness. The problem is that Alloy expressiveness and analysis capabilities are quite limited [13]: it has a simple type system with only integers; models in Alloy are static, and thus the approach presented in [13] can only be used to reason about static properties of the transformations (for example it is not possible to reason whether applying a rule r_1 before a rule r_2 in a model will have the same effect as applying r_2 before r_1); only ATL declarative rules are considered, etc. In our approach we can deal with all the ATL language constructs without having to abstract away essential parts such as the imperative section, basic types, etc. More kinds of analysis are also possible with our approach.

Other works provide formal semantics to model transformation languages using types. For intance, Poernomo [14] uses Constructive Type Theory (CTT) for formalizing model transformation and proving their correctness with respect to a given pre- and post-condition specification. This approach can be considered as complementary to ours, each one focusing on different aspects.

There are also the early works in the graph grammar community with a logic-based definition and formalization of graph transformation systems. For example, Courcelle [15] proposes a combination of graph grammars with second order monadic logic to study graph properties and their transformations. Schürr [16] has also studied the formal specification of the semantics of the graph transformation language PROGRES by translating it into some sort of non-monotonic logics.

A different line of work proposed in [17] defines a QVT-like model transformation language reusing the main concepts of graph transformation systems. They formalize their model transformations as theories in rewriting logic, and in this way Maude's reachability analysis and model checking features can be used to verify them. Only the reduced part of QVT relations that can be expressed with this language is covered. Our work is different: we formalize a complete existing transformation language by providing its representation in Maude, without proposing yet another MT language.

Finally, Maude has been proposed as a formal notation and environment for specifying and effectively analyzing models and metamodels [9,18]. Simulation, reachability and model-checking analysis are possible using the tools and techniques provided by Maude [9]. We build on these works, making use of one of these formalizations to represent the models and metamodels that ATL handles.

7   Conclusions and Future Work

In this paper we have proposed a formal semantics for ATL by means of the representation of its concepts and mechanisms in Maude. Apart for providing a precise meaning to ATL concepts and behavior (by its interpretation in rewriting logic), the fact that Maude specifications are executable allows users to simulate the ATL programs. Such an encoding has also enabled the use of Maude's toolkit to reason about the specifications.

In general, it is unrealistic to think that average system modelers will write these Maude specifications. One of the benefits of our encoding is that it is systematic, and therefore it can be automated. Thus we have defined a mapping between the ATL and the Maude metamodels (a *semantic mapping* between these two semantic domains) that realizes the automatic generation of the Maude code. Such a mapping has been defined by means of a set of ATL transformations, that we are currently implementing.

In addition to the analysis possibilities mentioned here, the use of rewriting logic and Maude opens up the way to using many other analysis tools for ATL transformations. In this respect, we are working on the use of the Maude Termination Tool (MTT) [19] and the Church-Rosser Checker (CRC) [20] for checking the termination and confluence of ATL specifications.

Finally, the formal analysis of the specifications needs to be done in Maude. At this moment we are also working on the integration of parts of the Maude toolkit within the ATL environment. This would allow ATL programmers to be able to conduct different kinds of analysis to the ATL model transformations they write, being unaware of the formal representation of their specifications in Maude.

Acknowledgements. The authors would like to thank Franciso Durán and José E. Rivera for their comments and suggestions on a previous version of the paper, and to the anonymous reviewers for their insightful comments and suggestions. This work has been partially supported by Spanish Research Projects TIN2008-03107 and P07-TIC-03184.

References

1. The AtlanMod Team: ATL (2010), http://www.eclipse.org/m2m/atl/doc/
2. Meseguer, J.: Conditional rewriting logic as a unified model of concurrency. Theoretical Computer Science 96(1), 73–155 (1992)

3. Clavel, M., Durán, F., Eker, S., Lincoln, P., Martí-Oliet, N., Meseguer, J., Talcott, C.: All About Maude - A High-Performance Logical Framework. LNCS, vol. 4350. Springer, Heidelberg (2007)

4. Eclipse (ATL), http://www.eclipse.org/m2m/atl/atlTransformations/

5. Jouault, F., Bézivin, J.: KM3: A DSL for Metamodel Specification. In: Gorrieri, R., Wehrheim, H. (eds.) FMOODS 2006. LNCS, vol. 4037, pp. 171–185. Springer, Heidelberg (2006)

6. Troya, J., Vallecillo, A.: Formal Semantics of ATL Using Rewriting Logic (Extended Version). Universidad de Málaga (2010),
   http://atenea.lcc.uma.es/Descargas/ATLinMaude.pdf

7. Bouhoula, A., Jouannaud, J.P., Meseguer, J.: Specification and proof in membership equational logic. Theoretical Computer Science 236(1), 35–132 (2000)

8. Stevens, P.: Bidirectional model transformations in QVT: Semantic issues and open questions. In: Engels, G., Opdyke, B., Schmidt, D.C., Weil, F. (eds.) MODELS 2007. LNCS, vol. 4735, pp. 1–15. Springer, Heidelberg (2007)

9. Rivera, J.E., Vallecillo, A., Durán, F.: Formal specification and analysis of domain specific languages using Maude. Simulation: Transactions of the Society for Modeling and Simulation International 85(11/12), 778–792 (2009)

10. Roldán, M., Durán, F.: Representing UML models in mOdCL. Manuscript (2008),
    http://maude.lcc.uma.es/mOdCL

11. di Ruscio, D., Jouault, F., Kurtev, I., Bézivin, J., Pierantonio, A.: Extending AMMA for supporting dynamic semantics specifications of DSLs. Technical Report 06.02, Laboratoire d'Informatique de Nantes-Atlantique, Nantes, France (2006)

12. Baresi, L., Spoletini, P.: On the use of Alloy to analyze graph transformation systems. In: Corradini, A., Ehrig, H., Montanari, U., Ribeiro, L., Rozenberg, G. (eds.) ICGT 2006. LNCS, vol. 4178, pp. 306–320. Springer, Heidelberg (2006)

13. Anastasakis, K., Bordbar, B., Küster, J.M.: Analysis of Model Transformations via Alloy. In: Baudry, B., Faivre, A., Ghosh, S., Pretschner, A. (eds.) Proceedings of the 4th MoDeVVa workshop Model-Driven Engineering, Verification and Validation, pp. 47–56 (2007)

14. Poernomo, I.: Proofs-as-model-transformations. In: Vallecillo, A., Gray, J., Pierantonio, A. (eds.) ICMT 2008. LNCS, vol. 5063, pp. 214–228. Springer, Heidelberg (2008)

15. Courcelle, B.: The expression of graph properties and graph transformations in monadic second-order logic. In: Handbook of graph grammars and computing by graph transformation, foundations, vol. I, pp. 313–400 (1997)

16. Schürr, A., Winter, A.J., Zündorf, A.: The PROGRES approach: language and environment. In: Handbook of graph grammars and computing by graph transformation: applications, languages, and tools, vol. 2, pp. 487–550 (1999)

17. Boronat, A., Heckel, R., Meseguer, J.: Rewriting logic semantics and verification of model transformations. In: Chechik, M., Wirsing, M. (eds.) FASE 2009. LNCS, vol. 5503, pp. 18–33. Springer, Heidelberg (2009)

18. Boronat, A., Meseguer, J.: An algebraic semantics for MOF. In: Fiadeiro, J.L., Inverardi, P. (eds.) FASE 2008. LNCS, vol. 4961, pp. 377–391. Springer, Heidelberg (2008)

19. Durán, F., Lucas, S., Meseguer, J.: MTT: The Maude Termination Tool (System Description). In: Armando, A., Baumgartner, P., Dowek, G. (eds.) IJCAR 2008. LNCS (LNAI), vol. 5195, pp. 313–319. Springer, Heidelberg (2008)

20. Durán, F., Meseguer, J.: A Church-Rosser Checker Tool for Conditional Order-Sorted Equational Maude Specifications. In: Proc. of WRLA 2010. LNCS, Springer, Heidelberg (2010)

Metamodel Matching Based on Planar Graph Edit Distance

Konrad Voigt and Thomas Heinze*

SAP Research CEC Dresden,
Chemnitzer Strasse 48, 01187 Dresden, Germany
{konrad.voigt,thomas.heinze}@sap.com

Abstract. A prerequisite for implementing a model transformation is a mapping between metamodel elements. A mapping consists of matches and requires the task of discovering semantic correspondences between elements. This task is called metamodel matching. Recently, semi-automatic matching has been proposed to support transformation development by mapping generation.

However, current matching approaches utilize labels, types and similarity propagation approaches rather than graph isomorphism as structural matching. In constrast, we propose to apply an efficient approximate graph edit distance algorithm and present the necessary adjustments and extensions of the general algorithm as well as an optimization with ranked partial seed mappings. We evaluated the algorithm using 20 large-size mappings demonstrating effectively the improvements, especially regarding the correctness of matches found.

1 Introduction

Model transformation is one of the fundamentals of Model Driven Engineering, driving not only code generation but also model integration. A model transformation, as the process of converting a source into a target model, requires a mapping to be formulated. A mapping is a set of semantic correspondences (matches) between metamodels. Nowadays, mappings are created manually which is an error-prone and time-consuming task. Therefore, support in terms of metamodel matching has been proposed recently [1,2,3,4,5]. Metamodel matching aims at a semi-automatic creation of mappings utilizing information such as labels, structure and types. However, the approaches proposed so far rely on a label-based approach focusing on types and similarity propagation. That means, their structural matchers are based on similarity propagation (e. g. from children to parents in case of a tree), rather than a structural comparison, i. e. a common subgraph. Since there is room for improvement in result quality [5], we propose to make use of the graph structure for matching.

---

* We would like to thank Prof. Uwe Aßmann of the Technical University of Dresden for supporting this doctorial work. The work was funded by means of the German Federal Ministry of Economy and Technology under the promotional reference "01MQ07012".

L. Tratt and M. Gogolla (Eds.): ICMT 2010, LNCS 6142, pp. 245–259, 2010.

The calculation of the maximal common subgraph as well as of the Graph Edit Distance (GED) are NP-complete [6]. Nevertheless, the NP-completeness problem can be tackled restricting the input to special graph properties. Requiring the graph property planarity, we propose to use a nearly quadratic $O(n \cdot \log d \cdot d^2)$ algorithm by Neuhaus and Bunke [7] from the area of fingerprint classification, which is an error-tolerant approximate GED calculation. We present its application, adjustments and evaluation for metamodel matching. Since the algorithm requires planarity, the metamodel matching constitutes three steps: (1) A planarity check, (2) a planarization, and (3) the graph edit distance calculation. In order to obtain better results we propose to use seed mappings for the GED matcher. A seed mapping is a set of correct mappings which serves as a starting point for similarity calculation. We propose user input by k-max degree mappings, i. e. k elements ranked by their number of adjacent edges.

Finally, we demonstrate the improvements of our approach by a comprehensive evaluation using 314 metamodels for the planarity check and planarization and 20 real-world transformations for the matching. Thereby, we integrated the graph edit distance matcher in our existing combining matching system Match-Box [5]. We systematically evaluated the impact of the GED by comparing our system with and without our GED matcher, the different types of graph representation, and finally the utility of k. To demonstrate the benefit of a metamodel matching system, we compare our results with the generic model matching approach EMF Compare [8] and the schema matching approach COMA++ as applied in [2].

We structure our paper as follows; in Sect. 2 we introduce the area of metamodel matching, discuss related work, and describe MatchBox. In the subsequent Sect. 3 we present the planarity check and planarization algorithm. This is followed by Sect. 4 presenting the original algorithm, our adjustments and extensions. It further presents our approach for k-max degree with partial user-defined mappings. Our evaluation is given in Sect. 5 presenting and discussing our results regarding the GED matcher quality. We conclude our paper by giving a summary and an outlook on future work.

2   Metamodel Matching and Related Work

The area of metamodel matching has recently received interest, so we will first give an overview of related work in matching and give afterwards an overview of our metamodel matching system MatchBox and describe possible graph representations for metamodels.

2.1   Related Matching Approaches

Model matching as the discovery of correspondences between elements is a domain independent approach on calculating model element similarity. It is applied for different purposes depending on the relation of the participating models. In case of two versions of the same model it is used for evolution, differencing, and comparison, if the two models are different it is used for data migration and synchronisation. Recently, it received interest being used to compare software models. According to the survey of Kolovos et al. [9] one differs between the following matching techniques: static identity-based (elements have static identifiers assigned on creation), signature-based (a signature from an elements properties is used), similarity-based (similarity assigned based on attribute matching), and customization support (useable only for a special type of models like UML). Representative systems are SiDiff [10] and EMF Compare [8].

A specialisation of model matching is metamodel matching, i.e. different instances of one metamodel (MOF) are considered. We restrict our approach to metamodel matching, because the domain specifics of this task allow for meaningful results as demonstrated by our comparison to EMF Compare (Sect. 5). An overview on ontology matching techniques is presented in the survey by Euzenat and Shvaiko [11]. These techniques, in context of metamodel matching, are represented in the following systems: string-based [1,2,3,4,5], linguistic resources [5], constraint-based [1,2,3,4,5], alignment reuse [2], meta information, data analysis and statistics, similarity propagation [1,2,3,4,5], taxonomy-based [1,2,3,4,5], repository of structures [2], and logic model-based. Consequently, there is no approach utilizing graph edit distance for matching.

These matching techniques are applied by metamodel matching systems, which can be grouped into sequentially or parallel systems. Sequential systems [3,4] follow the similarity flooding approach proposed by Melnik [12] propagate similarities in a graph between nodes applying a fix-point computation. Thereby, maching techniques are applied sequentially. In contrast, parallel systems [1,2] as our system MatchBox [5], apply the matching techniques independently and combine the separate results. A configurable combination is followed by the approach proposed in [13] targeting the use case of evolution.

These systems can benefit from the planar GED as an additional matching technique. Additionally, the fields of schema matching and ontology matching may make use of our results.

2.2   Metamodel Matching with MatchBox

In a nutshell, MatchBox takes two metamodels as input and produces a mapping as output. Figure 1 depicts an overview of MatchBox along with its four processing steps, each supported by a component. The process starts with the metamodel importer (1) which is responsible for an import of metamodels and models into our internal graph-based representation. The matching core (2) is an exchangeable component. It defines an interface that requests a similarity value between two model elements which is the task of matching. The matching techniques applied range from label-based similarities and data types to parent-child relations. Finally, the combination component (3) aggregates the results of each matcher to obtain the output mappings. For details please refer to [5].

We integrated the planar GED matcher in MatchBox making use of the import as well as the combination component. Finally, we measured the influence on the resulting quality (Sect. 5).

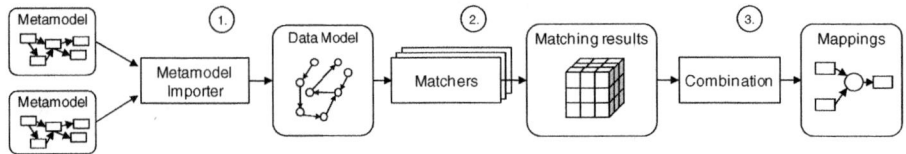

Fig. 1. Processing steps of the matching framework MatchBox

The planar GED matcher operates on an internal data model imposed by MatchBox. In contrast to the original version [5], the internal model has been changed to a graph representation. The graph consists of a set of labelled vertices connected by undirected edges which include the direction for later use. Due to the requirements of the planarization algorithm, two vertices are connected by maximally one edge. However, edges are aggregated, i. e. if there is more than one edge between two given vertices, a virtual edge is created aggregating the originals.

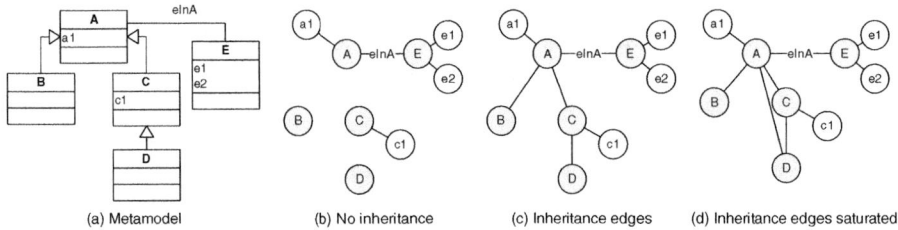

Fig. 2. Example for internal graph representation of metamodels

The mapping of metamodel elements on our graph representation is straight-forward: classes, packages and attributes are each mapped onto a vertex. References are mapped onto edges between participating classes. The mapping of inheritance is depicted in Fig. 2. According to the results of [4], we separate three different representations of inheritance:

(b) No inheritance: The inheritance is ignored, i. e. not reflected in the graph.
(c) Inheritance edges: The inheritance is reflected as an edge between the participating classes.
(d) Saturated inheritance edges: The inheritance edges modus is enriched by adding transitive inheritance edges (inherited inheritance).

These representations can be used in parallel with the reference graph, or be calculated separately. The evaluation of the different representations of inheritance is given in Sect. 5.

3   Planarity of Metamodels

The first requirement of the planar graph edit distance calculation is planarity. In the following, we will define the term planar graph and present established algorithms for a planarity check and planarization. Furthermore, we will present numbers demonstrating the non-planarity of some metamodels and thus the need for planarization.

An illustrative definition of planarity is, that a graph is planar, iff the graph can be drawn into the plane without two crossing edges. Such a drawing is called a planar embedding. Interestingly, a planar embedding defines an order on the vertices, thus ensuring a stable neighbourhood. This property is used by the GED algorithm. Graphs having no such embedding are called non-planar. Two well known examples are K_5 and $K_{3,3}$ The K_5 consists of 5 vertices which are all connected with each other. In contrast, the $K_{3,3}$ is partitioned into two groups of 3 vertices each, where each vertex of one group is connected to all vertices of the other group. These minimal non-planar graphs are used to check for planarity which is described in the following sections.

3.1   Planarity Check for Metamodels

The planarity check is a well-known problem in graph theory, so we selected an established algorithm by Hopfcroft and Tarjan [14], because of its linear runtime ($O(n)$). The algorithm combines the check for planarity with the embedding creation which is used during the matching.

We tested 314 metamodels for planarity; 70 from the ATL-Zoo[1] and 244 from the Atlantic EMF-Zoo[2]. It turned out that 56 out of 70 and 193 out of 244 metamodels are planar, i. e. in average 80 % of all metamodels are planar. However, some important metamodels like UML, WSDL, OCL or OWL are non-planar which raises the need to planarize them. Neglecting the trivial approach that deletes edges sequentially until planarity is achieved, we chose an efficient maximal planar subgraph algorithm.

3.2   Maximal Planar Subgraph for Metamodels

The planarity property can be established by removing vertices or edges. Preserving a maximal number of vertices for any graph is a NP-complete problem [15]. Therefore, we chose an approach where the number of edges is maximal. That means, if an edge that has been previously removed would be re-added, the graph would be non-planar. We applied the algorithm of Cai et. al. [15] granting a complexity of $O(m \log n)$ (m is the number of edges and n of vertices).

We applied the planarization algorithm to the metamodels of both Zoos. For non-planar metamodels in average 86 % of all edges are represented in the planar embedding. Comparing this to a spanning tree approach, the planarity approach offers more structural information. While in the planar graph 86 % of the edges

---

[1] http://www.eclipse.org/m2m/atl/atlTransformations/

[2] http://www.emn.fr/z-info/atlanmod/index.php/Ecore

Table 1. Comparison of edge count contained in a tree and a planar graph

	XHTML	WSDL	UML2	R2ML	RDM	OWL	OCL
#edges in tree	152	356	331	151	57	54	73
#edges in planar graph	208	426	428	198	91	85	93
$\frac{\#edges_{planar}-\#edges_{tree}}{\#edges_{original}}$	21.3	28.2	18.0	19.5	35.0	34.4	20.2

can be saved, a tree contains in average only 78 % of the edges. This can be further encouraged by the following Table 1, where some examples are listed (the percentage describes the gain in edges comparing a planar graph and a tree). For future work, a specific cost function can be applied, restricting the edges to be removed, e. g. to prefer a reference over a containment for removal.

The algorithms allow checking any given metamodel for planarity and performing planarization if necessary. The overall complexity of both operations is $O(m \log n)$ (m is the number of edges and n of vertices). The planarity enables the usage of the planar graph edit distance algorithm described in the following.

4   Planar Graph Edit Distance for Metamodel Matching

The graph edit distance algorithm we applied is a modified version of the approximation algorithm presented by Neuhaus and Bunke [7]. The algorithm is approximative, because it computes a lower bounded Graph Edit Distance (GED), instead of the minimal GED for two given input graphs. Thereby, the algorithm assumes planar labelled biconnected graphs.

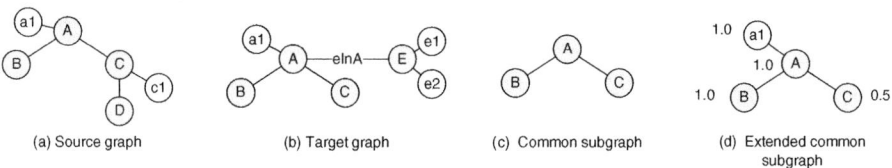

(a) Source graph   (b) Target graph   (c) Common subgraph   (d) Extended common subgraph

Fig. 3. Example of source and target graphs, a common sub graph, and our extensions

Figure 3 depicts a source (a) and target graph (b), an example output of the orginal algorithm (c), and an example outout of our extensions (d). The original output determines the common sub graph (A,B,C) as interpretation of the GED, omitting the vertex $a1$, because it violates the biconnectivity. Our extensions adds a similarity value in $[0,1]$ for each vertex as shown in Fig. 3 (d). Also we include all one-edge vertices in calculation thus adding $a1$ to the output graph.

In the following we will first introduce the original algorithm, then present our adjustments and extensions for metamodel matching. Finally, we present our k-max degree approach which uses partial user-defined matches as input. Since the seed mappings are based on selected elements presented to an user, we propose a simple and scalable heuristic for the selection of these elements.

4.1 Planar Graph Edit Distance Algorithm

The input of the algorithm is a planar labelled biconnected source and target graph. The output of the original algorithm is a common sub graph and the corresponding GED. The output in terms of similarity is therefore one or zero. One if a vertex (element) is part of the common sub graph or zero if not. The algorithm calculates the minimal GED to reach a nearly maximal common sub graph. There are two parameters which influence the GED calculation: the costs for deletion and insertion as well as the distance between two vertices. Finally, a seed match is needed denoting the starting point for calculation. To summarize, the algorithm consists of:

1. Input – Source graph G_s and target graph G_t
2. Output – Minimal GED and common subgraph
3. Distance function – Distance function for two vertices $dist(v_s, v_t)$
4. Cost function – Cost function for deletion $cost_{del}(v)$ and insertion $cost_{ins}(v)$ of a vertex v
5. Seed match – Seed mapping between a source and target vertex $v_s^0 \rightarrow v_t^0$

Listing 1 presents the algorithm in pseudo code. Starting with the seed match $v_s^0 \rightarrow v_t^0$ the neighbours of the source vertex $N(v_s)$ and the neighbours of the target vertex $N(v_t)$ are matched against each other. The results are matches between a set of source and target vertices, this serves as input for the next loop. The processing is performed until no match can be found, which occurs if no neighbours are existing or matching. Finally, all unprocessed vertices and edges are removed, thus constructing a common subgraph based on the minimal GED.

```
1    Input: G_s, G_t, v_s^0 → v_t^0
2    Variable:   FIFO queue Q
3    Add seed match v_s^0 → v_t^0 to Q
4    Fetch next match   v_s → v_t from Q
5      Match neighbourhood N(v_s) to the neighbourhood N(v_t)
6      Add new matches occurring in step 5 to Q
7    If Q is not empty, go to step 4
8    Delete all unprocessed vertices and edges in G_s and G_t
```

Listing 1. Planar graph edit distance algorithm in pseudo code

The match between both neighbourhoods ($N(v_s)$, $N(v_t)$) is calculated, using a matrix of all N-vertices' distances which is processed for minimal edit distance. Thereby, one takes advantage of the planar embedding which ensures that the neighbourhood of v_s, v_t is ordered. So, there is no need to calculate all distances for all permutations of all vertices of N(v) by applying any cyclic edit distance approach. Since the algorithm only needs to traverse the whole graph once, and the cyclic string edit distance based on the planar embedding has a complexity of $O(\log d \cdot d^2)$ [16], the overall complexity is $O(n \cdot \log d \cdot d^2)$ (d is the number of edges per node).

4.2   Adjustments and Optimizations

In order to apply the algorithm in context of metamodels, several adjustments and extensions are necessary. First, a seed match needs to be given. Therefore, we define the root package vertex match as input. We propose the following additional adjustments and explain them in detail afterwards.

1. Definition of a vertex *distance function* based on structural and linguistic similarity
2. *Dynamic parameter calculation* for weights of a distance function
3. *Removal* of invalid class-attribute and class-package matches
4. *Similarity calculations* during cyclic string edit distance calculation
5. *Processing of one-neighbour vertices*, i. e. classes and attributes

Distance Function We defined the distance function of a vertex as a weighting of structural and linguistic similarity, since this computation provides a good trade-off between quality and runtime. The linguistic similarity $ling(v_s, v_t)$ is the average string edit distance between the vertex and egde labels. Thereby, we make use of the name matcher of MatchBox as given in [5].

$$dist(v_s, v_t) = \alpha \cdot struct(v_s, v_t) + \beta \cdot ling(v_s, v_t) \wedge \alpha + \beta = 1$$

The structural similarity $struct(v_s, v_t)$ is defined as the ratio of structural information, i. e. the attribute count ratio $attr(v_s, v_t)$ and reference count ratio $ref(v_s, v_t)$, thus allowing for a fast computation.

$$struct(v_s, v_t) = \alpha \cdot attr(v_s, v_t) + \beta \cdot ref(v_s, v_t) \wedge \alpha + \beta = 1$$

The attribute and reference count ratio are defined as the ratio between the attributes respectively references of a source vertex v_s and target vertex v_t.

$$attr(v_s, v_t) = 1 - \frac{|count_{attr}(v_s) - count_{attr}(v_t)|}{max(count_{attr}(v_s), count_{attr}(v_t))}$$

Finally, we defined the cost for insertion and deletion as being equal, since both operations are equal for similarity calculation. Consequently, a vertex to be matched has to be deleted if no matching partner with a similarity greater than T can be found. The following threshold definition must hold to keep a vertex v_s:

$$sim(v_s, v_t) \geq 1 - cost_{del}(v_s) - cost_{ins}(v_t) = T$$

As an example, based on our evaluation data, we tested different T and obtained best results for $T = 0.74$. Moreover the weight of edges is reflected via their label similarity, because our experiments showed that this allows for better results than a numeric cost function.

Dynamic Parameter Calculation. The parameters α and β denote a weighting between the structural and linguistic similarity and can be set constant, e. g. to 0.7 and 0.3. For a dynamic parameter calculation we adopted the *Harmony* approach of Mao et. al [17]. Since the problem is to find maximal 1:1 matches between vertices, Harmony aims at calculating unique matches by evaluating combinations which allow for maximal similarity. This is computed in a matrix selecting the maximums of rows and columns deriving the ratio of unique and total matches. Indeed, we noted an improvement of more than 1 % using Harmony over a fixed configuration considering our evaluation in Sect. 5.

Invalid Match Removal. When a class is matched on an attribute or a package vertex the similarity results in zero. The same penalty applies to the match of contradicting inheritance or containment directions.

Similarity Calculation. Neuhaus and Bunke do not state which cyclic string edit distance to use for the neighbourhood matching. Therefore, we chose the approach of Peris and Marzal [16] which offers a run-time of $O(s^2 \log s)$ where s is the length of the strings to be matched and since it allows for weight assignments. Additionally, the algorithm also makes use of the planar embedding calculated before. While the distance is computed, we extended the algorithm making use of our similarities defined before and presenting them in the final result.

Additional Processing. The original algorithm only considers edges contained in biconnected components of a graph, because only then an ordering can be defined. That means, only vertices reachable by at least two edges are considered. Consequently, all attributes would be ignored. Therefore, we extended the algorithm by matching these vertices after the cyclic string edit distance for a specific vertex combination has been calculated. This affects the complexity only additive so it is still nearly quadratic.

4.3   Improvement by k-max Degree Partial Seed Matches

Neuhaus and Bunke stated possible improvements by one seed match, so we had a closer look on how to handle more seed matches. Following this, we investigated two possible approaches: (1) with or (2) without user interaction. The approach without user interaction is to use the default root package matches (one seed match). However, taking user interaction into account allows for further improvement in quality, but requires an additional effort, because a user has to define mappings for a given source and target mapping problem. Therefore, we decided to follow a simple and scalable approach which grants a maximum of information used.

To keep the interaction simple, we require the user to only give feedback once on a reduced matching problem. Consequently, we present the user a selection of source and target elements rather than letting him decide on the whole range of elements. That means, the user only needs to match a subset. The subset calculation by k-max degree follows a scalable approach by applying a simple heuristic. K-max degree is based on the rationale that the seed mapping elements should have the most structural information. Investigating our evaluation data we noted a normal distribution of edges per node, so the probability for vertices to match is highest if they have the highest degree and thus structural information. The computation can be done in linear time and therefore provides a scalable approach.

Matchable Elements Selection. We propose to select the k vertices with a maximal degree, i. e. the ranking of k vertices which contain most structural information. So for a given k and Graph $G(V, E)$ we define k-max degree as:

$$degree_{max}(G, k) = \{v_1, v_2, \ldots, v_k \mid degree(v_i) \geq degree(v_{i-1}) \wedge v_i \in V\}$$

Seed Matches. The user defined mappings yield information on matches and no-matches which are both used for the planar GED matcher. These seed matches are included into the algorithm by adding them to the list of all matches. The planar GED matcher makes use of them during the edit path calculation as well as during the cyclic edit distance calculation. That means instead of calculating a match as in Listing 1 line 5, the match is taken directly. The results show a considerable improvement which will be discussed next.

5   Evaluation

We want to show the quality of the results using the planar graph edit distance for metamodels. We systematically evaluated all parameters as given in Sect. 4. Our evaluation is based on a comparison of calculated mappings to pre-defined mappings. The latter are called gold-standards. A gold-standard is a set of correct matches between metamodels, i. e. a set of mappings. Since a transformation is an implementation of a mapping, we selected 10 transformations from the ATL-Zoo[3] as gold-standards. Additionally, we took the 10 mappings used in the evaluation of [2]. We chose both data sets, since they are publicly available and thus allow for a comparison to our results.

In order to describe the complexity of the mappings and participating meta-models we give an overview in Fig. 4. The diagram describes the size of the metamodels and their similarity. We show the number of matches between both metamodels mapped and the number of elements.

$$sim = \frac{2 \cdot \#matches}{\#elements_{source} + \#elements_{target}}$$

In contrast to other metamodel matching approaches [1,2,3,4], we provide a rather big set of 20 mappings ranging from 24 to 360 elements, with a similarity varying from 0.16 up to 0.66. On average the metamodels have a size of 145 with 27 matches and an average similarity of 0.36.

To evaluate mapping quality we use the established measures: precision p, recall r and F-Measure F which are defined as follows. Let t_p be the true positives,

---

[3] http://www.eclipse.org/m2m/atl/atlTransformations/

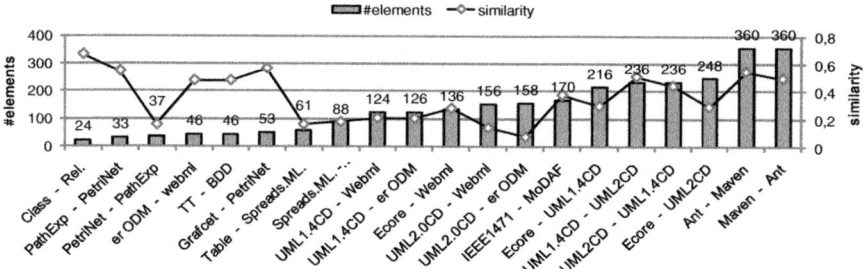

Fig. 4. Statistics for evaluation metamodels

i. e. correct results found, f_p the false positives, i. e. the found but incorrect results, and f_n the false negatives, i. e. not found but correct results. Then the formulas for these measures are:

$$p = \frac{t_p}{t_p + f_p}, \quad r = \frac{t_p}{t_p + f_n}, \quad F = 2 \cdot \frac{p \cdot r}{p + r}$$

Precision p is the share of correct results relative to all results obtained by matching. One can say precision denotes the correctness, for instance a precision of 0.8 means that 8 of 10 matches are correct. *Recall* r is the share of correctly found results relative to the number of all results. It denotes the completeness, i. e. a recall of 1 specifies that all mappings were found, however, there is no statement how much more (incorrect) were found. *F-Measure* F represents the balance between precision and recall. It is commonly used in the field of information retrieval and applied by many matching approach evaluations, e. g. [1,2,3,4,5].

The F-Measure can be seen as the effectiveness of the matching balancing precision and recall equally. For instance, a precision and recall of 0.5 leads to an F-Measure of 0.5 stating that half of all correct results were found and half of all results found are correct.

The evaluation consists of three incremental steps: (1) We start with a comparison of the graph edit distance matcher added to MatchBox using reference-based graphs. (2) Then we show further improvement by considering the inheritance graph using our GED matcher. Thereby, the results are merged with the reference-based GED. (3) Subsequently, we present our k-max degree approach showing its benefits. Finally, we summarize and compare our results.

5.1 Results for Graph Edit Distance Matcher

In order to calculate the results of MatchBox we first determined the optimal combination of matchers, i. e. the number and specific matchers along with a fixed threshold. A combination of 4 matchers yields the maximal results. Thereby, the original system uses the name, name path, parent, and leaf matcher (see [5]). These linguistic and similarity propagation-based matchers are configured with a fixed threshold of 0.35, which filters all matches below, and harmony-based

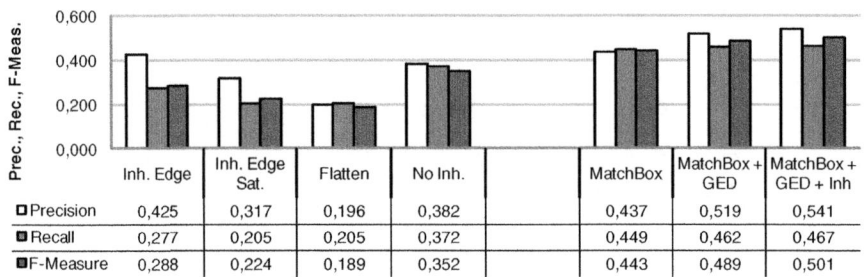

Fig. 5. Results for different inheritance modes using the GED matcher only

weights. This configuration leads to the following results: precision 0.437, recall 0.449, F-Measure 0.443; see Fig. 5 on the right (MatchBox).

Next, we exchanged the leaf matcher with our planar GED matcher. We first compared the graphs based on different inheritance representations. The overall results for matching with the GED only are depicted in Fig. 5 on the left. The best mode with an F-Measure of 0.352 is the representation based on no inheritance, i. e. reference edges are not mixed with inheritance edges. Adding a GED based on the reference graph without inheritance matching the complete 20 test sets is given in Fig. 5 on the right (MatchBox + GED). The numbers are: precision 0.519, recall 0.462, and F-Measure 0.489. Compared to the orginal MatchBox, this is an improvement of 0,082 (8.2 %) in precision, 0,013 (1.3 %) in recall, and 0,036 (3.6 %) in F-Measure.

Since the inheritance information would be discarded, we added a second planar GED matcher based on the inheritance edge graph. It is then combined with the results of the other matchers. The final numbers as in Fig. 5 (MatchBox + GED + Inh) are: precision 0.541, recall 0.467 and F-Measure 0.501. This leads to an improvement in F-Measure of 2.2 % w.r.t. the planar GED and of 5.8 % compared to the original MatchBox system. The main improvements are in precision (10.4 %), i. e. the mappings presented are more likely to be correct. In the following we will describe additional improvements using our k-max degree approach.

5.2   Result for k-max Degree Seed Matches

The evaluation of our k-max degree approach is based on the same set of test data as before. We applied only our GED reference matcher and GED inheritance matcher to measure the improvement of the calculation. We assume a one-time input by the user by giving correct matches ($Seed(k)$) for the given problem of k vertices. We took values for k from 0 to 20, because for greater k the values remain unchanged. The $k=0$ denotes the reference value, i. e. matching without seed mappings. The user-input was simulated by querying the gold-standards for corresponding mappings.

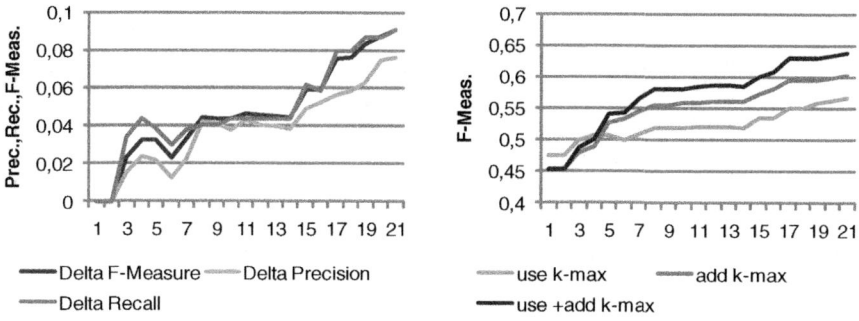

Fig. 6. k-max degree for varying k relative and absolute

Thereby, we separate the results into three series: (1) use k-max, (2) add k-max, and (3) use and add k-max. The first series should demonstrate the impact of seed matches on the similarity calculation. Therefore, we did not add the seed input matches after calculation. The second series preserves the seed matches by adding them, but does not use $Seed(k)$ as input for the GED. The third combines both presenting the results for a real-world usage, because a user is interested in all matches. The left side of Fig. 6 depicts scenario (1), i.e. using only the GED with k-max as input for calculation but not for the overall result. Thereby, the delta between $k = 0$ and k is shown to demonstrate the benefit for the GED matcher. The measurements are increasing, however they decrease at $k = 5$, because the structural vertices provide less correct additional information, than for $k = 4$.

However, in combination this is corrected by the other matchers. Figure 6 depicts the results on the right side for all three series in F-Measure. Increasing k improves the results and for $k = 3, 5, 8$ the slope is maximal which is due to the nature of our test data. Overall, we achieve a maximal improvement in F-Measure for $k = 20$ of 0,228 (22.88 %) and precision increases the most 0,291 (29.13 %), which shows that an input of maximal structural vertex mappings indeed increases correctness. We can also conclude, that the minimal k should be three, since our evaluation shows considerable increase from this on.

5.3   Summary of GED Results

Our evaluation based on 20 gold-standards has investigated the quality of the planar GED comparing it to the original MatchBox. Figure 7 depicts a comparison of the overall results, using our GED based on the reference graph, we noted an improvement of 0,082 (8.2 %) in precision and 0,013 (1.3 %) in recall leading to an overall improvement of 0,036 (3.6 %) in F-Measure. We then added our GED matcher based on the inheritance graph which demonstrated further improvements compared to our original system. Finally, we took the values for both GED matchers and a 5-max degree approach, where we chose 5 based on a conservative estimation of low effort for a user, which leads to further improvements w.r.t. the original system. The numbers are: 0,133 (13.3 %) for recall,

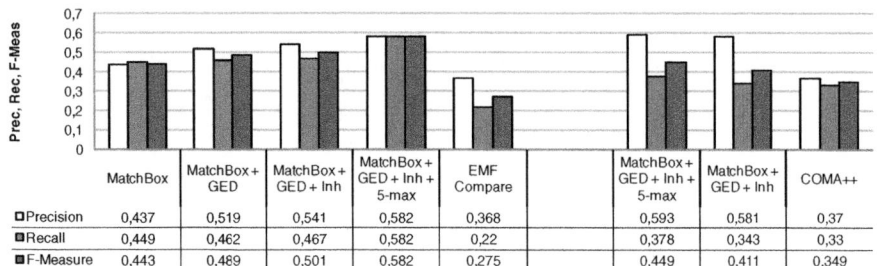

Fig. 7. Summary of evaluation and comparison to other approaches

0,144 (14.4 %) for precision and 0,124 (12.4 %) for F-Measure. That means using a fixed combination (no tuning) we achieved an improvement of 12.4% increasing the F-Measure from 0.41 to 0.54, i. e. a relative increase of 31.7%. Moreover, we achieve considerable results compared to the model matching system EMF Compare, applying our GED with $k = 0$ leads to an F-Measure of 0.582 whereas EMF Compare yields 0.275. The right side of Fig. 7 depicts a comparison to COMA++ as applied in [2] using their set of examples. Thereby, we have a gain of 0.211 (21 %) in precision and 0.062 (6.2 %) in F-Measure for $k = 0$. We conclude that a metamodel matching system should be preferred over a model, ontology or schema matching approach.

6   Conclusion and Future Work

Nowadays, metamodel, ontology and schema matching approaches mostly rely on linguistic and similarity propagation based approaches. We have presented an adoption of an approximate graph edit distance (GED) algorithm computing a common subgraph. The algorithm requires planar graphs, so we proposed and evaluated a planarity check and planarization algorithm for metamodel graphs. Subsequently, we presented the GED algorithm of Neuhaus and Bunke, its adjustments and extensions for metamodel matching. We proposed the k-max degree approach for further improvement of the matching quality. Thereby, we make use of k user input mappings ranked by the degree of elements. Finally, we evaluated our approach using 20 existing mappings and transformations. Our evaluation showed effective improvements of 0.13 (13%) in F-Measure using our graph matcher and 5-max degree user input.

Nevertheless, it needs to be explored which additional algorithms can benefit from planarity. An investigation of cost functions for planarization of metamodels can be interesting. Further the approach of using partial seed mappings shows promising results and needs to be evaluated especially w.r.t. usability and the amount and process of receiving input from a user. Finally, it is worth to investigate an application of the planar GED algorithm also on model level.

References

1. Lopes, D., Hammoudi, S., de Souza, J., Bontempo, A.: Metamodel matching: Experiments and comparison. In: Proc. of ICSEA 2006 (2006)
2. Kappel, G., Kargl, H., Kramler, G., Schauerhuber, A., Seidl, M., Strommer, M., Wimmer, M.: Matching metamodels with semantic systems - an experience report. In: BTW Workshops (2007)
3. Didonet Del Fabro, M., Valduriez, P.: Semi-automatic model integration using matching transformations and weaving models. In: Proc. of SAC 2007 (2007)
4. Falleri, J.R., Huchard, M., Lafourcade, M., Nebut, C.: Metamodel matching for automatic model transformation generation. In: Czarnecki, K., Ober, I., Bruel, J.-M., Uhl, A., Völter, M. (eds.) MODELS 2008. LNCS, vol. 5301, pp. 326–340. Springer, Heidelberg (2008)
5. Voigt, K., Ivanov, P., Rummler, A.: MatchBox: Combined meta-model matching for semi-automatic mapping generation. In: Proc. of SAC 2010 (2010)
6. Garey, M., Johnson, D., et al.: Computers and Intractability: A Guide to the Theory of NP-completeness (1979)
7. Neuhaus, M., Bunke, H.: An error-tolerant approximate matching algorithm for attributed planar graphs and its application to fingerprint classification. In: SSPR/SPR (2004)
8. Brun, C., Pierantonio, A.: Model differences in the eclipse modeling framework. Upgrade, Spec. Issue on MDSD IX (2008)
9. Kolovos, D.S., Ruscio, D.D., Pierantonio, A., Paige, R.F.: Different models for model matching: An analysis of approaches to support model differencing. In: ICSE 2009 Workshop on Comparison and Versioning of Software Models (2009)
10. Treude, C., Berlik, S., Wenzel, S., Kelter, U.: Difference computation of large models. In: Proc. of ESEC-FSE 2007 (2007)
11. Euzenat, J., Shvaiko, P.: Ontology Matching. Springer, Heidelberg (2007)
12. Melnik, S., Garcia-Molina, H., Rahm, E., et al.: Similarity flooding: A versatile graph matching algorithm and its application to schema matching. In: Proc. of ICDE (2002)
13. Garcés, K., Jouault, F., Cointe, P., Bézivin, J.: Managing model adaptation by precise detection of metamodel changes. In: Paige, R.F., Hartman, A., Rensink, A. (eds.) ECMDA-FA 2009. LNCS, vol. 5562, pp. 34–49. Springer, Heidelberg (2009)
14. Hopcroft, J.E., Tarjan, R.E.: Efficient planarity testing. J. ACM 21(4) (1974)
15. Cai, J., Han, X., Tarjan, R.E.: n o(m log n)-time algorithm for the maximal planar subgraph problem. SIAM J. Comput. 22(6) (1993)
16. Peris, G., Marzal, A.: Fast cyclic edit distance computation with weighted edit costs in classification. In: Proc. of ICPR 2002 (2002)
17. Mao, M., Peng, Y., Spring, M.: A harmony based adaptive ontology mapping approach. In: Proc. of SWWS 2008 (2008)

Surviving the Heterogeneity Jungle with Composite Mapping Operators*

Manuel Wimmer[1], Gerti Kappel[1], Angelika Kusel[2],
Werner Retschitzegger[2], Johannes Schoenboeck[1], and Wieland Schwinger[2]

[1] Vienna University of Technology, Austria
{lastname}@big.tuwien.ac.at
[2] Johannes Kepler University Linz, Austria
{firstname.lastname}@jku.at

Abstract. Model transformations play a key role in the vision of Model-Driven Engineering. Nevertheless, mechanisms like abstraction, variation and composition for specifying and applying reusable model transformations – like urgently needed for resolving recurring structural heterogeneities – are insufficiently supported so far. Therefore, we propose to specify model transformations by a set of pre-defined mapping operators (MOps), each resolving a certain kind of structural heterogeneity. Firstly, these MOps can be used in the context of arbitrary metamodels since they abstract from concrete metamodel types. Secondly, MOps can be tailored to resolve certain structural heterogeneities by means of black-box reuse. Thirdly, based on a systematic set of kernel MOps resolving basic heterogeneities, composite ones can be built in order to deal with more complex scenarios. Finally, an extensible library of MOps is proposed, allowing for automatically executable mapping specifications since every MOp exhibits a clearly defined operational semantics.

Keywords: Executable Mappings, Reuse, Structural Heterogeneities.

1 Introduction

Model-Driven Engineering (MDE) places models as first-class artifacts throughout the software lifecycle [2] whereby model transformations play a vital role. In the context of transformations between different metamodels and their corresponding models, the overcoming of *structural heterogeneities*, being a result of applying different modeling constructs for the same semantic concept [9,12] is a challenging, recurring problem, urgently demanding for reuse of transformations. Building and applying such *reusable transformations* requires (i) *abstraction mechanisms*, e.g., for dealing with arbitrary metamodels, (ii) *variation mechanisms*, e.g., for tailoring a reusable transformation to certain metamodels, and (iii) *composition mechanisms*, e.g., for assembling a whole transformation

---

* This work has been funded by the Austrian Science Fund (FWF) under grant P21374-N13.

L. Tratt and M. Gogolla (Eds.): ICMT 2010, LNCS 6142, pp. 260–275, 2010.

specification from reusable transformations. As a backbone, such reusable transformations are required to be offered by means of an *extensible library* being a prerequisite for reducing the high effort of specifying model transformations.

We therefore propose to specify horizontal model transformations by means of *abstract mappings* using a set of reusable transformation components, called *mapping operators* (MOps) to resolve recurring structural heterogeneities. Firstly, to reuse these MOps for mappings between arbitrary metamodels, i.e., *metamodel independence*, MOps are typed by the core concepts of meta-metamodeling languages, being classes, attributes, and relationships [6], instead of concrete metamodel types. Secondly, to resolve certain structural heterogeneities, MOps can be tailored by means of black-box reuse. Thirdly, based on a set of kernel MOps resolving basic heterogeneities, composite ones can be built in a simple plug & play manner in order to deal with more complex scenarios. Finally, a set of MOps is proposed, providing an initial library of reusable transformations encapsulating *recurring transformation logic* for the resolution of structural heterogeneities. The rationale behind is to follow an MDE-based approach, since abstract mappings can be seen as platform-independent transformation models abstracting from the underlying execution language. These abstract mappings can then be automatically translated to different transformation languages by means of higher-order transformations (HOTs) [17] since the MOps exhibit a clearly defined operational semantics thereby achieving *transformation language independence*. Please note that the presented kernel MOps supersede the MOps presented in our previous work [8], since the initial MOps suffered from two main problems. Firstly, the initial MOps were too fine-grained resulting in scalability problems. Thereby, they neglected the fact that a whole transformation problem can be partitioned into coarse-grained recurring sub-problems demanding for coarse-grained MOps too. Secondly, the initial MOps represented hard-coded patters and were too inflexible to form the basis for arbitrary composite MOps.

The remainder is structured as follows. Section 2 introduces an example exhibiting several structural heterogeneities, which are resolved by means of composite MOps in Section 3. Section 4 presents a MOps kernel providing the basic building blocks for composite MOps. Related work is surveyed in Section 5, a prototypical implementation is proposed in Section 6, and a critical discussion of the proposed approach with an outlook on future work is given in Section 7.

2   Motivating Example

Structural heterogeneities between different metamodels occur due to the fact that semantically equivalent concepts can be expressed by different metamodeling concepts. The ClassDiagram shown on the left side of Fig. 1, only provides unidirectional references to represent relationships, thus bidirectionality needs to be modeled by a pair of opposite references. In contrast, the ERDiagram explicitly represents bidirectionality, allowing to express relationships in more detail.

In the following, the main correspondences between the ClassDiagram and the ERDiagram are described. On the level of classes, three main correspondence types can be recognized, namely *1:1*, *1:n* and *n:1*, indicated by dotted

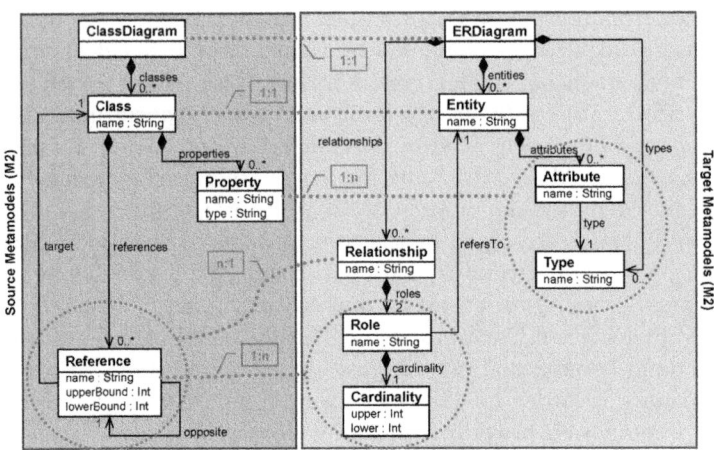

Fig. 1. Metamodels of the Running Example

lines in Fig. 1. 1:1 correspondences can be found (i) between the root classes ClassDiagram and ERDiagram and (ii) between Class and Entity. Regarding 1:n correspondences, again two cases can be detected, namely (i) between the class Property and the classes Attribute and Type and (ii) between the class Reference and the classes Role and Cardinality. Although these are two occurrences of a 1:n correspondence, there is a slight difference between them, since in the first case only for distinct values of the attribute Property.type, an instance of the class Type should be generated. Finally, there is one occurrence of a n:1 correspondence, namely between the class Reference and the class Relationship. It is classified as n:1 correspondence, since for *every pair* of References that are opposite to each other, a corresponding Relationship has to be established. Considering attributes, only 1:1 correspondences occur, e.g., between Class.name and Entity.name, whereas regarding references, 1:1 and 0:1 correspondences can be detected. Concerning the first category, one example arises between ClassDiagram.classes and ERDiagram.entities. Regarding the latter category, e.g., the relationship ERDiagram.types exists in the target without any corresponding counterpart in the source.

Summarizing, for the resolution of structural heterogeneities the fulfillment of the following requirements is desirable. Firstly, for allowing a transformation designer to focus on the correspondences in terms of abstract mappings, i.e., without having to cope with implementation details, abstraction from a concrete transformation language is preferable (cf. *abstraction by simplification* in Section 5). Moreover, for being able to cope with large transformation problems, a transformation designer should be empowered to focus on a specific structural heterogeneity at a certain point in time (cf. *abstraction by selection* in Section 5). Furthermore, even this simple example depicts that there are recurring kinds of correspondences demanding for reusable transformations between arbitrary metamodels (cf. *abstraction by generalization* in Section 5). Secondly, since equal correspondences (like the 1:n correspondences in the example) can be resolved in different forms, *tailoring mechanisms* without having to know the internals (black-box reuse) are desired. Thirdly, in order to be able to solve a transformation problem by a divide-and-conquer strategy adequate *composition mechanisms* are required. Finally, to ease the tedious task of specifying transformations, reusable transformations should be offered in an *extensible library*.

3   Composite Mapping Operators to the Rescue

The identified correspondences between metamodels (cf. Fig. 1) need to be refined to a declarative description of the transformation, denoted as *mapping*, which abstracts from a concrete transformation language achieving *abstraction by simplification*. To support transformation designers in resolving structural heterogeneities in the mapping, we provide a library of composite MOps. In this respect, reuse is leveraged since the proposed MOps are generic in the sense that they abstract from concrete metamodel types, thereby achieving *abstraction by generalization*. Thus, MOps can be applied between arbitrary metamodels since they are typed by the core concepts of current meta-modeling languages like Ecore or MOF. To further structure the mapping process we propose to specify mappings in two steps. Firstly, composite MOps, describing mappings between classes are applied, providing an abstract *blackbox-view* (cf. Fig. 2). Composite MOps select specific metamodel extracts to focus on when refining the mapping, providing *abstraction by selection*. Although attributes and references might be necessary to identify the correspondences in the blackbox-view, the actual mapping thereof is hidden in the *whitebox-view*. Secondly, in this whitebox-view the composite MOps can further be refined to specify the mappings between attributes and relationships using so-called *kernel MOps* (cf. Section 4).

We propose composite MOps (cf. Table 1), which have been inspired by a mapping benchmark in the area of data engineering [1], describing recurring mappings between relational and hierarchical schemas. Thereby we identified typical mapping situations being 1:1 copying, 1:n partitioning, n:1 merging, and 0:1 generating of objects, for which different MOps are provided. Since the mapping is executed on instance level, the actually transformed instance set should be configurable by additional conditions. Finally, inverse operators are defined, which allow to re-construct the original source object set.

1:1 Correspondences. MOps handling 1:1 correspondences map exactly one source class to one target class. Currently, two MOps are provided, being a `Copier` and a `ConditionalCopier`. A `Copier` simply creates one target object for every source object, applied in our example to map, e.g., the class `Class` to the class `Entity` (cf. Fig. 2(b)). Furthermore, it is often desired that a target object should only be created if a source object fulfills a certain condition, e.g., only if the `Class.name` attribute is not null. Therefore, the functionality of a `Copier` is extended to a `ConditionalCopier` that requires the specification of a condition, reducing the generated object set. Please note that there is no inverse

MOp for the `ConditionalCopier`, since it would require knowing the filtered instances in order to re-construct the original object set.

1:n Correspondences. MOps handling 1:n correspondences connect one source class with at least two target classes and therefore allow to split concepts into finer-grained ones. There are three MOps belonging to this category, being the `VerticalPartitioner`, the `HorizontalPartitioner`, and the `CombinedPartitioner`. In this respect, a `VerticalPartitioner` deals with the problem when attributes of one source class are part of different classes in the target, e.g., the attributes of the class `Reference` are part of the classes `Role` and `Cardinality` in the running example (cf. Fig. 2(d)). Besides this default behavior, aggregation functionality is sometimes needed. Concerning the running example, this is the case when splitting the `Property` concept into the `Attribute` and `Type` concepts, since a `Type` should only be instantiated for distinct `Property.type` values (cf. Fig. 2(c)). In contrast, a `HorizontalPartitioner` splits the object set to different classes by means of a condition, e.g., splitting `References` into unbounded (upperBound=-1) and bounded (upperBound≠-1) ones. As the name implies, a `CombinedPartitioner` combines the functionality of both operators, e.g., if a `Property.type` attribute should additionally be split into numerical and non-numerical types.

n:1 Correspondences. Since MOps handling n:1 correspondences merge several source objects, they require at least two source objects (not necessarily from different classes) to create a single target object, thus representing in fact the inverse operators of 1:n MOps. In this respect, a `VerticalMerger` merges several source objects that are related to each other by references into a single target object. The `VerticalMerger` in our example (cf. Fig. 2 (e)) has two connections to the class `Reference` and a condition expressing that two objects have to be opposites to each other to generate a single instance of the target class `Relationship`. In contrast, a `HorizontalMerger` builds the union of the source objects. Finally, the `CombinedMerger` again combines the functionality of the two before mentioned MOps.

0:1 Correspondences. MOps handling 0:1 correspondences are applied if the target metamodel contains classes without any equivalent source classes. For this reason we provide the `ObjectGenerator` MOp. Therefore mechanisms for

Table 1. Composite Mapping Operators

Correspondence	MOp	Description	Condition	Inverse MOp
1:1 - copying	Copier	creates exactly one target object per source object		Copier
	ConditionalCopier	creates one target object per source object if condition is fullfilled	✔	n.a.
1:n - partitioning	VerticalPartitioner	splits one source object into several target objects		VerticalMerger
	HorizontalPartitioner	splits the source object set to different target object sets	✔	HorizontalMerger
	CombinedPartitioner	combines behavior of VerticalPartitioner and HorizontalPartitioner	✔	CombinedMerger
n:1 - merging	VerticalMerger	merges several source objects to one target object	✔	VerticalPartitioner
	HorizontalMerger	creates union of the source object set		HorizontalPartitioner
	CombinedMerger	combines behavior of VerticalMerger and HorizontalMerger	✔	CombinedPartitioner
0:1 - generating	ObjectGenerator	generates a new target object without corresponding source object		n.a.

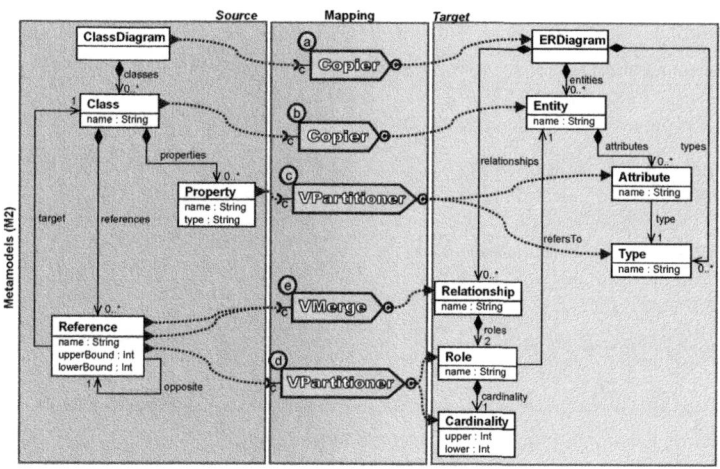

Fig. 2. Solution of the Mapping Example (Blackbox-view of MOps)

generating objects (and its contained values and links) are needed, which is the main contribution of the following section.

4   Specification of Composite MOps with Kernel MOps

In the previous section we introduced composite MOps to resolve structural heterogeneities in-the-large by using their blackbox-view. In this section we introduce so-called *kernel MOps* for mapping classes, attributes, and references in all possible combinations and mapping cardinalities which is the basis for resolving structural heterogeneities in-the-small. Subsequently, we discuss how kernel MOps are used to form composite MOps and show exemplarily how the whitebox-view is specified by means of kernel MOps.

4.1   Kernel MOps

In order to provide a MOps kernel, i.e., a minimal set of required MOps to overcome structural heterogeneities in-the-small, we systematically combined the core concepts of metamodeling languages, being (i) classes, (ii) attributes, and (iii) references with different mapping cardinalities, thereby complementing the work of Legler and Naumann [12] focusing on attributes only. Based on this rationale, the kernel MOps allow mapping source elements to target classes (2ClassMOps), target attributes (2AttributeMOps), and target relationships (2RelationshipMOps) (cf. first inheritance level of the kernel MOps layer in Fig. 3). On the second inheritance level we distinguish the following kernel MOps, according to different cardinalities.

1:1 Mappings. C₂C, A₂A, and R₂R MOps are provided for copying exactly one object, value, and link from source to target, respectively. Therefore, each of their *source* and *target* references point to the same Ecore concept in Fig. 3.

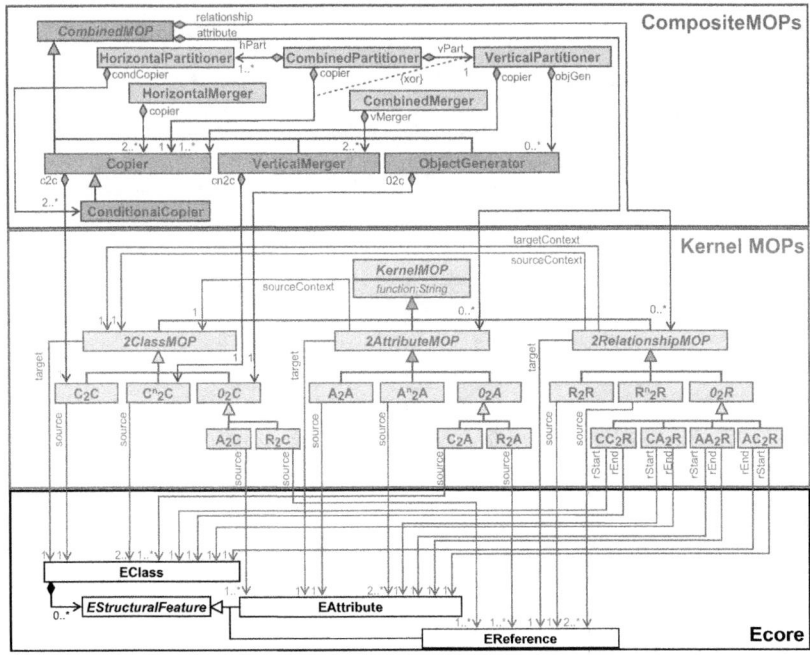

Fig. 3. Metamodel of Kernel and Composite MOps

n:1 Mappings. To resolve the structural heterogeneity that concepts in the source metamodel are more fine-grained than in the target metamodel, MOps are needed for merging objects, values, and links. For this, the MOps $C_2^n C$, $A_2^n A$, and $R_2^n R$ are provided that require a merge condition expressed in OCL, specifying how to merge elements, e.g., a function to concatenate several attribute values.

0:1 Mappings. Whereas source and target elements of kernel MOps dealing with 1:1 and n:1 mappings are all of the same type, i.e., pointing to the same Ecore concept in Fig. 3, 0:1 MOps ($0_2 C$, $0_2 A$, and $0_2 R$), bridge elements of different concepts, whereby the 0 indicates that there is no source element of equivalent type. Therefore, these MOps are intended to solve structural heterogeneities resulting from expressing the same modeling concept with different meta-modeling concepts – a situation which often occurs in metamodeling practice – and are therefore a crucial prerequisite to "survive the heterogeneity jungle".

MOps for 0:1 Mappings. In the following, we shortly elaborate on each concrete 0:1 MOp depicted on the third inheritance level in Fig. 3.

$0_2 C$ **MOps.** This kind of MOp is used to create objects out of values and links. In particular, the $A_2 C$ MOp is used for resolving the structural heterogeneity that in one metamodel a concept is expressed by an attribute, whereby the other metamodel defines the concept by an additional class. In the running example, this kind of heterogeneity occurs between the attribute Property.type and the class Type. Analogously, it might be the case that one metamodel has a reference between two classes whereas the other metamodel exhibits an additional class in between the corresponding classes. In such a case, for every link an object has to be created which is realized by the R_2C MOp.

0_2A MOps. Besides MOps for explicating source model concepts by means of classes in a target model, MOps are needed to generate values from objects and links. Concerning the first case, a target class may require a certain attribute, for which no corresponding attribute in the source class exists, e.g., an additional id attribute. In this case a value has to be set for every generated target object by a C_2A MOp since for every source object a value has to be generated. Concerning the second case, if an object has been generated from a link (cf. R_2C MOp) and the class of the generated object requires an attribute, we provide an R_2A MOp, which sets a value of an attribute of the generated object for every source link.

0_2R MOps. Finally, links may be generated on the target side which have no corresponding links on the source side, but are computable by analyzing the source model. Since links need a source and a target object, it is not sufficient to use A_2R and C_2R MOps, only, instead we need two elements on the left hand side of such MOps. By systematically combining the possible source elements used to generate target objects which are additionally linked, the following MOps are supported: CC_2R, AC_2R, CA_2R, and AA_2R whereby the first letter identifies the element used to generate the source object of the link and the second letter identifies the element used to generate the target object.

In contrast to composite MOps, we do not provide 1:n kernel MOps as they can be reduced to $n \times$ 1:1 correspondences and thus be again realized as a composite MOp. Furthermore, MOps handling 1:0 correspondences are not needed, since this means that there is a source concept without any corresponding target concept, i.e., no transformation action is required (in the forward direction).

4.2   Composition Model for MOps

To assemble the presented kernel MOps to composite MOps and to bind them to specific metamodels, every MOp has *input ports* with required interfaces (left side of the component) as well as *output ports* with provided interfaces (right side of the component), typed to classes (C), attributes (A), and relationships (R) (cf. Fig. 4). Since there are dependencies between MOps, e.g., a link can only be set after the two objects to be connected are available, every 2ClassMOp and every composite MOp (which contains 2ClassMOps) additionally offers a trace port (T) at the bottom of the MOp, providing context information, i.e., offering information about which output elements have been produced from which input elements. This port can be used by other MOps to access context information via *requiredContext* ports (C) with corresponding interfaces on top of the MOp, or in case of 2RelationshipsMOps via two ports, whereby the top port depicts the required source context and the bottom port the required target context (cf. Fig. 4). Since MOps are expressed as components, the transformation designer can apply them in a plug & play manner by binding their interfaces.

For composing kernel MOps we provide the abstract class `CombinedMOp`, aggregating `2AttributeMOps` and `2RelationshipMOps` (cf. Fig. 3). As we identified correspondences between classes in a first step, those kernel MOps dealing with the mapping of classes are an obligatory part of every composite MOp. Therefore, every composite MOp consists of one concrete refinement of the abstract class `2ClassMOp`, dependent on the composite MOps' number of correspondences, being a `Copier` for 1:1 mappings using a C_2C kernel MOp, a `VerticalMerger` for n:1 mappings using a C_2^nC kernel MOp, and an `ObjectGenerator` for 0:1 mappings using a O_2C kernel MOp, as depicted in Fig. 3. Furthermore, composite MOps can again be combined to more complex composite MOps, e.g., a `VerticalPartitioner` consists of several `Copiers` and `ObjectsGenerators`.

In this respect, the presented metamodel (cf. Fig. 3) makes the relationships between kernel MOps and composite MOps explicit thereby representing a conceptual model of heterogeneities, being a main advance compared to our previous work in [8] where no statements about interrelationships have been made.

4.3   Whitebox-View of Composite MOps

In Section 3 we only specified mappings between source and target metamodel classes in a first step, leaving out mappings for attributes and references. This is done in the second step, by switching to the *whitebox-view* of the composite MOps. Because each composite MOp sets the focus by marking involved metamodel classes for a specific mapping, switching to the whitebox-view allows to show only the metamodel elements which are relevant for this mapping. The transformation designer has to complete the mappings by adding appropriate kernel MOps to the composite MOp and by specifying their bindings to attributes and references. Thereby bindings of `2ClassMOps` are automatically set by analyzing the class bindings afore defined in the blackbox-view. To exemplify this, we elaborate on the whitebox-view of the `Copier` (cf. Fig. 4) and the `VerticalPartitioner` (cf. Fig. 5) by means of our running example.

Whitebox-View of Copier. The intention of a `Copier` is to transform one object and its contained values and links to a corresponding target object. Thus, a `Copier` generates one target object for every source object by the C_2C kernel MOp, representing the *fixed part* of the `Copier` (cf. both `Copiers` in Fig. 4) for which the bindings are automatically derived. The bindings of the *variable part*, i.e., arbitrary number of `2AttributeMOps` and `2RelationshipMOps`, are dependent on the specific metamodels. For example, the transformation designer has to use an A_2A kernel MOp to specify the correspondence between the attribute `Class.name` and `Entity.name`. The inclusion of attribute and relationship mappings results in additional ports compared to the blackbox-view (Fig. 2), which only shows class ports. As attributes only exist in the context of an object, the A_2A MOp depends on the C_2C MOp for acquiring context information.

For mapping references, `2RelationshipMOps` are employed in both `Copiers`. For example, the reference `ClassDiagram.classes` is mapped to the reference `ERDiagram.entities` using a R_2R MOp. As links require a source and a target object, the R_2R MOp is linked to the trace port of the C_2C MOp on top and to the trace port provided by the second copier at the bottom. Since the remaining references on the target side, i.e., `ERDiagram.types` and `ERDiagram.relationships`, do not have a counterpart reference on the source side, they have to be mapped by 0:1 MOps. Concerning links instantiated from the reference `ERDiagram.type`, the links' source object is an `ERDiagram` object which is created from a `ClassDiagram` object and the target object is a `Type` object created from a value of the `Property.type` attribute. These source elements are related by the path `ClassDiagram.classes.properties`. In order to reflect this in the target model, the user has to specify this path explicitly since otherwise only the cross product between the involved objects could be built. As the link's source was created on basis of a class and the link's target on basis of an attribute, a CA_2R MOp is applied. Finally, since `ERDiagram.relationships` links have to reflect the context of instances from class `ClassDiagram` and from class `Reference`, described by the path `ClassDiagram.classes.references`, we apply a CC_2R MOp.

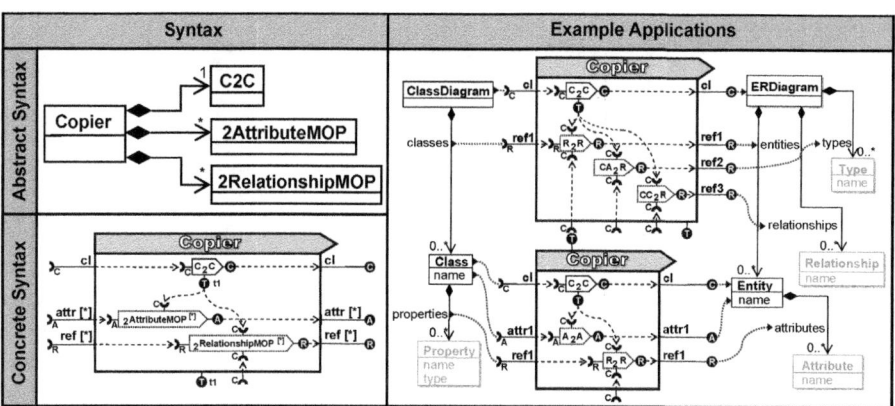

Fig. 4. Whitebox-View of Copier

Whitebox-View of VerticalPartitioner. Since in the general case the `VerticalPartitioner` only splits attributes of the source class to attributes in several different target classes, `Copiers` can be reused. As shown in Example Application 1 in Fig. 5, the first `Copier` creates `Role` objects and sets the value of the `Role.name` attribute and the second one creates `Cardinality` objects and sets the attributes `Cardinality.upper` and `Cardinality.lower`. Again the attribute mappings are specified by the transformation designer in the whitebox-view. Since there is no equivalent for the `Role.cardinality` link in the source model available, a link for every object pair has to be generated by the CC_2R MOp, which is automatically added to the `Copier` since it is always required. As the `Copiers` do not affect the instance set, there has to be a 1:1 relationship between the target classes. In case that the target classes are related by a 1:* relationship, the intention typically is to generate only one object per distinct value of a dedicated source attribute, e.g., only one `Type` object per distinct

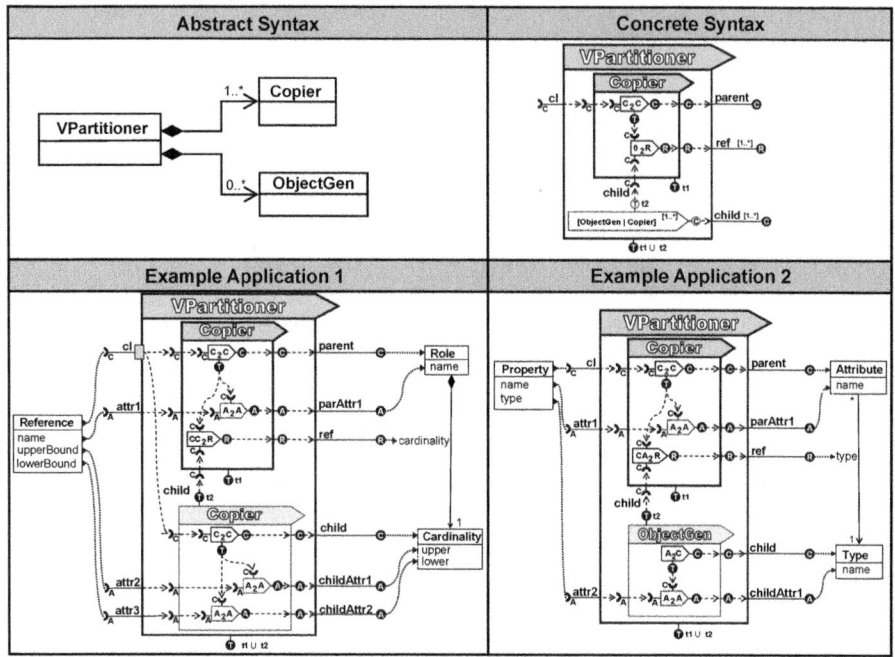

Fig. 5. Whitebox-View of VerticalPartitioner

`Property.type` value, which can not be achieved by a `Copier`. In order to generate the distinct objects the `ObjectGenerator` is applied, using an A_2C MOp to generate the according objects based on the `Property.type` attribute (cf. Example Application 2 in Fig. 5). In order to decide whether a new object should be created, i.e., an attribute value for which no object has been created up to now, the A_2C MOp queries its own context information.

5 Related Work

In the following, related transformation approaches are considered stemming not only from the area of model engineering, but also from data and ontology engineering since models can be treated as data, metamodels as schemas and transformations as a means for realizing data exchange. A similar analogy can be drawn for the area of ontology engineering. The comparison to our MOps is done in the following according to the introduced criteria (i) abstraction, (ii) variation, (iii) composition, and (iv) library of pre-defined MOps (cf. Table 2).

Concerning *abstraction*, different kinds of mechanisms have been investigated, namely (i) *abstraction by simplification*, (ii) *abstraction by selection* and (iii) *abstraction by generalization*. These terms are inspired by the general discussion of abstraction in [11]. In the context of model transformations *abstraction by simplification* denotes the removal of elements from a transformation language, abstracting language-specific details, e.g., for describing correspondences between classes. *Abstraction by selection* is the process of focussing on a certain part of the metamodels only, i.e., the transformation designer is enabled to specify a whole transformation in a divide-and-conquer manner, e.g., partitioning a certain Class into several others. *Abstraction by generalization* is interpreted in the model transformation context, i.e., allowing to focus on the generic transformation logic. This is currently mostly supported by generic types.

Table 2. Comparison of Transformation Approaches

	Transformation Approach	Abstraction			Variation			Composition			Library				
		By Simplification	By Selection	By Generalization	White-Box Reuse		Black-Box Reuse	Implicit	Explicit		Mapping Cardinality				Extensibility
					Copy-Paste	Inheritance			Internal	External	1:1	1:n	n:1	0:1	
Model Eng.	QVT Relations	control flow	✗	✗	✓	✓	✗	✗	when, where clauses	✗	✗	✗	✗	✗	✗
	TGG (Moflon)	control flow	correspondence nodes set focus	genericity (proposed)	✗	✓	✗	✗	✗	layers	✗	✗	✗	✗	✗
	VIATRA	control flow	✗	genericity	✓	✓	✗	✗	✗	ASMs	✗	✗	✗	✗	✗
	ATL (delcarative part)	control flow	✗	✗	✓	✓	✗	✓	lazy rules	✗	✗	✗	✗	✗	✗
	AMW	execution language	~	genericity	✗	✗	✗	✗	nesting	✗	✓	✗	✗	~	~
	MOps	execution language	Composite MOps set focus	genericity	✗	✗	✓	✗	context passing	✗	✓	✓	✓	✓	✓
Data Eng.	Clio/Clip	execution language	~	genericity	✗	✗	✗	✗	context passing	✗	✓	✗	✗	~	✗
	Mapforce	execution language	~	genericity	✗	✗	~	✓	✗	✗	✓	✗	~	~	✓
Ontology Eng.	MAFRA	execution language	✗	genericity	✗	✗	✗	✗	context passing	✗	✓	✗	✗	~	✗

With respect to abstraction by simplification, the approaches can be categorized into two groups, namely the ones abstracting from control flow only and the ones abstracting from the underlying execution language at all, thus focussing on the mapping specification, also known as schema mapping approaches from the area of data engineering. Regarding abstraction by simplification, only TGGs [10] provide support, since by defining the correspondence nodes, a focus on a certain metamodel part is set. The subsequent definition of the underlying graph transformation rule therefore just concentrates on this focused part of the metamodel. AMW [4], Clio/Clip [14], and Mapforce[1] provide only basic support in the sense that they allow to collapse certain metamodel parts. Concerning abstraction by generalization, TGGs, VIATRA [18], AMW, Clio/Clip, Mapforce and MAFRA [13] provide support by *genericity*. In contrast, our approach provides all kinds of abstraction mechanisms, being (i) *simplification* through abstracting from the underlying execution language, (ii) *selection* since the composite MOps set a certain focus, which can be concentrated on in the white-box view, and (iii) *generalization* through abstraction from the concrete metamodel since MOps are based on the meta-metamodel.

---

[1] http://www.altova.com/mapforce.html

With respect to *variation mechanisms*, the support for (i) white-box reuse, i.e., the implementation must be known in order to customize the reused components and for (ii) black-box reuse can be distinguished. In this context, mainly white-box reuse is supported so far by existing approaches. It is supported in the simplest form by copy-paste (QVT Relations, VIATRA, ATL [7]) as well as by inheritance (QVT Relations, TGGs, VIATRA, ATL). Regarding black-box reuse, only Mapforce provides basic support, e.g., by allowing to set parameters for string operators. On the contrary, MOps can be tailored without knowing the internals, thus realizing black-box reuse.

Concerning *composition mechanisms*, the approaches have been examined according to the criteria proposed by [3], distinguishing between (i) *implicit composition*, i.e., hard-coded mechanisms not adaptable by the transformation designer and (ii) *explicit composition*, i.e., composition can be explicitly specified by the transformation designer, further classified into (iia) *internal composition*, i.e., intermingling composition specification and rules and (iib) *external composition*, i.e., there is a clear separation between composition specification and rules. With respect to explicit composition mechanisms, all the approaches provide support except Mapforce. Regarding internal composition, most approaches follow this idea in different forms. Whereas QVT allows to describe composition by means of preconditions (when-clauses) and postconditions (where-clauses), ATL allows for the explicit calling of lazy rules. In contrast, Clio/Clip and MAFRA rely on data dependencies between the rules only, i.e., context passing. This is favorable, since the ordering of rules just depends on the data and therefore our approach also follows this idea. Concerning external composition, only TGGs and VIATRA follow this approach allowing for a clear separation between rules and composition specification in the simple form of layers (TGGs) or by the more sophisticated form of ASM (abstract state machine) programs (VIATRA).

Concerning the *library* aspect, only AMW, Clio/Clip, Mapforce and MAFRA provide a basic set of pre-defined components. In this respect, (i) the mapping cardinality, i.e., the cardinality supported by the offered MOps and (ii) the possibility to extend the pre-defined set of MOps have been investigated. With respect to mapping cardinality, only 1:1 mappings are supported by all approaches. More coarse-grained MOps, i.e., composite MOps (1:n, n:1, n:m) are neglected so far. Finally, for 0:1 mappings, i.e., the mapping between different metamodel concepts only basic support is provided. Regarding the extension of predefined MOps with user-defined ones, only Mapforce allows for the definition of new ones on the one hand by composing existing ones and on the other hand by writing a code script, i.e., the transformation designer has to define a MOp from scratch. Basically, also AMW could be extended by modifying the underlying metamodel and the HOT responsible for generating the executable ATL code. Nevertheless, this kind of extensibility is quite heavyweight and reserved to specialists. In contrast, our approach supports all kinds of mapping cardinalities and by offering a set of kernel MOps, the library can be easily extended by composing a new MOp out of kernel MOps or other composite ones.

6   Prototypical Implementation

This section elaborates on the prototypical implementation of the presented approach based on the AMMA platform[2]. In particular, we extended AMW [5] to specify mappings by using the presented MOps as well as a HOT [17] for generating executable ATL code [7] out of the mappings (cf. Fig. 6).

Extending AMW. The AMW framework provides a generic infrastructure and editor to declaratively specify weaving models between two arbitrary models. The editor is based on a generic weaving metamodel, defining generic weaving links, which can be extended to specify custom weaving links. The generic weaving links are mainly represented by the abstract classes WLink. For each kernel and composite MOp shown in Fig. 3, we introduced a direct or indirect subclass of WLink defining the properties of the MOp. In order to ensure context-sensitive mapping constraints, we provide basic verification support based on the EMF Validation Framework[3], e.g., every MOp has to be correctly connected to its source and target metamodel elements as well as to its context mappings.

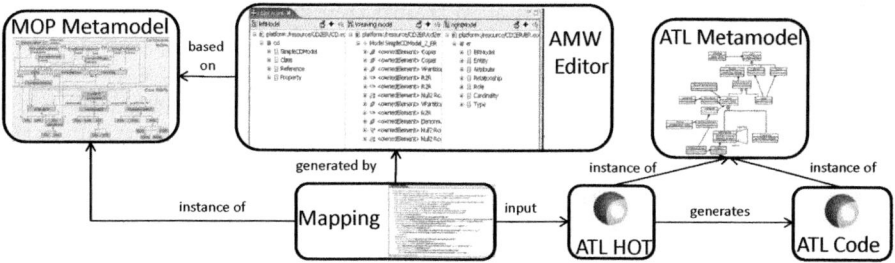

Fig. 6. Generating Transformation Code from Mapping Model

Execution of Mapping Operators. The extended AMW metamodel defines the abstract syntax of the mapping language, but does not provide means to specify the operational semantics needed for execution of mappings. Since we explicitly represent mappings as a model, we employ a HOT to compile the mappings into executable ATL code. For MOps dealing with 1:1, 1:n and n:1 mappings, declarative ATL code is generated in terms of matched rules. For MOps dealing with 0:1 mappings imperative code blocks are generated. Considering our running example, an A_2C MOp was applied to generate Type objects on basis of distinct Property.type values, for which a lazy rule is required. To ensure that the lazy rule is called only for distinct values, according trace information is needed. Since ATL provides trace information automatically for matched rules, only, we implemented our own, more flexible trace model for

---

[2] http://wiki.eclipse.org/AMMA
[3] http://www.eclipse.org/modeling/emf/?project=validation

providing trace information for every rule (irresponsible of the rule type) and for providing traces of values and links in addition to objects. For example, this specific trace information is needed to omit the creation of redundant Type objects in our running example. For 0:1 R-MOps it has to be ensured that the source and target objects of the link to be generated have already been established, before the link is set. Therefore, those links are created in an endpoint rule, which is called by the ATL engine just before termination. For more information on our prototype, we kindly refer the interested reader to our project homepage[4].

7   Critical Discussion and Future Work

A critical reflection of our MOps opens up several issues for future work.

Incorporation of Additional Modeling Concepts. Currently, only the most important concepts of modeling languages, i.e., classes, attributes and relationships have been considered. It would be highly desireable, however, to extend our MOp library to be able to deal also with concepts such as inheritance. We have already published first ideas in this direction in [8].

Effort Reduction by Matching Techniques. Our mapping approach consists of two steps being first the definition of mappings on class level which has to be further refined with attribute and relationships mappings. Since this refinement can be time-consuming, matching strategies [15,16] may be applied to automatically derive attribute and relationship mappings. Matching in this context may be especially beneficial since through setting a certain focus in the blackbox view, the search area is already restricted.

Impedance Mismatch Reduction by Other Execution Languages. The operational semantics of our MOps is defined using a HOT to ATL. Thus, there is an impedance mismatch between the abstract mapping specification and the executable code, which hinders understandability and debugging of the generated code. Therefore, the translation to other transformation languages should be investigated, trying to identify which transformation language fits best to the mapping specification. In this respect, the applicability of our own transformation language TROPIC [19] should be investigated as well.

Usability Evaluation. Kernel MOps provide rather fine-grained operators for overcoming structural heterogeneities. Nevertheless, they abstract from the intricacies of a certain transformation language, e.g., 0:1 MOps often require querying trace information or helper functions which require considerable effort in implementing manually. Therefore, the usability of our approach has to be investigated in further studies, evaluating the expected advantage.

---

[4] www.modeltransformation.net

References

1. Alexe, B., Tan, W.-C., Velegrakis, Y.: STBenchmark: Towards a Benchmark for Mapping Systems. VLDB Endow. 1(1), 230–244 (2008)
2. Bézivin, J.: On the Unification Power of Models. Journal on Software and Systems Modeling 4(2), 31 (2005)
3. Czarnecki, K., Helsen, S.: Feature-based Survey of Model Transformation Approaches. IBM Systems Journal 45(3), 621–645 (2006)
4. Fabro, M.D., Valduriez, P.: Towards the development of model transformations using model weaving and matching transformations. SoSym 8(3), 305–324 (2009)
5. Del Fabro, M., Bézivin, J., Jouault, F., Breton, E., Gueltas, G.: AMW: A Generic Model Weaver. In: Proc. of IDM 2005 (2005)
6. Hull, R., King, R.: Semantic Database Modeling: Survey, Applications, and Research Issues. ACM Comput. Surv. 19(3), 201–260 (1987)
7. Jouault, F., Allilaire, F., Bézivin, J., Kurtev, I.: ATL: A Model Transformation Tool. Science of Computer Programming 72(1-2), 31–39 (2008)
8. Kappel, G., Kargl, H., Reiter, T., Retschitzegger, W., Schwinger, W., Strommer, M., Wimmer, M.: A Framework for Building Mapping Operators Resolving Structural Heterogeneities. In: Proc. of UNISCON 2008, pp. 158–174 (2008)
9. Kashyap, V., Sheth, A.: Semantic and schematic similarities between database objects: A context-based approach. The VLDB Journal 5(4), 276–304 (1996)
10. Koenigs, A.: Model Transformation with Triple Graph Grammars. In: Bruel, J.-M. (ed.) MoDELS 2005. LNCS, vol. 3844, pp. 120–127. Springer, Heidelberg (2006)
11. Kramer, J.: Is abstraction the key to computing? Com. ACM 50(4), 36–42 (2007)
12. Legler, F., Naumann, F.: A Classification of Schema Mappings and Analysis of Mapping Tools. In: Proc. of BTW 2007 (2007)
13. Maedche, A., Motik, B., Silva, N., Volz, R.: MAFRA - A MApping FRAmework for Distributed Ontologies. In: Gómez-Pérez, A., Benjamins, V.R. (eds.) EKAW 2002. LNCS (LNAI), vol. 2473, pp. 235–250. Springer, Heidelberg (2002)
14. Raffio, A., Braga, D., Ceri, S., Papotti, P., Hernández, M.A.: Clip: a visual language for explicit schema mappings. In: Proc. of ICDE 2008, pp. 30–39 (2008)
15. Rahm, E., Bernstein, P.A.: A survey of approaches to automatic schema matching. The VLDB Journal 10(4), 334–350 (2001)
16. Ramos, R., Barais, O., Jézéquel, J.M.: Matching Model-Snippets. In: Engels, G., Opdyke, B., Schmidt, D.C., Weil, F. (eds.) MODELS 2007. LNCS, vol. 4735, pp. 121–135. Springer, Heidelberg (2007)
17. Tisi, M., Jouault, F., Fraternali, P., Ceri, S., Bézivin, J.: On the Use of Higher-Order Model Transformations. In: Paige, R.F., Hartman, A., Rensink, A. (eds.) ECMDA-FA 2009. LNCS, vol. 5562, pp. 18–33. Springer, Heidelberg (2009)
18. Varró, D., Pataricza, A.: Generic and meta-transformations for model transformation engineering. In: Baar, T., Strohmeier, A., Moreira, A., Mellor, S.J. (eds.) UML 2004. LNCS, vol. 3273, pp. 290–304. Springer, Heidelberg (2004)
19. Wimmer, M., Kusel, A., Reiter, T., Retschitzegger, W., Schwinger, W., Kappel, G.: Lost in Translation? Transformation Nets to the Rescue!. In: Proc. of UNISCON 2009, pp. 315–327 (2009)

Author Index